The Galley Conjectural Tree

—— traditional or historic affiliation
▪▪▪▪ suggested affiliation
⚓ Royal Galley borne or quartered in Arms

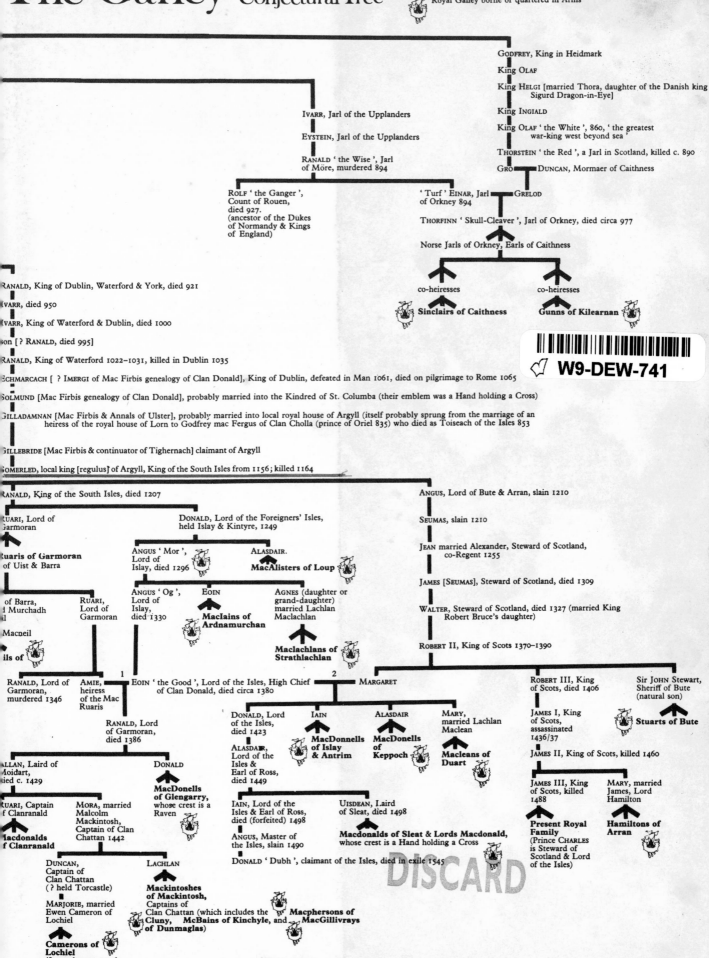

GODFREY, King in Heidmark

King OLAF

King HELGI [married Thora, daughter of the Danish king Sigurd Dragon-in-Eye]

King INGIALD

King OLAF 'the White', 860, 'the greatest war-king west beyond sea'

THORSTEIN 'the Red', a Jarl in Scotland, killed c. 890

GRO —— DUNCAN, Mormaer of Caithness

IVARR, Jarl of the Upplanders

EYSTEIN, Jarl of the Upplanders

RANALD 'the Wise', Jarl of Möre, murdered 894

ROLF 'the Ganger', Count of Rouen, died 927. (ancestor of the Dukes of Normandy & Kings of England)

'Turf' EINAR, Jarl of Orkney 894 —— GRELOD

THORFINN 'Skull-Cleaver', Jarl of Orkney, died circa 977

Norse Jarls of Orkney, Earls of Caithness

co-heiresses ⚓ **Sinclairs of Caithness**

co-heiresses ⚓ **Gunns of Kilearnan**

RANALD, King of Dublin, Waterford & York, died 921

IVARR, died 950

IVARR, King of Waterford & Dublin, died 1000

son [? RANALD, died 995]

RANALD, King of Waterford 1022–1031, killed in Dublin 1035

ECHMARCACH [? IMERGI of Mac Firbis genealogy of Clan Donald], King of Dublin, defeated in Man 1061, died on pilgrimage to Rome 1065

SOLMUND [Mac Firbis genealogy of Clan Donald], probably married into the Kindred of St. Columba (their emblem was a Hand holding a Cross)

GILLADAMNAN [Mac Firbis & Annals of Ulster], probably married into local royal house of Argyll (itself probably sprung from the marriage of an heiress of the royal house of Lorn to Godfrey mac Fergus of Clan Cholla (prince of Oriel 835) who died as Toiseach of the Isles 853

GILLEBRIDE [Mac Firbis & continuator of Tighernach] claimant of Argyll

SOMERLED, local king [regulus] of Argyll, King of the South Isles from 1156; killed 1164

RANALD, King of the South Isles, died 1207

ANGUS, Lord of Bute & Arran, slain 1210

SEUMAS, slain 1210

JEAN married Alexander, Steward of Scotland, co-Regent 1255

JAMES [SEUMAS], Steward of Scotland, died 1309

WALTER, Steward of Scotland, died 1327 (married King Robert Bruce's daughter)

ROBERT II, King of Scots 1370–1390

RUARI, Lord of Garmoran

DONALD, Lord of the Foreigners' Isles, held Islay & Kintyre, 1249

Ruaris of Garmoran of Uist & Barra

ANGUS 'Mor', Lord of Islay, died 1296 ⚓

ALASDAIR. **MacAlisters of Loup** ⚓

of Barra, d Murchadh

RUARI, Lord of Garmoran

ANGUS 'Og', Lord of Islay, died 1330 ⚓

EOIN **MacIains of Ardnamurchan** ⚓

AGNES (daughter or grand-daughter) married Lachlan Maclachlan

Macneil

ils of ⚓

Maclachlans of Strathlachlan ⚓

RANALD, Lord of Garmoran, murdered 1346

AMIE, heiress of the Mac Ruaris

1 EOIN 'the Good', Lord of the Isles, High Chief of Clan Donald, died circa 1380

2 MARGARET

ROBERT III, King of Scots, died 1406

Sir JOHN Stewart, Sheriff of Bute (natural son)

RANALD, Lord of Garmoran, died 1386

DONALD, Lord of the Isles, died 1423

IAIN **MacDonnells of Islay & Antrim** ⚓

ALASDAIR **MacDonells of Keppoch** ⚓

MARY, married Lachlan Maclean

JAMES I, King of Scots, assassinated 1436/37

⚓ **Stuarts of Bute**

ALLAN, Laird of Moidart, died c. 1429

ALASDAIR, Lord of the Isles & Earl of Ross, died 1449

Macleans of Duart ⚓

JAMES II, King of Scots, killed 1460

RUARI, Captain of Clanranald

MORA, married Malcolm Mackintosh, Captain of Clan Chattan 1442

DONALD **MacDonells of Glengarry**, whose crest is a Raven ⚓

IAIN, Lord of the Isles & Earl of Ross, died (forfeited) 1498

UISDEAN, Laird of Sleat, died 1498

JAMES III, King of Scots, killed 1488

MARY, married James, Lord Hamilton

Macdonalds of Clanranald ⚓

ANGUS, Master of the Isles, slain 1490

Macdonalds of Sleat & Lords Macdonald, whose crest is a Hand holding a Cross ⚓

Present Royal Family (Prince CHARLES is Steward of Scotland & Lord of the Isles) ⚓

Hamiltons of Arran ⚓

DUNCAN, Captain of Clan Chattan (? held Torcastle)

LACHLAN

DONALD 'Dubh', claimant of the Isles, died in exile 1545

MARJORIE, married Ewen Cameron of Lochiel

Mackintoshes of Mackintosh, Captains of Clan Chattan (which includes the **Cluny, McBains of Kinchyle,** and **of Dunmaglas**) ⚓

Macphersons of MacGillivrays ⚓

Camerons of Lochiel (formerly quartered the Galley) ⚓

THE HIGHLAND CLANS

SIR IAIN MONCREIFFE
OF THAT ILK   Albany Herald

The dynastic origins, chiefs
and background of the Clans
and of some other families
connected with Highland history

with photographs by DAVID HICKS

THE HIGHLAND CLANS

 Bramhall House   NEW YORK

Produced by Design Yearbook Ltd., 21 Ivor Place, London N.W.1.
Published by Barrie & Rockliff, 2, Clements Inn, London W.C.2.
Designed by Ian Cameron.
House Editor: Elizabeth Kingsley-Rowe.
Text set by Harrison & Sons (Westminster) Ltd., 20/22
Bedfordbury, London W.C.2.
Printed and bound by N. V. Grafische Industrie Haarlem, Holland.

Designed by Ian Cameron.
House Editor: Elizabeth Kingsley-Rowe.
mcmlxvii
© Sir Iain Moncreiffe (Text) and Design Yearbook Ltd.
This edition published by Bramhall House,
a devision of Clarkson N. Potter, Inc.
Printed and bound in the Netherlands.

a   b   c   d   e   f   g   h

Photographs by David Hicks, assisted by Peter Briault.

Additional photographs as follows:

Peter Theobald: pages 12(both), 19(b. right), 22(b), 29, 33, 34, 55(b.rt.), 57, 59(both), 60, 68(both), 69 (t. & b.), 71, 75, 76, 77, 78, 89, 91, 102, 111, 112, 113, 115(t.), 116(both), 118, 119, 120, 124(both), 126, 130(t.), 132(both), 133, 134(t.), 135(t.), 136(all), 137(both), 138(b.), 142(b.), 145, 147, 151, 154, 155, 156(t. & b.1), 159(b.), 165, 179(b.), 183, 184, 185(right), 186, 196, 198(both), 200, 203(b.), 206, 211(both), 214(t.), 217, 220(b.), 234, 236, 238.

Alberto A. Weissmüller: 114, 115(b.r.), 182.

John Bush: 46, 54, 96, 97(t. & r.), 98(b.), 210(l. & b.), 212(l.), 214(b.), 226, 231, 232(centre & b.).

Ian Yeomans: 58, 94, 130(b.).

Camera Press Limited: 240(b.).

The Daily Telegraph: 234(r.).

North of Scotland Hydro-Electric Board: 31, 181, 202, 203(t.).

Aberdeen Journals Limited: 78(b.).

The Boy Scouts Association: 74(b.):

By courtesy of Tom Scott of Edinburgh and by permission of the Clan Donnachaidh Society: 41(t.).

The Highland News Limited, Inverness: 128.

Crown Copyright: reproduced by permission of the Ministry of Public Building and Works: 242, 245.

Reproduced by gracious permission of Her Majesty the Queen: 24.

The American Embassy: 159(t.), 199.

The British Museum: 176.

Dr Douglas Simpson: 16(b.), 52(l.).

The National Museum of Antiquities of Scotland: 13, 14(b.), 61, 80(t.r.), 213, 218.

John Dewar & Sons Limited: 14(t.).

Sir Anthony Wagner, Garter Principal King of Arms: 195.

From The Scottish National Portrait Gallery:
   30, 47, (by permission of the Earl of Wemyss)
   50
   169 (by permission of the Honble. Robin Sinclair)
   197
   224 (by permission of Major James Drummond-Moray of Abercairny)
   227 (by permission of the Duke of Atholl)
   239 (by permission of Sir David Ogilvy of Inverquharity).

Sir Hew Hamilton-Dalrymple of North Berwick: 11(t.).

The Countess of Sutherland: 28.

Mr. P. A. Macnab: 179(t.).

The Royal Commission on Ancient & Historic Monuments of Scotland: 66(b.l.).

The Scottish Tourist Board: 67.

The Scottish Field: 219(both).

Clan Badges drawn by Joy Bedford.

Drawings on pages 46 and 81 by Jacque Solomons.

The author also wishes to thank the many kind friends who allowed him access to their houses and who lent pictures or photographs which he wished to use as illustrations.

Contents

CORRIGENDA

p. 59:   first caption, line 2.   *for* 12th February *read* 13th February
p. 138:   first çaption, line 3.   *for* Chief of Clan Ay *read* Chief of Clan Shaw

Rear endpaper: The Lyon
  delete AED ANRADHAN (and following note) *and replace by* ANROTHAN
  delete the generation marked (?NIALL)
  for AEDH 'the splendid' *read* AEDH 'the splendid' an Buírrche
    (The Buffalo)
  reverse the positions of MAOLMUIRE *and* DUGALL, *with their descendants,*
    to make Madmuire the elder brother
  move GILLACRIST *and his descendants down a generation, making him a*
    younger brother of FERCHAR *and* SUIBANE

Foreword

A couple of years ago, while staying with *Mac Chalein Mor* to shoot roe in a drive with Scottish deer-hounds to clear the young timber plantations in Glenshira, I was given access to the many neat note-books at Inveraray on West Highland history and clan genealogy that contained the life-work of that scholarly recluse, the late Duke Niall of Argyll. Everything was unfinished and unpublished. It all seemed such a waste.

I realised that I too had been doing the same sort of thing: more than thirty years spent in collecting material for an exhaustive book on the clans and families of Scotland, highland and lowland alike—impeded by simultaneous work on the influence of the Dawn Religion and sacral royalty, on subsequent civilisation in general and on British custom in particular. Recently, David Hicks had also taken a number of photographs to illustrate another of my projected works: on the historic homes of the present-day lairds associated with the Highlands, who still hold some of the lands they held at the time of the sixteenth-century Parliamentary Rolls. Duke Niall's unfinished notes made it clear that these tasks cannot adequately be completed in anybody's otherwise busy lifetime.

It therefore seemed better to write something now than everything never. This book is the result. So it is not meant to be a disciplined work of scholarship. Nor does the layout permit space for references. It's more like a note-book of random jottings about this vast subject. The length of an article has nothing to do with historical importance, but usually only indicates that I've more fairly new stuff to write about one clan or family than about another. Thus the mighty MacLeods and the massacred Lamonts are already extensively written up in the excellent histories published by their active Clan Societies, but little has been written before about such interesting clans as the Maclachlans and the McCorquodales. And time has prevented any research as yet into the history of such families as Polson and Swanson (branches of Mackay and Gunn), MacNicol of Portree (otherwise Nicolson), Rankin (hereditary pipers to Maclean of Coll), Maclaverty and MacSporran (respectively tatlers and purse-bearers to the Lords of the Isles). But we do try to give a panoptic view of the clans in particular and of Highland history in general.

A lot more work needs to be done by Gaelic scholars, like the Rev. John McKechnie, who can collate the Irish annals and MacFirbis's genealogies with the Highland genealogical papers (often with several generations obviously omitted) that are already printed or gradually being made available for research. Far more will probably be known about clan origins when the work of such modern scholars as Professor G. W. S. Barrow, Professor Archie Duncan and Dr. Grant Simpson can be fully considered: although unfortunately mediaeval genealogy is only incidental to their work as historians. Meanwhile, I have been greatly helped by the draft county maps of feudal superiorities in the thirteenth century so generously made available to me by their compiler: Major John Weir, Keeper of MSS. in Glasgow University Library.

So many other people have helped that it's impossible to thank them all. My wife, for instance, is responsible for most of the typing errors. Of all those who were kind about the illustrations I'm especially grateful to Sir Anthony Wagner, Garter Principal King of Arms, who has allowed us to reproduce a part of his unique Balliol Roll even though it's at present awaiting special editing before general publication. Then there is Ian Cameron, who has undertaken the layout of a book made difficult by the length of the pictures' captions. But above all, I must thank Miss Elizabeth Kingsley-Rowe (a genealogically interesting specimen as a cousin of Kingsley who wrote *The Water Babies*), who has been the driving force behind getting the book completed in time and space—and who, as a result, has had skilfully to edit our over-lengthy captions. Finally, David Hicks and I are especially indebted to two Chiefs who had us to stay and provided us with bases from which to operate. One is Lochiel, perhaps the most talented of a long line of remarkable Chiefs. The other is Lord Lovat, of whom Winston Churchill wrote to Stalin (quoting Byron) that Lovat was the mildest-mannered man that ever scuttled ship or cut a throat.

Of course the book is intended to appeal to clannish pride. But it should always be remembered that the Highland clan system produced vertical as opposed to horizontal social distinctions. A Maclean or a Campbell, a Cameron or a Mackintosh, were distinguished by features which cut clean across class. Although people often speak of 'old families', in fact no family is older than any other. What is meant is that the particular families called 'old' have managed to maintain their identity and retain records of their past longer than the majority of other folk. In England and abroad, this is too often true only of a limited aristocracy. In the Highlands, however, everybody was eventually descended one way or another from several of the great historic royal clans. Nor did parental disregard of the canonical laws of marriage bar innocent children from membership of the clan. At a meeting of the Standing Council of Scottish Chiefs, while discussing the Succession Bill, the present writer pointed out that illegitimacy did not *necessarily* in Scotland exclude a son from succession even to a chiefship, if covered by a parental nomination accepted by the Crown—and that this applied in fact to a fellow chief present. After the meeting two other chiefs (neither of them the one I had in mind) came up to me separately and protested: ' I've never been called a bastard in public before '

All the same, this book stresses the sacral royal and dynastic origin of the founder chiefs, and thus of the clans themselves: the ultimate biological unity with the Sovereign that accounts for ' Highland pride ' and loyalty. The end-papers should make this meaning clear. Also, a short history of a clan must be based on some account of its chiefs, just as a short history of a realm tends to concentrate on the doings of its kings. (Incidentally, the royal title was not King of Scotland but *King of Scots*, as Chief of Chiefs of the whole family of Scots throughout the world). Economic and social history can better be studied in the works of Dr. I. F· Grant, and by reading *Scottish Studies*, the twice-yearly publication of the School of Scottish Studies run by Mr. Basil Megaw for Edinburgh University.

Again, any Perthshireman is conscious of the overlapping of the Highlands and the Lowlands. So some of the families who held lands in both parts of Scotland tend to be given extra space, as their history is usually omitted altogether from standard clan books. Indeed, had there been more time and space, I would have included accounts of such other ' overlapping ' names as Rose of Kilravock, Brodie of Brodie, Dunbar of Westfield, Erskine of Mar, Spalding of Ashintully, Ramsay of Bamff, Fothringham of Fothringham, Lyon of Glamis, Haldane of Gleneagles and Stirling of Keir: though it would perhaps be a bold man that tried to write anything new about such an ' overlapping ' family as Innes of that Ilk, whose historian and scion is the present Lord Lyon King of Arms—Sir Thomas Innes of Learney, author of *The Tartans of the Clans & Families of Scotland* (Edinburgh 1947) and editor of Frank Adam's *The Clans, Septs & Regiments of the Scottish Highlands* (Edinburgh 1952). I should perhaps

mention at this point that the following crest badges appearing in this book have not yet been recorded in Lyon Register: Galbraith, Gunn, Macaulay, Macfie and Macquarie.

Readers who want to follow up a particular clan or family should refer to Margaret Stuart's *Scottish Family History* (Edinburgh 1930), supplemented by Joan Ferguson's *Scottish Family Histories held in Scottish Libraries* (Edinburgh 1960). Much fascinating detail about the rarer surnames is to be found in Dr. George Black's *The Surnames of Scotland* (New York Public Library 1946). A good short general history of the Highlands is W. R. Kermack's *The Scottish Highlands* (Edinburgh 1957). The pioneer work on the older castles of the Highlands and Lowlands alike is of course MacGibbon & Ross, *The Castellated & Domestic Architecture of Scotland* (Edinburgh, 5 vols. 1887–1892)— on which we have drawn for some of our illustrations— but which should be read in conjunction with the present-day works of Dr. W. Douglas Simpson, who has kindly allowed us to use two of his drawings. Highland dress is examined in J. Telfer Dunbar's *History of Highland Dress* (Edinburgh 1962). The selection of tartans for the present work had to be made while I was temporarily abroad, and so that difficult task fell upon my editors. However, those who want to study tartan further should read Lady Hesketh's *Tartans* (London 1961). We received a lot of kind help from Mr. R. E. Hutchison of the Scottish National Portrait Gallery and Mr. Stuart Maxwell of the National Museum of Antiquities of Scotland. Finally, I can hardly miss this opportunity of warmly recommending my own coloured map, *Scotland of Old*, illustrated by Don Pottinger and published by John Bartholomew & Son, of Edinburgh.

Iain Moncreiffe of that Ilk.
Easter Moncreiffe, Perthshire, July 1967.

The Highlands

North of the Forth and the Clyde is the true Scotland that once had her capital at Scone. This was the old Gaelic-speaking kingdom of Alba, later known in ' Scots ' as Albany in rather the same way as Moscow-ruled Russia was known as Muscovy. This was Scotland as she stood before she assimilated the Cumbrian Welsh from the Clyde to the Solway and conquered the Northumbrian English from the Forth to the Tweed: before the wily lawyers and clerks of Glasgow and Edinburgh retaliated by getting their grips on the North and gradually eroding the Celtic culture and Gaelic language of their erstwhile conquerors.

Within the ancient land, there has never been quite such a clear-cut distinction between the highlands and the low-lands as has perhaps had to be made by many writers obliged to generalise. Tartan was worn in the lowlands as well as in the highlands, although of course highland dress was not worn in the lowlands as it is a hill dress. Every-where the Scots are of mixed race: Picts mingled with Gaels from Ireland, Norsemen from Scandinavia, Britons from Strathclyde, Angles from Northumbria, Normans and Flemings and Franks from the Continent. The Hebridean clan of MacLeod is of Norse origin, the Sutherlands were Flemish, while in the conquered territory south of the Forth such families as Dundas and Dunbar (and probably Home) were Gaels. Intermarriage had already scrambled the Scottish genealogical egg by the dawn of our national history.

Moreover, there were always families who held land both in the highlands and the lowlands. While they were tem-porarily a younger branch, for example, the present line of the Frasers of Lovat made their principal home at Strichen in lowland Buchan, but they always held land also at Abertarff in highland Stratherrick. Again, the Wemyss family belong to the Clan Macduff, the oldest known of all our surviving Gaelic clans, and because they held lands in the highlands the then Laird of Wemyss appears on the parliamentary Roll of Highland Landlords in 1587. Yet they have held lands in lowland Fife since time immemorial, and have made their home there at Wemyss itself since the eleven hundreds. As late as the sixteenth century the Lords Glamis in Strathmore spoke Gaelic as well as English, and

The Fair City of Perth, long the capital of Scotland, and still her natural geographical centre. Here Parliaments were held, and the kings inaugurated on the Stone of Destiny (or later, crowned) in the old Pictish capital at Scone, a little to the north across the Tay. In the foreground is Moncreiffe Island, held by the Moncreiffes until the end of the last century. The two open spaces beyond it are the two famous ' Inches ' of Perth, once islands in the marshes (Inch is from the Gaelic *innis*, an island). There is an unsubstantiated local tradition that they were given to the City of Perth in the fourteenth century, in return for the right to a family burial vault in St. John's Kirk, by the earliest known Provost of Perth: John Mercer of Aldie, M.P., Ambassador to England and France.

    ' Folk say the Mercers tried the toun to cheat,
      When for *twa inches* they did win *sax* feet '.

We are reminded that Perth was then a leading seaport, for Provost Mercer himself was robbed when shipwrecked in England, as a result of which his son Andrew Mercer, Bailie of Perth, gathered a mixed fleet of Scottish, French and Spanish vessels, and raided the English coast until defeated in 1378 in a naval battle by Sir John Philpot, Lord Mayor of London. From the Mercers' heiress springs the present Lord Lans-downe.

It was an old Norse and Anglo-Saxon custom to fight ' Trials by Combat ' on a special island called a *holmgang*, and the nearest *holmgang* to the mediaeval Parliaments at Scone or Perth was the North Inch: while our old parliaments (as opposed to councils) were most usually summoned when trials for high treason were impending. So it was on the North Inch that trials by combat were usually fought in Scotland. The most famous was the ' Battle of the Clans ' in 1396, which the present writer believes was fought between the Mackintosh Shaws of Clan Chattan and the Cummins: in the presence of King Robert III. One night in 1437, however, Sir Robert Graham swept down on to Perth at the head of a picked raiding party of his highlandmen, and slew King James I himself. Thereafter, Scone and Perth were less often the centre of Scottish national affairs.

in the eighteenth century highlanders from as far afield as Glenmuick on Deeside took the surname of Lyon and acknowledged the Earl of Strathmore in the lowlands of Angus as their chief.

All the same, there was of course an ever-increasing difference. This appears for instance in the mediaeval historian Wyntoun's chronicle, in various Acts of Parliament too, and in the late sixteenth-century ballad lamenting the slaughter by Huntly of the bonnie Earl of Moray—' Ye hielands and ye lawlands, and whaur hae ye been?'. This distinction gradually became more and more marked as the Gaelic language retreated into the highlands and islands and as, after the Union of the Crowns, English gold was able to give the King more strength to control, through his Privy Council, his unruly subjects throughout the low country in Scotland. Blood feuds between the great lowland Names were stamped out, leaving clan warfare isolated in the highlands. King James VI was able to write from Whitehall that where his ancestors had been hard pressed to rule by the sword, he could rule by a stroke of the pen.

Although the original Scots were Gaels, yet ' Scots ' is an English tongue. The blood of both was a mixture of Celt and Teuton: but the Gaelic-speaking mountain folk were increasingly thought of as a dangerous nuisance by the ' Scots '-speaking lowlanders. The well-armed hillmen had traditions and customs, a costume and a music all their own, and a language which seemed literally ' barbarous ' to the businesslike burgesses and canny countrymen of the low ground.

Sir Robert Dalrymple, who married the Hamilton heiress of Bargany in 1707, and was son of Lord President Dalrymple of North Berwick. He belonged to one of the greatest and most powerful of the Lowland Whig families, but is wearing a tartan dressing-gown in his own home.

Although heather, peat hags and bracken cover so much of the highlands today, in the old days vast tracts of the hill-country were wooded. Intensive efforts are now being made to revive forestry in the highlands, both by the Forestry Commission and by such timber-enthusiasts as Lord Dundee. Yet almost until modern times a great part of what is now moorland was covered by the eerie Caledonian Forest. A few remaining woods of this forest are to be seen in the Black Wood of Rannoch in the Robertson

The Bonnie Earl of Moray's corpse, shewing his every wound in detail, taken by his mother's orders immediately after he was slain by the Gordons. He was surrounded at night in his castle at Donibristle in Fife by the Gordons under Huntly, who had a royal commission to arrest him. The castle was set on fire, but held out under the hereditary Sheriff of Moray (Dunbar of Westfield) while the earl made his escape. Unfortunately, the silken tassel in his cap took fire, and he was tracked down in the darkness. As Gordon of Gight (the poet Lord Byron's ancestor) slashed his face, the dying earl exclaimed: ' You have spoilt a better face that your own.' The earl's mother, Lady Doune (a Campbell of Argyll), extracted several bullets with her own hands from her son's corpse and ordered this portrait of the atrocity to be painted— it is referred to in a contemporary report by the English Ambassador— before dying herself of burns sustained in the fire. The picture is now at Darnaway Castle.

country in Glenstrathfarrar in the Lovat country and at Rothiemurchus in the Grant country (where reindeer – long extinct in Scotland, except for some obtained from Lappland in 1790 by the 4th Duke of Atholl, which did not thrive – have been reintroduced as an experimental research project by the Reindeer Council of the U.K., mainly in Glenmore Forest Park). In these and other patches are continued what was once the native woodland of the highlands, dominated by the true Scots fir, which has survived by reseeding naturally. But the rest of the huge Caledonian Forest had similarly regenerated itself century after century until, after the population explosion in the highlands during the seventeen and eighteen hundreds, vast areas were denuded by man.

There used also to be in the highlands deciduous forests of oak and alder. Oak in Rannoch was long used for smelting. But little attempt has been made to replant hardwoods because they grow so slowly. Forestry is now in the hands of either the Forestry Commission, who must have a fairly rapid turnover to justify themselves, or of the

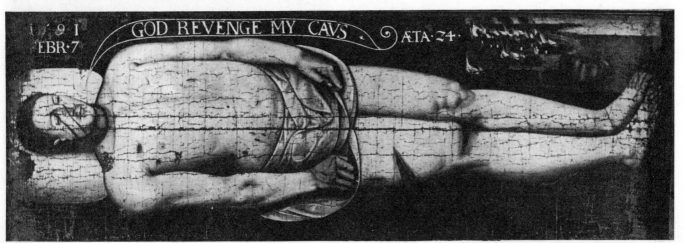

The forest of Rothiemurchus.

lairds, who must make a foreseeable profit in order to maintain the economy of their estates. So the highlands are now being re-afforested with conifers—particularly the larch. This was introduced into the highlands in 1737 when Menzies of Culdares brought three larches back from the Tyrol and presented them to Lord George Murray, who in turn gave them to his brother, the 2nd Duke of Atholl. 'At first they were treated as hothouse plants, which condition not suiting them, they were planted out in 1738.' The Atholl family encouraged the larch, about 20 million trees being planted by the 4th Duke; and in 1883 the 7th Duke of Atholl, visiting Japan, brought back seedlings of the Japanese larch which he planted near Blair Castle. Quite accidentally, these were cross-pollinated with the European larch and produced the hybrid larch which, being ideally suited to the Scottish climate, has become the standard tree for Scottish forestry.

Until late in the seventeenth century, wolves roamed the highland forests. Mary Queen of Scots was present at a hunting party in Atholl when, in addition to 360 red deer and some roes, 5 wolves were killed. The last wolf in the highlands is often said to have been killed by Lochiel in 1680, but in fact a female wolf with her cubs was slain in a cave in Sutherland perhaps as late as 1743. Now that the wolf has gone, the fierce Scots wild-cat remains as the largest savage wild animal in Britain. *Felis catus* has never yet successfully been tamed, and is quite unlike the domestic cat both in character and appearance. The present Farquharson chief has a striking sporran made from the pelt of a large wild-cat trapped at Invercauld. One of the rarest of all British mammals—the pine marten—is also still occasionally trapped by accident in the highlands. Such an unfortunate accident has at least provided a very fine pine marten sporran for a Mackenzie chieftain: Lord Cromartie. The capercailzie (the Gaelic ' old gaffer of the woods ') became extinct in the eighteenth century, and was reintroduced successfully by the Marquess of Breadalbane. It is a purely woodland bird and so (contrary to recent uninformed opinion) nobody was ' cleared ' to make way for its revival. Golden eagles still fly, and ptarmigan in

the high peaks, while the rare osprey has returned to nest in Badenoch. But the blackcock and the ' moor-fowl ' or grouse are above all the birds of the Highlands.

Life was primitive in the old clan days. The shallow soil of the highlands was broken with a crude spade-plough worked by foot, the *cas-chroim*. The main crops on the cultivated low ground were barley and oats, which provided bread and porridge, but potatoes became an important supplement by the second half of the eighteenth century. Flax was also grown. On the more level ground it was possible to use horse-drawn ploughs with four small horses abreast and a highlandman walking backwards between the centre animals to guide the plough from stones. The staple summer dish of the clans was a mixture of milk and whey, also oatcakes and porridge, augmented by fish caught locally. On the West Coast and in the Isles, whale and seal steak occasionally gave variety to the fish diet of the mainland: salmon, trout and pickled herrings. Geese and poultry were kept. Meat was eaten more in the winter, also salted butter, crowdie, and skim-milk cheese. The surplus in livestock formed the principal highland trade: cattle, horses (far more than is generally realised), sheep, goats and pigs. Indeed, the money obtained from the sale of hides, wool and especially of livestock in the Lowlands and the South was for centuries the Highlanders' constant source of income.

But the martial clans' prestige was based above all on cattle (like other pastoral warrior races as far afield as the Masai and the Watutsi). Many barrels of pickled beef were exported annually to the Continent: and a fascinating book has been written on the well-worn drove roads that carried the bestial through many a dangerous territory to

Sixteenth-century brooch of the MacIver Campbells of Ballochyle, bearing the Campbell *gyronny* coat-of-arms with two blank quarters, the leopard's heads for MacIver, and the initials MC. It is now in the National Museum of Antiquities of Scotland, in Edinburgh.

such famous cattle-markets as the Falkirk 'tryst' and that at Crieff in Perthshire. The animals were normally pastured on the moorland near the cultivated land in the broad straths and narrow glens. On the higher ground, even highland cattle were only hardy enough to be loosed for a few summer weeks. The stone huts whose ruins are still to be found throughout the mountains were never permanent habitations, but were the summer shielings put up to shelter the women and children who enjoyed their annual outing as cattle herders. When the brief summer was over, they returned to their settlements around the small arable patches far below the high ground. At the onset of winter, beasts were slaughtered to provide barrels of salt meat, two or three households often sharing one carcase, and the making of haggis ensured that nothing at all was wasted. Even 'braxy' mutton from sheep found dead on the hillside was eaten. The cattle that were spared for breeding were bled alive to give the raw material—fresh blood—to be mixed with oatmeal for 'black pudding'. By Spring they were often so weak that they had to be man-handled out to pasture in the 'lifting time'.

Cattle always meant prestige. From ancient Celtic times cattle raids were looked on as a sort of sport or test of prowess. The highlanders saw little wrong in it, unless they had been paid tribute for 'protection'. The late W. C. Mackenzie put their viewpoint thus: 'The animals were made by God; they derive their food direct from God's pastures, on which man has expended neither labour nor money; therefore the animals are the common property of mankind. If we steal our neighbours' cattle to-day, our neighbours will steal ours tomorrow, and so we are quits; and as for the Sasgunnaich (Lowlanders), well, their country belonged to our forefathers, so it is a land where every Highlandman can take his prey.'

So cattle raiding was regarded by the otherwise very law-abiding Gaels as quite distinct from ordinary theft: it was simply up to the other side to try and prevent them from succeeding. Thus from pre-Christian times onwards the famous *boroma* or cattle tribute levied by the high kings of Ireland on the kings of Leinster was never handed over without a battle. And, in times when a certain amount of blood-letting was thought a reasonable show of vigour, the heir to a highland chiefship was expected to have led at least one cattle raid before his succession. This practice of cattle raiding added a word to the English language: ordinary 'mail' meant 'rent', so 'black mail' was the name originally given to the illegal levy made by high-landers on cattle raiders from other clans to allow them free passage through their territory—or alternatively, levied as 'protection money' on Lowland neighbours.

But life was not as primitive as all that. For the Gaels, being naturally resourceful, made full use of their natural resources.

The clansfolk usually built their own wee houses, and often made their own pottery and shoes. In all districts, there were of course carpenters, wrights, blacksmiths, armourers and weavers: hence surnames like Macintyre and Gow. Tailors and shoemakers used to travel, making suits or shoes in their patrons' houses. There were itinerant stocking merchants as late as the nineteenth century. There was a considerable linen industry, from home-grown flax and mostly for the home market. Beautiful 'waulking songs' remind us of the part played by the women in fulling the cloth.

The salmon fishing industry was and is still a valuable source of income to the eastern Highlands. From the Beauly, Spey, Ness and other rivers, the Frasers of Lovat, Stuarts of Moray, Gordons of Huntly, Mackenzies of Sea-forth and the Gairloch, all exported smoked, salted or dried salmon to the Continent: the Inverness merchants who acted as middlemen sending the fish in Inverness-built ships as far afield as the Netherlands, France and Italy. Sea fishing was even more lucrative. The chiefs and chieftains usually put up the money to provide the fishing-boats, and the merchants generally bartered for the catch—cod, herring, ling, skate—with oatmeal, iron, wine, brandy, and tobacco.

Timber was floated down main rivers like the Spey and the Tay, and sold in the Lowlands. Oak bark was used for tanning, and much leather was sent abroad. Until Canada was opened up to the fur trade by the French in the seventeenth century, the Highlands exported to the Continent many thousands of furs annually: mostly fox, pine marten and weasel skins. The 12th Earl of Sutherland set up saltpans, and also started the coal-mining at Brora, early in the seventeenth century. About the same time, slate quarrying for export to the Lowlands was begun in Mull and elsewhere.

For local consumption, heather ale was brewed in the home from very early times. By the sixteenth century frequent mention is made of *brogac*, 'the stimulation', a sweetened malt liquor whose production (anyway in Inverness) had to be repeatedly restricted to prevent a grain famine. About this time whisky, 'the water of life', began to take over in Inverness, and soon private stills were started by lairds and tacksmen all over the Highlands—suppressed from the eighteenth century onwards by harsh revenue demands that only led to illegal distillation. In the seventeenth century, the Islesmen had a dangerous 'stop-the-breath' whisky, four times distilled from oats, also a milder whisky, only thrice distilled, called *trestarig* (from the Danish words *tröst*, 'comfort', and *arak*, 'distilled spirit'). The chieftains and tacksmen drank a great deal of claret, but the Privy Council laid down a scale for them, anyway in the Hebrides, and strictly limited the import of to grow long for the purpose; but their grand ambition is to adorn their harps with great quantities of silver and gems, those who are too poor to afford jewels substituting crystals in their stead. Their songs are not inelegant, and, in general, celebrate the praises of brave men; their bards seldom choosing any other subject.' At the *ceilidhs*, poetry and legendary epics were declaimed by bards and story-tellers. There was also music and dancing, solo and collective singing. Their outdoor games were curling and shinty.

The ancient instrument of the Celt was the *clarsach* or harp. But although bagpipes are obviously very ancient in the Highlands, as with hill-folk in other countries, there is little mention of the pipes until the sixteenth century, when Alasdair 'Crouchback', 8th Chief of MacLeod (1481–1547), founded the famous College of Piping at Borreraig in Skye for the MacLeod chiefs' hereditary pipers, the MacCrimmons, the greatest pipers of all Gaeldom. It took between eight and twelve years to qualify at this college. A piper played during a raid made in about 1600 by the Stewarts of Atholl on Coupar Angus, and thereafter the pipes were so regularly used in battle as to be banned in 1747 as an 'instrument of war'. Sometimes the Highlanders danced reels or solo to the pipes or the Jew's harp.

Late mediaeval *clarsach* or harp of the Robertsons of Lude.

The Macnab (1734–1816), by Raeburn. Francis Macnab, 16th Chief of Macnab, in his uniform as Lt-Colonel of the Royal Breadalbane Volunteers, to whom he used to give his commands ' in voluble and forcible Gaelic'. He courted a lady in vain, even though he ' told her as an irresistible charm that he had the most beautiful burying-ground in the world ' (the Macnab chiefs are buried on the island of Inchbuie, ' the Yellow Isle' in the river Dochart, which is covered with Scots pines, larches, beeches and sycamores). So he never married, although he had thirty-two children and it was rumoured that several lasses in the district got ' the bad disorder' from him. He had his own distillery at Killin; and Heron, who toured Perthshire in 1792, wrote that The Macnab produced the best whisky to be found in Scotland.

wine. However, a late sixteenth-century writer tells us of the Islesmen: ' They boil the flesh with water poured into the paunch or skin of the animal they kill, and in hunting sometimes they eat the flesh raw, merely squeezing out the blood. They drink the juice of the boiled flesh. At their feasts they sometimes use whey, after it has been kept for several years, and even drink it greedily.'

The Highlanders were immensely hospitable. They loved their *ceilidhs*, which were held ' by the light of the peat-fire flame' in the townships on winter evenings. The same sixteenth-century writer says: ' Instead of a trumpet, they use a bagpipe. They are exceedingly fond of music, and employ harps of a peculiar kind, some of which are strung with brass, and some with catgut. In playing they strike the wires either with a quill, or with their nails, suffered

At other times they danced to 'mouth music' or, particularly during the eighteenth and nineteenth centuries, to the fiddle. The greatest were the Atholl fiddlers, Neil Gow (1727–1807) and his son Nathaniel Gow (1766–1831), who composed many strathspeys and country dances.

In the highlands, funerals have always been great ceremonies. Over 5,000 men, horse and foot, attended the 6th Lord Lovat's funeral in 1633. During the American War of Independence, in 1779, the celebrated Scots-American naval raider Paul Jones sailed into Loch Dunvegan, only to hasten back to sea again because he mistook a funeral procession for an armed body of clansmen marching to defend the castle. At Sir Malcolm MacGregor of Mac-Gregor's funeral in 1879, the procession in Balquhidder was several miles long. At the conclusion of the 8th Duke of Atholl's burial service in 1942, after a motor procession from Dunkeld to Blair, Atholl Highlanders, Hillmen, Curlers and Freemasons, also men of the Scottish Horse and the Canadian Forestry Corps, filed round the grave, the masons dropping in sprigs of acacia and the Atholl Highlanders sprigs of juniper, while others drank to His late Grace and poured oblations of whisky. And a great gathering of Campbells attended the State Funeral of the 10th Duke of Argyll in 1949, when his coronet nearly fell off his coffin and his styles and titles were proclaimed by a royal herald wearing a tabard. In the old days, a *coronach* or lament used to be wailed by the women. Led by the principal mourner, the others then danced through the night of the 'wake'. Burials were followed by speeches and much drink—Charles Robertson of Auchleeks was drowned when he fell through the ice on Loch Tummel while returning drunk from a funeral, early in the eighteenth century.

Most of the chiefs and greater chieftains necessarily pos-

Part of a Processional Roll prepared for a herald's guidance at the State Funeral of George Gordon, 1st Marquis of Huntly, in 1636.

sessed a stone stronghold. A few of these still survive, much adapted or enlarged as their modern homes: Hebridean castles like those of Maclean at Duart and Macneil at Kisimul and MacLeod at Dunvegan—and on the mainland, those of Atholl at Blair, Sutherland at Dunrobin, Perth at Stobhall, Rattray at Craighall, Farquharson at Invercauld, the Cromartie Mackenzies at Castle Leod, the Campbells at Cawdor and the Ogilvys at Airlie. Picturesque ruins remain of such other strongholds as that of Clanranald at Eilean Tioram, Glengarry at Invergarry, MacIain of Ard-namurchan at Mingarry, Argyll at Inchconnel, the Gordons at Huntly, Lamont at Toward, McCorquodale at Loch Tromlie, Macfarlane at Eilean-a-Vow, Colquhoun at Rossdhu, Menzies at Castle Menzies, the Shaws of Rothie-murchus at Loch-an-Eilean and the Sinclairs at Girnigoe.

But a chief who lived at a sufficient distance from any unpleasant neighbours usually moved out of his tower. Whenever it was safe, he naturally preferred to live in a house. Chiefs therefore tended either to abandon or else to convert their strongholds as soon as it was possible for them to live more comfortably. In the seventeenth century, the Mackay chiefs lived in the charming House of Tongue. In the eighteenth century, Macneil of Barra moved out of Kisimul Castle into a modest Georgian house at Eoligarry. Achnacarry, the home of Lochiel, which was burnt by the Government troops in 1746, appears to have consisted of two stone gable ends with a wooden house built between them: though earlier chiefs had lived in the tower of Tor-castle.

We are told in the Dewar MS. that in the age of King

The old 'Laird's House' at Pitcastle in Atholl, former home of the royally-descended Robertson chieftains of Pitcastle. Now roofless, it is the typical four-roomed house of a sixteenth-century 'bonnet laird'. On the ground floor was Pitcastle's sitting room, and a twenty-foot long public room that was partitioned to allow for a kitchen and passage. Carved fir panelling from these once *painted* partitions, together with the nail-studded front door with its triangular peep-hole, has been taken to Blair Castle for preservation: and probably dates from the time of Duncan Robertson of Pitcastle, who sat on a local assize with six more Robertsons and eight other Athollmen to try a Stewart murderer in 1602. An inside stone staircase led to Pitcastle's own bedchamber, but there is only an outside stair (shewn in the illustration) to the general bedroom, also on the upper floor.

James VI 'Macfarlane of Arrochar had a castle on the island of Inveruglas and another in Eilean a' bhùtha, but his dwelling-house was in Tarbert at a place called the Cladach Mor, Big Strand, at the side of Loch Lomond. . . . The house was but thirty-four feet long and thirteen broad, inside. It contained but three rooms: a kitchen, a sitting-room and a pantry, and the pantry was in the middle of the house. The kitchen-fire was on the middle of the floor and a hole right over it in the roof allowed the smoke to escape. The fire of the sitting-room was near the gable and a stone with a smooth surface behind it. A chimney-top made of twigs and daubed with clay was above the fire of the chamber to let out the smoke. The rafters of the house were about three feet asunder. Beams of cleft oak placed close together and covered with sods formed a loft above the laird of Arrochar. There was but a single window with six panes in the chamber. There was one window with four panes in the kitchen, on the front of the house, and there was a window-hole at the back, which was shut with boards when the wind blew through it. There was another window-hole in the pantry shut with boards, which was opened when anything was to be done there. The house was thatched with bracken.'

The tacksmen or leading gentlemen of the clan lived in pleasant but not very large houses. Nowadays they would often be considered mere cottages. For although the ordinary gentlemen were well educated and in many cases most polished, they lived close to their people and anyway could not afford grand houses. For instance, as a Baron, the MacLaren chieftain of Wester Invernenty had local powers of life and death, but he still went ploughing with

the rest. In 1736, Stewart of Invernahyle wrote to Atholl's factor: 'Rob Roy's youngest son . . . came with a gunn and pistle to the Town of Drumlich where John McLaren, Baron Stoibchon and Wester Innernenty liv'd, and the said Baron with two of his neighbours being att the pleugh, this youngest son of Rob Roy's, called Robert, came to the pleugh, and without any provocation, as the Baron was holding the plough, shott him behind his back, of which wound he dyed that night.'

Simpler still were the 'black houses', which were thick-walled rubble cottages, often consisting of a single room with no window. Usually they had no gables, and their roofs were pitched at a low angle, supported by longitudinal beams over coupling timbers and usually springing from the inner part of the ledges formed by the tops of the four walls. The hearth was in the centre of the floor, and some of the peat-smoke could escape through a chimney-hole beside the roof-tree. Turf, rushes or heather were the usual thatching materials, although latterly straw was used. The custom was that the walls belonged to the laird, but the roofing to the cottar, who took it with him if he removed When the thatch had grown too old, it was used for manuring the infield. A clay and wattle partition often provided a second room, used to shelter livestock (who entered by the same door) in bad weather. Even Dunvegan itself was originally just a great long 'black house' surrounded by a curtain wall, and the present Macneil of Barra found the ashes of the mediaeval central hearth when he was restoring

Dunvegan Castle, as it was in the time of Leod, name-father of the MacLeods, during the thirteenth century. The curtain wall and well still exist, as also does the sea-gate, which until the middle of the eighteenth century was the only entrance to the castle. The long-hall of those days was like a great 'black-house' (with a central hearth as at Kisimul), but has long since been replaced by an ever-changing complex of buildings. This reconstruction was drawn by Dr. Douglas Simpson.

the ruined (and always until now, chimneyless) Great Hall of Kisimul Castle.

Buchanan wrote of the Hebrideans in 1582: 'In their houses, also, they lie upon the ground; strewing fern, or heath, on the floor, with the roots downward and the leaves turned up. In this manner they form a bed so pleasant, that it may vie in softness with the finest down, while in

A typical 'black house' in the Hebrides. The thatch is held on by a fishing-net weighted with stones.

salubrity it far exceeds it.' He adds that when they 'travel in other countries, they throw aside the pillows and blankets of their hosts, and wrapping themselves round with their own plaids, thus go to sleep'. It is recounted that when the great Sir Ewen Cameron of Lochiel (1629–1719) was snowbound on the open hills at night while out wolf-hunting, he kicked away a snowball which his heir had made up to rest his head on, asking angrily if his son had grown so soft that he could not sleep without a pillow?

Up to the sixteenth century, the bare-legged clansmen or 'redshanks' wore pleated tunics to the knee, usually dyed with saffron. They had great mantles or plaids, apparently of tartan, their favourite colours being purple and blue until the mid-sixteenth century, when dark browns became popular for camouflage. Mediaeval chiefs sometimes wore plate-armour under their armorial surcoat. But as late as the sixteenth century the chieftains tended to wear a distinctive 'yellow war coat', of thickly padded and quilted linen, and their followers' bodies were often protected by leather jerkins in place of armour. On the whole, however,

Tomb effigy at Iona of a Maclean chieftain of Coll, shewing his kilted war-coat and conical helmet or *clogaid*.

their defensive armour consisted of a conical 'iron head-piece, and a coat of mail, formed of small iron rings, and frequently reaching to the heels'. They carried bows, with barbed arrows that were difficult to extract from a wound, Lochaber axes (with a hook at the end of the staff, for dragging an enemy from his horse) and long two-handed swords. These claymores or 'big swords' usually had quatrefoils ornamenting the end of their upward-sloping crossguards.

By the seventeenth century, however, these claymores had been cut down to form basket-hilted broadswords. A round Celtic shield of leather on wood, often with a central spike, called a targe, was carried on the left arm; and a dirk was held point downwards in the left hand. The Roll of Arms for the Earl of Atholl's following in 1638 appears to indicate some connection (perhaps only sufficient means) between the wearing of a targe and the ownership of a gun or pistol. One entry on that roll shows a Highlander still in possession of a coat-of-mail. But it was already rare, for the MacGregor chief's brother, who was killed at the battle of Glenfruin in 1603, was nicknamed Iain *Dubh nan Luireagh*: 'Black John of the Mail-Coat'. Arm-pit knives were carried for practical use, but the black stocking-knife or *sgian dubh* is first illustrated in Raeburn's celebrated

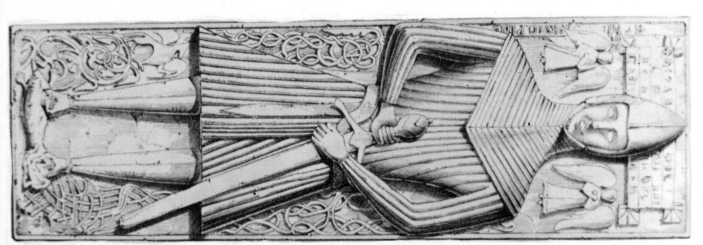

Targe of James Stewart, 4th of Ardvorlich, who was wounded by mistake by a party of Camerons when he took part in Atholl's operations against Argyll in 1685. It is probably the only contemporary targe in existence that still has its original spike.

portrait of MacDonell of Glengarry, who appears to have a knife and fork together in his stocking; although Stewart of Ardvorlich has what he believes to be seventeenth-century examples of a similar knife and fork, flattened for the leg but now lacking the sheath. Its introduction into regimental uniform gave it its modern vogue. Bye-knives and forks were also often carried, side by side or one above the other, in the scabbards of dirks. The Highland pistol, of which the finest were made at Doune, is usually distinguished by a ball-trigger (a round knob in place of a normal trigger) and by having no trigger-guard. Screwed into the butt, there is often a pricker for cleaning the touch-hole.

By the seventeenth century, the ancient tartan mantle of the clansmen had developed into the great belted plaid, which was itself divided in the eighteenth century into kilt and short plaid, worn over a dyed shirt. Belted plaids were often cast off in battle, much to the horror of lowland or foreign foes, who called the highlanders 'naked savages'. This was hardly fair, as they tied their shirt-tails between their legs before going into action. From at least the sixteenth century, the King, great nobles and mounted chieftains wore 'short Highland coats' over tartan trews which combined breeks and hose in a single close-fitting garment: the plaid being belted over all.

The antiquity of clan and family tartans is much in dispute. It seems certain that there were some in existence before the Jacobite Risings, possibly even from the sixteenth century (when the Macleans had an annual rent payable in ells of black, white and green cloth: the colours of their present tartan); and Garth implies that old war tartans existed. But if family or district tartans did exist so early, they were certainly not consistently worn. However, family or estate *tweeds* (such as the Atholl grey or the Dalhousie tweed) have existed for upwards of a century, but are certainly not worn constantly by those who have a right to them. The same applies to regimental tweeds, such as that of the Scots Guards which is already about a century old.

By the reign of Queen Anne, the Grants had a red and green uniform *war* tartan, but contemporary paintings show that they wore whatever they fancied in civil life. There are reasons for supposing that the Red Murray, or Murray of Tullibardine, hangings on a bed at Blair Castle have survived from the late seventeenth century; and what looks very like the same sett appears on the plaid of Norman, 22nd Chief of MacLeod (whose grandmother was sister of

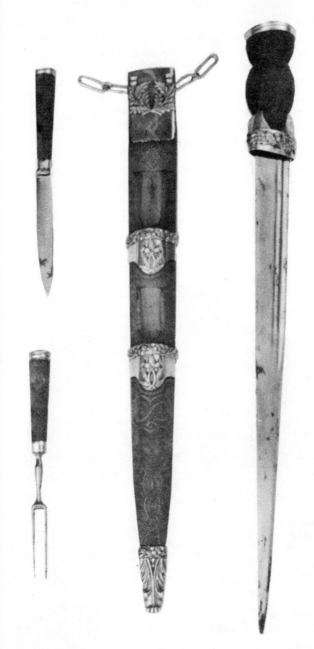

the 1st Duke of Atholl and who was brought up partly in Perthshire), in his famous mid-eighteenth century portrait in the pose of Apollo Belvedere, by Allan Ramsay. And in 1768, Sir Robert Murray Keith wrote from Dresden, where he was British Envoy, for ' a plaid of my colours '. In his case, the tartan was probably regimental, and several clan tartans undoubtedly began as regimental tartans when chiefs raised clan regiments in the eighteenth century. The Gordon clan tartan, for example, was designed originally for the Gordon Highlanders by adding a yellow stripe (which their old rivals the Black Watch infuriatingly refer to as a ' yellow streak ') to the old Government or Black Watch tartan.

The distinguishing mark of kings or chiefs in many parts of the world, from Africa to America, is the wearing of eagle's feathers. Dr. Johnson wrote of the young Laird of Coll and his clansmen that ' He did not endeavour to dazzle them by any magnificence of dress: his only distinction was a feather in his bonnet '. The convention has long been established that a chief wears three eagle's feathers, the chieftains of cadet branches wear two, and the gentlemen of the clan may wear one feather. The Sovereign, as Chief of Chiefs, wears four. These distinctions are followed by the Royal Company of Archers (who used to wear tartan uniforms). Their Captain-General wears three eagle's feathers, their officers two, and the ordinary Archers of the Queen's Body Guard wear a single feather.

When chiefs went about, they were accompanied by a body of armed clansmen known as their ' tail '. Besides an adequate following of armed men, it included the bard or *seanachaidh* (historian), the henchman (the chief's personal

Dirk with carved heather-wood hilt and sheath, mounted in its present form in 1822 for Sir Evan MacGregor of MacGregor. The blade is older, and the silver mounting is inscribed ' Major Evan MacGregor, Aid de Camp to H.R.H. Prince Charles, Sept. 1745 '. Major Evan, whose son Sir John eventually became 18th Chief of Clan Gregor, was younger brother of Robert MacGregor of Glencarnock, Chieftain of the Children of the Mist, who commanded the MacGregors in the 1745 Rising. It was Evan MacGregor who, with a long gun (' she was so heavy that no man could carry her above a mile at once ') fired the first shot at Cope's army the day before Prestonpans. ' The Prince thought much of this, that we got the first blood of them.' Duncan MacGregor, who was present as an officer, wrote years afterwards to Evan's son, Sir John, about the MacGregor regiment at the battle of Prestonpans itself: ' Captain Duncan MacGregor was wounded through the thigh, Captain James Mor MacGregor was wounded thro' the thigh, Captain Malcolm MacGregor got his two legs broken, twenty-one private men were wounded and one shot dead upon the spot. We pursued the retreating army a mile and a half . . . The Prince came and took Glencarnock in his arms, and Captain Evan, and told them to gather the whole Clan MacGregor upon the middle of the Field of Battle. There was a table covered and the MacGregors guarding him at dinner, every man got a glass of wine and a little bread. Your Father and Uncle sat down with him, the rest of the Chieftains took it amiss that the MacGregors got this honour, but it was dear bought . . .'

This illustration also shews the bye-knife and fork carried in the scabbard.

Pictish stone in Strathpeffer, carved with the world-wide royal symbol of an eagle.

body-guard, as Gold Stick is to the Queen), the *bladaire* or tatler (the chief's ' mouthpiece '), the harper or piper, and even a special man to carry their chief dry-shod over fords—the chief was as tough as they were (as witness the Great Lochiel), but they liked to do him this honour, shedding lustre on the whole clan. A great magnate like Atholl, just like his Lowland counterparts such as Douglas, was attended in Edinburgh by followers who wore his crest hung around their necks (rather like decanter-labels)', as can be seen, for instance, in Chambers' eighteenth-century print of the Riding of the Scottish Parliament in 1685. From this there were evolved the modern clan badges, which consist of the chief's crest surrounded by a strap-and-buckle bearing his motto. These badges are usually made of silver, and have been worn in the bonnet since the nineteenth century.

The older badges were the lucky plants of the clans. The idea of a sacred plant is very ancient, going back to the Dawn Religion in the New Stone Age. Family plants are found as far afield as among the Japanese samurai. And there was an ancient Greek who, fleeing from a battle-field, came on a field of clover and stopped to be slain rather than tread on his family plant. The Hay mistletoe at Erroll is referred to in Frazer's monumental work, *The Golden Bough*. The Moncreiffe oak-leaves appear on a stone carving of the 12th laird's heraldic ' mantling ' by 1634.

A silver pine-cone button from Sir Gregor MacGregor of MacGregor's evening kilt coat. It is the plant-badge of Clan Gregor.

After the 1745 Rising, one of the Government witnesses at the trial of Lord Lovat gave evidence that 700 Frasers had paraded at Castle Dounie wearing the Jacobite white cockade and sprigs of yew in their bonnets. There is still a great yew in Stratherrick, where the Stratherrick Frasers cut their plant badges—the Frasers in the Aird got their yew badges from Tomnahurich, which was the main Fraser gathering-place. In the seventeenth and eighteenth centuries, the Macdonalds marched to war behind a bunch of heather tied to a pole. In 1678 ' the Glencow men were verie remarkable, who had for their ensigne a faire bush of heath, wel spred and displayed on the head of a staff '; and in *The Grameid* in 1691, James Philip says of the Macdonalds in Dundee's Jacobite host two years before: 'These all being chiefs sprung from the blood of Donald, they . . . carry into battle, as the emblem of their race, a branch of wild heather hung from the point of a quivering spear.'

Another interesting survival from ancient times is that certain ' beasts ' have always been considered sacred, dedi-cated to that spirit of royalty which represents the whole symbolic feeling of the nation. For example, Edward II of England protected by statute the whole of the dolphin

family, and also protected the sturgeon under the mistaken impression that it was a form of dolphin. That is why the sturgeon is the fish that most people think of as Fish Royal, and all sturgeons caught in English waters are sent to The Queen. But in the Celtic world, especially among the ancient Gaels, the salmon was the sacrosanct royal fish. When one Irish king overthrew another, he used to kill the salmon in his enemy's royal fishpond. Ancient Irish kings wore the salmon as a brooch. Even today the Duke of Argyll, his son Lord Lorne, and the Campbells of Lochnell, the branch who have long been the nearest heirs, are

Velvet doublet of the present *Mac Chailein Mor*'s son and heir Ian Campbell, Marquis of Lorne, shewing as silver buttons the sacred royal salmon of the ancient Gaels, worn by the Argyll family as ultimate successors in the female line of the local Kings of Argyll: the ' Border of the Gaels '. His wife Iona, Marchioness of Lorne, is daughter of Sir Ivar Colquhoun of Luss, present Chief of the Clan Colquhoun.

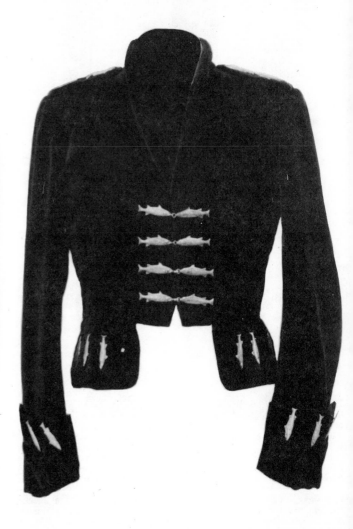

regarded as having a special right to wear silver salmon as the buttons on their doublets. When the late Duke of Argyll as a young man went to stay with the late Duke of Atholl, the younger members of the Atholl family went up to his bedroom, cut off his silver salmon doublet-buttons and replaced them with real sardines stuck on to pieces of cardboard; thus continuing the ancient feud between the Atholl and Argyll families into modern times as what social anthropologists would call a ' joking relationship '. So salmon fishing was reserved to the Crown, whose revenues were thus augmented by the ability to grant charters of particular salmon fishing, like ordinary grants of land. Until the sixteenth century, too, the King of Scots was always accompanied by a live lion, the royal ' beast ' of Scotland, and there was a Lyon's Den in every royal palace.

From the most ancient times known to us, it was perhaps one of the main purposes of ceremonial pageantry to inculcate religious concepts or ethical principles within the growing community. But after the Reformation (which in Scotland occurred in 1560) an extreme reaction against elaborate ritualism drove almost all beauty and colour out of Highland church life for a long time. It's sad, for instance, to realise that the lost pre-Reformation Scottish sacred music was famous throughout Europe. The lovingly carved statues of holy men (which is all that ' saint' actually means) were smashed, though now once again we have a statue of a holy man, John Knox, outside St. Giles' Cathedral. The popular emotional need for colourful ceremony found outlets in other ways, often secret. It was in the time of the learned theologian King James VI (who was himself made a mason in what is now Lodge Scone and Perth) that Freemasons began the process that led to the formation of purely speculative as opposed to operative Masonic Lodges: for Freemasonry inculcates the highest brotherly and indeed divine ethical principles through the beautiful symbolism of its ritual. The present Lord Macdonald, Chief of the great Clan Donald, is a past Grand Master Mason of Scotland, as was the late Sir Iain Colquhoun of Luss, Chief of the Clan Colquhoun.

A more sinister result of the suppression of all colour in religion after the Reformation, was a marked revival of the witch cult. People talk about ' witch-hunts ' nowadays as if there never were any underground witches. But indeed there were, and many, though not necessarily always those unfortunates who were hunted out and ' pricked ' as such. Of course, many vestiges of the Dawn Religion, the sacrificial cult of the divine king (that venerates the continuity of the embodied life-force), survive in Christian ceremonial: the magic of the old rituals being translated poetically to express new and more abstract meanings (see the present writer's *Blood Royal*). Other traces continue, such as touching wood, not walking under a ladder (Woden's sacrificial scaffold), or the keeping of an animal mascot. But in the sixteenth and seventeenth centuries more sinister rites underwent a marked underground revival. It must be remembered that witchcraft was the primaeval religion, the fertility cult (that perceives divinity in the spark of life), with its symbolic worship of the Horned One, and that men as well as women could be witches: joining in the secret covens of thirteen grouped around the ' devils ' (local priests of the Fertility Spirit) scattered throughout Scotland.

Men of the highest rank joined with the most humble in these pagan rites. The Lord Lyon King of Arms was burnt at the stake for witchcraft in 1569; while King James VI's cousin Francis Stuart, Earl of Bothwell, was the Devil of the North Berwick witch-coven in 1589, and used his occult power to plot the king's death. In the same year, Hector Munro of Foulis, Chief of the Clan Munro, called in some local warlocks and witches to save his ailing life by casting his approaching death on to his younger half-brother, George Munro of Obsdale, as a Substitute Victim. The principal witch, Marian McIngarrath, dug a grave in which the Munro chief lay down at midnight, wrapped in blankets, and was covered over lightly with green turf fastened down with withes, ' probably cut from a rowan tree, to guard the spot from evil spirits '. His foster-mother Christian Neil then ran the length of nine riggs (over a mile) to consult with the local Devil, and then returned; whereupon the witch Marian asked her if she had made her choice, and the chief's foster-mother spoke the grim doom that ' Mr. Hector was her choice to live and his brother George to die '. The chief then literally returned from the grave to Foulis Castle. That he was called ' Mr.' at this date implies that he had graduated at a University; and it seems clear that he had profited by his education, for his reliance on witchcraft proved sound. His brother George duly died in 1590, and he himself recovered from his long illness in time to stand trial for murder and witchcraft. Naturally he was acquitted, but his poor witch-doctor, the unhappy sorceress Marian McIngarrath, was strangled and burnt at the stake, with the rest of her coven, after duly confessing under torture. Her highly successful skill was derived from an Old Norse magic ritual of pagan times, that had lingered on underground through the centuries. The last Highland witch to be burnt at the stake was so executed in 1722, at Dornoch in Sutherland.

Today, perhaps our most everyday reminder of the gay witches' ' sabbaths ' is the popularity of round reels. From the cave rites of the New Stone Age, and throughout aeons of time, on through the Bronze and Iron Ages into the eighteenth century, a basic religious ceremony continued all over Europe, and certainly in the Highlands. A mixed circle of both sexes danced round and round a central figure, who played on pipes or a flute, or sometimes (in more sophisticated days) even on a fiddle. This central figure was the Fertility Spirit's local priest and representative—a man dressed up full hairily in horns and a tail, Pan's living image. Nobody could deny there was something rather beastly about him. As the dance went on, the worshippers became gayer and gayer, in fact in their fine

The *Clach Dearg* or ' Red Stone ', the charm of Ardvorlich. In 1722, the celebrated heraldist Nisbet reckoned the then *Mac Mhic Bhaltair* to be Chieftain of all the Stewarts of Balquhidder because he possessed this sacred Charm Stone. From forty miles around, the worried owners of sick cattle used to bring kegs of spring water to Ardvorlich. ' There the Lady of Ardvorlich took the Charm, dangled it by its chain in the water and swirled it round three times, reciting a Gaelic incantation the while. After the Charm was taken out of the water, it was necessary for the owner of the beasts to take his keg back to his animal to drink; and shortly afterwards it would recover. One other obligation had to be observed; the man carrying the keg was not allowed to enter any building with the keg on his way home . . . ' It is a ball of rock crystal mounted in bands of silver with a Celtic pattern. It was probably part of a reliquary, and the family tradition is that it was brought back from a Crusade. Of course Ardvorlich's direct ancestor Alexander, 4th Steward of Scotland (1214–1283) was a Crusader, but any charm brought back by him would obviously have descended to the senior line of the Royal Stewarts. However, it could have been brought back from a much later Crusade. For instance, Sir Colin Campbell of Glenorchy went on a Crusade as a Knight of Rhodes (what is now called a Knight of Malta) in the fifteenth century, and brought back a similar charm stone, listed in a Glenorchy inventory c.1600 as ' ane stane of the quantitye of half a hen's egg set in silver, being flatt at the ane end and round at the uther and lyke a peir, whilk Sir Coline first laird of Glenurchy woir when he fought in battel at the Rhodes agaynst the Turks, he being one of the Knychtis of the Rhodes.' So it seems possible that Ardvorlich's more recent ancestor, whom King James III in 1465 called ' our beloved kinsman, James Stewart of Albany, natural son of the late James Stewart, son of Murdach Stewart, late Duke of Albany ', accompanied Glenorchy in his ' caravan ' against the Turks—or else took part in some similar Crusade—and brought back the blessed Charm Stone of Ardvorlich.

frenzy definitely abandoned. Perhaps that is why the poet Gray called them our 'rude forefathers'. Christianity had overthrown the newer gods far more easily than it conquered Pan and his beguiling pipes. So much so, that while all false gods were 'devils' to the Christians, yet it was the image of the Horned One himself that they usually depicted as 'The Devil'. The spirit of fertility became to ecclesiastical thought especially identified with Evil, and soon the catholic words 'sin', 'immoral' and 'licentious' took on a narrowed meaning that is perhaps behind many of our psychological, social and religious problems today. In 1489, the Inquisitors (who were all men) sensibly found that 'witchcraft is more natural to Women than to men, on account of the inherent wickedness of their hearts'. Nor is it surprising to find that Wine (or any intoxicant brew) and more especially Song were in exuberant demand at the witches' sabbaths. It is said that the witches, for instance, used to dance as late as the sixteenth century under the arches of the old bridge at Avignon: '*Sous le pont d'Avignon, on y danse tout en rond*' still has a fine diabolical ring. But by the eighteenth century such dances survived in the Highlands only as popular reels. The eightsome reel in its present form was evolved out of the old round reels by two Murrays, the 6th Duke of Atholl and the 7th Earl of Dunmore (whose son the 8th Earl, by the way, won the Victoria Cross) in the nineteenth century. The innocent mainstay of every Highland ball, the dancers still circle round a central figure; and as each successive man jigs alone in the middle, he raises his arms crescent-wise like antlers above his head, in a Stone Age symbol of the Horned One. But that is all. The pipe-major's piercing pipes are not the pipes of Pan.

A contemporary of the Wizard Earl of Bothwell and of the witch Marian McIngarrath was the famous Brahan Seer, many of whose remarkable prophecies still await fulfilment. 'Second Sight' undoubtedly exists in the Highlands, in the sense that if the many witnesses to its existence were witnesses instead to a crime, somebody would be

A 'sheila-na-gig' figure, built into the wall of the late mediaeval church of Rodil on the island of Harris, once the burial place of the MacLeod chiefs. These very ancient fertility symbols were often incorporated in old churches. After Harris passed from the MacLeods of Dunvegan in the nineteenth century, it was held for some time by the Murray earls of Dunmore, cadets of Atholl, and the present Earl is a Gaelic-speaker and piper who keeps up his connection with the island. The then Earl of Dunmore built Amhuinnsuidh Castle in North Harris in 1868. But Lady Dunmore is said not to have entirely approved of the sheila-na-gigs at Rodil, and to have made her gamekeeper shoot at them.

Aluminium works on the slopes of Ben Nevis in the Cameron country, the highest mountain in the British Isles (4,406 feet). On the summit the snow never melts. There is a prophecy that Cameron of Lochiel will hold his lands 'as long as there is snow on Ben Nevis'.

convicted on the overwhelming volume of their corroborative evidence. This also applies, of course, to the Loch Ness Phenomenon, better known as the Monster or 'Nessie'. We are told in a MS. History of the Campbells of Craignish, written c. 1717–1722, to cite but one instance, about ' the MacViccars being Rectors of it (Kilmun) but very lately before (1540), and from whom the old Parsons of Kilmalew, and Barons of Brenchellie, so famous for the surprizeing Gift of Prophesie inherent to that Race of the MacViccars for many ages '. It is hard to find the natural explanation for Second Sight, except perhaps on the basis of J. W. Dunne's *Theory of Time*.

It is easier, of course, to account for visionary dreams of *past* events, by the theory of Ancestral Memory. A moment's reflection will shew that a general ' folk memory ' is impossible, for a man can no more inherit a memory from some unrelated person than he can inherit the colour of his eyes from him. But he does inherit the colour of his eyes, and indeed all his other basic features, mental and physical, in a jumble from his myriad ancestors: and every now and then things slip into a recognizable shape and someone is the ' spitting image ' of some ancestor: as for instance the late ninth Baronet of Moncreiffe closely resembled the first Baronet of Moncreiffe, who was born in 1626. It does not seem impossible that in our subconscious mind we similarly inherit a jumble of memories, occasionally falling into shape in the same picturesque way. This would account for many of the emotional prejudices, not always attributable to environment, that sway individuals for apparently very ancient historical or religious reasons about which they nevertheless usually have never heard. An interesting Highland case of visionary dreams is that of the late James Fraser, cartwright in Beauly, who shortly before the Second World War related to Charles Ian Fraser of Reelig, the meticulously careful Highland scholar, a dream which often recurred to him, and of which Reelig sent an account to the present writer shortly before his death in 1963. The cartwright proceeded to give such an account of the fatal battle of *Blar-na-Leine* by Loch Lochy in 1544 (when *Mac Shimi* and almost all the Frasers were slain fighting the Clanranald) as very few scholars could have compiled. Some of his details, though obvious in retrospect, had not generally occurred to anybody before. Other details can be corroborated from certain obscure sources, but it seems improbable for various reasons that this particular cartwright or any friend of his could have undertaken the necessary research. And his description of the contemporary costumes, equipment, and methods of fighting could scarcely be bettered. Reelig, though naturally sceptical, was unable to resist the impression that he was telling the truth. The Fraser clansmen were much inter-bred in their own clan country, and James Fraser the cartwright probably descended over and over again (through cousin-marriages within his own ancestry) from a particular Fraser eyewitness of the battle: so that his recurring dream could possibly well be an example of Ancestral Memory.

Another survival from ancient times was the *crois taraidh* or ' Fiery Cross ', the Scottish successor of the Old Norse ' fire arrow '. Two pieces of wood were charred at the upper end and then fastened together to form a Cross, to which was attached a rag dipped in sheep's or goat's blood. Being both burnt and bloody, the Cross represented Fire and Sword. In time of war, the chief or chieftain sent it in relays throughout every township and clachan in his territory. Each successive bearer, usually mounted on a garron pony, shouted out as he passed, a single word: the name of the Gathering Place. The normal gathering place of

the Grants was ' Craigellachie ', of the Campbells ' Cruachan ', of the Robertsons ' Fea Choire '. Every able-bodied clansman thereupon seized his weapons and hurried to the appointed spot. Thus mobilisation was very rapid.

The Fiery Cross was used all over Scotland as late as the sixteenth century. Before the battle of Pinkie in 1547, when the English had invaded Scotland, ' the Governor of Scotland . . . caused certane herauldis and pursevauntes with all possible diligence pas throch all the partis of the realme with a fyrie croce bering fyre on the heid of it in thair handes, as the use of that realme hes bene in all gret extremiteis, chargeing all maner of man alswell spirituall as temporall of the aige betuix saxtene and saxtie bodin with armour in feare of wear to repair towart Mussilbruch with all possibill haist.' The last occasion on which the Fiery Cross called clansmen to war was in 1746, when Lord George Murray sent it out through Atholl in his attempt to retake Blair Castle from the advancing Hanoverians. But the Fiery Cross went out once again, during the General Election of 1820, and 800 Grant clansmen mobilised immediately and marched on Elgin to protect their Chief and his sisters, who had been blockaded in their townhouse there by an urban mob belonging to the opposite political party from that for which the Chief's brother was the candidate. The startled townsfolk gave no further trouble, except doubtless to vote as they pleased.

In time of peace, the chiefs gathered their clansmen periodically, to practise mobilisation and to make sure they were properly equipped and fit to fight. ' It was these ordinary people who formed the fighting men of the district in time of war, for the Scottish chiefs depended upon the loyalty and love of their own clansmen rather than on hired men-at-arms. Little countries of their own, the great districts were often at war with one another—but at least they knew their enemy and why they were fighting, and the casualties were nothing compared with those in the wars brought about by the existence of the vast agglomerate States of today.'

Gatherings called ' wapenschaws.' or weapon-shews were held both by highland chiefs and lowland lairds for the inspection of weapons, since they were responsible for the defence of their own territory and, in time of war, for the defence of Scotland. At these Gatherings, it was customary to hold Games at which feats of athletic prowess were performed by the local clansmen. For strength and alertness were prized by these warrior herdsmen. There were foot races and trials of strength, tossing the caber and putting the weight. Often, the opportunity was taken of driving the red deer for the great ' hunts ', when young clansmen learnt to use country in a martial way while collecting in the deer to pass the cross-bows or guns in the butts. In 1715, at Aboyne on Deeside, the Earl of Mar held a famous hunting party which emphasised the dual purpose of highland gatherings: hunting combined with preparation for war. The great hunt was attended by many of the peers and chiefs and, as a result of their deliberations, their host gathered his men in the Braes of Mar, raised the Jacobite royal standard, and began the 1715 Rising.

In time of national emergency, such as the Jacobite Risings, harsh measures were employed by the authorities on either side to force out those few who hung back, just as is done by the State in modern conscript War. The present writer was distressed, during the Second World War, to sit on the court-martial that tried a gipsy deserter, who had been conscripted and sent most unsuitably to the Grenadier Guards. Nevertheless, the unfortunate gipsy had to be sentenced to a term of imprisonment, for the country was at war and the State had so ordained. After the 1745 Rising, many clansmen wisely pled that they had been forced out by threats of burning their roof-trees, and there is no doubt that such threats combined with public opinion to bring out some unwilling men on both sides. On the other hand, Stewart of Garth tells us (of such chiefs as Grant, who thought it right, and MacLeod, who thought it wise, to support the Government cause in 1745) that: ' The sound arguments that prevailed with the Chiefs, who could comprehend them, had no influence on their followers who were, in this instance, more inclined to follow their feelings than listen to reason. Of this, the behaviour of the clan Grant was an instance. Eleven hundred men pressed forward to offer their services, on condition that their Chief would lead them, to support, what they styled, the cause of their ancient Kings. Afterwards, when it was found necessary to pay a compliment to the Royal General [i.e. Cumberland] by meeting him at Aberdeen, all the Chief's influence could only procure ninety-five followers to attend him; a Chief, too, much beloved by his people. In the Isle of Skye, likewise, Sir Alexander Macdonald (father of Chief

King George IV, by Wilkie. He had a great respect for his High-landers and, in 1822, was the first *de facto* Sovereign to visit Scotland since 1651. The present writer believes that he was also the lawful Jacobite Sovereign.

Baron Macdonald) and the Lairds of Macleod, Rasay, and others, had 2,400 men ready, when expresses arrived from Culloden. The former remained at home with his men, Macleod obeyed the summons of the President [Forbes of Culloden, Lord President of the Court of Session] whose arguments had such influence. Though Macleod is described by this great law officer as the only man of sense and courage he had about him, his influence over his followers failed so completely, when they discovered that his opinion was different to their own, that he could not command the obedience of more than 200 men, although upwards of 1,000 men, consisting of his own people, the Laird of Rasay's, and other gentlemen, were ready at Dunvegan Castle. These, and several circumstances which occurred at that period, are of themselves sufficient to prove, that the Highlanders were not those slaves to the caprice and power of their Chiefs that they have been supposed; and that, on the contrary, as I have already noticed, the latter were obliged to pay court, and yield to the will and independent spirit of their clans. These facts also refute a general opinion, that those who engaged in the Rebellion were forced out by their Chiefs and Lairds.'

After the failure of the 1745 Rising, gatherings were frowned on for over half a century. But after the accession of King George IV, who wore the kilt (as did his brothers), had a special affection for the Highlanders and was the first Sovereign to set foot in Scotland for 171 years, local Gatherings and Games were held once more. His niece, Queen Victoria, loved the Highlands (where she made her own favourite home) and actively fostered the Games. At first, the authorities were a little worried, as when rowdyism occurred and swords were drawn at the Caledonian Society's gathering in Inver Park at Dunkeld in 1826. But although some, like the annual Atholl and Breadalbane Gathering, included processions of armed highlanders—the Lonach Gathering on Donside still does—the emphasis now moved more and more away from war and on to the Games. Nowadays, the old warlike training of the horse-men, ' tilting at the ring ', is performed on motor-bicycle or jeep-back. Tossing the caber, putting the weight, and throwing the hammer, still continue. Piping and dancing were always features of these gatherings, and so the High-land Games once more became the annual meeting-place of the local community. It is sad that the smaller local Gatherings are now being quite deliberately taxed out of existence (by the decision of a recent Tory Government) despite the vigorous protests of all lovers of the Highlands, at a time when special tax privileges are being accorded to an alien game of the English, called cricket.

Law and order was maintained in the highlands through two sorts of jurisdiction—the feudal power of the barons and the traditional authority of the chiefs. To some extent the two forms overlapped, as many chiefs were also barons. For example, Lochiel and Duart were baronies held of the Crown, as were Struan and Strathlachlan and Foulis. The Mackintosh was Baron of Moy under the bishopric of Moray, while other barons held their jurisdictions under the earldoms of Atholl and Erroll. A laird was a tenant-in-chief of the Crown, while a baron was somebody whose jurisdiction included powers of ' pit and gallows '. A barony was a unit of government and jurisdiction over a specified area, of which the baron was the local administrator. His duties in keeping the law included the powers of life and death for capital crimes, but his principal work was in day-to-day local organisation and social welfare.

The greatest Highland magnates even possessed the rights

of Regality, with powers wider than those of the king's own Sheriff Courts (and they were usually the local hereditary Sheriff as well). For instance, the Atholl family had their Regality Courts at Logierait, where they were advised in a great council chamber by what amounted to a local parliament of nearly a hundred Atholl gentlemen, 'many of them of great landed property'. Stewart of Garth tells us of this Atholl 'feudal parliament' that it assembled in 'a noble chamber of better proportions than the British House of Commons'.

The feudal laws, which the barons themselves had enacted in Parliament, obliged them to provide certain facilities, such as a mill for their people, and to see that their heirs received adequate education to fit them for their baronial duties. A specified number of times each year, a baron had to hold a Baron Court. Those who held directly of

Lochiel's *cromag* or crook. The patriarchal chiefs were regarded as the shepherds of their people, and indeed the Gaelic expression for the Lord of the Isles was the Shepherd of the Isles: *Buachaille nan Eileanan*.

still looked to him as patriarch, but also to individual members of the clan who had settled outside clan territory, and to the 'broken men' who had given him their *calp* (a bequest of their best beast) or who had adopted the chief's clan surname to secure his protection.

In view of the chiefs' traditional powers, the Scots Privy Council was wont to hold such of them as it officially recognised, responsible for the actions of all people of their clan or name. In this case, the Crown styled them, e.g. the Laird of MacGregor, even if they were not tenants-in-chief, the theory being that they held their clan, though not their lands, directly of the Sovereign. In the sixteenth century, the Government took hostages from them. In the seventeenth century, it made chiefs find cash security for their clansmen's good behaviour. By the eighteenth century, a 'bounty' or pension was sometimes paid by the Government to chiefs, in return for the task of keeping their clansmen under control. In 1714 the MacGregors, then a chiefless and broken clan, even went so far as to elect a remote cadet as 'Chief', simply in order to get the pension for them, with a secret agreement that he should split a third part of any pension received among the three chieftains—Roro, Glengyle and Bracklie—who each really claimed the true chiefship.

Often clansmen went to their own chief with a problem, and accepted his jurisdiction or arbitration, even if he did not have a legal title to his lands and they themselves were living elsewhere. A chieftain like MacDonell of Keppoch lived on lands which were not properly held of the Crown, nor at times by any good charter, yet his influence carried far beyond the bounds of his territory. In 1744 Cameron of Lochiel entered into an agreement with the MacDonell chiefs of Glengarry and Keppoch to deal with crime among their clansmen 'within proper districts of our estates (or where our authority among our followers and dependents will extend and reach)', and in accordance with this agreement, for example, Lochiel appointed a depute to deal with any offenders among the Camerons who had settled far away in Ardnamurchan, although it was former Clan Donald country then long in Campbell possession and nominally subject to Campbell jurisdiction.

Clan discipline was sometimes rather summary. The following incident occurred during the 1745 Rising. 'When (MacGregor of) Glencarnock and (Cameron of) Lochiel were at breakfast in the morning, they heard shooting on the brow of the hill, Lochiel said to Glen "What shooting can be in the hill?" Glencarnock answered "I shall tell you that the Camerons are shooting sheep on the hill".

Sir James Colquhoun, 20th of Luss (1647–1676), M.P., the 'Black Cock of the West', wearing his robes as a Scottish feudal baron.

the baron, called the 'goodmen', were divided into assizes which assessed the guilt or innocence of those brought before them. Over the Court there presided the baron himself, or more usually the Baron Bailie appointed by him. If the assize found somebody guilty, the sentence or doom was pronounced by the Deemster. The baron himself could sit in the court instead of his Bailie but could only be there as the judge, not as part of the assize or jury. He could however mitigate the sentence. A witch found guilty by an assize at Slains in 1597, for instance, was nevertheless freed by the 9th Earl of Erroll who was presiding; though the poor woman was later re-arrested and burnt by the less kindly burgesses of the City of Aberdeen. The assizes at the Baron Court also determined questions of local administration, such as 'should the Lang Craig be laboured, or should it lie fallow?'.

The jurisdiction of the chiefs *as such* was very different from that of the barons. By ancient custom, the chief was father and head of the family of all his clansmen, who therefore accepted his patriarchal rulings. His influence extended not only to the younger branches of his family who had acquired territories of their own elsewhere and

Right-hand pistol of a pair carried by Donald Cameron, the 'Gentle Lochiel', in the 1745 Rising. Interlaced Ls for 'Lochiel' on the butt. He was Master of Lochiel in the Jacobite peerage, as his father, who was still living in exile, had been created Lord Lochiel by the Old Chevalier.

"God forbid" said Lochiel "it is the MacGregors". Says Glen "I shall lay forfeit one hundred guineas that it is not the MacGregors". With this the two left breakfast, and drew their pistols and vowed if they were Camerons that Lochiel would shoot them and if MacGregors that Glen would shoot them; and by great fortune, passing the head of the avenue, there was a Cameron with a sheep upon his back; Lochiel fired at the fellow, and shot him thro' the shoulder, there he fell, the two went on a good way further but they got not a MacGregor yet.'

Lochiel could not have shot the man in his capacity as Baron of Lochiel, because he would have had first to call the case before his own Baron Court to obtain a conviction and give sentence before punishment could be administered. He was simply shooting him as his Colonel and as the chief of his clan, and the tough Camerons in general accepted that he was doing right: they knew 'the Gentle Lochiel' well enough to know that though it was rough, in time of war it was justice. In the Government Army at that time, such an offender, if not shot to death instead, could have been given several hundred lashes of the cat-o'-nine-tails on successive days and would doubtless often have died under the torture.

Before the North of Scotland came to be considered as in some way different from the South, the Gaelic world had itself been divided by the quarrel between the Stewart kingdom, the heartland power, and Macdonald's realm, the western coastal power, which had originally been a local kingdom under the high king of Norway. Macdonald still regarded himself as King of the Isles under the Scottish high-kingship, but was regarded as Lord of the Isles by the mainland power. Moreover, Macdonald was also Earl of Ross and therefore held much of the northern mainland of the Highlands. Although this division between Macdonald and Stewart spheres of influence is blurred, it gave rise to a fairly well-defined social distinction between systems of land tenure adopted under the two régimes.

The parts of the highlands always held directly of the King of Scots, like Atholl, were feudalised at the same time as the rest of Scotland. Land was then held on a feu (the word is the same as fee) which implied security of tenure. A chief like Robertson of Struan, holding land feudally of the Crown, often feued some of it out to his own cadets, who in turn thus acquired security of tenure—and so on downwards. Eviction from land held feudally was impossible except on such grounds as rebellion. An even more

outright concession to a cadet was to grant him lands in 'ward', which 'primarily involved service in the field without any regular payment whatsoever. But when a vassal was a minor the superior drew the whole profits of the lands. This was a most valuable perquisite, though, of course, its yield was uncertain. But ward had one disadvantage in the highlands. Custom entitled a chief anyway to the support of his clan; thus, in making a grant to a cadet, he was really giving away something for nothing.' But clansmen with ward-holdings were as secure as the feuars, in fact more so.

But Macdonald of the Isles had held the Hebrides and the earldom of Ross, a vast highland area including what is now called Inverness-shire, as an almost independent realm until nearly 1500. In these wilder highlands, a chief like Macdonald of Clanranald would usually grant to a younger son not a feu but a tack, which was a form of lease. The tack was often given for life. More usually it was for three generations. When this time was up, the then tacksman could try to buy the land in if his branch had done well enough and prospered. Sometimes this was accomplished by way of wadset, when his chief 'pawned' the land for a capital sum and did not redeem it. Otherwise, he was shifted to a smaller tack, but was nevertheless provided for within the clan country. As a result, the more distant a tacksman's relationship to the chief, the less land he held, unless he had managed to make and save enough to buy it in for himself; for there were always younger sons of later generations pressing for the land. However, until the end of the seventeenth century, this system encouraged the feeling of clanship; and the members of the clan did expect the chief ultimately to provide for them.

Indeed, the chief administered a clan 'welfare state'. Thus, when the 21st Chief of MacLeod died in 1707, twenty-six widows were receiving pensions from the Dunvegan rents, and his successor took over the duty of looking after 'the widows and crippled folk of the clan'. Again, we are told of Macneil of Barra in 1695 that: 'When a tenant's wife in this or the adjacent islands dies, he then addresseth himself to the Macneil of Barray . . . Upon this representation, Macneil finds out a suitable match for him; and the woman's name being told him, immediately he goes to her, carrying with him a bottle of strong waters for their entertainment at marriage, which is then consummated. When a tenant dies, the widow addresseth herself to Macneil in the same manner . . . If a tenant chance to lose his milk-cows by the severity of the season, or any other misfortune: in this case Macneil of Barray supplies him with the like number that he lost. When any of these tenants are so far advanced in years that they are incapable to till the ground, Macneil takes such old men into his own family, and maintains them all their life after.'

When the Lordship of the Isles was overthrown and the Earldom of Ross also annexed to the Scottish Crown, all Macdonald's grants of land to the native inhabitants became invalid. This, as also the system of tacks in those parts of the Highlands which he had ruled, enabled the triumphant Scottish government to make attempts at dispossessing ancient but troublesome clans by unfairly granting feudal charters of their lands to strangers. The charters themselves were all right, and gave security, but often to the wrong clan. Also, some chiefs were deliberately forced or inveigled into debt and their lands then foreclosed on, under the Scottish legal system that was incomprehensible to them and to their clansmen. The Campbells of Argyll in the West, and the Gordons of Huntly in the East, were the main instruments of Government policy at first. Then came the Jacobite forfeitures of the eighteenth century. Later, ' progressive ' schemes to modernise the highlands by putting in sheep farms were helped by the same system of tacks which made evictions easy. Those highland families who had feus of their lands could not be evicted, providing they were held securely in feu by charter confirmed by the Scottish Crown. Therefore the Clearances were only completely possible in those parts of the highlands that had never been properly feudalised down to a fairly low level.

Of course, small holdings were never feudalised anywhere in the highlands. The tacksmen sometimes sub-let crofts to smaller tenants who were called mailers because they paid mail or rent. Later these mailers tended to become crofters holding their land directly of the Laird. Often these were joint tenants (see, for instance, the Judicial Rentals of the MacLeod Estates 1664, of the Macdonald Estates 1733, and the Mackinnon Estates 1751). Joint leases of up to three hundred acres of moorland and a little green pasture were often held by townships of tenants. These townships usually also divided annually by lot their much smaller arable acreage which was in ' runrig '. The infield was kept manured, but the outfield was simply ploughed until it was exhausted and then left to recover under grass. Such tenant families would keep two to twenty milk cows, several garron ponies and from twenty to two hundred sheep or goats.

In peacetime, the gentlemen of the clan had duties in attendance on their chief. In wartime, they officered its fighting force. In Islay, for example, each merkland maintained one gentleman in ' meat and cloth ', who did no ordinary manual labour but had to be in constant readiness as one of the laird's household, ready both with service and advice. But, contrary to much woolly thought in modern times, the land was always theoretically the chief's or laird's, subject to customary obligations, for ' the idea that " there is no partnership in women or land " is of long standing in the highlands: *cha bhi bràithreachas mu mhnaoi no mu fhearann.* '

In times of war, the ordinary tenants formed the bulk of the chief's fighting force. Many were true clansmen whose genealogies went back at least nominally to the forefather of the whole clan. To the crofters this was important, because the chief and his branch chieftains accepted the usual Celtic moral obligation to ward off famine from their kindred and to provide a share in the ancestral lands for every descendant of the common ancestor. The system lasted until a Whiggish statute of the Scottish Parliament in 1695 eventually brought about the end of runrig tenure of the land. ' Nor is it difficult to date from the passing of this Act that break-up of the Clan system in its agrestic character, not reached, in its patriarchal aspect, until after 1746. '

The rest of the fighting force was made up of new-comers who had sought the chief's protection. For example, when the MacGregors massacred the MacLarens, slaying their chief and temporarily breaking the clan, many MacLarens went to the neighbouring chieftain, Campbell of Glenorchy, and offered him their *calp*. This was the best beast or steed in each clansman's possession at the time of his death, in return for which he and his heirs were protected, provided they followed that chief or chieftain. *Calp* was abolished by statute in 1617.

Attached to the tacks and crofts were usually a number of cottars who helped to labour them in return for a couple of cows and sufficient land of their own to sow a boll of oats. They were originally not true members of the clan but incoming ' broken men ' or else descendants of the once unfree *nativi*, doubtless mostly of Pictish stock, who were attached in ancient times by ' direction of labour ' to the soil of the country. But they too intermarried with the clansmen and other followers of the chief and, by the end of the seventeenth century, the whole of the chief's following was so much inter-related that everyone had come to be regarded as a member of the clan. This communal spirit was reinforced by the custom that the chieftains had of boarding out their own children to foster-parents, so that they were brought up to share the everyday lives of their people in the households of ordinary clansmen. But, by the middle of the seventeenth century, fosterage had begun to become honorary, and some chiefs nominally fostered their sons with honoured members of the clan, who took on certain financial or other obligations to the child without actually having to bring him up in their homes.

Yet, curiously enough, fosterage was originally a royal custom from pagan times, when a king was expected to be slain as a sacrifice by his successor. For the concept of clanship goes far back into the Celtic world, particularly into ancient Ireland. Each community was a little kingdom, for it was thought quite natural that there should be local kings acknowledging greater kings, indeed several grades of king. But it was the local king who actually administered his own local kingdom: the paramountcy of the greater kings being a matter of prestige rather than of government. Ancient Ireland contained a hundred, and Norway about thirty, little kingdoms. In what is now Scotland, there are said to have been seven kingdoms, excluding Argyll, the Orkneys, and everything south of the Forth and Clyde. There were Kings of Atholl, Kings of

The Royal Footprint carved in the rock at Dunadd, in the sacred inauguration place of the ancient Dalriadic dynasts who were Kings of Argyll. At his inauguration, each successive king placed his own foot in this footprint of his royal ancestors.

Strathearn (Fortrenn), Kings of Moray, Kings of Argyll and Kings of Strathclyde. We still talk of the **Kingdom of Fife**. There is no reason to suppose that people were less happy when they enjoyed local autonomy and were able to know their sovereign personally, as in Monaco and Liechtenstein today. The *Benelux* economy does not require that the Kingdom of the Belgians and the Grand Duchy of Luxembourg should be merged politically in the Realm of the Netherlands. But it seems that only very sophisticated people can distinguish between economic and political union: and so the greater kingdoms gradually swallowed up the little ones during the Middle Ages.

Whether Celtic or Norse in origin, the pagan kings were sacred beings. At his inauguration, each king had to go through various religious rituals, as a result of which he and his people felt that the Lucky Spirit of the community entered and dwelt in the king's body. This is what was meant when it was said that the royal families descended from the gods. Since this Lucky Spirit's human casket could not be allowed to decay, such kings were periodically

---

A great Irish chieftain in his national dress: Sir Niall O'Neill, 2nd Baronet of Killeleagh, Lord Lieutenant of Armagh, who was mortally wounded as the Colonel of O'Neill's Dragoons, fighting for the Jacobite Cause at the battle of the Boyne in 1690. His portrait by J. M. Wright in 1680 (now in the Tate Gallery, though a slightly different version of it is at Dunrobin Castle) is unique, in that it depicts a great Irish noble in the Erse costume of that period; with his 'wild Irish' fringed cloak, curious but beautifully adorned Erse apron, long red hose, pointed brogues, Celtic dirk, basket-hilted broadsword, great oval shield of studded red leather, gold-tipped black javelin, and elaborately-tooled red leather conical cap with the flowing plumes of an Irish chieftain. Sir Niall descended in the direct male line from King Domnall 'the Young Ox' O'Neill, elder son of Aodh 'Athlone', King of the North of Ireland (1030—1033), whose younger son An-rothan was ancestor of the Highland chiefs of Lamont, Maclachlan, Macneil, MacEwen and other clans of Cowall and Knapdale in Scotland.

sacrificed or slain by their rightful successors. Christianity, with its emphasis on Our Lord being the once only and final sacrifice, put an end to open king-slaying, although in practice Celtic kings went on being slain by their successors up to the eleventh century. Indeed, of the MacCarthy of Muskerry branch of the ancient royal house of Munster, we are told that ' the MacDonough MacCarthys kept up the custom of family murders' apparently as late as the sixteenth century. ' The attempt by each heir on the life of the successive dynasts of Muskerry seems to have been looked on with the religious fervour accorded by the Romans to the arena and by moderns to boxing contests. When the then Lord of Muskerry was slain by his heir in the sixteenth century, the murder was described as his being " slayne by his cosen Donaghe McOwen *who had the best challenge* to Muscrye ".' A similar state of affairs can be observed among the Kings of Scots, until the sons of Saint Margaret ganged together against all comers, and put a stop to it.

After the adoption of Christianity, the kings continued to receive the awe that had rightly been accorded to their sacrificial position, for it was felt that they still symbolised the Spirit of their people. As the supreme patriarch, the High King, whether in Ireland or in Scotland, was regarded in the Gaelic world as head of the whole national family: the Chief of Chiefs. In Ireland, the local kings of the Gaels were gradually brought under the English Crown. In 1515, a report to Henry VIII observed that ' ther byn more than 60 countryes, called Regyons, in Ireland, . . . some region as bygge as a shyre, some more, some lesse; where reygneith more than 60 Chyef Capytaynes, wherof some callyth themselffes Kynges, some Kynges Peyres, in their langage, some Prynceis, some Dukes, some Archedukes, . . .: and every of the said Capytaynes makeyth warre and peace for hymself, and holdeith by swerde, and hathe imperiall jurysdyction within his rome, and obeyeth to noo other person.' Although even the Macdonalds had stopped styling themselves kings by the sixteenth century, the situation in the Highlands was not so far different: and it is important for a proper understanding of the clans to realise that their chiefs, like the ' Chyef Capytaynes ' of Ireland, were also of dynastic origin. Indeed, the seventeenth-century Wardlaw MS. tells us of the Highlands that ' all our chiftens derive themselves from kings and princes '. The Lord Lyon will still only allow crest-coronets (which are in fact open crowns) to Chiefs.

This royal background is of great importance in understanding Highland pride. For the clan were the ' children ' of the chiefs, and the chiefs were the scions of the prehistoric Blood Royal. By the Middle Ages, the local kings had become earls or mighty lords, like the Earl of Strathearn who reigned ' by the Indulgence of God ', or the Lord of the Isles, who was called the Shepherd of the Islands (*Buachaille nan Eileanan*). Nobody was ever made an earl in mediaeval Scotland, who was not either a king's son or cousin, or else married to a king's daughter or cousin, except in the case of local dynasts also of royal stock. The earls created between Flodden and the Union were equally drawn from the old nobility. Until the late seventeenth century, only earls (and the newer ranks of marquess and duke) wore coronets or open crowns, as ' cousins of the Sovereign ', and had the royal ermine on their robes: and the full ceremonial style of an earl, proclaimed for instance at state funerals in the old days, is ' Most Noble and Puissant Prince '. When the Queen makes an ex-Prime Minister an earl, she is making him an honorary cousin of the Royal Family, and it would of course be a meaningless honour if, for example, Her Majesty's own brother-in-law were not also made Earl of Snowdon. There was no need to create the Duke of Edinburgh ' Prince Philip ', since all dukes and earls are princes. That is why royal princes are called after their dukedoms or earldoms as soon as they are bestowed on them. It is only because we have nobody called ' prince ' who is not already an earl, outside younger sons of the Royal Family who have not yet been given peerages, that the idea has gained ground that ' prince ' is a separate (supposedly higher) rank than duke or earl.

The local dynasts' younger branches, in the male or female line, were settled in appanages. Their heads were the ' captains ' or chiefs who held the actual thanages, often converted into baronies in feudal times. The word ' chief ' is Norman-French, and was introduced into Scotland by the chiefs of great Norman families like the Bruces and Hays and Lindsays. It has long been used to translate the different words by which at various periods the Highlanders have designated the heads of their clans, although the earlier translation was ' captain ' in the sense of headman (from Latin *caput*, a ' head ') and still survives in the formal style of two of the greatest chiefs: the Captain of Clan Chattan and the Captain of Clanranald. (These should not be confused with the captains of castles, such as the Captain of Dunstaffnage.) In very early charters, the

Kildrummy Castle, mediaeval centre of the great highland Earldom of Mar, that included Deeside and Donside, territory of the Forbes, Gordon and Farquharson clansmen. The Earldom of Mar is the oldest surviving peerage in Britain, dating from before peerages were created by the Crown, and the family of the present 30th Earl of Mar are simply styled, e.g. ' Lady Janet of Mar '. It has passed through several heiresses over the centuries. But the Erskines, who had inherited the earldom through an heiress in 1438, were unjustly deprived of it by the Crown until 1565, as a result of which the head of the Erskines in the male line has been recognised as also holding a separate earldom of Mar from 1565, and is now styled the Earl of Mar & Kellie. The two Earls of Mar should, however, not be confused.

head of the clan is called the *toiseach* which was then translated into English as ' thane ', and his territory (the clan's appanage) was called a thanage. Also, in some fourteenth-century charters, there appears the ancient Erse style *ceann-cineal*: head of the cenel or cineal, an older word in normal use than clan. The Cenel Conaill, for example, were the kindred of St. Columba and the ruling dynasty of Tirconaill (' Conall's Land ', conquered by their ancestor King Conall *Gulban* in the fifth century) in Ireland. Similarly, before 1256 the last of the male line to hold the earldom of the old Earls of Carrick (a branch of the ancient Princes of Galloway) nominated by a special charter his brother's son Sir Roland of Carrick to the position of ' kenkynol ' (*ceann-cineal*) of the old dynastic clan of Carrick—a position inherited from Sir Roland by the powerful Kennedy chiefs who were locally known as late as the sixteenth century as the ' Kings of Carrick '. When the gypsies first came to official notice under their celebrated Faa' or Fall dynasty, King James V granted the then Faa' a charter with a jurisdiction of life and death over all the ' Egyptians ' in Scotland, and styled him ' Earl of Little Egypt ': so it is perhaps interesting that the Privy Council in their turn styled him ' Captain of the Egyptians ' as though he were a Highland chief.

The title ' chief ' is now applied by custom only to the head of a whole Name—with certain exceptions, notably the heads of the principal branches of the royal Clan Donald, also sometimes those of the royal clan of Stewart, and the head of the Clan Fraser of Lovat, long separated from his Lowland kindred. The heads of branches are called ' chieftains '. Where chieftains held their lands directly of the Crown and not of their own chiefs (e.g. Campbell of Breadalbane or Maclean of Ardgour), they

Sir Iain *Glas* Campbell of Glenorchy, *Mac Chailein mhic Dhonnachaidh*, afterwards 1st Earl of Breadalbane, known to his enemies as 'Slippery John'. The identification of this portrait has been disputed, but for various reasons the present writer does not doubt it. This is perhaps the earliest surviving painting of a highland chieftain in his national dress, and was taken by J. M. Wright c.1680 as a comparison picture to that of Sir Niall O'Neill, the Irish chieftain. 'Slippery John' bought up the debts of the childless 6th Earl of Caithness, got a bond from him of his titles and estates, and after the earl's death managed to get a charter recognising himself as Earl of Caithness in 1677. The rightful 7th Earl opposed him in force at the head of the Sinclairs, so he and 700 of his Campbells marched north, invaded Caithness, and defeated the Sinclairs in battle. As his own men were dressed like him, in belted plaids, while the Sinclairs preferred to wear the trews, the Campbells of Glenorchy mocked the Sinclairs for their costume—and before the battle Glenorchy's piper, Finlay MacIver, taunted them with his specially composed tune *Bhodach nam Brigeis:* 'Gaffers in Trousers', now known as Breadalbane's Salute. The Sinclairs continued resistance, and King Charles II intervened. 'Slippery John' gave up the Earldom of Caithness, and in 1681 was created Earl of Breadalbane and Holland instead.

did not always follow their chief in political matters—but usually branches of the same surname acted collectively in matters affecting the affairs of their clansmen. This was true of the Lowlands, too, up to the seventeenth century; but continued in the Highlands until after Culloden.

Younger sons were settled within the appanage that formed the clan territory. Their children in turn settled there, and thus the clan took roots. For the word *clan* simply means 'children', and originally each clan was made up only of the immediate descendants of the man after whom it was named. Thus the Clan Donald were the actual descendants of King Donald, who was Lord of the Isles in the thirteenth century; and the Macnabs, 'Sons of the Abbot', were the family of the hereditary Abbots of Glendochart. As there was little emigration, and as it was considered the moral duty of the chief to provide a portion of land within the appanage for every genuine

member of his clan, generation after generation the land was divided up, with the smaller portions going on the whole to the more remote relations. These naturally intermarried with the other inhabitants of the district, and so the whole people of each territory gradually came to feel themselves related to the chief. Although this feeling was often fictional in the male line, it was usually very real in the female line. So, by 1746, MacDonell of Keppoch, a chief of the Blood Royal of the Isles with an ancestry going back to the gods, could refer naturally to his armed tenantry (in his dying words at Culloden) as 'the children of my tribe': *clann mo chinnidhmi.*

People often speak of 'old families'. In fact, of course, no family is older than any other, and what is really meant is that the particular families called 'old' have managed to maintain their identity and retain records of their past longer than the majority of other folk (to cite the present writer's Scottish genealogical introduction to the 1952 edition of Burke's *Landed Gentry*). People also speak loosely of 'blood running thin', as though a long-recorded family had in truth a longer descent than an unrecorded family— and sometimes they talk about 'new blood', when what they refer to is just as 'old blood' as anybody else's but happens to be (for better or maybe for worse) of unknown origin. It's also fashionable to talk about 'the accident of birth', as if it were by some accident that the nuptials of *Mac Chailein Mor* produce a typical Campbell, and not a Macdonald nor even a baboon. It is no accident that Winston Churchill was not a Russell, that Bertrand Russell is not an Alexander, or that Field Marshal Alexander is not a Churchill: indeed, their fathers would have eyed their wives' friends suspiciously had they turned out so. But it is, however, a true accident of birth that Sir Winston Churchill was not Duke of Marlborough, that Bertrand Russell is not Duke of Bedford, or that Field-Marshal 'Alex' is not Earl of Caledon: for it was by chance that elder brothers existed and survived. Similarly, it must not be forgotten that ultimately the true Highland clansmen descended just as much from their dynastic name-father as the chief himself did. When King George II asked to see a Highland soldier, two Black Watch privates, Gregor McGregor, 'commonly called Gregor the Beautiful', and John Campbell, son of Duncan Campbell of the family of Duneaves in Perthshire (a cadet of Glenlyon), were sent to London. 'They displayed so much dexterity and skill in the management of their weapons, as to give perfect satisfaction to his Majesty. Each got a gratuity of one guinea, which *they gave to the porter at the palace gate as they passed out.* They thought that the King had mistaken their character and condition in their own country.' For Private Gregor McGregor was as much a descendant of the original chief, Gregor of Golden Bridles ('Royal is my Blood'), as was the then Chieftain of the Children of the Mist; and Private John Campbell could trace his descent from Great Colin as easily as could the Duke of Argyll himself.

Prince Charles Edward's rescuers, Miss Flora Macdonald and her attendant Neil MacEachan, were just as much the descendants of Somerled, King of the Isles, as were Clanranald and Sir Alexander Macdonald of Macdonald themselves. And the tremendous vigour of the old kings burst out repeatedly in the humblest of their scions. Neil MacEachan's son, for instance, born in exile, became that Alexandre Macdonald, Duc de Tarente, whom Napoleon made a Marshal of France. But it was an advantage to them psychologically, that the main line of their chiefs always held on, with their family records, in the old clan country: for it enabled all of the clan to feel part of a continuous and traceable history, to have the knowledge of belonging to a truly historic family—abroad too often limited to a narrow upper class, but in the Highlands the prerogative of all. Even the famous Macfie race of tinklers bear ' one of the oldest and most interesting Gaelic personal names we possess '. Furthermore, a man's daughter is just as much his child as his son is—and a descent in the female line is still a descent: nobody could have been born at all if any single one of his myriad ancestors had died in infancy. The present writer doubts whether even one of the gallant clansmen who fought at Culloden could ever have been born to be there at all, had King Kenneth mac Alpin been strangled in his cradle. ' Butcher ' Cumberland might well have reflected that this would have been an excellent thing, were it not that His Royal Highness also descended, many many times over (through cousin-marriages within his own ancestry), from the same King Kenneth mac Alpin.

Descents link downwards in the social scale. Kings married across the oceans, nobles across the counties, but

Cruachan, the mountain beneath which the Campbells had their original gathering-place on Loch Awe. Now it has a reservoir storing eight million units of electricity; and two-thirds of a mile inside Ben Cruachan is an underground power station of four hundred megawatt capacity, inclined shafts rising through the mountain rock from the power station to the reservoir. Surrounding mountain peaks can be seen rising through the mist behind Ben Cruachan.

until modern times ordinary folk married near to home. So the likelihood, for example, of a particular Mackay clansman of today descending from a particular Clan Donnachaidh clansman of the fourteenth century is infinitely remote. But it is not at all unlikely that the same Mackay clansman should descend from King Robert Bruce. If he had any descent in the female line (with so much intermarriage in Strathnaver) from Niall ' of the Bass ', Chief of Mackay in 1433, he would therefore also descend from Niall's mother Elisabeth of the Isles, daughter of Macdonald himself, and her mother was in turn a daughter of King Robert II, grandson of King Robert Bruce. Similarly, the likelihood of a particular Clan Donnachaidh (Robertson) clansman of today descending from a particular Mackay clansman of the fourteenth century is equally remote. But it is most improbable that the same Robertson clansman would not descend (through local intermarriage in Atholl) from the prolific Stewarts of Garth, whelps of the Wolf of Badenoch, himself a son of King Robert II, the grandson of King Robert Bruce. Indeed, it is most improbable that there is any Highland chief today who does not descend from King Robert Bruce, nor any other Highlander who does not descend from King Kenneth mac Alpin, who united the Picts and Scots. It is the royal stock that is genealogically as well as politically the unifying force

that makes all Scotsmen true kinsmen. So the royal style was patriarchal not territorial, for it embraced Scotsmen everywhere into the national family: not 'King of Scotland' but 'King of Scots'. Today the Queen, the reigning descendant of Queen Victoria and Mary Queen of Scots, of Robert Bruce and Malcolm *Ceann-mor* and Kenneth mac Alpin, as also of the ancient dynasts of the Picts and Scots, the Norse and Britons, is the head of this national family: the Chief of Chiefs, who freshly incarnates the Spirit of Caledonia.

The clans are thus simply the historic branches of this national family. So it is not surprising that the Highlander, whose clan can be traced back to one of the ancient royal houses of pre-Christian times, and whose nostalgically-remembered territory was an appanage—the clan's special portion of an immemorial realm—and not a purchased estate, usually has a great pride in his ancestry and a deep love of his homeland. This feeling is by no means for the Highlands in general. When Burns wrote ' My heart's in the Highlands ' he was expressing no Highland sentiment. A Highlander would feel, my heart's in Appin, or in Atholl (' cam' ye by Atholl? '), or in Lochaber (' maybe to return to Lochaber no more ')—but historically speaking, he might have been only too willing to take Fire and Sword to the neighbouring districts. ' Cruachan ' means nothing to a Grant, nor ' Craigellachie ' to a Campbell: but reversed, their significance is intense. For each branch of the national family—anyway in the Highlands—prefers its own home ground.

Chiefs were called most usually after the namefather of the clan, e.g. MacGregor, ' the Son of Gregor '. In English, from at least the sixteenth century onwards, there was a tendency either to call the chief ' the Laird of MacGregor ' or else ' MacGregor of that Ilk '—treating his clan as if it were his estate, which indeed the Crown did when it took hostages from him even when he wasn't a Crown tenant—a style which in the eighteenth and nineteenth centuries got Englished still further into ' MacGregor of MacGregor ' (luckily, to avoid confusion, the present chief has the Christian name of Gregor, and is easily remembered as Sir Gregor MacGregor of MacGregor). In popular conversation, chiefs are often called ' The ' in English: the first reference to the Clan Gregor chief as such appearing in the seventeenth-century *Black Book of Taymouth*, ' although not righteous heir to the MacGregor '. A MS. of the reign of James VI tells us ' How the MacLeoid of the Lewes was with his whol trybe destroyed ', and The Chisholm appears in the Inverness Council records of 1654, as soon after does The Dallas. A rather more modern example is an entry in Sir Frederick Ponsonby's Game Book for 23 August 1911: ' Moy Hall. 7 guns. The King, The Mackintosh, Ld. Tullibardine, Ld. Lovat, Sir C. Cust, Angus Mackintosh and F.P.—1009 grouse '. But sometimes chiefs were called in English after their appanage, e.g. Lochiel or Glengarry, though in that case they always had a Gaelic patronymic too. Lochiel was *Mac Dhomnuill Duibh*, ' the Son of Black Donald '; and Glengarry was *Mac Mhic Alasdair*, ' the Son of the son of Alexander '. The Robertson chief was called Struan (or sometimes Struan Robertson, to distinguish him from the Murray laird of Strowan), but the Perth Hunt were perhaps unnecessarily emphasising his position as chief when the then Robertson of Struan was entered in their minutes on 30 September 1862 as ' The Struan '.

The surname of the dynastic clan spread only gradually throughout their territory. For example, the Earls of Lennox were mighty rulers, sprung from ancient royal stock. They had a younger branch, who received as their

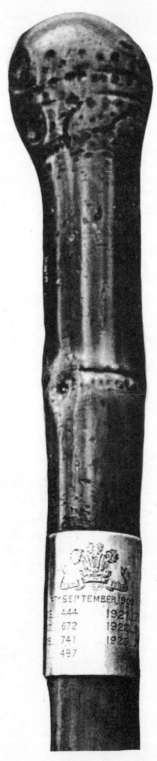

Walking stick presented by the Prince of Wales (afterwards King George V) to The Mackintosh in 1909, to the inscription on which was added the bag of grouse on each successive later Royal Visit to Moy. The King held at least one Privy Council at Moy, and Lloyd George held a Cabinet Meeting there, while staying with The Mackintosh, Lord Lieutenant of Inverness-shire.

appanage Arrochar in the Lennox. The head of this branch in the early fourteenth century was called Bartholomew. So his descendants were naturally called Macfarlane, which (of course) means ' Son of Bartholomew '. They became chiefs of the ruling clan in the Arrochar district. Their younger branches were also settled there. They too came to be called Macfarlanes. To repeat, more and more of the people in the district intermarried with them until—although they might not actually all be called Macfarlane—they all regarded themselves as belonging to the clan and as being related to the chief, in whose country they were living and of whom they were holding their own homes.

The ordinary highlanders did not necessarily have the same surname as their chief, although they often adopted it latterly. Indeed, until a late stage, most highlanders did not take fixed surnames at all. When they did, some clans like the Campbells, Cummings, Frasers and Mackenzies encouraged them to take the name of the chief's family. All the same, clan surnames were not nearly as widely adopted as many people suppose. For example, the mass of the ordinary people who made up the clan regiments in the '45 had very different names from the clan surname. The officers mostly did have the same name as the chief, but they were usually tacksmen and therefore almost certainly relations.

Thus there is only a half-truth in the popular idea that all the people in a given area had the same name and belonged to the same 'tribe'. Certainly they felt that they belonged to the local clan: and, for instance, highlanders who lived in the Robertson country would have Robertson relations and would tend to hold their land of Robertson lairds. But the clan was not a great tribe of people all called Robertson living from prehistoric times in one area and electing a chief called Struan. Quite the opposite, the area was held by Struan, descendant of its ancient dynasts, and he threw his branches like roots downward. They radiated out and gradually absorbed everyone else. Just as the system was becoming really tribalised—when Keppoch referred to his clansmen at Culloden as 'the children of my tribe'—it was broken.

When the Whig revolution took place in Britain at the end of the 1680's, its strongest opponents were the Irish and the Highlanders. Although perhaps they had suffered most from the Government in the past, they showed enormous loyalty to it in adversity and fought like fiends. They defeated the Whig army at Killiecrankie, although it was commanded by a Highlander, Lord Reay's cousin General Hugh Mackay of Scourie. Seeing what a great danger the military organisation of the Highlanders could be, the Government (inspired not so much by the Campbells as by the Dalrymple Master of Stair) attempted to teach them a lesson of terror with the massacre of Glencoe. But the action boomeranged. For it was so horrifying that the propaganda worked against those who had attempted to make use of the massacre as an 'object lesson' to the clans. In the upshot, Sir Thomas Moncreiffe of that Ilk, as Clerk of the Exchequer (i.e. permanent head of the Treasury) signed a special authorisation for compensation to be paid to the surviving Macdonalds of Glencoe.

In 1715, the Government felt the power of the highland broadsword to such an extent, that they began to realise that the Highlanders had to be subdued in order to bring them within the organisation of the rest of the British Isles. Forts were built at Fort George in Inverness, halfway down the Great Glen at Fort Augustus, and at the south-western end of the Great Glen at Fort William, all three called after members of the Hanoverian royal family. Block-houses were erected, garrisons installed, and General Wade, a humane and charming man who got on very well with the Highlanders, started building roads and the delightful humpbacked 'Wade bridges' as his lines of communication through the Highlands. Officially, Highlanders were disarmed after the '15 Rising, but they concealed their weapons in the thatch of their houses and wherever else they could. Again in 1745 (as it seemed to the English) these

Fort George, near Inverness, built by the Government to dominate Clan Chattan and the Frasers of Lovat.

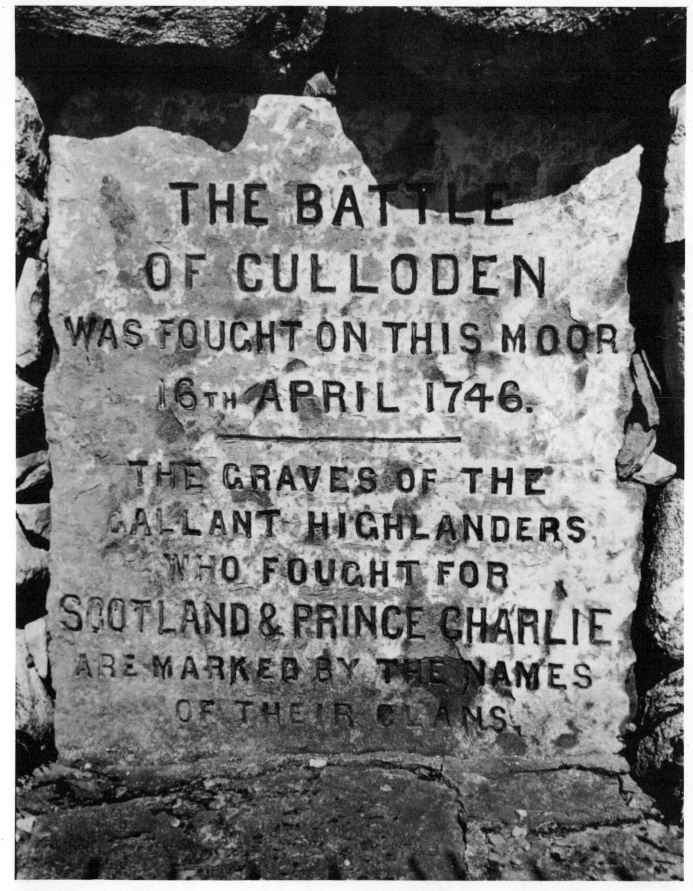

Memorial on the battlefield of Culloden.

gibbering aborigines, speaking an alien tongue, dressed in strange garb, bearing the sort of shield their ancestors might have borne against Julius Caesar, came rushing down, albeit in comparatively small numbers, but this time as far as Derby, chasing everybody before them. The Central Government was now so disturbed that it took a great deal of trouble to lessen the power of the Highlanders ever to do such a thing again.

In 1747, the heritable jurisdictions of the great chiefs were abolished by Parliament, against the votes of the majority of Scottish members of both Houses and contrary to the express terms of the Treaty of Union (which surely should only lawfully be modified by a majority of the

Scottish representatives: else what was the point of negotiating the Treaty at all). It is said that this freed the people, but in fact the disappearance of the Baron Courts removed their traditional share (as members of assizes) in local government and turned the former units of administration into ordinary estates. And it is not clear why a local bailie appointed by the Duke of Atholl, who was dependent on local feeling, and was administering local customary law, should always be supposed worse than a sheriff substitute politically appointed by the Crown without local knowledge. Certainly, when the troubles came, the Government sheriffs took little account of local popular feeling. These old local jurisdictions would of course have died a natural death in the nineteenth century, but for quite different reasons.

The century following the overthrow of the clans in 1746, saw an unparalleled population explosion in the Highlands, that led inevitably to great hardship. Excluding Orkney and Shetland, which are outside the Highlands, the 'Crofting Counties' are Argyll, Inverness-shire, Caithness, Sutherland, Ross and Cromartie. Their total population in 1755, i.e. at the time of the overthrow of the clan system, was 216,952. Today their total population is slightly larger: at the 1961 census it was 241,389. But the chaotic period of population explosion in these counties was in the first half of the nineteenth century. In 1801, *before* the 'Clearances' it had risen to 255,993. In 1851, *after* the Clearances, it had risen by about another thirty per cent to the unprecedented figure of 334,475. These figures, coming at a time when the Industrial Revolution was changing the whole economy of the country, give some idea of the problem with which Highland estate administration was faced at this period. Different lairds tried to meet the situation in different ways. But whatever method was tried, the situation remains the same. Cattle economy on the high ground is no longer economic. Sheep failed when the Napoleonic Wars' blockade came to an end. Except for some subsidised crofters, folk no longer live in the narrow glens, whether 'cleared' or not, but are settled in the broader fertile straths or in the coastal districts. However, industry never took root in Highland hearts so long as they were rooted in the Highlands. Men of Highland descent flourish in great cities from Glasgow to Toronto. But in the Highlands they could not accustom themselves to urban life. Burghs like Inverness were planted by alien merchants; and even a cathedral town like Dunkeld was never a large place.

Emigration took away only a part of the expanding surplus population. At first the chiefs and chieftains, feeling their clansmen belonged to the Highlands, tried to dissuade their people from emigration. Burns, who did not really understand Highlanders (though his romantic sympathy for them is even more lyrically moving today than ever) attacked Lord Breadalbane for trying to discourage his own people from emigrating from the glens to the New World. Later, as the population explosion continued, some lairds, who found the pressure of economics made them unable to give their surplus population an adequate subsistence, assisted emigration out of their own pockets. As the Highland economy staggered from crisis to crisis, harsh measures were as ineffectual as the old ways in dealing with the situation. Mr. John Prebble, perhaps the most recent authority on the worst Clearances, suggests that if the hard-pressed lairds had followed the wise advice of Sir John Sinclair of Ulbster, greatest and best of the chieftains in Caithness, a 'slow and considerate change' could have made the conversion to sheep a benefit to the small tenants, with 'native shepherds among the Highlanders' acting as herdsmen in common to joint townships pooling their holdings and capital. It is an historically emotional disaster that this was not tried: even though retrospective commonsense tells us that it, too, would probably not have worked. A further and postponed disadvantage is that 'sheep monoculture in the Scottish Highlands has been slowly destroying fertility for the last 150 years or more, by eating out the finer grasses, leaving coarser grasses and bracken to predominate'. As it was, when cattle proved uneconomic, Lowland-run sheep farms cleared the higher straths—not only to fail in their turn, but actually to encourage a further increase in the population who had been shifted to the lower ground.

Colonel David Stewart of Garth (himself a whelp of the Wolf of Badenoch) wrote in 1822: 'While the country was portioned out amongst numerous tenants, none of their sons were allowed to marry till they had obtained a house, a farm, or some certain prospect of settlement, unless, perhaps, in the case of a son, who was expected to succeed his father. Cottagers and tradesmen were also discouraged from marrying, till they had a house, and means of providing for a family. These customs are now changed. The system of throwing whole tracts of country into one farm, and the practice of letting lands to the highest bidder, without regard to the former occupiers, occasions gloomy prospects, and the most fearful and discouraging uncertainty of tenure. . . . Having now no sure prospect of a permanent settlement, by succeeding to the farms inherited by their fathers, nor a certainty of being permitted to remain in their native country *on any terms*, they marry whenever inclination prompts them. The propriety of marrying when young, they defend on this principle, that their children may rise up around them, while they are in the vigour of life, and able to provide for their maintenance, and that they may thus ensure support to their old age; for no Highlander can ever forgo the hope that, while he has children able to support him, he will never be allowed to want. . . . If a poor man's family are under the necessity of going to service, they settle among themselves which of their number shall in turn remain at home, to take charge of their parents, and all consider themselves bound to share with them whatever they are able to save from their wages.'

During this difficult century, some estates felt obliged to reintroduce (until 1886) the old pre-Culloden convention in the form of an actual prohibition to marry on the estate without leave, properly granted on evidence of economic ability to support a family. The lairds of course applied a rather similar rule to their own children in the 'cut-him-off-with-a-penny' Victorian mode: as happened to the late Cluny Macpherson's father. Today, perhaps only young officers of the Brigade of Guards are still thirled in such a way. For example the present Lords Lovat, Bute, Forbes and Ogilvy, the Master of Lovat, The Menzies, Maclean of Duart, Colquhoun of Luss, Rattray of Rattray, MacGregor of MacGregor (and for that matter, the present writer) have all, while subalterns in the Scots or other Foot Guards, been obliged to apply for permission if they wanted to marry; a permission that is by no means automatically granted.

When the Clearances came, some of the wholesale evictions were caused by avarice, some by economic pressure on the debt-burdened lairds, yet others (what is the worst of all) by Good Intentions. To this last and nastiest category belonged the notorious Sutherland Clearances, ordained and expensively paid for out of his own pocket for purely doctrinaire reasons by an English liberal 'planner', the Marquess of Stafford (later created Duke of

Sir Gregor MacGregor of MacGregor, Chief of the Children of the Mist, a skilled mechanic and parachutist.

Sutherland) who was horrified to find his wife's 'tenantry' living like Afghans in their huddled huts up the glens, and zealously removed them against their will but 'for their own good' to light industries in the coastal areas. The population of Sutherland increased during these Clearances from 23,117 in 1801 to 25,793 in 1851, but the methods adopted (unknown to the Sutherland family) by the factors in carrying out this 'redeployment' of 'local labour' were unnecessarily insensitive and bitterly oppressive. There is nothing such a planner understands less, nor is annoyed by more, than heart-felt 'sentimental reasons' for passionately wanting to go on doing what *he* in his Olympian certainty considers non-utilitarian, uneconomic or irrational. Scotland's loss was the Commonwealth's gain, as we are reminded in Andrew Dewar Gibb's *Scottish Empire* (London 1937). Mr. Ian Grimble, a sensitive and up-to-date researcher into these particular Clearances, said in a recent speech that Karl Marx had found them 'very much to the purpose as he rummaged about in the British Museum piling up evidence for *Das Kapital*'. The present writer, when he worked in Russia in 1946, observed Stalin's brutal 'Clearances' of whole nations like the Volga Germans and the Crim Tatars as an irony of history, since they were brought about ultimately by Marx.

The Clearances in general took several forms. Some were not total evictions (and the distinction is not always sufficiently made in works on the subject) where the dispossessed had to leave the district for ever; but were instead examples of planning within a district, people being moved from black-houses in glens and resettled in other accommodation on another part of the same estate—rather like the 'slum clearances' carried out by modern town councils, often with equal harshness in the case of old folk naturally attached to their old homes, however decrepit. In other cases, chiefs who had struggled not to evict their clansmen fell so much into debt in the effort, that their creditors did it for them. Thus Lord Macdonald, a kindly chief who adhered to the patriarchal school, who had 'spent all his resources on the relief of destitution' among his people during the Potato Famine of 1846, found himself in the hands of his creditors, who formed themselves into a body of Trustees and forced him to clear part of North Uist: though he insisted on remitting arrears of rent, taking crop and stock at valuation, and himself paying to assist the resulting emigration. Another Clan Donald chief, Mac-Donell of Glengarry, who had been obliged by the Highland economic collapse to sell Invergarry and emigrate to Australia, wrote from the Antipodes during the Potato Famine to remit until better times all rent from his remaining tenants in Knoydart, for he looked on them 'less as tenantry than as children and followers': but his hard-faced Sassenach widow, less MacDonell-minded but equally hard-pressed for cash, afterwards went back on his wishes. Tragically enough, none of the coercion was really necessary, for the people would eventually have gone anyway, as they have done equally from the estates that never cleared.

In many cases, clansmen emigrated together, often led by a chieftain or even sometimes by their chief himself. Thus, in the middle of the eighteenth century, some of the Mackintoshes of Borlum (descended from the 16th Chief of Mackintosh) led 200 clansmen in an organised emigration to Georgia, where they were settled south of Savannah along the north bank of the Altamaha River, to act as a buffer between the English colonists and the Spaniards of Florida. From one of their leaders (through a later marriage to a charming Creek squaw) descends Waldo E. McIntosh, present Principal Chief of the Creek Nation: 20,000 redskins in Oklahoma and Indiana. A Macneil chieftain emigrated from Vatersay off Barra at the head of 370 Barra men in 1802, settling in America, whence his great-grandson has returned as the present Chief of the Clan Macneil to restore their ancestral sea-girt stronghold. The Macnab, having negotiated with the Canadian authorities for a tract of some 81,000 acres in the New World, emigrated at the head of his clan to Canada. Here things went wrong tribally speaking, through his ignorance of Canadian as opposed to Scots law, when it came to the obvious point when a particular 'clever' clansman had to take him either for his natural patriarch or else for a 'testy tyrant'; indeed, much controversial research might be required to determine whether it was ever possible to transplant something of the pre-Culloden clan system to the New World, but common-sense tells us that it was doomed everywhere in its pristine forms. But a cousin and later chief, Sir Allan MacNab (1798–1862), became Prime Minister of Canada.

However, many reactionary chiefs and chieftains were horrified altogether by the Clearances. Struan Robertson refused to clear: now his heir has no land in Scotland and has to live in Jamaica. Mackenzie of Cromartie (heir of the forfeited Jacobite earl) not only refused to evict anyone—the County of Cromartie was formed from the family estates—but also sheltered and settled as many refugees as he could from the local evictions over his border (the 'Ross of Balnagowan' laird of his day was an interpolating Lowlander called Ross—ultimately 'de Roos'—in no way related to the old chiefs of the local Clan Ross). By an ironic somersault of history, the present talented and socially-conscious Countess of Sutherland is the descendant of the Cromartie who sheltered the victims of those Clearances. Other chiefs, like Lord Lovat, who disapproved of the clearances, improvised temporary shelter for refugees from elsewhere, until they could provide more permanent accommodation for them on another part of their estate. But in the end, nobody would endure the hardships of the high ground in a modern world, and the mountain-tops were left to their oldest inhabitants: the red deer and the ptarmigan.

Other clans met the economic crises in what can only

be called a truly clannish way. The MacLeods typify this. In the late eighteenth century the whole MacLeod economy was in a state of collapse, for chief and clansmen alike. The 23rd Chief tried desperately to persuade his impoverished clansmen not to emigrate: ' besought them to love their young chieftain, and to renew with him the ancient manners . . . and promised to do everything for their relief which in reason I could '. They did love him, and the tacksmen of the clan came forward of their own accord and entered into a voluntary obligation to pay a 7½ per cent increase in rent, ' in the hope that it may enable MacLeod and his Trustees to re-establish his affairs and preserve the ancient possessions of his family . . . on condition that, as our principal motive for coming under the voluntary obligation is our attachment to the present MacLeod, to the standing of the family, and our desire of their estate being possessed entire, we shall be freed therefrom if we shall have the misfortune to lose him by death, or if any part of the estate be sold '. This just enabled the estate to be maintained, and they then made provision for an allowance to the MacLeod chief himself, but he would not accept it, preferring instead to join the Army and seek his fortune in prize money at war. He raised personally the 2nd Battalion of the Black Watch, becoming its first Lieutenant-Colonel, and soon rose to be Second-in-Command of the whole Indian Army, where he had many adventures. Thus had the clan saved their chiefly heritage.

The other side of the same coin was shown two generations later. The 25th Chief of MacLeod ruined himself ' in 1846 in his efforts to succour his people in the great Potato Famine. The potato was the staff of life of the greater part of the population of Skye at that time; and when the crop entirely failed for two years, more than two-thirds of the inhabitants were destitute. MacLeod of MacLeod and his wife laboured to help and encourage his people. He beggared himself in providing food and work for them, so that at the age of thirty-seven he had to take a junior post in the Home Office in London in order to support himself and his family; and it was only in his old age that he was able to live in Skye '. Meanwhile, Dunvegan Castle was ' stripped of all that could be sold, pictures, plate and furniture ', to raise funds to feed his starving clansmen. Although he had had no legal obligation to do anything, Norman MacLeod of MacLeod had acted as a true Chief, and the Skye folk have never forgotten him.

Disaster after disaster struck the Highlands. For a while, in the first quarter of the nineteenth century, it seemed as though kelp might save the Western Isles and the mainland coastal districts. Kelp was the seaweed industry, introduced in 1765. Seaweed was exported to England as a rich fertiliser. Seaweed was also at first cut and burnt to produce soda. After 1823, when the Leblanc process was discovered in England, kelp was still used to produce iodine. It had subsidiary uses in the manufacture of soap and glass: and indeed the *algae* industry has been revived in the Hebrides today by Campbell-Preston of Ardchattan and Lochiel's brother, Colonel Charles Cameron—among the many modern by-products being, the writer understands, lovely red cherries for cocktails. The disadvantages of the kelp industry 150 years ago are said to have been that the seaweed was all taken up for industrial purposes, when previously it had been an essential source of agricultural manure, and that labour was similarly diverted from agriculture: but in fact when kelp failed, agriculture proved to be no adequate substitute. For a while, the Hebridean economy boomed. Macdonald of Clanranald (who has rather unfairly been accused of ' clearing ' when in fact he moved some black-houses to another part of the estate in the course of landscape gardening) became prosperous enough—at one glorious moment, £18,000 a year in solid golden sovereigns—to join White's and to be fêted as ' Clanronald Macdonald ' in Almack's: London's most exclusive night-club ever. Suddenly, he was broke. All had to be sold. He was gone. The new landlords began clearing at once. A sad saying was blown away in the wind: ' To whom shall I make my complaint, and no Clanranald in Moidart? '.

For, when the tariff protection that was saving the coastal economy was removed in the Whiggish interest of Free Trade, the last buttress of Hebridean life collapsed. Nearly two centuries before, the Brahan Seer had predicted that *Nuair a bhitheas maor nan ordagan mora agus dall nan ceithir-meoraibh-fichead comhla ann am Barraidh, faodaidh MacNeill Bharraidh 'bhi deanamh deiseil na h-imirich*: ' when the big-thumbed Sheriff-Officer and the blind man of the twenty-four fingers shall be together in Barra, Macneil of Barra may be making ready for the flitting '. And so it came to pass. The irascible General Roderick Macneil of Barra went bankrupt when the kelp industry failed as a result of the Government's Free Trade policy, a big-thumbed sheriff officer crossed over from South Uist (sharing the ferry with a well-known but decidedly unwelcome blind man who had twelve fingers and twelve toes) to serve the writ upon him, and in 1838 the island of his forefathers was taken from him and sold to absentee proprietors. Nothing the chiefs or the clansmen could do would suffice against the forces of economy when the Government (however objectively) was on the other side.

All this might have been the end of the clan idea, had not Pitt the Elder realised that the Highlands held an enormous reservoir of well-behaved martial men who were not being used. More than a century earlier, the Mackay chief Donald, 1st Lord Reay (commemorated in the beautiful MacCrimmon pibroch *Domhnall Dual Mac Aoidh*, ' Donald the Real Mackay ') had raised a regiment of several thousand Highlanders first for the Danish Service, and then for the Swedish Service, to assist the Protestant Cause in the Thirty Years War. There was a Gaelic saying:

Na h-uile fear a theid a dhollaidh
Gheibh e dolar o MhicAoidh

' Whoever is down on his luck, can still get a dollar (thaler) from Mackay.' The exemplary character of these Highland mercenaries is perhaps not sufficiently remembered. Monro's *Expedition* (London 1637) has many anecdotes shewing that their good conduct when billeted on civilians was as remarkable as their courage. At this period, the senior general of the Scottish mercenaries in the Swedish Service was one of the present writer's favourite forefathers, Field-Marshal Sandy Leslie, afterwards Earl of Leven (his mother was a Stewart girl in Rannoch), ' the old, little, crooked souldier ' who issued and rigidly enforced a proclamation ' forbidding the firing of any dwelling-house, hewing down fruit trees, killing a yielding enemy, outrages on women, &c., and stating that " murther is no less intollerable in the time of War than in the time of Peace ".' Throughout the rest of the seventeenth century and the first half of the eighteenth century other Mackays officered the Scots-Dutch Brigade in the service of the Netherlands, doubtless recruiting many of their men from their own clan territory. From 1704 to 1712 the Scots Guards had a Highland Company, who wore tartan and belted plaids, spoke Gaelic and were stationed at Inverness. This Highland Company Scots Guards was the first unit in the British Army to have a piper on their authorised establishment.

'The first quadrille at Almack's'. Left to right: the Marquess of Worcester, the Countess of Jersey, Clanronald Macdonald and the Marchioness of Worcester. Genealogically, the dancing figures are interesting, since three of them were natural scions of Blood Royal in the direct male line. Lord Worcester, though surnamed Somerset, was really a Plantagenet, sprung from Fulk of Anjou, King of Jerusalem, through King Edward III, knight-armoured victor of Crécy and Poictiers. Lady Worcester, surnamed FitzRoy, was a Stuart, ultimate outcome of King Charles II's sport with the Duchess of Cleveland. 'Clanronald Macdonald' (as Harriette Wilson calls the third dancer in this picture) came of a race less sophisticated but also more anciently royal, the line of Somerled, King of the Isles, slain by treachery in the twelfth century. Reginald George Macdonald, nineteenth Chief and Captain of Clanranald, was like Lord Worcester a member of White's and of Parliament.

By the Regency, Almack's (they say it was an anagram and that its founder's real name was MacCall) had become 'the seventh heaven of the fashionable world'. At ten golden guineas each, tickets for the weekly balls were almost unobtainable, as their distribution was determined by 'a feminine oligarchy less in number but equal in power to the Venetian Council of Ten'—Ladies Castlereagh, Jersey, Cowper, Sefton and Willoughby d'Eresby, with the Princesses Esterhazy and Lieven—the capricious lady-patronesses, who black-balled gaily and daily. This unbridled committee of women, two foreign ambassa-dresses among them, met weekly in their special 'blue chamber' at Almack's, to twist to their liking the social lives of such gentlemen as were in London during the season. Their coveted vouchers of admission were so much the talk of their generation, that in 1822 when Canning was given the Foreign Office with as ill a grace as possible by his reluctant king, George IV, the new Foreign Secretary compared it to receiving a

ticket for Almack's, and finding written on the back, 'Admit the rogue'. And Captain Gronow of the First Guards, apparently himself in favour with the lady-patronesses, noted with some satisfaction that of the three hundred officers serving with the Foot Guards in 1814, only about half a dozen managed to secure tickets of admission. On one occasion, the Iron Duke of Wellington himself was turned away for trying to enter in trousers, sans culottes.

The great Atholl fiddler, Nathaniel Gow, greatest of Highland violinists, was often booked with his band to play at Almack's weekly subscription balls, where 'the highest life in London' danced reels and Scottish country dances to such tunes as Hamilton House and the twa De'ils; while popular engravings of Raeburn's old Neil Gow (Nathaniel's father), fiddling briskly in his tartan trews, were hung up in several English country-house lavatories. Nathaniel Gow composed many lively or melancholy airs himself, and half a dozen collections of Scottish country-dance music published in the last century are prefaced by the advertisement 'As danced at Almack's'.

But towards the end of 1814, two new dances were introduced from the Continent: the waltz by Countess Lieven (thought at first rather shocking, as the partners were clasped in each other's arms instead of jigging separately, as in the old country dances and in popular present-day dances), and the quadrille by Lady Jersey. In that year, at the age of twenty-nine, the plain-spoken Lady Jersey (who had forty thousand a year) was at the height of feminine fashionable power; and it is significant of the extent to which Highland valour and Macpherson's Ossian and Sir Walter Scott's romances had made their mark on the world of fashion, that Lady Jersey should have been dancing her own special dance with Clanranald himself at what was to her perhaps one of the most important moments in her personal history.

Later, but still early in the eighteenth century, half a dozen Independent Companies, attached to no regiment, policed the Highlands as a Watch, called Black from their dark tartan to distinguish it from the ordinary redcoats: and in 1740 they were embodied together into the famous regiment still known as The Black Watch.

After the suppression of the 1745 Rising, Pitt saw the opportunity of raising Highlanders for military service in the wars abroad. Between 1757 and 1762, when peace was concluded with France, nine new Highland regiments were raised. Although penniless and landless, the Master

of Lovat, for instance—styled only Fraser of Lovat since his father's execution but still Mac Shimi to his loyal clans-men—was able to raise 600 men of his own within a few weeks; his neighbours raised more men; and in 1757 'Colonel Fraser of Lovat' sailed for America in command of 1,460 men of the 78th Fraser's Highlanders, whom he led up the Heights of Abraham to the taking of Quebec, where Wolfe himself died in the arms of a Fraser High-lander. Ironically, the conquest of Canada removed the French menace from the American colonists, and thus indirectly led to the American War of Independence. Once

A son of Colonel the Honble. Archibald Fraser of Lovat, wearing tartan about the time his father (with Lord Graham) had secured its restoration by Parliament in 1782. Late in life, Colonel Fraser of Lovat, the 18th *Mac Shimi*, formed the impression that he had become a turkey and, on arrival in his carriage on a visit to the Grants of Rothiemurchus, could not be induced to leave it as he was sitting on some eggs. However, like any other bird, he left them for a moment to relieve the calls of nature, whereupon the eggs were broken and some live chicks placed among them. Finding the eggs apparently hatched on his return, Lovat relaxed and was happily persuaded to enter the Grants' house.

The Government, however, continually broke its engagement promises to the private soldiers. This sometimes led to what the English called 'mutinies', usually settled by the good sense of the clan officers being combined with their chiefs' possession of what was then known as 'interest', that is the power to be heard by the officials of the Central Government. A typical example is perhaps that of the privates of the 2nd Battalion of the Black Watch, whom the Government (contrary to the terms of their enlistment) proposed in 1786 to draft into other units in India. Their Commanding Officer, the 23rd Chief of MacLeod, wrote immediately to the Commander-in-Chief: ' I have to observe to Your Excellency that this is the first time ever that this regiment was drafted, and that we were raised upon the idea of being exempted from that misfortune. My own Company are all of my own name and Clan, and if I return to Europe without them I shall be effectually banished from my own home, after having seduced them into a situation from which they thought themselves spared when they enlisted into the service . . . I must entreat Your Excellency to allow me to carry them home with me, that I may not forfeit my honour, credit, and influence in the Highlands, which have been exerted for His Majesty's service. ' MacLeod's firm request was granted, but the rumours of Governmental ill-faith can have done no good to future recruiting.

When tartan and the kilt were banned—by the hated Dress Act of 1747, repealed through the efforts in Parliament of Montrose's and Lovat's heirs in 1782—only Government soldiers were allowed to wear Highland dress: though a number of civilian portraits shew us that the Act was not rigidly enforced after the first few years of Southron panic. Perhaps it is from those martial days that there still exists a convention that only black (and never brown) shoes are worn with the kilt. So far, the last of what might be called clannish regiments were the Lovat Scouts and their rivals the Scottish Horse, raised and commanded by Lord Lovat and by the Duke of Atholl's heir during the Boer War.

The present Duke of Atholl's father was killed commanding the Scottish Horse in Italy during the Second World War; and the Scottish Horse regimental tie is black with gold stripes in threes, based on the gold and black paling of the Atholl coat-of-arms.

The achievements of the Highland regiments did much to win the Highlanders a national respect that has never waned. All the same, inter-clan feeling at the end of the eighteenth century was still vicious and bitter. Macdonalds hated Campbells, MacLeods feuded with Macdonalds, Mackenzies with MacLeods. Then came Sir Walter Scott, to whom Scotland in general and the Highlands in particular owe more (psychologically) than it's now fashionable to acknowledge. Sir Walter commanded the respect of Europe, indeed of the whole civilised world, and he used this position to make what had seemed squalid really picturesque. His magic made a silk purse out of our sow's ear. In his heroic prose—then a most unusual novelty— he suddenly took the meanness out of old Scottish feuds, and made them seem romantic in retrospect.

' Sir Walter Scott was backed by King George IV, whom it is now so smart to mock, but who as our most sympathetic Sovereign since the seventeenth century gave Scotland back her rightful place at last. Everybody felt that somehow the King was the heir of the Jacobite as much as the Hanoverian tradition. And they were more right, even from the strictly legalistic point of view, than is now perhaps generally realised. Up to the Wars of Independence, it had been possible to be a 'man' of two or three different realms

again, the Government appealed to the Fraser chief, now ' General Fraser of Lovat' and restored to his ancestral lands; and in 1775 he raised 2,340 men for the 71st Fraser Highlanders, six other chiefs (including Mackintosh of Mackintosh himself) being amongst his officers: this regiment wore the red hackle long before the Black Watch established it as their own exclusive privilege.

Among the clan regiments to survive longest were the Seaforth Highlanders, raised in 1778 in Ross-shire and the Hebrides by the Mackenzie chief: the Cameron Highlanders, raised in 1793 in Lochaber by the Cameron chieftain of Erracht; the Gordon Highlanders, raised in 1794 in Badenoch and elsewhere by the Marquis of Huntly (some would say by the kiss given to each recruit by his mother, the fetching Duchess of Gordon); also the Argyll Highlanders, raised in 1794 in Argyllshire by the Campbell chief, and amalgamated in 1881 with the Sutherland Highlanders, who had been raised in 1800 in Sutherland and Ross-shire by the Countess of Sutherland's cousin, General Wemyss of Wemyss: this last regiment formed the gallant ' Thin Red Line' at Balaclava. These regiments were so much family and clan affairs, that between 1793 and 1827, for example, no less than eleven officers of the Cameron Highlanders were the sons, brothers, nephews or grandson of General Sir Allan Cameron of Erracht who originally raised the regiment.

simultaneously; but by the fourteenth century it had become settled law (in both England and Scotland) that a person who was not born in the liegeance of the Sovereign, nor naturalised, could not have the capacity to succeed as an heir—he was in the strictest sense 'illegitimate', though not of course born out of wedlock. This legal incapacity of aliens to be heirs applied to all inheritances, whether honours or lands. The effect of the succession opening to a foreigner in Scotland was that, if he had not been naturalised or if his case was not covered by some special statute, the succession passed to the next heir 'of the blood', who thus became the only 'lawful' heir. It was of course always open to the Sovereign to confer an honour or an estate on a foreigner; the rule of law merely prevented aliens from being 'lawful heirs' to existing inheritances. In Scotland, this law was modified in favour of the French from the sixteenth century, but was otherwise rigorously applied until the Whig Revolution of 1688, after which it was gradually done away with by the mid-nineteenth century. It was precisely because of this law that Queen Anne found it necessary to pass a special Act of Parliament naturalising all alien-born potential royal heirs under her Act of Settlement of the throne. But of course, from the Jacobite point of view, no new statute could be passed after 1688, and the old law remained static until the death of the Cardinal York in 1807. At that time, his nearest heir in blood by the old (and therefore continuing Jacobite) law was not—as is sometimes supposed—the King of Sardinia, for the royal Sardine had not the legal capacity to be an heir in Scotland, unless naturalised (e.g. by marriage to the Sovereign) which he was not. The nearest lawful heir of the Cardinal York in 1807 was, in fact, curiously enough, King George III himself, who had been born in England (and therefore in the technical liegeance of James VIII). It is ironic that poor good King George, who has recently been proved not to have been mad at all, but to have suffered from an unusually acute form of a rare physical (and not at all mental) malady called porphyria that was unknowingly maltreated beyond the human breaking-point by his doctors, appears (according to even more recent research) to have inherited that disability from his Stuart ancestors, who fortunately suffered from this painful bodily toxin in a much milder form. However, his descendant, our present Queen, is the lawful Jacobite sovereign of this realm: as was Queen Victoria (who made her favourite home in Scotland) and King George IV before her.

The former bitterness of the old feuds became a 'joking relationship', and the revived War Gatherings became colourful Games. They were neither ignored nor suppressed, but simply changed from backwardness and bitterness into pageantry and fun. Those who seek to detribalise Africans in the beneficial interests of modernising their *standard of living*, might perhaps also consider their *pride* and, as Sir Walter did for us, adapt rather than abolish 'quaint' customs. Men will die for the Colours, but not for an extra ten bob a day. Nobody is burnt alive any more at the pagan fire festival still celebrated on All Hallow E'en, but the English get a lot of fun out of burning the effigy of poor Guy Fawkes (who shared the present writer's views about the value of Parliament) on the nearest available date. No longer is it an issue whether a job should go to a Macdonald or a Campbell, but each clan still enjoys its historic identity and cultivates its own roots. The annual Argyllshire Gathering at Oban makes no distant clan tremble lest the Campbells are Coming, but is instead an opportunity of visiting the Campbells and their former Maclean foes in surroundings of gaiety and colour.

The characteristic form of Scott's novels—the historical

background, the straightforward hero, the kindly folk who help him, the lack of sex, the girl whose hand is eventually won like a school cup—has been continued by a series of Scottish writers through R. L. Stevenson, S. R. Crockett, Neil Munro (so closely related, we are told, to the ducal house of Argyll), D. K. Broster, John Buchan, Compton Mackenzie, and so to Nigel Tranter. Throughout their works, honour and decency are preferred to slickness and cynicism: and the Spirit of Caledonia is never debunked merely in order to lend the emphasis of shock to some ephemeral point. These are not, of course, ordinary portrayals of real everyday life: but stones on the cairn which represents so many many honourable Scotsmen, High-

Sir Iain Moncreiffe of that Ilk, as Albany Herald and an Advocate, leaving the Parliament House in Edinburgh after attending a special sitting of Lyon Court.

landers and Lowlanders alike.

By the second half of the nineteenth century, the clan as a method of social organisation had disappeared from Scotland. Opinionated judges, confronted with the simple question whether somebody inheriting a particular estate was a member of the Clan Chattan—a question as easily to be solved by any qualified expert as whether somebody belongs to the Transport & General Workers Union— waffled for a long time about clan warfare (as if ' children ', which is what *clan* means, didn't equally exist in time of peace) and then held that the whole clan concept was no longer known to the law. But there was life in the old clans yet. Indeed, Lyon Court regards anyone who takes a clan surname as being as it were ' naturalised ' into that clan, so that if he is granted Arms (the symbols of the Name) they will always allude to the basic coat borne by its chief. Clansmen at home sometimes tend to take their history for granted. But clansmen far afield in Glasgow or Birmingham, Toronto or Brisbane, Chicago or Wellington, can find in their history those roots that give them identity and distinguish them from being merely numbered ants in some enormous, though enormously useful, urban ant-hill.

In England and on the Continent, the feeling of belonging to a great historic family is too often confined to a limited aristocracy. Not so in Scotland. As the Countess of Erroll, hereditary Lord High Constable of Scotland and Chief of the Hays, wrote in 1964: ' In too many countries the great historic families are separated from the mass of the people, but in Scotland we have been fortunate in that pride of Name has never depended on wealth and rank, and in that the clan tradition has always prevented class barriers from arising to divide our proud nation. The fact that the Grahams have a ritual head in the Duke of Montrose and that Lords Huntly and Aberdeen are Gordons, in no way makes a Graham or a Gordon superior in class to their fellow Scots. In the same way, all the bearers of great Scottish Names share alike in their ancient traditions. It is this brotherhood within clan or Name which links all Scots together and is so marked a feature of our countrymen wherever they may be. We are all one family of Scots, the branches of that family being the clans and Names, and the Chief of Chiefs our Queen.' And Dame Flora MacLeod of MacLeod wrote in the Clan MacLeod Magazine that ' her dear clan family ' is ' beyond and outside and above divisions between nations, countries and continents. . . . it takes no note of age or sex, rank or wealth, success or failure. The spiritual link of clanship embraces them all '.

The effective expression of this continuing clan sentiment was the establishment of the Clan Societies and the Clan Associations, a full list of which throughout the world is to be found in the *Scots Year Book*, edited by the present writer. At the apex of this vast clan pyramid there is the Standing Council of Scottish Chiefs, which meets annually in the capital, and with whom the Queen, as Chief of Chiefs, had luncheon during a Royal Visit to Edinburgh some years ago. There are today about 1,700 Scottish Societies and Associations, with many branches at home, in Canada, Australia, New Zealand and the United States—indeed all over the World. *An Comunn Gaidhealach* keeps our Gaelic poetry and song alive in its *Mod*. The Scottish Tartans Society, with their headquarters in the Tolbooth at Stirling, seek to gather under one roof all authoritative information about tartan; and the Lord Lyon King of Arms has an official Register of Tartans recorded by the various chiefs and chieftains. The 1745 Association keeps alive the memory of the gallant Jacobites who lost all for what they believed to be the rightful Cause. While overseas Scotsmen

Decanter specially designed by a craftsman of the Scottish Crafts Centre and presented by Sir Edward Reid to the Clan Donnachaidh Society. It is engraved with the coat-of-arms of Struan Robertson, Chief of the Clan Donnachaidh. His supporters, the Serpent and Dove, allude to the clan's belonging to the Kindred of St. Columba, through their descent in the direct male line from King Duncan [slain by Macbeth], son of Crinan, hereditary Abbot of Dunkeld.

in general tend to join the local Caledonian Society or St. Andrews Society, those of Highland descent also belong to their own Clan Society—and recollect wherever they are the proud traditions of sea-wrack or heather, peat-fire or droving, feud or massacre, that gave their very names to the hills and glens where their forefathers made Highland history. In this way, the clan society fulfils a social and indeed emotional function. For it transcends religion and politics, class and status, success and failure, bringing as their natural right to all clansmen everywhere all the regal pride and historic colour that so justly surround the tartan.

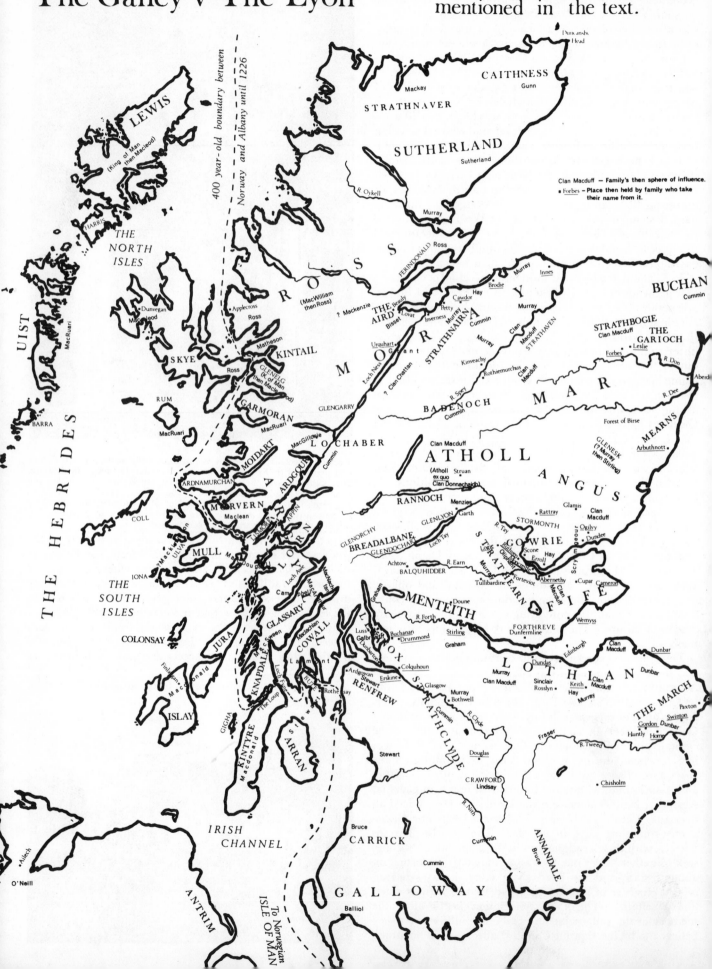

THE THIRTEENTH CENTURY
The Galley v The Lyon
To illustrate clans and families mentioned in the text.

Clan Macduff — Family's then sphere of influence.

▪ Forbes — Place then held by family who take their name from it.

400 year-old boundary between Norway and Albany until 1226

LEWIS (King of Man then Macleod)

HARRIS

THE NORTH ISLES

UIST

Dunvegan MacLeod

SKYE

Applecross

Ross

Matheson

KINTAIL

GLENELG (K. of Man then Macleod)

RUM

MacRuari

BARRA

MacRuari

GARMORAN

MacRuari

MOIDART

MacGillonie

GLENGARRY

LOCHABER

Cummin

THE HEBRIDES

COLL

ARDNAMURCHAN

ARISAIG

ARDGOUR

MORVERN

Maclean

APPIN

LISMORE

LORN

MULL

MacDougall

ULVA

IONA

THE SOUTH ISLES

COLONSAY

JURA

Finlaggan

Macdonald

KNAPDALE

Macsween

GIGHA

ISLAY

The Loup

KINTYRE Macdonald

ARRAN

IRISH CHANNEL

ANTRIM

To Norwegian ISLE OF MAN

O'Neill

Ailech

STRATHNAVER

CAITHNESS

Duncansby Head

Mackay

Gunn

SUTHERLAND

Sutherland

R. Oykell

Murray

R O S S

(MacWilliam then Ross)

FERINDONALD Ross

? Mackenzie

THE AIRD

Beauly

Lovat

Bisset

Inverness

Urquhart

Loch Ness

Grant

? Clan Chattan

Petty

Cawdor

Murray

STRATHNAIRN

Cummin

M O R A Y

Brodie

Innes

Hay

Murray

Clan Macduff STRATHAVEN

BUCHAN

Cummin

STRATHBOGIE Clan Macduff

THE GARIOCH

Forbes ▪ Leslie

R. Don

Aberdeen

Kinveachy

Rothiemurchus

Clan Macduff

BADENOCH Cummin

R. Spey

M A R

R. Dee

Forest of Birse

MEARNS

GLENESK (? Murray then Stirling)

Arbuthnott

Clan Macduff

A T H O L L

(Atholl ex quo Clan Donnachaidh) Struan

RANNOCH

Menzies

GLENLYON Garth

A N G U S

Rattray

Glamis

Clan Macduff

STORMONTH

GLENORCHY

BREADALBANE

GLENDOCHART

Loch Tay

R. Tay

Logie

GOWRIE

Ogilvy

Dundee

Scone

Achtow

R. Earn

BALQUHIDDER

STRATHEARN

Kilspindie

Oliphant

Errol

Hay

Scrymgeour

Tullibardine

Murray

Fortevioit

Abernethy

Clan Macduff

Cupar

Cameron

FIFE

Wemyss

MENTEITH

Doune

R. Forth

Graham

Stirling

FORTHREVE Dunfermline

Buchanan

Drummond

Graham

Luss

Galbraith

Dunbarton

Colquhoun

LENNOX

Edinburgh

Clan Macduff

Dunbar

Dundas

Murray

Clan Macduff

L O T H I A N

Sinclair

Keith

Rosslyn

Hay

Clan Macduff

Murray

THE MARCH

Paxton

Swinton

Gordon Dunbar

Huntly Home

Ardgowan

Stewart

Erskine

RENFREW

Glasgow

Murray

Bothwell

STRATHCLYDE

R. Clyde

Stewart

Douglas

R. Nith

Fraser

R. Tweed

Chisholm

Bruce

ANNANDALE

Bruce

CARRICK

Cummin

GALLOWAY

Balliol

The Highlands and Brae country of Scotland in the 16th century: to illustrate the spheres of influence of clans and families.

The Clans

The Clan Macduff

Although the main power of the Clan Macduff was in Fife, and ' Macduff' was not usually used as a surname, except by the MacDuffs in Perthshire, its chiefs (the Earls of Fife) were of such power and influence throughout the eastern highlands, that some understanding of its history is necessary to any consideration of the origins of several later clans.

Certainly, the chiefs of the Clan Macduff held rich lands in the Lowlands of Fife, Stirlingshire, East Lothian and Midlothian. But they also held far more extensive lands in the Highlands of Perthshire, Banffshire, Inverness-shire and Moray. Among the branches of the Clan Macduff were the families of Wemyss, Spens and Abernethy, also perhaps Cameron, Scrymgeour, Fernie, Kilgour, Syras and Scott of Balweary (who anyway married the Syras heiress). In fairness to the Duffs of Muldavit, afterwards Dukes of Fife, who were small landowners in Banff in the fifteenth century, their unproved claim to be a branch of the Clan Macduff of Fife is not so improbable as it might seem at first sight, when it is remembered that the original Macduff clan had great estates in Banffshire in the Middle Ages.

In the highlands of Perthshire, as early as the twelfth or thirteenth century, the Earls of Fife held the hill district of Strathbran, where David MacDuff, Baron of Fandowie, still appears in 1594 and 1602. ' Alexander McDuff, brother to Balanloan ', is named in a list of Gentlemen on the Atholl Estates who took part in the Rising of 1745 (the Jacobite Duke of Atholl was created Lord Strathbran by the Old Chevalier in exile); and the MacDuffs of Bonhard in Perthshire recorded in the nineteenth century Arms which clearly allude to a Fife and Atholl connection. Indeed, in the late thirteenth century the Earls of Atholl, just north of Strathbran, were themselves a branch of the Clan Macduff, holding also the Aberdeenshire district of Strathbogie.

Above all, the mediaeval Earls of Fife held vast Highland districts (including Strathavon), in the Cairngorms and on the Spey, in the counties of Inverness-shire, Moray and Banffshire. These lands bordered on Badenoch, haunt of the Clan Chattan, and lay on both sides of Rothiemurchus, cradle of the Clan Mackintosh. It is not therefore unreasonable to accept the Mackintosh claim to be themselves a branch of the Clan Macduff: and the *lyon rampant* appears in the first and fourth quarters of their shield on the earliest surviving Mackintosh seal, that of Alexander Mackintosh, Thane of Rothiemurchus in 1481. The *lyon* is still borne, *red on gold*, by The Mackintosh and his cadets, such as Shaw of Tordarroch and Farquharson of Invercauld.

It is suggested that the first two known chiefs of the Clan Macduff, Constantine and Gillemichael Macduff, successive Earls of Fife in the second quarter of the twelfth century, were brothers; and that their father Duff had been a predeceasing eldest son of Aethelred (Gaelicised as *Aedh*), last hereditary Abbot of Dunkeld and first Earl of Fife—of the Kindred of St. Columba who had inaugurated the King of Scots in the early days of the Celtic Church in Scotland. The Kindred of St. Columba had themselves attained the throne in 1034. Aedh or Aethelred was son of King Malcolm III and Saint Margaret. Although he was elder brother of King Edgar, King Alexander I and King David I, he was presumably debarred from the throne either through infirmity or as an Abbot. He probably derived his position in Fife from a marriage to the sister and heiress of Maelsnechtai, King of Moray, who was Chief of Clan Duff as grandson of Queen Gruoch, herself the heiress of the line of King Duff (killed 967) which was appanaged in the ' kingdom of Fife '.

The abbot-earl Aedh probably died in about 1128, after which the Moraymen rose in several attempts to put his surviving sons successively upon the throne. This was in keeping with the old laws of the Gaels,

The round Tower of Abernethy, built for the Columban monks of the Celtic abbey, of which a branch of the Clan Macduff (cadets of the Earls of Fife) were hereditary Abbots. Abernethy was the most sacred place of the Picts, probably dedicated to the goddess-spirit Brigid—in Christian times to St. Brigid. The present writer supposes that the pagan Pictish kings, whose throne-name appears to have been Bruide, incarnated a male manifestation of this spirit.

Francis, afterwards rightful 7th Earl of
Wemyss, with his wife Catherine, daughter of
the 2nd Duke of Gordon, ' Cock of the North '.
Painted by Allan Ramsay in 1745, he is
wearing trews and plaid, broadsword and
dirk. His elder brother David Wemyss, Lord
Elcho (who was, curiously enough at that
date, an Old Wykehamist) raised for the
Jacobite Cause a troop of Horse Guards,
consisting of about a hundred ' all gentlemen
of family and fortune ' in blue coats with red
waistcoats and cuffs, and was with Prince
Charles Edward at Culloden. On the death
of their maternal grandfather, the notorious
Colonel Francis Charteris, ' Rapemaster-
General of Great Britain ' (who was drummed
out of the British Army for cheating at cards
and out of the Dutch Army for theft, but made
a vast fortune at gambling before the populace
cast dead dogs and offal into his grave at his
funeral), Francis Wemyss inherited his great
wealth, and took the name of Charteris (pronounced ' Charters ' and derived from
Chartres in France), succeeding as rightful 7th
Earl of Wemyss on Lord Elcho's death in
exile in 1787. His descendant is the present
David Charteris, Earl of Wemyss & March,
K.T., Chairman of the National Trust for
Scotland and a former Lord High Commissioner to the General Assembly of the
Church of Scotland.

But the ancient lands and barony of Wemyss,
with its beautiful castle, were settled on the
younger brother of both Lord Elcho and the
7th Earl. This brother, James, thus became
Wemyss of Wemyss and Chief of the Name,
and was forefather of the present Captain
Michael Wemyss of Wemyss, who still lives
in Wemyss Castle, at West Wemyss. The
great Wemyss estates were known as Wemyss-
shire in the Kingdom of Fife. The Wemyss
family, besides belonging to the premier clan
of the Scottish Gaels, the Clan Macduff,
often had interests in the Highlands. In 1587,
the then Laird of Wemyss appears on the
parliamentary Roll of Highland landlords,
and as late as 1800 the famous Sutherland
Highlanders were raised by General William
Wemyss of Wemyss, whose mother had been
the only daughter of the sixteenth Earl of
Sutherland.   Indeed, a corridor of Wemyss
Castle is still carpeted with Sutherland tartan
instead of Wemyss tartan.

Wemyss Castle at West Wemyss in the Kingdom of Fife, home of Michael Wemyss of
Wemyss, Captain late Royal Horse Guards
(the Blues), the descendant of Gillemichael
Macduff, Earl of Fife ' by the Grace of God '
(c.1129–1135).   His wife, Lady Victoria
Wemyss, is sister of the Duke of Portland and
was a God-daughter of Queen Victoria. This
castle was built by Sir John of the Wemyss,
who inspired Wyntoun to write his famous
Chronicle and who died about 1428, and has
been much added to and altered throughout
the last five and a half centuries. Mary Queen
of Scots was staying here with the Laird of
Wemyss in 1564/5, when she first met her
future husband ' Darnley '. The older castle
of the family was at East Wemyss, where its
ruins are known locally as ' Macduff's Castle '.
King Edward I of Scotland stayed a night
there in 1304 during his occupation of Scotland. His unwilling host, Sir Michael of
Wemyss, joined in the Rising of King Robert
Bruce, and in 1306 King Edward wrote to Sir
Aymer de Valence (Guardian of Scotland)
that he was not pleased with Sir Michael,
directing Sir Aymer to destroy his manors and
lay waste his lands, ' or worse if possible '.
In the cliffs below ' Macduff's Castle ' are two
of the famous Wemyss caves (Wemyss is from
the Gaelic *uamh* meaning ' cave '), in which
are ancient or Pictish markings on the rock-
face. This sketch of Wemyss in 1792 shows
the present Wemyss Castle looking across the
Firth of Forth to Edinburgh Castle.

which would have preferred the MacAedh brothers before their Macduff
nephews. The Macduff earls therefore supported the line of King David I
and King Malcolm IV, and were accorded by them in return the premier
position in the realm.   Since ' Macheth ' (MacAedh) was sometimes
confused with ' Macbeth ', it seems possible that the historic Macduff
support of the boy King Malcolm IV against Macheth is the origin of
the tale of a legendary Macduff's support of King Malcolm III against
Macbeth, that gave rise to Shakespeare's famous but misleading play.

Anyway, the Clan Macduff was the premier clan among the Gaels of
mediaeval Scotland. Its chief, the Earl of Fife ' by the Grace of God ',
bore a *red lyon on gold*, a coat-of-arms only appropriate to a branch of the
royal house of Scotland senior even to that of the reigning kings themselves.
He was treated as almost a sacred personage, being placed first after the
King in all gatherings, speaking first in Council and Parliament, and

leading the van in battle (which among the ancient Gaels was the duty of an abbot bearing a holy reliquary, like the Ark of the Covenant in biblical times). Indeed, the chieftains of the most important cadet branch of the Clan Macduff were hereditary Abbots of Abernethy.

The Earl of Fife and the Abbot or Lord of Abernethy were both ' Capitals of Law of the Clan Macduff ': the Gaelic is *toisech-dior*, literally ' thane of law ' or ' law-chief '. This celebrated law was that all manslayers within the ninth degree of kin to the earls of Fife could claim sanctuary at the Cross of Macduff near Abernethy, and secure remission by paying a fixed compensation to the victim's family. Above all, the chiefs of the Clan Macduff had the right of enthroning the king on the Stone of Destiny at Scone; and after Edward I had carried off the Stone to Westminster, King Robert Bruce himself underwent a second Coronation in order to be crowned by a member of the Clan Macduff (Fife's sister, whom the English kept in a cage in public as a reprisal). After the last Earl of Fife (who was also the Regent Albany) was beheaded and forfeited in 1425, the Clan Macduff right of crown-bearing passed to the Lord Abernethy, who (through two heiresses) was then the Red Douglas and is now the Duke of Hamilton. The plain shield of a *red lyon on gold* is still borne by Wemyss of Wemyss, whose line have lived at Wemyss itself in Fife since the twelfth century, and who spring in the direct male line from Gillemichael Macduff, Earl of Fife more than eight hundred years ago.

Hamilton

The Hamiltons first impinged on the Highlands about the end of the thirteenth century, when their ancestor Gilbert may have married the widow of the Chief of the Galbraiths in the Lennox; but it was not until the fifteenth century that they became great Highland landowners, and their main sphere of influence was of course always in the Lowlands.

Their ancestor Sir Walter fitz Gilbert (i.e. Walter son of Gilbert) of Hameldone—perhaps from Hameldone Hill in the North of England, where the Scots were to be defeated in 1402—held lands in Renfrewshire by 1294. From his Arms and name, he was probably related to the great Scoto-Norman baronial house of Umfraville, earls of Angus at this time, who descended from the heiress of the ancient Celtic dynasts of Angus but who also held a wide fief in the North of England. After Bannockburn, he joined King Robert Bruce, who thought him an important enough acquisition to grant him immediately in 1314/5 the lands of Dalserf (forfeited by the Cummins) and soon afterwards gave him also the Barony of Cadzow, now called Hamilton after the family.

At Cadzow was eventually the magnificent Hamilton Palace, now pulled down, and there still survives there a famous herd of half-wild park cattle (as at Chillingham in Northumberland). These herds of white cattle were long thought to be the nearest survivors in appearance to their ancestral aurochs, the extinct wild ox of Europe: but they appear in fact to have only become semi-albinos through partial domestication (it has been suggested deliberately bred albino for ancient sacrificial purposes) and to be ultimately related to the dark ancient British breed called the black Pembroke, in turn related to the black Spanish fighting-bulls.

His son, Sir David fitz Walter of Hamilton, 2nd lord of Cadzow, who sat as a Baron in King David II's Parliament, was captured with that king by the English at the battle of Nevill's Cross in 1346; and ' considered of so much importance that he was placed in the custody of the Archbishop of York, who was enjoined not to deliver him up without a special mandate from King Edward '. He was only freed on payment of a heavy ransom. In 1445, the sixth lord of Cadzow was made a Peer of Scotland as Lord

Hamilton, in the days when lords were first being distinguished from other barons in Scotland.

James, first Lord Hamilton, brought the family to the Highlands by his marriage in about 1474 to the princess Mary of Scotland, sister of King James III. The unfortunate princess had been happily married to Thomas, Master of Boyd, 'the most courteous, gentlest, wisest, kindest, most bounteous knight' and 'fairest archer, devoutest, most perfect, and truest to his lady'; and the king had made him Earl of Arran, giving them the island of Arran for her dowry. But his father, the Regent Boyd (from whose younger son descended William Boyd, Earl of Kilmarnock, beheaded as a Jacobite after Culloden, and the present Gilbert Boyd, Lord Kilmarnock), suddenly fell from power in 1469, and the family fled into exile in Burgundy. After her beloved husband's death, the princess returned to Scotland, where the king gave her hand in marriage to Lord Hamilton, then an elderly widower. In 1484, after the murder by the Montgomeries of the young 2nd Lord Boyd (her son by her first marriage), her heir was James, 2nd Lord Hamilton, the son of her second marriage. This was of immense importance to Scottish history, as throughout the sixteenth and seventeenth centuries the Hamilton chiefs were often the nearest heirs presumptive to the throne.

In 1503, 'resplendent in the costume of white damask flowered with gold of which we hear in the Treasurer's accounts', Lord Hamilton was created Earl of Arran, and given the island with the earldom. The island of Arran had come to the Stewarts (his royal mother's family) with an heiress of the house of Angus, son of Somerled, King of the Isles (slain 1164). So the Hamiltons ultimately held the island of Arran because of their Gaelic and Norse royal blood: and they have quartered the Hebridean dynastic Black Galley in their coat-of-arms ever since.

Thenceforward, the history of the Hamiltons was on an international plane. James Hamilton, 2nd Earl of Arran, Regent of Scotland for the infant Mary, Queen of Scots, was created Duc de Châtelherault by the King of France in 1548/9. The subsequent history of this duchy is rather interesting. If it survived various forfeitures during the Franco-British wars of the seventeenth and eighteenth centuries (but under the various Republics that would apply to every other French title), the old royally-granted dukedom of Châtelherault is now held by the heir male of the family, James Hamilton, 4th Duke of Abercorn: who should really be the Premier Duke of France from the Royalist point of view (the next senior

The Honours of Scotland at St. Giles's Cathedral. In 1953, for only the second time since the Union between Scotland and England, the sacred Honours of Scotland—the Crown, the Sceptre and the Sword of State—were borne in public through the streets of the capital. The present Duke of Hamilton (who was wearing the kilt as usual) is seen bearing the Crown in his capacity as Lord Abernethy, a chieftain of the Kindred of St. Columba who inaugurated the Queen's ancestor King Aidan more than 1,400 years ago. The Earl of Crawford, Chief of the Lindsays, bears the Sceptre as premier earl 'upon the place' (his rival, Mar, an older earldom though of lower precedence, not being present). The Countess of Erroll, Chief of the Hays, stands between the Queen and the Duke of Edinburgh, carrying her silver baton of command and wearing her state robes as Lord High Constable of Scotland. Her deputy as bearer of the Sword, the Earl of Home (afterwards Prime Minister), is seen passing between Prince Philip and Lady Erroll's personal officer-of-arms, Slains Pursuivant, who is wearing a cloth-of-silver tabard embroidered with her coat-of-arms, the three red escutcheons of the Hays. Beside Slains Pursuivant stands the young Master of Rollo, her page; and Lord Home is attended by his own page, John Hamilton, Lord Binning.

surviving dukedom, Uzès, only dating from 1565). On the other hand, in 1864, the Emperor Napoleon III 'maintained and confirmed' his cousin the 12th Duke of Hamilton in the title of Duc de Châtelherault, presumably for not cutting him in the Bois (as with Dorset in *Zuleika Dobson*). The Duke was the Emperor's cousin, because his mother, the Duchess of Hamilton, was a daughter of the reigning Grand Duke of Baden by his Grand Duchess, Stephanie de Beauharnais: but Hamilton was then neither heir male (the Duke of Abercorn) nor heir general (Lord Derby) of the first Duc de Châtelherault. So the only logical conclusion of Napoleon III's action must be that the Dukes of Hamilton became Napoleonic dukes of Châtelherault with retrospective precedence from 1548/9; and it can therefore be argued that the present Duke of Hamilton should really also be the Premier Duke of France from the imperial Bonapartist point of view. Such are the pedantic jokes that enable us to confuse law and history.

Throughout the sixteenth century, the Hamiltons were at feud with the Stuarts of Lennox (descended from the first Hamilton earl of Arran's sister) about the succession to the throne—the Lennox Stuarts claiming that the 1st Earl of Arran's marriage was invalid. In 1526, after the Hamiltons of Arran defeated the Stuarts of Lennox at the battle of Manuel, Sir James Hamilton of Finnart, the 'Bastard of Arran', murdered in cold blood his cousin John Stuart, Earl of Lennox (Darnley's grandfather), after the earl had surrendered and given up his sword: he then set 'his mark'—a slash across the jaws—on many of Lennox's party who were his captives. A fiery but talented nobleman, who had spent some years at the Court of France, the Bastard of Arran was later the talented architect of the Renaissance front at Falkland Palace. But after getting his Lutheran cousin, Patrick Hamilton, Abbot of Fearn, burnt at the stake (really for having a dangerous rival claim to the Earl of Arran's for the throne), the Bastard was 'framed' as having been 'art and part' in an old plot against King James V; and after being worsted in a duel fought as a Trial by

Combat between himself and his accuser (Patrick Hamilton's avenging brother), the poor Bastard was unfairly beheaded for treason. It is said that this remarkable architect's ghost returned to haunt the king's dreams, foretelling his doom and the deaths of his two sons, the poor little elder brothers of Mary Queen of Scots. The Bastard's brother John Hamilton, Archbishop of St. Andrews, was hanged by the Reformers under the Regent Lennox in 1571. But by then the succession dispute had been settled by the marriage of Lennox's son Henry Stuart, Duke of Albany and King Consort of Scotland (whom English historians will persist in calling 'Lord Darnley', though we never did), to Mary Queen of Scots.

The other Hamilton feud in the sixteenth century was with the 'Red Douglas' earls of Angus about precedence. The Earl of Angus claimed place before even dukes, as one of the two Premier Peers of Scotland (the other was the Earl of Erroll as hereditary Lord High Constable). This precedence was probably based on his right of bearing the Crown, as Lord Abernethy—a right derived from his female-line ancestors, the hereditary Abbots of Abernethy, who were the principal branch of the premier Clan Macduff after the downfall in 1425 of the Regent Albany, last Earl of Fife: the clan who had had the duty of enthroning each king upon the Stone of Destiny. The Earls of Angus had their burial place at Abernethy— always the key to an ancient priority. When told that it was proposed to create Huntly a duke, the redoubtable Archibald Douglas, 6th Earl of Angus (step-father of King James V) observed to the Queen Regent, 'if he is to be a duke [duck], I will be a drake'. The Hamiltons, as heirs presumptive to the throne, felt that they should be accorded the first place. As early as 1520 there occurred the famous bloody brawl called 'Cleanse the Causeway', when the Douglas and Hamilton 'tails' chanced to come head on in the narrow High Street of Edinburgh, and Angus's men drove Arran clean out of the city. In 1599 Lord John Hamilton (who appears on the parliamentary Roll of Highland Landlords in 1587, as his elder brother Arran had long been mad) was made Marquis of Hamilton, together with Huntly. They were the first two ordinary marquises in Scotland, which then had no dukes either except the king's Stuart cousin Lennox: earl having always been the highest normal—and indeed semi-royal—rank. The Douglas earls of Angus continued to protest that they had a right to 'the first place and vote of parlement'. In 1633, the then Angus gave up the privilege in return for being made Marquis of Douglas, but afterwards it was pointed out that under a charter of 1631 he was only liferented in the earldom and couldn't give up the right for his heirs. The question is still of legal interest, as the two Premier Peers of Scotland—the Constable and the Earl of Angus—are the two hereditary Lords Assessors who advise the Lord Lyon King of Arms on matters of fact as opposed to law. Even though the then Hamilton became a duke in 1643, and the Dukes of Hamilton have long been Premier Dukes of Scotland, the dispute can now never be resolved, as through the marriage of the Duchess of Hamilton in her own right to the Marquis of Douglas's son in 1656, the present Duke of Hamilton is also (in the direct male line) Earl of Angus. But whether he is a Premier Peer as Duke of Hamilton or as Earl of Angus, he carried the Crown of Scotland in 1953 as Lord Abernethy.

The later history of the Hamilton family is so well-known that it is unnecessary to write about it here, since it is more concerned with the Lowlands than the Highlands. And although their Highland territory, the island of Arran, passed to the Grahams in 1895 through the marriage of Lady Mary Douglas-Hamilton to the sixth Duke of Montrose (whose daughter, Lady Jean Fforde, has given Brodick Castle to the National Trust for Scotland), the present Douglas Douglas-Hamilton, 14th Duke of Hamilton, K.T., P.C., G.C.V.O., A.F.C. (the champion 'boxing Marquis' who was the first airman to pilot an aeroplane over Mount Everest) has taken an active interest in trying out such experimental industries as shark-fishing (for oil) off the Western Isles, and always wears the Highland dress on national occasions when he welcomes the Queen as Her Majesty's hereditary Keeper of the Palace of Holyroodhouse.

Stewart

The Stewarts take their name from the hereditary office of Steward of Scotland, granted to their ancestor Walter fitz Alan by King David the Saint (1124–1153). This was the greatest office in the realm, and after the Stewarts became Kings of Scots themselves from 1371, it was settled for ever on the heir apparent to the throne. So today, Prince Charles is Great Steward of Scotland still, because he is the female-line descendant of Walter fitz Alan, the first Stewart. In the thirteenth century, the 4th Steward of Scotland (a crusader) married the heiress of the lord of Bute, of the royal house of the Isles—and another of Prince Charles's dignities is that of Lord of the Isles.

Fitz is the Norman-French for 'son' (French *fils*); and Walter's father was Alan fitz Flaald, Sheriff of Shropshire, son of Flaald fitz Alan, who became hereditary Steward of Dol in Brittany when his own elder brother perished on the First Crusade in 1097. Their first traceable ancestor Alan, a Breton noble living in about 1045, was also hereditary Steward of Dol: and the family appear to have been connected with the Counts of Dol and Dinan who were a branch of the ancient ruling dynasty of Brittany. As Brittany was colonised from Britain, it seems probable that their original ancestors were Ancient Britons of high rank, and so it is especially interesting that the first monarchs of united Great Britain should have been the chiefs of the Stewart clan.

The Stewart plant-badge, oak, may well have been in the family from pre-heraldic times, for it was also a badge of the English earls of Arundel who descended from Walter fitz Alan's elder brother. These earls of Arundel became the Premier Earls of England; where later, scions of the House of Stewart—legitimate and illegitimate, and often under other assumed surnames—held thirteen dukedoms: three of which (Richmond, Grafton and St. Albans) still survive. Scions have also held three French, one Italian and ten Spanish dukedoms, the hereditary offices of Admiral of the Indies and Grand Constable of Navarre, have given France a Grand Constable and several Marshals, have received three Cardinal's hats, and have given two Prime Ministers to Great Britain; as well as fourteen sovereigns to Scotland of whom five also reigned in England.

In Scotland, the first four dukes and the first marquis ever to be created

Tomb effigy of 'the Black Stewart': Sir John Stewart, hereditary Sheriff of Bute from 1385, natural son of King Robert II, and ancestor (through John Stuart, 3rd Earl of Bute, K.G., Prime Minister of Great Britain, 1762–1763) of the present John Crichton-Stuart, 6th Marquis of Bute, hereditary Keeper of Rothesay Castle for the Prince and Steward of Scotland (Prince Charles). The Stewarts held the island of Bute because their Crusader forefather Alexander, 4th Steward of Scotland (1214–1283) married the daughter of Seumas mac Angus, lord of Bute, of the old royal house of the Isles. So Lord Bute's lands in the island have come to him by descent for over a thousand years. Incidentally, the name James (*Seumas*) came into the family in the same way, and was later made famous by seven (or eight) Stewart kings all called James.

Lochindorb Castle, stronghold of the Wolf of Badenoch: King Robert III's redoubtable brother Alexander Stewart, Earl of Buchan. When the Bishop of Moray excommunicated the Wolf for deserting his wife in favour of his mistress, he burnt the town of Forres and the Cathedral of Elgin in 1390. The Wolf's effigy in armour is still behind the high altar of Dunkeld Cathedral in Atholl, where he left many natural descendants, whose heads were the Stewarts of Garth. The principal cubs of the Wolf, still living in Atholl, are the chieftainly litter at Balnakeilly—where they have prowled and prowled around since the reign of Mary Queen of Scots. The present heir of Balnakeilly won the Military Cross with The Rifle Brigade, and his younger brother exchanged his ancestral wolfskin for a bearskin, and became Regimental Adjutant of the Scots Guards.

52

A pictorial reconstruction of Doune Castle, in Menteith, built by Robert Stewart, Duke of Albany, who was Regent of Scotland (1388–1420). He was son of King Robert II, and forefather in the direct male line of the present John Stuart, 19th Earl of Moray, who still owns their lovingly-preserved but long un-inhabitable castle, and whose son Lord Doune lives in a charming Regency house at Doune Lodge nearby. Albany and his nephew Rothesay were the first two dukes ever created in Scotland, both royal Stewarts and both on the same day, 28 April 1398. The castle is especially interesting, as it is organised for possible defence by mercenary men-at-arms and not by trusted clansmen. So the Duke's quarters are in the tower on the right, over the guardroom and gatehouse, controlling completely the portcullis and thus all entry. The quarters for distinguished guests, always a danger in Scotland, are placed quite separately in the tower on the left. In between the two towers is the Great Hall and the accommodation for the garrison: placed between himself and his guests, but unable themselves to gain access to the duke's quarters or the gatehouse. For there were deliberately no internal communications between the three parts of the castle. Doune Castle was so called because it was built on the site of the older *dun* of Menteith, where the ancient Celtic earls of Menteith had their stronghold. The Regent Albany held the *dun* because his wife was the Countess of Menteith in her own right, and so Lord Moray's connection with the Doune of Menteith goes far back beyond the dawn of history.

Grandtully Castle in Atholl, stronghold of the Steuarts of Grandtully, who could raise 300 men before the '45, is still the home of their Steuart-Fothringham descendants. The late Laird of Grandtully commanded the 2nd battalion Scots Guards in both battles of Monte Camino in 1943; now a battle honour on the regiment's Colours.

were all Stewarts, and at one time or another Stewarts have held the earldoms of Angus, Arran, Atholl, Bothwell, Buchan, Bute, Caithness, Carrick, Fife, Galloway, Mar, March, Menteith, Moray, Orkney, Strathearn and Traquair; and the present dukes of Lennox and Buccleuch, though they bear other surnames, are really Stewarts in the male line.

The main Lowland branches of the Stewarts today are that of the 12th Earl of Galloway, Lord Lieutenant of the Stewartry of Kirkcudbright and former Grand Master Mason of Scotland (who claims descent from Sir John Stewart of Bonkyl, slain fighting for Wallace in 1297, younger son of Alexander, 4th Steward of Scotland), and that of Sir Guy Shaw-Stewart of Ardgowan, 9th Baronet, M.C., Lord Lieutenant of Renfrewshire (the original Stewart territory in Scotland), the descendant of Sir John Stewart of Ardgowan, natural son of King Robert III.

Archibald Stuart, 19th Earl of Moray, bestrides the Highland Line both in Menteith and in Moray. He springs in the direct male line, through the Lords Doune and Avandale, from the two Dukes of Albany, Regents of Scotland 1388–1424: the first duke being younger son of King Robert II. There is reason to suppose that his immediate ancestor, the 2nd Duke of Albany's grandson, was in fact legitimate, but accepted letters of legitimation with his elder half-brothers in 1479 because of the political dangers of belonging lawfully to the Blood Royal of the fallen House of Albany. In 1580 James Stuart, Master of Doune, became 2nd Earl of Moray in right of his wife, the daughter of another James Stuart, 1st Earl of Moray, Regent of Scotland and natural brother of Mary Queen of Scots. Known as the 'Bonnie Earl of Moray', a sad lute-tune and old ballad laments the 2nd Earl's violent death at the hands of the Gordons. From him, there descends the present Earl.

There are other branches of the Stewart clan settled in the Highlands. John Crichton-Stuart, 6th Marquis of Bute, hereditary Keeper of Rothesay Castle, descends from Sir John Stewart, hereditary Sheriff of Bute from 1385, known as 'the Black Stewart' and a natural son of King Robert II. Lord Bute's uncle, Lord David Stuart, was a signatory to the modern Covenant in favour of Home Rule for Scotland. The Stewarts of Appin in Lorn spring from an allegedly illegitimate son of John Stewart, Lord of Lorn (slain by the MacDougalls in 1463), of the branch descended from the 4th Steward of Scotland's younger son, Sir John Stewart of Bonkyl, slain fighting for Wallace in 1297. To this branch belonged also the 'Black Knight of Lorn', ancestor of the extinct Stewart earls of Atholl (from whose heiress came the Stewart Murray dukes of Atholl), and his brother Alexander was ancestor of the Steuarts of Grandtully in Atholl, now represented in the female line by the Steuart-Fothringhams.

Other families in Atholl were the Steuarts of Ballechin, founded by Sir John Stewart, natural son of King James II, and the Steuarts of Cardney, scions of a natural son of King Robert II. Perhaps the most numerous Stewarts in Atholl, however, were the branches of the Stewarts of Garth,

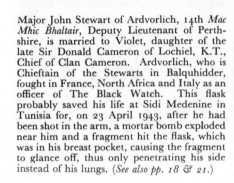

Skull believed to be that of James Stewart, Earl of Moray and Regent of Scotland (shot in 1569/70 by a Hamilton whom he had wronged). He was the natural son of King James V, and half-brother of Mary Queen of Scots. His daughter Elizabeth Stewart, Countess of Moray in her own right, brought the earldom to her husband James Stuart, Lord Doune, who thus became the 'Bonnie Earl of Moray'. When the Moray Aisle in St. Giles's Cathedral was opened after the First World War, this skull was sent to the late Francis Stuart, 18th Earl of Moray (an ex-fighter pilot ace from the earliest war days of the Royal Flying Corps), who had the cranium mounted as a drinking-cup on silver acorn legs (oak being the Stuart plant-badge). But, as it tends to leak, it's better for keeping nuts in on the sideboard. The 18th Earl was elder brother of the present Earl and of James Stuart, 1st Viscount Stuart of Findhorn, who was Secretary of State from 1951 to 1957.

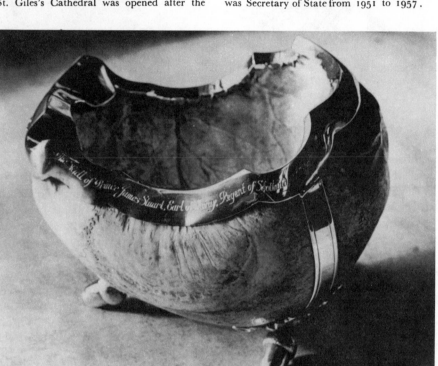

Major John Stewart of Ardvorlich, 14th *Mac Mhic Bhaltair*, Deputy Lieutenant of Perthshire, is married to Violet, daughter of the late Sir Donald Cameron of Lochiel, K.T., Chief of Clan Cameron. Ardvorlich, who is Chieftain of the Stewarts in Balquhidder, fought in France, North Africa and Italy as an officer of The Black Watch. This flask probably saved his life at Sidi Medenine in Tunisia for, on 23 April 1943, after he had been shot in the arm, a mortar bomb exploded near him and a fragment hit the flask, which was in his breast pocket, causing the fragment to glance off, thus only penetrating his side instead of his lungs. (*See also pp. 18 & 21.*)

The weapons of the 'Mad Major' James Stewart of Ardvorlich. His broadsword and backsword cross *an gunna breachd*, 'the Speckled Gun' (with its magic stock), with which he shot a marauding Macdonald of Glencoe, and the dirk with which in a fury he murdered his friend Lord Kinpont in 1644.

When his mother was pregnant with him in 1589 some of the Children of the Mist came to Ardvorlich and played rather a nasty practical joke on her. While she was out of the room getting meat and drink for them, they put her brother's severed head on the table and when she returned they were offering it bread and cheese (they were cross with him because as Forester Depute of Glenartney, he had cut off some MacGregor poachers' ears). At this sight, Lady Ardvorlich went mad, fleeing from the house into the woods and hills, and giving birth to the Mad Major beside a little loch on Beinn Domhuill, still called the Woman's Loch.

Her husband, Alasdair Stewart of Ardvorlich, promptly hanged a dozen MacGregors on an oak tree at Meovie (where their skeletons were accidentally unearthed by roadmen in 1810) though, in their dire need later, he was fined heavily for sheltering some refugee Gregarach; and when the Mad Major grew up, he harried the MacGregors too. He also slew a marauding Macdonald of Glencoe, who was grappling on the ground with an Ardvorlich dairymaid, with a skilful shot from his Speckled Gun. In 1642 his younger son Alexander was beaten up with bludgeons loaded with lead, by fellow students at St. Andrews, and died some months later. Another son, Harie Stewart, was mortally wounded fighting for Montrose at Tippermuir in 1644, when the godly enemy attacked them very unsuccessfully to the war-cry of 'Jesus and no quarter', selected by their 'Christian' ministers.

The Mad Major was present with Montrose, but soon afterwards fell out with the Grahams, apparently because their ally Alasdair 'Colkitto' MacDonell's men had harried his lands; and in a fury he dirked his best friend John Graham, Lord Kinpont, eldest son of the 7th Earl of Menteith. He had to flee to the enemy camp, where he was well received by Argyll: and his adventures were the basis for Sir Walter Scott's *Legend of Montrose*. After his death, the Mad Major's enemies were still determined to have at him. His kith, kin, clansmen and dependants set out with the coffin on their five-mile journey to Dundurn. 'The party had barely got half way when word came that his enemies intended to ambush the funeral cortège . . . So they hastily dug a hole near where they were and " shoughed him in ", and later when the country was quieter they dug him up and gave him a proper burial in the little chapel at Dundurn, where his father and his successors to the present day lie buried beside him.' A stone now marks the spot where the Mad Major's body was temporarily interred.

sprung from a natural son of Alexander, Earl of Buchan, known as the the 'Wolf of Badenoch' and younger son of King Robert II: Colonel David Stewart of Garth, writing in 1822, tells us of the Wolf's son, James Stewart of Garth, that 'There are now living in the district of Athole, within its ancient boundary, 1,835 persons of the name of Stewart, descendants of this man, in the male line, besides numbers in other parts of the kingdom'. The principal chieftains of this stock left in Atholl are the Stewarts of Balnakeilly, now represented by Mrs. Stewart-Stevens and her son Lt-Colonel Ralph Stewart-Wilson, M.C. The Stewarts of Ardvorlich in Balquhidder still hold their old lands beneath Ben Vorlich by Loch Earn, and descend from a natural son of the wild lord James *Mor* Stewart, the only one of the 2nd Duke of Albany's sons to escape being beheaded with their father in 1425. Their present chieftain, Major John Stewart, 14th of Ardvorlich, has written an excellent clan summary in his book *The Stewarts* (Edinburgh 1954).

It is, however, hardly necessary to remind people of the history of a clan whose chiefs included Mary Queen of Scots and Bonnie Prince Charlie.

'La Belle Stuart' posed as the model for Britannia on our pennies. She was Frances Stuart, grand-daughter of the 1st Lord Blantyre, and perhaps the only lady at Court who refused the advances of the gallant King Charles II Stuart (grandson of Henri IV, the *Vert Galant* who was one of France's most celebrated lovers). She preferred to marry Charles Stuart, Duke of Richmond & Lennox, K.G., hereditary Lord Great Chamberlain and High Admiral of Scotland, who was drowned at Elsinore while Ambassador to Denmark: after too good a dinner aboard a visiting British frigate, he fell between the warship and the boat that was to take him ashore. The King of Denmark sent her husband's body home to her, with a mourning present, 'in a new ship richly adorned, the sails and ship all black'. The Duchess of Richmond and Lennox left a large sum of money to buy an estate for her own cousin Alexander Stuart, Lord Blantyre. It was used to purchase from the Maitlands their lands and castle of Lethington, promptly renamed Lennoxlove. A Scottish country dance is still called 'Lennoxlove to Blantyre'.

Cairn marking the site of the judicial murder of James Stewart of the Glens, sentenced to be hanged by a Campbell assize at Inveraray (the Campbell capital) presided over by Argyll himself as Lord Justice General (the only instance of his presiding personally at any criminal trial) in mistaken revenge for the murder in 1752 of Colin Campbell of Glenure, 'the Red Fox', whom they thought had been shot by another Stewart but who was in fact possibly shot by a Cameron. This is perhaps the last instance of a blood-feud between clans: Campbells *v.* Stewarts of Appin. (See also p. 57.)

The Clan Donald

The great Clan Donald, long the mightiest of all the clans, derive their surname from Donald of Islay, whose father Ranald mac Somerled was King of the Isles and Lord of Argyll and Kintyre (1164–1207). Each successive Lord of the Isles descended from Donald bore the Gaelic style of *Mac Dhòmhuill*, 'the Son of Donald', but Macdonald was not used as an ordinary surname by the family or their clansmen until the sixteenth century: the earlier surname used being 'of the Isles' or just plain 'Isles', and cadets being otherwise called either by their patronymic or a nickname, e.g. 'Alasdair of the Isles', 'Alasdair mac Iain' or 'Alexander Johnson', or just plain 'Alasdair the Warty'—rather than Alexander *Carrach* Macdonald of Lochaber, in the more modern form. But he would be referred to often enough as a *Domhnullach*, i.e. 'one of the Clan Donald'.

Donald of Islay's father, King Ranald, was son of King Somerled (who was slain campaigning against the King of Scots in 1164) by the daughter of King Olaf of Man. The genealogies of both King Somerled and King Olaf require much further research. But it may be suggested that both sprang from the Norse kings in Ireland through two different 'sons' of Ivar,

Lord Macdonald, as Lord Lieutenant of Inverness-shire, presenting the Chief of Clanranald to the Queen in 1956.

Mingarry Castle, stronghold of MacIain of Ardnamurchan, descended from Iain *Sprangach* 'the Bold', younger brother of King Robert Bruce's firm friend, Angus *Og* Macdonald, lord of Islay. Ardnamurchan Point marked the northernmost limit of the South Isles.

King of Dublin, who sacked Dunbarton in 870—and that King Ivar himself descended through King Ranald Higher-than-the-Hills (in whose honour Thiodolf wrote the famous *Ynglingatal*) from the Norse Ynglingar dynasty: and therefore through such saga-hallowed kings as Halfdan the Stingy and Eystein the Fart from the seventh-century Ingiald Ill-Ruler, last of the Frey-born Yngling pagan sacral 'Peace-Kings of Uppsala' in Sweden, associated with human sacrifice of royal victims from within their own sacred family and claiming descent from the male manifestation of the ancient goddess Nerthus, whose emblem was the Galley.

King Somerled's descent from the House of Ivar depends on the reasonable identification of his great-great-grandfather Imergi (as given by the seanachies) with the Iehmarc of the Anglo-Saxon Chronicle, one of the three kings who submitted to Canute when he invaded Scotland and who was obviously Echmarcach ('Horse-Rider' in Gaelic, and pronounced Margadr by the Norse), King of Dublin on and off from 1035 to 1052.

Colour plate
Castle Stalker in Appin, built by Duncan Stewart, 2nd of Appin (1497-1512). He was the King's Chamberlain in the Isles, and King James IV is said to have stayed with him there. *Caisteal Stalcaire* means the Castle of the Deer-Stalker or the Wild-Fowler, and the king is said to have gone with *Mac Iain Stiubhart* to falconry or the chase. Between the Jacobite Risings, the Government garrisoned the castle against the Stewarts of Appin themselves, and it has long been a ruin. But work is in progress to make it habitable again, as its new owner claims Stewart descent in the female line.

The Massacre Monument in the village of Glencoe. Here, on 12 February 1692, the unsuspecting Macdonalds of Glencoe were murdered at dawn in midwinter by the Government troops who had been billeted on them in the most friendly manner for the past fortnight. *Mac Iain*, their aged chieftain, was murdered in his bedroom: his widow escaped, stript naked, to die of cold. Their massacre was deliberately engineered by John Dalrymple, Master of Stair, to terrorise all clans who did not agree with his revolutionary politics. He was joint Secretary of State for Scotland to William of Orange, who strongly supported the ' plan . Stair originally wanted to massacre all the Camerons and all the MacDonells of Glengarry as well. Argyll and Breadalbane necessarily had to be let into the secret of the Government's plan, or part of it. But the Campbells in general have perhaps received too large a share of the blame, simply because the actual troops employed (though very few of the officers or men were Campbells at all) happened to be a company of Argyll's Regiment and were commanded by Robert Campbell of Glenlyon. A snowstorm prevented other troops from coming up in time for the blame to have fallen more heavily instead on more senior Government officers, Colonel Hamilton and Major Duncanson, who did not belong to Clan Campbell. It was a Government measure ordered bureaucratically by progressive Whigs, ' liquidating ' reactionary Jacobites as vermin, and a fine example of ' planning '. Ever since, the *Nine of Diamonds* has been known as ' the Curse of Scotland ', for the Dalrymple coat-of-arms has nine lozenges on its saltire. The writer is happy to add that it was Sir Thomas Moncreiffe of that Ilk, as permanent head of the Treasury, who signed the order for the payment of compensation to the victims of the massacre.

Tobar nan Ceann, the ' Well of the Heads ' near Invergarry. Here the clan poet, Iain *Lom* MacDonell, washed the severed heads of seven of the ruffians who had murdered his chieftain, Alasdair MacDonell, 12th of Keppoch, in 1663. The poet had composed a bitter lament, the *Murt na Ceapaich*, and (having appealed in vain to Lord MacDonell and Aros, the Glengarry chief) secured an effective vengeance party from Sir James Macdonald of Sleat. The poet presented the washed heads to Glengarry; and in the nineteenth century Alastair MacDonell, 15th of Glengarry, erected over the spring a monument inscribed in English, Gaelic, French and Latin, capped with a carving of the seven heads bound by their hair to a dirk.
Colour plate
In the mountains of Skye, where the MacLeods and Macdonalds fought each other with two-handed swords, bows and arrows, for centuries.

So it may be significant that as late as 1263 the isle of Arran was ineffectually assigned by the King of Norway to another Margadr who must necessarily have been of Somerled's line.

But the old Gaelic seanachies believed Somerled to be a Gael in the male line, and certainly King Somerled *Gillebride's*-son and King *Echmarcach* Ranald's-son will have descended from Gaelic princesses, as their names show. The probability is that Somerled descended from one or more heiresses of the royal house of Lorn (perhaps one of them married Godfrey mac Fergus, the ninth-century prince of Oriel who came from Ireland to the help of King Kenneth mac Alpin in Argyll, and is traditional ancestor of Somerled; and one of King Echmarcach's line married their heiress). Anyway, Somerled first appears as the *regulus* or sub-king of Argyll under Scotland before he also established himself as a *rex* or king in the South Isles under Norway.

King Somerled himself reigned over the South Isles from Bute to Ardnamurchan Point, as well as being ruler of Argyll, Lorn and Kintyre on the mainland. But after his death, the Norse system was unfortunately followed whereby his territories were split up among his various sons and their descendants, who sometimes styled themselves kings and sometimes lords. When the whole of the Hebrides were ceded by Norway to Scotland in 1266, they were divided into four great administrative groups. Skye and Lewis were placed under the overlordship of the Earl of Ross, and the other three island groups under Somerled's descendants: MacDonald in Islay, MacRuari in Uist and MacDougall in Mull.

In the fourteenth century, Donald of Islay's branch, the Macdonalds, acquired all the South Isles and part of the North Isles. Islay they held already. Mull and its adjacent islands were given to them by the Bruce kings, when the MacDougalls of Lorn were forfeited for supporting the Balliol cause. Uist with its adjacent isles as far south as Barra, together with the great mainland district of Garmoran including Moidart and Knoydart and Morvern, came to ' Good John of Islay ' (Eoin Macdonald, styled Lord of the Isles from 1354) through his first marriage to the heiress of the MacRuaris. Her inheritance he gave out to Ranald, his son by her, to be held under Donald, whom he nominated to be next Lord of the Isles and who was son of his second marriage to a daughter of King Robert II.

Ranald was ancestor of the great Clanranald, with its younger branch, the MacDonells of Glengarry, who all remained loyal to the line of his younger half-brother Donald as High Chief of Clan Donald. From Donald's younger brother Iain *Mor* the Tanist (assassinated in 1427), who married the heiress of the Bissets of the Glens of Antrim in Ireland, sprang ' Clan Donald South ': the Macdonalds of Islay and Kintyre, and the present McDonnell earls of Antrim. From another of Donald's own younger brothers, Alasdair *Carrach* or ' the Warty ', came the Macdonells of Keppoch on the mainland. The MacIains of Ardnamurchan, and the MacIains or Macdonalds of Glencoe (who were to suffer that notorious massacre at the orders of the Master of Stair) had already branched off

This is probably the oldest surviving likeness of a Macdonald. It shows the mighty Ranald, founder of Clanranald, eldest surviving son of Eoin *Macdonald*, Lord of the Isles. Ranald died at Eilean Tioram Castle, ' his principal residence ', in 1386, and was buried in Iona. He is depicted bearded, wearing his quilted ' yellow war-coat ', and a Celtic conical helmet with chain-mail to protect his neck and shoulders, and is armed with claymore and dirk and battle-axe. This broken Cross-shaft from the little island of Texa, off Islay, is inscribed HEC EST CRUX REGNALDI JOHIS DE ISLA: This is the Cross of Ranald (the son) of Eoin of Islay. Ranald was son of the Lord of the Isles by his first marriage, to Amy, heiress of the royal house of Mac Ruari: and he succeeded her in the great lordship of Garmoran, including all Moidart, Arisaig, Morar and Knoydart, together with the superiority of the islands of Harris, the Uists, Eriskay, Barra, Rum and Eigg, to which his father added the superiority of Ardgour, Sunart and lands in Lochaber; altogether a vast inheritance between the Great Glen and the Outer Hebrides. In return, at his father's request, Ranald resigned the High Chiefship of Clan Donald and the Lordship of the Isles to his younger half-brother Donald (ancestor of the present Lord Macdonald), whose mother was a Stewart princess, daughter of King Robert II. From Ranald, there descended the powerful Captains of Clanranald (the older style for a chief), and their haughty cadets the MacDonells of Glengarry. Ranald's other distinguished descendants included Flora Macdonald, Napoleon's Marshal Macdonald (Duc de Tarente) and the great Highland poet *Alasdair Mac Mhaighistir Alasdair*: whose ' longest work, the " Blessing of the Ship "— the description of a voyage by the galley of Clanranald—has been described as the finest sea-poem written in Britain '. The present Chief is Ranald Macdonald, 23rd Captain of Clanranald, who is also Jacobite titular 10th Lord Clanranald. (*See also pp. 38 & 78.*)

before this period.

Donald, Lord of the Isles (1387–1423), unsuccessfully claimed by force of arms the earldom of Ross in right of his wife. But in 1435 it was given to his son Alasdair Macdonald, Lord of the Isles, who thus acquired the overlordship of Skye and Lewis, the only part of the Hebrides not hitherto under Macdonald sway. He also acquired Ross and much of modern Inverness-shire. Thereafter, the four administrative divisions of the Hebrides (for which see R. W. Munro's fascinating edition of *Monro's Western Isles of Scotland*, Edinburgh 1961) were Islay, Mull, Skye, and Lewis (to which the whole 'Long Island' could now be attached).

The Irish annalists style the Macdonalds *kings* in the fashion of the Gaels, and Macdonald's Kingdom was then at its height. As ruler of the Isles, he presided over the Council of the Isles on Eilean 'a Comhairle, the island in Loch Finlaggan near his castle in Islay. He had his own officers-of-arms, Islay Herald and Kintyre Pursuivant. As Earl of Ross, he had other officers-of-arms, Ross Herald and Dingwall Pursuivant: for his northern capital was at Dingwall, where the local assembly or Tingwald had been held since Norse times.

Thenceforward many mainland clans, such as Mackintosh and Cameron, Mackenzie and Matheson, Ross and Munro, acknowledged Macdonald's authority: until the earldom of Ross was forfeited to the Scottish Crown in 1475. But the Hebridean clans—Maclean and Macneil, MacLeod and Mackinnon, Macquarie and Macfie—continued to remain loyal to Macdonald for long after the follow-up annexation of the Lordship of the Isles itself in 1494 by the Stewart kings of Scots, who themselves descended from the heiress of a rival branch of the House of Somerled. Since then, the heir to the throne has always held the title—Prince Charles being the present Lord of the Isles—although the Hebridean clans went on rising in vain attempts to restore Macdonald rule until the death in 1545 of the last Lord of the Isles's grandson Donald *Dubh* Macdonald. The civilisation of the Hebrides never recovered from the loss of their Home Rule.

The difference in outlook between the centralising government and the world of the Gaels is perhaps summed up by an entry in 1499 in the Annals of Ulster, recording the ' execution ' in Edinburgh of what the Scots government would have called Sir John Macdonald of Duniveg with his son John and his grandsons Ranald and Donald: ' A sad deed was done in this year by *the king of Scotland, James Stewart. Eoin Mac Domhnaill, king of the Foreigners' Isles*, and Eoin the Warlike his son, and Raghnall the Red and Domhnall the Freckled, were executed on one gallows the month before Lammas '.

After the downfall of Macdonald's kingdom, the other different clans went their own way, feuding amongst themselves, while the great chieftains of the Macdonald royal stock also became chiefs of separate clans. Clan-ranald still had his great inheritance. Islay was over-run by the Campbells, and only Largie and the Antrim branch survived. Glengarry for a while acquired the chief position through marriage to the heiress of Lochalsh, the senior surviving representative of the Lords of the Isles. But Sleat descended in the male line from the last Lord of the Isles's half-brother, Hugh Macdonald of Sleat in Skye, and in the late seventeenth century was recognised by the Privy Council as Laird of Macdonald.

After the 1715 Rising, the Barony of Sleat was forfeited and, after careful Government enquiries among the various Clan Donald chieftains, when it was restored, it was renamed the Barony of Macdonald. Thereafter the Sleat baronets were styled Macdonald of Macdonald and were eventually created Lords Macdonald in 1776. But a family arrangement in the nineteenth century, confirmed by a private Act of Parliament, had the ultimate effect of dividing between two brothers the baronetcy and chiefship of Sleat from the peerage, high chiefship and territorial barony of Macdonald. As a result, Alexander Macdonald of Macdonald, 7th Lord Macdonald, present Lord Lieutenant of Inverness-shire and former Grand Master Mason of Scotland, who still holds wide lands in the Isle of Skye, was in 1947 officially recognised as the High Chief of all Clan Donald.

Invergarry Castle, ruined stronghold of the MacDonells of Glengarry. The far side of the castle overlooks Loch Oich. Glengarry's crest is the Raven, sacred bird of Woden and thus of his ancestors the Norse sea-kings of the Isles: and the Glengarry clan gathering-place was called *Creagan an Fhitich*, the Raven's Rock. The present Air Commodore Aeneas Mac-Donell of Glengarry, C.B., D.F.C., R.A.F., *Mac Mhic Alasdair*, is one of the few survivors among the fighter pilots who won the Battle of Britain, and of whom Churchill said that never had so many owed so much to so few. From 1956 to 1958 the 22nd Chief was British Air Attaché in Moscow.

Duntulm Castle in the Isle of Skye, a stronghold of the Macdonalds of Sleat, Chiefs of Clan Uisdean. They descended from Uisdean of the Isles, half-brother of the last Lord of the Isles, and younger son of Alasdair *Macdonald*, Earl of Ross and Lord of the Isles (who died at Dingwall in 1449). Because the rightful High Chief (Donald *Dubh*) had so long been an inaccessible prisoner of the Government, it was felt that the succession had devolved upon the Chiefs of Sleat (the pronunciation is shewn by the saying that in the House of Macdonald the slates are on top): 'this certainly was the view taken by the vassals of the Isles in 1539, when the Chief of the Clan Uisdean once more unfurled the ancient banner and determined to lay claim to and take possession of the time-honoured heritage of his sires'. Donald *Gruamach* 'the Grim' of the Isles, Chief of Sleat, was promptly proclaimed *Macdonald* and led a Rising to restore the Lordship of the Isles. He arrived at Eileandonan, Mackenzie's castle in Kintail, which was not expecting him and had a garrison of only three. But Duncan MacRae, one of Mackenzie's 'Shirt of Mail', took aim from behind the battlements and shot Donald the Grim in the leg. The fiery royal chief impatiently tore out the arrow, severing his own main artery with the barb, and so the Rising ended in his premature death on a nearby sand-bank. Donald the Grim's son, 'Dusky' Donald *Gorm* (literally

'the Blue'), probably died in exile in England, while seeking an alliance with the Tudor king against their common 'Auld Enemy': Scotland. There is a well-known tale (copied by other clans about their own chiefs, but most appropriate in the case of this, the greatest of clans) that when Donald *Gorm* was in London at this time he was asked to the Lord Mayor's Banquet and placed rather too near the wrong side of the salt, as if he were a simple squire. Halfway through the banquet, somebody told his host that he was in fact a great prince in his own country, at that very moment negotiating a treaty with King Henry VIII, and so the anxious Mayor immediately sent a message asking Donald *Gorm* to come and sit at his right hand. The reply is famous: 'Tell the Lord Mayor not to be fashing himself. Wherever *Macdonald* is sitting, that is the head of the table.'

In 1689, the then Chief of Sleat was appointed a Commissioner of Supply as the Laird of Macdonald; in the same year his lands were referred to as the Barony of Macdonald, and he was also described as Sir Donald Macdonald of that Ilk: all signs that at last the Crown recognised once again a High Chief of all Clan Donald—and that the slates were still on top of the House of Macdonald. The then chief was forfeited for taking part as a Jacobite in the 1715 Rising, and when they were restored to his heir in 1727, they were erected anew into the free Barony

of Macdonald for him as Alexander Macdonald of Macdonald. The 9th Baronet was created an Irish peer as Lord Macdonald in 1776.

Godfrey, 3rd Lord Macdonald, was in a difficult position. His mother, the heiress of the old Anglo-Norman family of Bosville of Thorpe in Yorkshire, had wanted the two families kept separate. He himself eventually married a natural child of King George III's brother (the Duke of Gloucester & Edinburgh) by an affair with the Earl of Tyrconnel's daughter. Lord Macdonald's eldest son born to this lady was only legitimated in Scots Law (but not in English law, which applied to his peerage) by their subsequent marriage, whereas their younger son, born after the marriage, was undoubtedly legitimate by birth. 'Lord Macdonald sought, like a practical and commonsense Scot, to separate again the Skye and Yorkshire inheritances of Macdonald and Bosville respectively. Holding the view that his first-born son was illegitimate, he hit upon the very sensible expedient of settling upon him the Yorkshire estates and making him Bosville of Thorpe and Gunthwaite with the appropriate Bosville coat-of-arms, whilst the Skye estates, including the territorial barony of Macdonald and the Irish peerage of Macdonald, all descended to . . . the first son born after the ceremony of marriage.' As a result, the high chiefship of Clan Donald remained with the title of Lord Macdonald and the vast territorial Barony of Macdonald in the Isle of Skye, while the more valuable (though smaller) estates in Yorkshire went to the son who took the name of Bosville. The matter was difficult, as the elder son had expected to be Lord Macdonald until suddenly told of his position at his father's death, while the other son coveted the rich Yorkshire farmlands more than the barren Skye moorlands. So a special private Act of Parliament had to be passed in 1847 to regulate the position in accordance with their father's settlement.

However, seventy-eight years later, when the then Lord Macdonald was mad and could not act for himself, the romantically-minded wife of the then Squire of Thorpe felt an injustice had somehow been done, and in 1910 a decreet of the Court of Session was obtained establishing that her husband's grandfather had been legitimated by Scots Law. As a result he took up the old family baronetcy (created in 1625, and now the Premier Baronetcy of Nova Scotia) and was officially recognised as Chief of Sleat, i.e. Chief of Clan Uisdean. They and their children all assumed the surname 'Macdonald of the Isles'. This has been criticised, since younger children do not usually use the family designation. But if some method had been found of indicating that this was not meant to be the chiefly designation, but a collective surname, such as by hyphenating Macdonald-of-the-Isles (as with the special surname granted as a battle honour to the family of General Ross-of-Bladensberg), the idea was in this particular case not so very absurd: for the surname of the whole family until the seventeenth century was 'of the Isles' or just 'Isles', and *not* 'Macdonald'—rather like the surname 'of Mar', borne by cadets of the Earl of Mar.

The late Chief of Clan Uisdean, Sir Somerled Macdonald of Sleat, represented the Baronets of Nova Scotia—as the Premier Baronet—when the Honours of Scotland were carried before the Queen to St. Giles's Cathedral in 1953. He wore tartan trews, for he had lost a leg while leading the Company he commanded through one of Rommel's minefields in the Western Desert, and years after the war (in which he had won the Military Cross), Sir Somerled died of his wounds. Meanwhile, in 1947, after very careful investigation of this complicated problem, the Lord Lyon King of Arms officially recognised the present Lord Macdonald (who succeeded to 90,000 acres in Skye) as High Chief of all Clan Donald: under whom are the Chiefs of Sleat, Clanranald, Glengarry and Antrim.

FORTITER

MacAlister

MacAlister means Son of Alasdair, the Gaelic for Alexander. The principal family of the name, the MacAlisters of the Loup in Kintyre, descended from Alasdair *Mor*, younger son of Donald of Islay, Lord of the Isles, from whom the mighty Clan Donald derive their name. Donald himself was son of Ranald, King of the Isles, Lord of Argyll and Kintyre, who died in 1207 and belonged to the Celto-Norse royal house of the Hebrides.

According to the Irish *Annals of the Four Masters*, Alasdair *Mor* himself was slain in battle in 1299 against his kinsman Alasdair MacDougall, Lord of Lorn. The style of the MacAlister chiefs of Loup was *Mac Eoin Duibh*, 'Son of Black John', after a fifteenth-century chief. The chiefs of the MacAlisters of Loup moved to the lowlands at the beginning of the nineteenth century, after inheriting an estate in Ayrshire through an heiress. The principal cadets were the MacAlisters who were hereditary Constables of Tarbert Castle, the key to Kintyre, and the present MacAlisters of Glenbarr who still live in Argyll.

The Alexanders, who settled in Clackmannanshire in the sixteenth century, held their lands of Menstrie there under the Earls of Argyll and claimed descent from the Clan Alister. These Alexanders of Menstrie became viscounts in 1630 and Earls of Stirling from 1633 to 1739—also Viscounts of Canada, the first earl having been earlier granted the Lordship of Nova Scotia and been instrumental in the foundation of the Order of Baronets of Nova Scotia. In 1631 the Viscount of Stirling was actually acknowledged as chief of Clan Alister by Archibald MacAlister of Tarbert. The Scottish family of Alexander who settled in Ulster in the seventeenth century and became Earls of Caledon reasonably claim descent from the Menstrie line. If these various affiliations were to prove correct, the present Field-Marshal Earl Alexander of Tunis would be shown to descend in the direct male line from the old Royal House of the Isles: whose martial ancestor King Somerled shook the whole might of Scotland eight hundred years ago.

Menstrie Castle, held under the Earls of Argyll by the Alexanders, afterwards Earls of Stirling, who claimed descent from the Clan Alasdair in Kintyre, and were acknowledged as Chiefs by MacAlister of Tarbert himself in 1631. From the Menstrie family, the Alexander earls of Caledon in turn claim descent.

Tarbert, a royal castle of which Argyll is the Hereditary Keeper, and of which an important branch of the Macalisters were the Hereditary Constables on his behalf. A *tarbert* (or drawboat) is a place where the old Vikings found they could drag a boat across on rollers. This particular Tarbert between the Loup and Loch Fyne is of historic importance, because in 1093 King Magnus Bare-Legs of Norway agreed with King Malcolm *Ceann-mor* of Scotland that the Hebrides formed part of Norway and the mainland belonged to Scotland—and the test of what was Norwegian was to be whether a ship with its rudder in position could sail round it. As the peninsula of Kintyre was 'a large land and better than the best island in the Hebrides', King Magnus secured it by having his own dragon-ship dragged across the mile of dry land from East Loch Tarbert to West Loch Tarbert, with himself at the tiller. As a result, Kintyre later formed part of the Macdonald Lordship of the Isles, and it was not until the seventeenth century that the mainland power of the Campbells was able to conquer it.

Morrison

Morrison means 'Son of Maurice', and in the Hebrides was used as the English form for *Mac Ghille Mhuire*, 'Son of the Devotee of St. Mary'. An Irish family called O'Muircheasain (from The O'Neill's country) also settled as bards in the island of Harris by the time of Sir Ruari *Mor* MacLeod of Dunvegan, who had campaigned in Ireland for The O'Neill against Queen Elizabeth I; and they too later Englished their surname as Morrison.

The chiefs of the Morrison clan in the Hebrides were the hereditary Brieves of the island of Lewis, where they had their stronghold at Dun Eystein and their big house or *Tigh Mór* near Habost in Ness, the extreme north of the whole 'Long Island'. We are told that at one time their jurisdiction was wide, extending 'over the Hebrides from Islay to the Butt of Lewis, and on the opposite coast to the Ord of Caithness'. A brieve or brehon (Gaelic *Britheamh*) was the local judge in the sense of hereditary arbiter, awarding compensation for injury and settling disputes brought to him voluntarily by the parties, handing down legal custom from generation to generation, also expounding, interpreting and teaching the customary laws. These laws among the Gaels, known as the Brehon Laws, may be studied in Dr. John Cameron's *Celtic Law* (Edinburgh 1937),

Five Penny Ness in the Morrison country, showing the coastline immediately south of the Brieves' stronghold of Dun Eystein.

though the influence of Norse custom on the Hebrides has to be taken into consideration, and so the Manx laws should also be examined. The Brieve's 'Courts were usually held on the side of a hill where they were seated on green banks of earth'.

According to the traditional genealogists, the Morrison chiefs descended from Ceadhain mac Mhuirich, a cadet of the Clan Donald dynasts called MacIain of Ardnamurchan (and thus in the direct male line from Somerled, King of the Isles, slain 1164). He is said to have married the heiress of the original Morrison chiefs in about 1346, when 'the haughty heiress persuaded him to change his surname to Morrison and he became one of the best brieves of Lewis'. They derive the original line of Morrison brieves from Gillemoire, natural brother of Leod of Dunvegan (thirteenth-century forefather of the MacLeods), a cadet of the Norse royal house of the Isle of Man and the Outer Hebrides, which still reigned in Lewis at that time.

The Morrison brieves of Lewis lived in accord with their kinsfolk the MacLeod lords of Lewis; until the then brieve cuckolded Ruari MacLeod of Lewis, and confessed openly on his death-bed in 1566 that it was himself who had fathered Lady Lewis's eldest son. The Mackenzie Tutor of Kintail married a daughter and 'heiress' of the spurious 'son', and ultimately claimed the island of Lewis. In the long war that followed between the Lewis MacLeods on the one side, and the Mackenzies and

Morrisons on the other, the MacLeods were overthrown and the Mackenzies secured the island. However, in the course of the struggle, Iain *Dubh* Morrison, the then Brieve, was slain in 1601 by the MacLeods; who later captured and executed his eldest son and successor, Malcolm *Mor* Morrison.

It is doubtful whether the Brieves exercised any judicial authority after 1595 or so; and the last mention of a Brieve of Lewis is in 1616, when Letters of Fire & Sword were granted to the Tutor of Kintail against 'Donald MacIndowie Brieff', the then Morrison chief, who had been causing trouble. For the Mackenzies, after their victory, would stand no nonsense from their erstwhile allies. Thereafter the Brieves of Lewis are heard of no more.

But in the present century, the Morrisons have come into their own again. Two Hebridean Morrisons have been made Peers of the Realm. William Morrison, 1st Viscount Dunrossil, of a branch of the Morrison clan settled in North Uist, was Speaker of the House of Commons and then died in 1961 as Governor-General of Australia. And John Morrison, 1st Lord Margadale, who was Chairman of the powerful '1922 Committee' of Conservative back-benchers (and whose mother was a descendant of the famous Elizabethan hero, Sir Richard Grenville of *The Revenge*), owns the island of Islay, which was once the home of the Norse sea-kings and also of the Clan Donald chiefs, from a combination of both of which families the Morrison chiefs claimed descent.

The Butt of Lewis, extreme northernmost point of the whole 'Long Island'. This was the bleak limit of the *Mac Ghille Mhuire* clan country. John Morrison of Ruchdi, in the Vallaquie district of the island of North Uist, appears (from the traditional Gaelic pedigree which children used to be compelled to memorise) to be the present representative of the O'Muircheasain chieftains whose *dun* was on the little isle of Pabbay off Harris. He is an ophthalmic surgeon, and has been officially recognised as chief of the Clan.

MacLeod

MacLeod means ' Son of Leod ', derived from an Old Norse name Liotr apparently meaning ' ugly ' but perhaps akin to the Anglo-Saxon word ' leod' meaning ' prince '. There was a Jarl Liotr in Orkney in the tenth century, and another Leod was hereditary Abbot of Brechin in about 1132. But MacLeod tradition tells us that the clan's name-father Leod was younger son of Olaf the Black, King of Man and the North Isles, who held sway in the island of Lewis from 1187 to 1237 and whose son Magnus, last Norse king of the Isle of Man (died 1265) also held Glenelg on the mainland. Certainly both Lewis and Glenelg passed to the MacLeods. However, it is possible that Leod sprang from King Olaf's brother Ivar.

These Norse kings were of the house of Godred Crovan, King of Man, Dublin and the whole Hebrides—the great ' King Orry ' of Manx tradition, he had fought under King Harald Haardrade of Norway against the Anglo-Saxons at Stamford Bridge in 1066; died in Islay in about 1095, and is still remembered in the modern Gaelic song ' Godred Crovan's Galley '.

There seems little doubt that this Norse dynasty of Man and the Hebrides sprang from the mighty Ynglingar royal stock, whose ferocious royal ancestors are traced back in the sagas through King Halfdan the Stingy to King Olaf Tree-Hewer (sacrificed to Woden by his own people in Norway during a time of famine), son of King Ingiald Ill-Ruler who lived in the seventh century and was last of the Frey-born pagan ' Peace-Kings of Uppsala ' in ancient Sweden. These celebrated sacral Peace-Kings were associated with human sacrifice of royal victims from within their own dynastic family, which claimed descent from incarnations of the spirit Frey (the god after whom Friday is named), the male manifestation of the very ancient goddess Nerthus or ' Mother Earth ', whose sacred emblem was

The MacLeod bull's head crest, under a window of St. Clement's Church at Rodil in Harris, rebuilt by Alasdair *Crottach*, 8th Chief of MacLeod, early in the sixteenth century. The horizontal string course of black schist, which is diverted around the bull's head, is traditionally a mourning band for the MacLeod chief who died while the building was in progress. A black bull is a very ancient symbol of royalty as far afield as Mecklenburg and Zululand, and a black bull's head often symbolised the death of an enemy chief. The Ancient Egyptians used to sacrifice a black bull and load its head with curses, transferring to it the guilt for the sins of their community. The Zulus used to kill a bull with their bare hands before going to war with the enemy king whom it symbolised. As late as 1916, the Metropolitan of Athens excommunicated a bull's head, representing Venizelos who had plotted against King Constantine of Greece, and the bull's head was then ceremonially stoned. A black bull's head was set before the young Douglas chief at the royal table in Edinburgh Castle before his summary execution in 1440. A decade or so earlier, the Mackintosh guests massacred the feasting Cummins at the entry of a black bull's head, which was to have been the signal for their own chief's doom. So the MacLeod crest is a very ancient royal emblem, as befits scions of the old pagan Norse sea-kings, and may represent victory over a rival royal line.

Alexander MacLeod of Dunvegan's tomb in St. Clement's Church at Rodil (made for himself in 1528): i.e., Alasdair *Crottach's* tomb.

Dunvegan Castle, perhaps the most famous of all the highland chiefs' strongholds, has been occupied continuously by the same family for the last seven centuries. Twenty generations of MacLeod chiefs have lived in the castle. Its ancient walls and towers rise sheer from the summit of a rocky crag above a sea-loch in the Isle of Skye. The rock falls some thirty feet to the sea-beach on three sides of the Castle, which occupies the whole of the summit, a full quarter of an acre, and is protected on the landward side by a fosse sixty feet wide but no longer as deep as in the Middle Ages. This fosse is now crossed by a bridge to the modern entrance, but until the eighteenth century the only way into the Castle was by the Sea Gate, where a steep and curving flight of rough stone steps leads steeply upwards in the slope of the rock. This famous castle is said to have become the chief stronghold of the MacLeods through the marriage of their name-father Leod, who already held Harris (the southern peninsula attached to the island of Lewis) and part of Skye, to the heiress of the Norse seneschal or *arminn*, MacArailt or Harald's Son, who held Dunvegan and the rest of Skye early in the thirteenth century. Leod himself built the Sea Gate and the curtain wall at Dunvegan.

The castle is seen from Loch Dunvegan. During the American War of Independence, the celebrated Scots-American raider Paul Jones (one of the founders of the U.S. Navy) sailed into the loch in 1779, but hastened back to sea because he mistook a funeral procession —that of the forefather of the present dynamic life peer, Dr. George MacLeod, recent Moderator of the General Assembly of the Church of Scotland and founder of the Iona Community—for an armed body of clansmen marching to defend the Castle. A few years later General Norman MacLeod, 23rd Chief, made a fortune in India and thought it wise to crown the seaward curtain wall of Dunvegan Castle with its present battlements which are designed for cannon. (*See also p. 16.*)

the Galley. At the dawn of heraldry, the Black Galley was the emblem of the old Manx kings, and it was quartered by the MacLeods of Dunvegan until the seventeenth century, when they adopted instead a quartering of the Three Legs of Man.

We are told that Leod, who already held Harris (the southern peninsula attached to the island of Lewis) and part of Skye, acquired Dunvegan Castle by his marriage to the heiress of the Norse seneschal or ' arminn ', MacArailt or Harald's Son, who held Dunvegan and the rest of Skye early in the thirteenth century. Since then, Dunvegan has been occupied continuously by the same family for more than seven centuries. Twenty generations of MacLeod chiefs have lived in the castle, and it is still the home of the present 28th Chief, Dame Flora MacLeod of MacLeod.

Leod's two sons founded the two great branches of Clan Leod: known as the Siol Tormod and the Siol Torquil. Torquil's descendants held the island of Lewis until they were overthrown by the expanding Mackenzies (claiming through a bogus heiress) at the beginning of the seventeenth century: but younger branches of the Siol Torquil held Assynt and Cadboll on the mainland rather longer, and the island of Raasay until 1846. The Siol Tormod held the peninsula of Harris, also Glenelg on the mainland, and still hold Dunvegan Castle in Skye. The head of the Siol Tormod appears as MacLeod of that Ilk by the sixteenth century: i.e. as MacLeod of MacLeod, chief of the whole Name.

Dr. I. F. Grant, whose able history of the clan should be read by all MacLeods, has summed up their character at Dunvegan: ' Throughout the history of the MacLeods there runs a thread of tenacity that worthily fulfils their motto, " Hold Fast ". In nothing is this staunchness better shown than in the maintenance of the bonds uniting the chief and his clansmen. In no other clans have such ties been so consistently maintained. Samuel Johnson and Boswell described how they had survived the break-up of Highland society following the '45. The archives in the Muniment-room show how faithfully the chiefs continued to fulfil their obligations. Doctors

Looking from Macdonald country in Skye across to the island of Raasay. MacLeod of Raasay, a chieftain of the Siol Torquil (the MacLeods of the Lewes), bore the Gaelic title of *Mac Ghille Chaluim*. The first separate MacLeod of Raasay was *Gillechaluim Garbh* or 'Rough Malcolm' MacLeod, younger brother of Ruari MacLeod, 10th of the Lewes, the last undisputed Chief of the Siol Tormod before the troubles came upon them at the end of the sixteenth century. Raasay managed to survive their destruction; but in 1846 the 11th chieftain was obliged to sell the island, and the present MacLeod of Raasay lives in Australia.

Sligachan Bridge, with the Cuillins in the Background. 'Warty' Alexander or Alasdair *Carrach* MacDonell, lord of Lochaber (the early fifteenth century ancestor of the chieftains of Keppoch) is said to have been slain with many of his men in a desperate battle by Loch Sligachan, after his retreat had been cut off when his galleys were seized by a MacAskill leader (the MacAskills were a race of warriors who adhered to MacLeod of Dunvegan).

'MacLeod's Tables'. The tale goes that a MacLeod chief (perhaps Alasdair 'Crouchback', 8th Chief of MacLeod from 1481 until about 1547) 'visited the Scots Court and a Lowland noble sneeringly suggested that he must be impressed by the magnificence of what he saw. The Highland chief replied that he had a finer hall, table and candlesticks at home. The king was present and a wager was made. Next year the king and his Court visited the Hebrides (perhaps the celebrated Royal Visit of 1540, when King James V kidnapped and imprisoned as hostages most of the chiefs who came to 'welcome' him) and MacLeod conducted them to the top of the higher of the two flat-topped hills opposite Dunvegan, known as MacLeod's Tables. In that magnificent setting a banquet was **served** by the light of blazing torches held by **stalwart** clansmen and it was agreed that **MacLeod** had won his wager.'

The Fairy Flag of the MacLeods, still at Dunvegan. This ensign is of oriental Mediterranean silken fabric, more than a thousand years old, and very carefully stitched in the darns: possibly a saint's shirt kept to bear in peace or war as a lucky relic. The MacLeods suppose it to have been given them by the Fairies. But it seems more likely that it is in fact the famous sacred 'Land-Ravager' flag that King Harald *Haardrade* ('Hard-Counsel') of Norway brought back from his days as Captain of the Varangian Guard at Constantinople, and which he is known to have left behind with the ships in which the MacLeods' ancestor Godred *Crovan* (afterwards King of Man and the Isles) escaped after their defeat at Stamford Bridge by King Harold of England in 1066.

The Fairy Flag was doubtless often carried into battle *furled*, by its hereditary keepers; whose bodies after death were placed on a special grating to disintegrate beneath the lid of their stone family coffin at Rodil in Harris, the ashes of each immediate predecessor being shaken through the grating to join their ancestors' ashes below. But the MacLeods believe that the flag was only to be *unfurled* in time of gravest peril, and then on only three occasions—and that this has already been done twice, on both occasions when Alasdair Crouchback, 8th Chief of MacLeod (1481–1547) was battling against Clanranald. However, there is a tale that it was once unfurled to check a cattle plague. In 1799 the iron chest containing the flag was improperly forced open out of curiosity by the factor, during the absence of General MacLeod of MacLeod (the 23rd Chief), whereupon a prophecy of the Brahan Seer was fulfilled and the chief's heir perished when his warship was blown up at sea. In 1938, when a wing of Dunvegan Castle was on fire, the flames checked and ceased their destruction at the very moment that the Fairy Flag was carried past on its way to safety.

The head of Loch Harport in Skye, once the country of the MacLeods of Talisker. The present MacLeod of Talisker, the nearest chieftain of the original male line of Siol Tormod, lives in Australia; and generously pledged his loyalty to Dame Flora MacLeod of MacLeod at her accession. His ancestor, Sir Ruari MacLeod, 1st of Talisker (a younger son of Sir Ruari *Mor* MacLeod, 16th Chief of the clan) was Tutor of MacLeod and raised the clan to fight for King Charles II against Oliver Cromwell. At the fatal battle of Worcester in 1651, seven hundred MacLeod clansmen fell on the field or were slain trying to escape through hostile England. The appalling losses suffered by the clansmen made all future Chiefs of MacLeod reluctant to risk their people in the later Risings.

were maintained (in the fine tradition of the old Lordship of the Isles), education was fostered and heavy expenditure incurred in road-making. MacLeod's private post to Edinburgh was for long a boon to the community. Grain was imported in times of scarcity. Agricultural improvements kept pace with the most enlightened in the country; and the MacLeod estates were never sullied by the blot of " clearing " the people from their holdings. On the side of the clansmen the love and veneration of their chiefs and of Dunvegan has continued. . . . The bonds of affection that unite the present chief, Flora MacLeod of MacLeod, and her clansmen in all the airts of the world is indeed a living tie that neither mountains nor a waste of seas can divide.'

And Dame Flora herself has written in the Clan MacLeod Magazine that her ' dear clan family ' (there are 20,000 MacLeods in the United States alone) is ' beyond and outside and above divisions between nations, countries and continents . . . it takes no note of age or sex, rank or wealth, success or failure. The spiritual link of clanship embraces them all '.

Mackinnon

It seems hard to doubt that the Mackinnons belonged to the kindred of St. Columba. Mackinnon means 'Son of Fingon', and the earliest references to the Clan Fingon relate them to the island abbacy of Iona, while their original homeland was in the north of the neighbouring island of Mull. The plant-badge peculiar to the Mackinnons (apart from *pine*, which they share with other clans sentimentally linked to 'Clan Alpin') is *St. Columba's flower*.

Iona Abbey was founded by Saint Columba in 563, and thereafter the abbots were chosen from his kindred: the Cenel Conaill or descendants of the saint's great-grandfather, King Conall Gulban, founder of the Irish realm of Tirconaill. By mediaeval times, the kings of Tirconaill bore the surname of O'Donell, and their coat-of-arms displayed the saint's arm holding a Cross in the hand. The abbacy of Iona fell into decline after the Viking raids, and from the ninth century the chief abbots of St. Columba's kindred were those of Kells and later of Derry in Ireland and those of Dunkeld in Alba.

In 1164, when the royal house of the Isles, semi-independent satellites of Norway, were threatened with absorption into the expanding Scottish realm of Alba, King Somerled invited the Irish chief *coarb* of St. Columba to accept the abbacy of Iona; but in vain, for naturally the saint's kindred in Ireland would not allow the Columban primacy to pass back to the Hebrides. So, by the thirteenth century, Ranald, King of the Isles, had followed the Scottish kings' example and introduced the Benedictine Order to Iona. This led to long-standing dissension between the monks who preferred the way of the old Celtic Church, with married abbots of the Founder's Kin administering the abbey estates, and those who adhered to the new Benedictine rule encouraged by the Roman Church. In 1204, for instance, the northern Irish Columban clergy led by two bishops and two abbots raided Iona, demolished a monastery erected on Columban land by the new Benedictine abbot, and proclaimed the then Abbot of Derry (a descendant of St. Columba's brother) to be also Abbot of Iona. The clan's name-father Fingon appears from the Gaelic MS. genealogies to have lived in the thirteenth century, at this critical time for the Columban family. He must have been of high birth and evidently of the Founder's Kin. For from the fourteenth century almost until the Reformation, tacit local resistance to the new order at Iona seems to have rallied behind the Clan Fingon. And The Mackinnon quarters the hand holding a Cross.

In 1358/9 the then chief, Niall son of Gillebride Mackinnon, had a brother Fingon who was chosen to be the mitred Abbot of Iona, in spite of immediate opposition from the papacy (at Avignon), which only confirmed his election nearly forty years later, in 1397. Abbot Fingon, known as the 'Green Abbot', followed the ancient Celtic custom of regarding clergy as free to marry, and had several children by the lady of his choice. His grandson Fingon Mackinnon ('of noble birth' though also the son of a priest and an officially unmarried lady) used influence at Rome in 1426 to be released from his oath not to get himself admitted a monk at Iona, where he soon followed in his grandfather's footsteps. 'He took as his concubine a lady . . . with her mother's full consent, and . . . he also proceeded to lay violent hands on the goods of the said monastery'. At Iona, too, is the magnificent Celtic cross erected by Lachlan Mackinnon, father of the last abbot: Iain Mackinnon, who died in 1500 and whose elaborate tomb effigy can still be seen in Iona Cathedral. After Abbot Iain's death, the Roman church solved the succession problem by giving the abbacy of Iona in perpetual *commendam* to the successive Bishops of the Isles.

The historians of the Isles call the Green Abbot 'a subtle and wicked

Shattered shaft of Mackinnon's Cross on Iona, erected in 1489 by Lachlan Mackinnon, father of the last Abbot of Iona.

Tomb effigy at Iona, of Iain Mackinnon, last Abbot of Iona, who died in 1500. 'Before the Cathedral was renovated the teeth and bones of this Abbot were to be seen where his tomb is, having been brought to the surface by the action of worms.'

AUDENTES FORTUNA JUVAT

councillor' who plotted against the Lord of the Isles, as a result of which his brother, the then Mackinnon chief, was executed—perhaps by the Maclean chief on Macdonald's behalf. It certainly appears to have been in the fourteenth century that the Mackinnons lost to the Macleans much of their territory in Mull where, however, they retained Mishnish with their castle at Dunara. It was perhaps at this time that the Lord of the Isles agreed in an indenture with the Lord of Lorn that the keeping of the key castle of Cairnburgh off Mull was not to be given to any of the Clan Fingon. About this period, on the other hand, the Mackinnons acquired in the Isle of Skye the great district of Strathairdale—twenty-six miles long by six miles wide, including Broadford, together also with the island of Scalpay—probably through inter-marriage with the MacLeods of Dunvegan, whose original arms they quarter (the triple-towered castle and the Manx galley). But a late sixteenth-century report on the Isles tells us that Strathairdale was given to Mackinnon by the Lord of the Isles ' for to be judge and decide all questions and debates that happens to fall between parties through playing at cards or dice or sic other practice ', which was perhaps related to Mackinnon's particular office, as one of the barons in the Council of the Isles under Macdonald rule, of being in hereditary charge of all weights and measures in the Hebrides.

After that, the centre of Mackinnon power was in Skye, with their chief's castles of Dunakin (at Kyleakin) and Dunringill, and later their house at Kilmorie—until the sale of the last of their lands for debt in 1791.

Castle Maoil or Dunakin, 'Haakon's Dun' by Kyle Akin, the Mackinnon chiefs' stronghold commanding the *caol* (kyle) or straight between Skye and the mainland.

Maclean

VIRTUE MINE HONOUR

Mac'lean means 'Son of Gillean', and the clan take their name from their ancestor Gillean of the Battle-Axe, a thirteenth-century warrior whose lineage is traced through a Celtic abbot of Lismore and the royal house of Lorn from the ancient Gaelic kings of Dalriada. The old genealogies attach them to the line of King Lorn's great-grandson Baodan, whose descendants the Cenel Baodan were appanaged in the district now known as Morvern, but which was still called 'Kinnel Bathyn' when Argyll was formed into a sheriffdom in 1292. Morvern was long Maclean country.

By the middle of the next century their chiefs were already related to the ruling dynasty of the Isles, for in 1367 Lachlan *Lubanach* Maclean had to obtain a papal dispensation legalising his marriage to Mary, daughter of the great Macdonald, Lord of the Isles, as they were otherwise too closely related according to canon law. We are told it was a love match 'by her inclination of yielding', and that he had gained her father's approval after kidnapping him in a bold exploit, in which he slew the Mackinnon chief. Certainly he was taken into high favour with the Lord of the Isles, from whom he received wide lands in Mull, where the Mackinnons had formerly been in possession, and in other islands. This descent from the ruling dynasty of the Isles was the foundation of Maclean power in the Hebrides, and so the Black Galley of the old Norse sea-kings can be seen among the quarterings on the Maclean chief's banner that still flies over Duart Castle, which dominates the Sound of Mull. The castle itself appears on record by 1390, and the Keep was probably built by Lachlan *Lubanach* Maclean of Duart, but the great curtain walls seem much older.

The ruins of Breacachadh Castle, mediaeval stronghold of the Macleans of Coll, on the island machair in a sea-bay. The oldest part probably dates from the time of their founder, 'Rough' Iain *Garbh*, son of Lachlan 'the Big-Bellied' Maclean of Duart in the fifteenth century. Beyond it is their charming Georgian house with its two curving wings, all rather spoilt by the later addition of sham battlements but also now fast falling into ruin. Here Maclean of Coll's eldest son Donald entertained Dr. Johnson and Mr. Boswell in 1773, when he was chieftain of about a thousand islanders on Coll alone, and also held Rum and part of Mull as well. Dr. Johnson wrote of young Coll (who was drowned in the following year), 'He is as complete an islander as the mind can figure. He is a farmer, a sailor, a hunter, a fisherman'; and of his islanders, 'The inhabitants have not yet learned to be weary of their heath and rocks but attend their agriculture and their dairies without listening to American seducements ... At Coll there is no wish to go away'. But the island prosperity collapsed with the rest of the Hebridean economy, and in 1848 Alexander Maclean of Coll, the last *Mac Iain Abraich* to rule the island, was obliged to sell his four hundred-year-old patrimony and emigrate to Natal in South Africa. The new proprietors, faced with the general population explosion (the numbers had risen from about 1,000 in 1773 to 1,400 in 1840, an increase of 40 per cent.), 'cleared' in 1852, bringing the population back to normal, and introduced dairy farmers from Ayrshire, as 'cheese-making throve because of the limey soil. Coll cheese became famous enough to find its way on to the menu of the House of Commons'. All the same, the population fell by 1958 to about 170, mainly of incomer farming stock. However, the present Stewart of Coll descends in the female line through the Stewarts of Appin from the old Kings of the Isles. In modern times, a Maclean of the Coll chieftainly stock won the Victoria Cross. But far away on the island of Coll, the walled burial ground of their forefathers tumbles sadly neglected: for the Macleans themselves are gone despite their wish.

The eastern entrance to the Sound of Mull, that flows between the mainland and the Isle of Mull, is commanded by the great black massive strength of Duart Castle. This was once the stronghold, and is still the home, of Maclean of Duart, Chief of Clan Gillean. Looking across from Duart to the mainland opposite, there can be seen on one hand the ruins of Dunollie Castle, held by the Mac-Dougall chiefs, and on the other Ardtornish Castle, where the High Chief of Clan Donald held sway as Lord of the Isles. On the landward side, Duart Castle is protected by great windowless curtain walls, thirty feet high and nearly ten feet thick, enclosing the residential buildings around two sides of a courtyard bounded on the seaward side by the Great Tower of the Keep. Beyond the curtain walls, the castle was further protected by a deep fosse cut in the rock. The castle itself appears on record by 1390, and the Keep was probably built by Lachlan *Lubanach* 'the Wily' Maclean of Duart, but the great curtain walls seem much older.

In the sixteenth century, Hector *Mor* Maclean of Duart appears to have made the extensive additions to the Great Tower. In 1540 he was kidnapped by King James V in person, when he went aboard the royal flagship, anchored off Duart in the Sound of Mull during a royal cruise through the Hebrides. In 1604 Duart Castle had to be temporarily surrendered to the King's Commissioner; and five years later Hector *Og* Maclean of Duart himself with most of his fellow Hebridean chiefs (except Macneil of Barra and MacLeod of Dunvegan who prudently stayed away) were kidnapped at a dinner given by the king's Lord Lieutenant on board ship off Aros in the Sound of Mull. Duart was only released on harsh terms, among the mildest of which were the destruction of almost all his galleys, the banning of all firearms and two-handed swords, and the compulsory education of his children under Privy Council direction. By the Statutes of Icolmkil, however, which followed on the chief's release, Maclean of Duart was allowed to import four tuns of wine a year (the Statutes banned wine to the clansmen) and to retain eight gentlemen in attendance in his household at Duart Castle, a larger number than any other island chief. In 1631 the chief's heir was created a Baronet of Nova Scotia. After his succession, he enlarged Duart Castle, where his initials SLM 'for 'Sir Lachlan Maclean', and the date 1633 can still be seen over the great doorway. It was probably he and his immediate predecessors who built the residential quarters in the north wing of the castle courtyard at Duart.

In the reign of Charles II, Argyll got a judicial decree for debt, putting him in possession of all the Maclean chief's territory. The chief was a little child, and his Tutors were only partly successful in an attempted alliance with Lord MacDonell and Cameron

For a long time the Macleans of Duart had to face the rivalry of another branch of the clan, the Maclaines of Lochbuie, and many strange legends are told of the struggle between the two houses: how Hector *Mor* Maclean of Duart (grandson of the chief who fell in 1513 with the 'Flowers of the Forest' on Flodden Field) supported Iain the Toothless Maclaine of Lochbuie in suppressing a rising led by Lochbuie's only son, Ewen of the Little Head, who was slain and whose ghost 'the Headless Horseman'

of Lochiel against Argyll. Maclean of Brolas, as Tutor of Duart, therefore sent out the Fiery Cross and 'did convocate together armed men with swords, hagbuts, pistolls, durks and other weapons invasive, and munitione bellicall'. When the Sheriff-Depute of Argyll arrived to take over on behalf of the Campbells, he was repulsed by shots from within Duart Castle, while outside it the Macleans had mustered 'seven score armed men, armed with fyre-locks, swords and targets, in a posture ready to feight, with their plaids throwne from them, standing and drawne up hard by the house of Dowart'. So in 1674 Argyll obtained official Letters of Fire and Sword against them, and the Campbells prepared to invade their country. A brief respite after Argyll's downfall in 1681, when, however, the Government claimed Duart as part of the forfeited Campbell estates, was followed by Argyll's restoration at the Whig Revolution of 1688. Duart Castle was bombarded ineffectively

from the sea by English warships, while Sir John Maclean of Duart was away leading his clan to fight for the Jacobite cause under 'Bonnie Dundee' at Killiecrankie. But the overthrow of the Jacobites enabled the Campbells to invade Mull with 2,500 men, and at last to secure Duart Castle.

In the reign of King Edward VII, the ruined stronghold was re-acquired by the Macleans, and restored under the guidance of the architect Burnett. A remarkable feature is the great plate glass window of the Sea Room, with a magnificent view out over the Sound of Mull, introduced without spoiling the bleak strength of the castle's sea-face. Many Macleans from all over the world helped towards the great cost of restoration, and after a Clan Gathering in 1912 their ancient home was once again inhabited by their chief, Sir Fitzroy Maclean of Duart, *Mac Ghill' Eathainn.*

still rides abroad whenever a Maclaine of Lochbuie is about to die; and how Hector *Mor* then interned Iain the Toothless on the island of Cairnburgh, away from ordinary women so that he could have no new heir, but allowed him an ugly and ill-shapen maidservant by whom Iain had a son, Murdoch the Stunted, who escaped to Ireland and after many adventures returned to become ancestor of the later Maclaines of Lochbuie.

As long as Macdonald ruled the Lordship of the Isles, the Macleans were among his most loyal supporters. 'Red Hector of the Battles' Maclean of Duart was killed commanding under the Lord of the Isles at Harlaw in 1411. Other Chiefs of Clan Gillean often commanded his armies and war fleets, and acted as Seneschals of the Isles. When Macdonald's son, Angus *Og*, supported by most of the Clan Donald chieftains, rose in rebellion against his father, the Lord of the Isles was backed by all the Maclean chieftains: Duart himself, Lochbuie and Ardgour (ancestor

Tombstone of 'the Rider' at Iona. It is among the other Maclean chieftains' tombs, and is reputed to be that of Ewen 'of the Little Head' MacLaine, yr. of Lochbuie, who was killed in battle against his own father—Iain the Toothless—and Maclean of Duart. As 'the Headless Horseman', his ghost still rides abroad to presage the death of a Mac-Laine of Lochbuie: his most recent appearance was in the twentieth century. His half-brother, Murdoch the Stunted, was legitimated in 1538 and was ancestor of the present chieftain.

of Sir Fitzroy Maclean, the 'Balkan brigadier' of our own time), whose galleys were defeated by the Macdonald rebels in the cruel sea-battle of Bloody Bay in the north of Mull in 1481. Angus *Og* would have hanged the Maclean chief, who was taken prisoner, but Clanranald had him spared, ' saying he would have none to bicker with if Maclean was gone'. However, some fifty Maclean survivors who got ashore were smoked out of their cave and butchered, since when it has had the grisly name of the ' Cave of the Heads '.

At this period, Macdonald was still a semi-sovereign prince and his great island nobles styled themselves and their heirs in the mode used by peers on the mainland: ' Lord Maclean ' and the ' Master of Duart '. In 1501 King James IV took the field in person against Hector *Odhar* Maclean of Duart, who held out for the true Lord of the Isles until special artillery and the Scottish Royal Navy were brought against him. So long as there remained any hope of maintaining the island principality, the Macleans continued to rally to the rightful Lords of the Isles; and they carried on the struggle against Scotland intermittently, often in alliance with Scotland's other ' auld enemy ' England, until the death in 1545 of the last Macdonald claimant.

But after the downfall of the Lordship of the Isles, the Macleans gradually submitted to the Scottish Crown and as early as 1496 their lands of Duart were erected into a feudal barony by King James IV. From this period their chiefs began to be at feud with the different branches into which Clan Donald broke up, as the Macleans struggled with the Macdonalds to fill the vacuum left by the fallen Lords of the Isles.

In the sixteenth century, the coveted prize of Hebridean diplomacy and warfare was the trade-route with Ireland, that ran from Craignish on the mainland of Argyll, across Jura and Islay, to Lough Foyle in Ulster. A long war therefore ensued between the Macleans and the Macdonalds for the control of Jura and Islay. This feud culminated in the disastrous battle of Tràigh Ghruineard in Islay in 1598, when Sir Lachlan *Mor* Maclean of Duart was slain with an elfin-bolt by a little black fairy man whose services he had spurned. It is said that Sir Lachlan Maclean had gone to a conference with the Macdonalds, ' without armour, in a silk dress, and with a rapier at his side. Along with him were his second son and the best of their kin in their holiday garb, and with little other arms than their hunting knives and boar spears, but although set upon by an ambush of nearly seven hundred men they made a desperate defence '. The Herculean Sir Lachlan was promptly avenged by his sons in a terrible massacre of the Islay folk lasting three days, but his death, which had been presaged by a fiery comet as befits the doom of princes, was a great loss to his clan. After his death, the Macdonalds and Macleans were alike weakened by the feud. The initiative in the Hebrides passed to the Campbells, who had played a waiting game, and it was Argyll who finally secured control of the trade-route with Ireland.

Perhaps typical of the links between Scotland and Ireland at this time was the life of Catherine Maclean, who was a civilized Gaelic aristocrat ' not unlernyd in the Latin tong, speakyth good French, and is sayd some lytell Italyone '. She was Duart's sister and Argyll's widow: she then married The O'Donnell, ruler of Tirconail, but was captured by another great Irish dynast, The O'Neill, ruler of Tyrone, who made her his mistress and kept her ' chained by day to a little boy, and only released to amuse her master's drunken leisure '. Duart's sister was thus a Scottish countess dowager and an Irish queen in distress. She had sons by both Calvagh O'Donnell and Shane O'Neill, and in the next generation Duart's sons led a strong force of Macleans to raid Ireland on behalf of their O'Neill cousins. These cousins were overthrown by another member of their dynasty, the famous Red Hugh O'Neill, Earl of Tyrone and last native King of Ulster, who sought to drive the English out of all Ireland. To avenge their cousins profitably, the Macleans offered to raise two thousand men and sail in their own galleys against Red Hugh, if Queen Elizabeth of England would pay their expenses. Meanwhile, Duart asked for English gold in payment

Family targe of the Macleans of Ardgour.

Family frame containing a photograph of Catriona Maclean, present Maid of Ardgour, with her parents (above) and two of her sisters (right).

Sir Charles Maclean of Duart, 11th Baronet of Morvern and 27th Chief of the Clan Maclean, who is Lord Lieutenant of Argyll and Chief Scout of the Commonwealth.

Waterfall at Allt Coire Lair, above Loch Cluanie. In this district, the territories of the MacDonells of Glengarry, Mackenzies of Kintail, Frasers of Lovat, The Chisholm, and the Grants of Glenmoriston, all intermingled.

Ardgour House. Behind the Georgian house is 'Maclean's Towel', the waterfall at Ardgour. There is a prophecy that the Macleans will hold Ardgour until Maclean's Towel runs dry. Nearby is the copse, said to mark the spot where the MacMasters of Ardgour were slaughtered by Donald Maclean, 1st Chieftain of Ardgour, son of Lachlan 'the Big-Bellied' Maclean of Duart (whose father, 'Red Hector of the Battles', was the Maclean chief slain at the battle of Harlaw in 1411), when he conquered their territory five centuries ago. The last MacMaster fled to the Corran ferry, but the ferryman refused to help him, seeking to curry favour with the conquering Macleans. Donald Maclean slew them both, remarking that if the ferryman was willing to betray his late masters in need, he would be of no use in his own service. Among Donald's descendants today is Sir Fitzroy Maclean, 1st Baronet, M.P., 'the Balkan Brigadier', who was parachuted into Yugoslavia to help Tito against the Nazis, and who is married to Lord Lovat's sister.

The Jacobite monument in Glenfinnan. Here in 1745 the Jacobite Duke of Atholl & Rannoch raised Prince Charles Edward's standard, and the Rising began. The Macdonalds of Clanranald were the first clan to rise for the Prince, and were already assembled here in their own country when Lochiel's pipes were heard and the Clan Cameron arrived to join them.

for stopping Macdonalds from joining Red Hugh, and apparently arranged with Clanranald a demonstration in which he intercepted and 'captured' 900 of Clanranald's men on their way to Ireland through Mull: in this way, nobody got hurt and Duart doubtless split the reward with Clanranald.

In 1603, King James VI of Scotland inherited the English throne, and with it access to the records of Tudor transactions with the island chiefs. From this time onwards the Maclean power began to wane, and the Campbells were on the move into the Hebrides. However, in 1631 the chief's heir, Lachlan Maclean of Morvern, was created a Baronet of Nova Scotia. The new baronet occupied Iona, but was soon obliged to restore it to the bishop. He also enlarged Duart Castle.

The Macleans remained loyal to the Stewart kings throughout the civil wars of the seventeenth century, and (although by then Duart had lost his lands) the Maclean clansmen came out under their chiefs or chieftains as staunch Jacobites in the Risings of the eighteenth century. But the Macleans incurred heavy debts in the royalist cause, and Argyll cunningly bought up all the claims against Duart. With great legal skill, and by making use of his power to sue in his own courts (the Campbell chief held great judicial offices in the West), Argyll managed to multiply Duart's indebtedness into a vast sum and eventually to get a judgement putting him in possession of all the Maclean territory. The Macleans tried to hold out by force, and for a while were successful. Duart Castle was bombarded ineffectively from the sea by English warships, while Sir John Maclean of Duart was away leading his clan to fight for the Jacobite cause under 'Bonnie Dundee' at Killiecrankie in 1689. But the overthrow of the Jacobites enabled the Campbells to invade Mull with 2,500 men, and at last to secure Duart Castle, which was garrisoned for a while, but eventually allowed to fall into ruin.

Sir John held out in the island castle of Cairnburgh until 1692, when he went into exile. Although Duart Castle was lost, he raised the clan again for the Jacobite Cause in the 1715 Rising. His son, Sir Hector Maclean of Duart, 5th Baronet, was created Lord Maclean in the titular Jacobite Peerage by 'the King over the Water' in 1716. A keen freemason, while in exile Sir Hector founded the Grand Lodge of France at Paris, with its Ecossais *Degrees*, and was its first Grand Master in 1736 (his successors were the Jacobite 'Earl of Derwentwater', the Duc d'Antin, and Louis de Bourbon, Comte de Clermont). In 1745 he was imprisoned by the Government in Edinburgh Castle, and so the clan was commanded for him in the Rising by Maclean of Drimnin, who was killed at Culloden (*Kaid* Sir Harry Maclean, Commander-in-Chief of the Sultan of Morocco's Army at the end of the nineteenth century, was a Maclean of Drimnin: and the Sultan's military pipe-band still have Maclean tartan bags and streamers on their pipes).

It was not until 1911 that the ruins of Duart were recovered by the Chiefs of Clan Gillean, and restored with great care. At a celebrated Clan gathering on 24 August 1912, their ancient home was once again taken possession of by the then Chief, Sir Fitzroy Maclean of Duart, 10th Baronet, K.C.B.: a Hussar colonel who had ridden with the Light Brigade in the Crimean campaign and who died a centenarian. His grandson, Sir Charles Maclean of Duart and Morvern, 11th Baronet, present Chief of Clan Gillean and Lord Lieutenant of Argyll, who was mentioned in despatches while commanding a squadron of tanks in the Scots Guards during the Second World War, is now Chief Scout of the Commonwealth.

Eilean Shuna in Loch Linnhe, the island home in 1679 of the Macleans of 'the Race of the Iron Sword', from whom springs the present Lt-Colonel Neil McLean, D.S.O., former M.P. for Inverness-shire and wartime guerrilla leader in Ethiopia and Albania: recently engaged in the Yemen. These Macleans descend from a younger son of Lachlan *Bronnach* 'the Big-Bellied' Maclean of Duart, chief of the clan, who died after 1472.

As the Macleans struggled with the Macdonalds to fill the vacuum left by the fallen Lords of the Isles, they entered into an uneasy alliance, often cemented by intermarriage, with the Campbells of Argyll on the mainland. These marriages did not always succeed in their object. For instance Lachlan *Cattanach* Maclean of Duart became bored with his wife, Lady Catherine Campbell, Argyll's sister, so he marooned her on a dangerous rock that is covered at high water and, supposing her drowned, reported her death to the Campbells. Unknown to him, she had been rescued by some passing fishermen and taken to the Earl of Argyll. She was avenged in 1523 by another brother, the Thane of Cawdor, who surprised Maclean of Duart on a visit to Edinburgh, where he dirked him in bed. The Lady Rock is still visible at low water, washed by the sea out in the Sound of Mull between Lismore and Duart. Three generations later, Sir Lachlan *Mor* Maclean of Duart employed Spanish soldiers from the Armada galleon *Florida* that was blown up by an English-paid secret agent (called Smollett) in Tobermory Bay with several Maclean hostages aboard. King Charles I granted the wreck to the Marquis of Argyll, and the Duke of Argyll is still trying with divers to raise her treasure from the sunken wreck.

Macquarie

The surname Macquarie is from the Gaelic: ' Son of Guaire ', and Guaire itself is an old Celtic personal name meaning Proud. The chiefs of the clan were the Macquaries of Ulva, an island off Mull.

According to the old genealogies, their forefather Guaire was brother of Fingon, the ancestor of the Mackinnon chiefs. This seems probable, since the Mackinnons at one time dominated the isles of Mull and Iona, which in turn surround Ulva. In this case, the Macquaries are likely to have been, at least in the female line, of the kindred of Saint Columba. The saint himself was of course a prince of the royal house of Tirconaill in Ireland, descended from Niall of the Nine Hostages, High King of Ireland, who was reigning at Tara when the Roman legions left Britain.

In 1463 Iain Macquarie of Ulva witnessed a charter of Macdonald, lord of the Isles and earl of Ross, apparently as one of the members of the Council of the Isles. But after the downfall of the Lordship of the Isles, the Macquarie chiefs supported the Macleans of Duart who now dominated Mull. In 1651, Macquarie of Ulva was slain with most of his clansmen, supporting the Macleans in King Charles II's cause against the Cromwellians at the fatal battle of Inverkeithing.

Lachlan Macquarie was the last real 'lord of Ulva's Isle', which he was obliged to sell in 1778, dying in Mull at the age of 103. His kinsman, General Lachlan Macquarie, was the most famous Macquarie of all. He was Governor of New South Wales in Australia for twelve years, being sent out to succeed 'Mutiny on the Bounty' Bligh, who had been forcibly deposed by the officer commanding the local troops. General Macquarie did everything in his power to help the transported convicts to become good settlers when emancipated, and his popularity is reflected in the naming of the Macquarie River and many other places in Australia. He died in 1824, and was buried in Mull.

Tombstone of a chieftain at Iona, traditionally that of a Macquarie chief of Ulva, but recently deciphered as that of Brice Mackinnon. He is wearing the quilted saffron highland war-coat; girded with his sword-belt in the old comfortable way, around the loins and not the waist.

His shield has the Hebridean royal *Galley*, indicating a descent from the old Norse Kings of the Isles. The beasts on his shield had been mistaken for wolves, as 'Ulva' is from the Old Norse for 'Wolf's Isle'.

Macfie

We are told by Dr. George F. Black in his invaluable life-work *The Surnames of Scotland*, that Macfie is ' one of the oldest and most interesting Gaelic personal names we possess '. ' Its plan and concept ', says Dr. Gillies, ' go far away beyond those of even our old names ' (*Place-names of Argyllshire*, p. 82). Dr. Black derives Macfie through Mac duffy from *Mac Dhuibhshith*, ' Son of Dubhsith ', a name meaning ' Black (one) of Peace '. But he himself reminds us that there was a family on the island of South Uist in the Hebrides known as *Dubh-sidh* or ' Black Fairy ' (*sidh* can equally mean ' elf ') from a tradition that they had been in touch with the fairy folk. And the Macduffies or Macfies were also a Hebridean clan.

The chiefs of the clan were the Macfies of Colonsay, an island which afterwards passed to the Macdonalds and Campbells and then to the McNeills, and is now held by Lord Strathcona.

It has been suggested that the Macfies were connected with the Dubhsidhe who was Lector of Iona in 1164, and as abbatial appointments tended to be kept in the family, the Macfies may therefore have been related to the sacred clan who became the Mackinnons. Certainly the church on Colonsay was dedicated to St. Columba, to whose kindred the Mackinnons probably belonged. On the other hand, there are those who say the Macfies descend from a seal-woman.

In 1463 Macfie of Colonsay appears as a member of the Council of the Isles that advised the great Macdonald rulers, and in 1531 a later Macfie of Colonsay was cited for treason, being still a firm supporter of the forfeited Lordship of the Isles. Dean Monro, writing in 1549, tells us that ' McDufi-fithe of Collinsay ' also held part of the isle of Jura. He later refers to him as ' ane gentle Capitane callit Mcduffhye '—gentle meaning here well-born and captain being the old style for a chief—and observes that Colonsay is seven miles long by two broad: ' ane fertile Ile, gude for quhyte (white) fishing, with ane paroche Kirk '.

After the downfall of the Lords of the Isles, the Macfie chief adhered to the Macdonalds of Islay. So it may be that the little dark fairy-man who is said to have slain Sir Lachlan *Mor* Maclean of Duart with an elfin-bolt when the Macleans invaded Islay in 1598 was not so much a *dubh-sidh* as a *Mac Dubh-sidh* or Macfie. Murdoch Macfie of Colonsay had been captured (with Macdonald of Sleat and Macleod of Dunvegan) when Maclean of Duart surprised and defeated MacDonnell of Islay in 1587. Strange tales are told about this Macfie chief and his Black Dog, and how he eventually met his death at Maclean hands, killed by an arrow-shot while taking refuge in a cave still called *Slochd Dubh Mhic a' Phi*. In 1609, the then Macfie of Colonsay was one of the Hebridean chiefs who were forced by the Government's Commissioner, the Bishop of the Isles, to agree to the ' Statutes of Iona ' that so curtailed their ancient highland way of life.

The Macfies continued to support the Macdonalds of Islay, and in 1615 Malcolm Macfie of Colonsay rose in support of Sir James MacDonnell of Islay, Chief of ' Clan Donald South ', on whose destruction the Government was determined. The Campbells (to whom Islay had been promised) secured the eventual submission of another chieftain of Clan Donald South, Colla *Cioteach* (left-handed or sinister), the original ' Colkitto ', who captured the Macfie chief and handed him over to Argyll. In 1623, to add injury to insult, Colkitto slew Malcolm Macfie of Colonsay (whom he found hiding under a pile of seaweed) and others of his clan, and took the island for himself. In this way, during the course of the seventeenth century, the island passed out of Macfie hands.

Macfie of Colonsay was also hereditary custodian of the Records of the Isles—but these, also, like the Macfie chiefs themselves, have long since vanished. On Colonsay, a family of crofters represents the family today.

The beautifully carved stone Celtic tomb-slab of Murchard Macfie of Colonsay, chief of the clan, who died in 1539 and was buried on the neighbouring island of Oransay, which also belonged to the Macfies. The fine craftsman who made it signs his name, and most skilfully incorporates the Macfie coat-of-arms, *a Sword above a Galley*, in his intricately simple design. The sword is a superb example of the old Highland two-handed claymore, with its cross-guard ending in four-ringed quillons. Above, Scottish deerhounds are attacking a stag accompanied by two hinds.

Am Binnean Crom, The Hangman's Rock on the isle of Colonsay, where the Macfies held sway until the seventeenth century. Note the hole for the rope. All interested Macfies should read J. de V. Loder's *Colonsay and Oransay* (Edinburgh 1935).

VINCERE VEL MORI

Macneil

The Macneils take their name from Niall, a chief who lived in the thirteenth or early fourteenth century, and who belonged to the dynastic family of Cowall and Knapdale. They descended from the Irish prince Anrothan, who married a daughter of the local king in the eleventh century, as we are told in the old Irish Gaelic MS. genealogies. Other branches of the same dynastic family became the Maclachlans, Lamonts, MacSwins, and MacEwens: all in the same district.

Anrothan himself was a son of Aodh O'Neill, King of the North of Ireland (1030–1033), whose ancestry was the most distinguished in the world of the Gaels: going back through Niall 'Black-Knee', High King of Ireland (killed in battle against the Norsemen in 916) to Niall 'of the Nine Hostages', the pagan High-King of Ireland when the Romans were still in Britain. Scholars accept his ancestry back as far as the fourth century A.D., when the family were already sacral Kings of Tara.

In the Middle Ages, the island of Gigha off the coast south of Knapdale was held by MacNeill chieftains, who also held Taynish on the mainland. They were in a key position as hereditary Keepers of grim Castle Swin in Knapdale during the fifteenth and sixteenth centuries. To this branch belonged the McNeills of Colonsay (another Hebridean island) 1700–1904, and Ronald McNeill, 1st Lord Cushendun, who in 1928 was Acting Foreign Secretary.

It was probably in the fourteenth century that the clan gained another group of islands, this time in the Outer Hebrides—the remote island of Barra with its many surrounding isles including Mingulay, together with Boisdale in South Uist. Barra and South Uist had formed part of the vast possessions of the great house of MacRuari, scions of the old Celtic-Norse sea-kings of the Hebrides. As late as 1373 their heiress's son Ranald, ancestor of the Macdonalds of Clanranald, still held the superiority of Barra. But the banner of Macneil of Barra displays a quartering of the Black Galley, the emblem of the MacRuaris as a branch of the Blood Royal of the Isles, and there seems no doubt that the Galley descended to the Macneils, together with the characteristic name of Ruari and indeed the island of Barra itself, through a female-line descent from the House of MacRuari.

Jane McNeill, Countess of Dalkeith. Painting by John Merton, R.A. Lady Dalkeith descends from Torkill MacNeill of Gigha, Chief of Taynish in 1449, through the McNeills of Colonsay: one of the most talented families of the Highland aristocracy. Her father is grandson of the late Sir Malcolm McNeill, Chairman of the Local Government Board of Scotland, brother of Major-General Sir John McNeill, V.C., G.C.V.O., K.C.B., K.C.M.G., 9th Laird of Colonsay, who won the Victoria Cross in the Maori War and was Equerry to both Queen Victoria and King Edward VII. Their father, Alexander McNeill of Gigha, was brother of Duncan McNeill, 1st Lord Colonsay, P.C., Lord Justice General of Scotland (who was made a Peer in 1867) and of the Right Honble. Sir John McNeill, P.C., G.C.B., 8th Laird of Colonsay, British Envoy to the Shah of Persia; and uncle of Ina McNeill, Duchess of Argyll (Lady-in-Waiting and personal Private Secretary to Queen Victoria), who died in 1925 and is buried, with her husband the eighth Duke, beneath sculptured marble tomb effigies in Iona Cathedral.

Castle Swin, on Loch Swin in Knapdale, held in the fifteenth century for the Lords of the Isles by the MacNeills of Gigha, chieftains of Taynish. The original Suibhne after whom the castle was named was probably the thirteenth-century chieftain of that name who was akin to the MacNeills, Maclachlans and Lamonts.

'The castle on an island in the sea on an island in the sea' is Kisimul Castle, the gem of the Outer Hebrides. This picturesque stronghold was the lair of the pirate Chiefs of Clan Neill, the Macneils of Barra, and hard alongside it there can still be seen cut into the rock the berth for 'Kisimul's Galley', famed in Gaelic song. Beyond the galley berth is the old yair or catchment that trapped fish as the tide fell; and also on a rock outside the curtain walls of the castle are the ruins of the galley crew's guard house. The castle itself crowns a tiny rock, sea-girt in land-locked Castlebay, a lagoon of Barra. Within the wall defences were the Great Tower or Keep entered only by an internal drawbridge formed by its own door hinged at the bottom and set eighteen feet above the ground, a small subsidiary garrison building whose upper floor gave access to the keep drawbridge when the tower door was lowered, the old kitchen, the present chief's residential building, the Great Hall with its harpers' gallery, the guard tower with the pit or prison, and the Chapel. The Great Hall is of the earliest period of castle building, for it had no chimney fireplace, but simply the ancient central hearth of a type dating back to Viking times, with the peat-smoke finding its own way out as in the old Hebridean black houses. In the old days, Macneil's sennachie (sometimes called 'the chief druid') used to sound a great horn from the battlements of the castle, and proclaim out across the wild Atlantic: 'Hear oh ye people, and listen oh ye nations! The great Macneil of Barra having finished his meal, the princes of the earth may dine now.' This is identified by scholars with a very ancient royal ritual of Oriental origin, and was doubtless brought to the remote Outer Isles by Macneil's female-line ancestors, Viking sea-kings in contact with the East.

Barra means the 'Isle of Saint Barr,' and it has been suggested that the saint after whom the island was called was not St. Fionn Bharr, the founder of Cork, but St. Barr-fhionn, great-grandson of King Niall of the Nine Hostages. It's therefore interesting that the Macneils also claim descent from Niall of the Nine Hostages, who reigned as high king of Ireland at Tara in about 400 A.D., when Ireland was still pagan, and who raided Britain in Roman times. The great ironwork lanterns set up in Kisimul Castle by the present Macneil of Barra bear the red hand of O'Neill surrounded by nine fetterlocks, emblems from the quartering on his banner that commemorates this descent from King Niall of the Nine Hostages.

In 1409 Macneil bore the Christian name of Ruari, previously unknown in the family, and his son Gilleonan's MacRuari ancestry was evidently remembered in the local Barra tradition that he descended from 'thirty-three Ruaris' in succession who had held the island before him. In 1427 Gilleonan Macneil of Barra received a charter of Barra and Boisdale from the Lord of the Isles, though both were in the heart of the old MacRuari territory inherited by the powerful Clanranald. The charter implies that the Macneil right to this territory had come through Gilleonan Macneil's mother, the daughter of Fearchar Maclean, and so it may perhaps reasonably be suggested that *her* mother was an heiress of the MacRuaris: descended from Ruari, whose father was Ranald, King of the Isles (1164–1207).

As late as 1530, Torkill MacNeill of Gigha was referred to by the Privy Council as 'chief and principal of the clan and surname of Macnelis'. But, as the power of Gigha declined in the days of Campbell expansion into the Inner Hebrides, so did that of Barra far away in the Outer Hebrides increase: and Macneil of Barra has now long been officially recognised as Chief of the whole Clan and Name.

At first Macneil of Barra supported Macdonald even against the Macleans of Duart, as when he rallied to the Lord of the Isles against whom a plot had been contrived by the Mackinnon chief's brother Fingon, the 'Green Abbot' of Iona, who enlisted the aid of Duart and Dunvegan, yet was foiled. But even before the downfall of the Lordship of the Isles, Macneil made a close alliance with the powerful Macleans of Duart to resist Clanranald, who only finally conquered Boisdale from Macneil after a couple of centuries of intermittent warfare. Such wars, the old Barra folk believed, were heralded by the appearance of drops of blood in the 'spring and fresh water well' near the church of Kilbarr in the north of the island.

When the King of Scots at last overthrew the Lord of the Isles, Macneil received a Crown charter in 1495 confirming him in possession of Barra

Colonsay House on the Isle of Colonsay, in the time of Duncan McNeill, Lord Colonsay. The older part was built by Malcolm McNeill of Colonsay in 1722, and a stone above the front door is carved with his initials and those of his wife, Barbara Campbell, daughter of the 10th Captain of Dunstaffnage. As it was built on the site of the pre-Reformation cemetery of Kiloran Abbey, the housekeeper was naturally haunted at first by the ghost of 'Charlie of the Chickens', *Tearlach nan Eoin*, wearing his winding-sheet, until his bones were dug up by the factor from their undignified position beneath the new kitchen hearthstone and re-buried elsewhere.

In 1745, we are told that a Jacobite officer was sent 'to sound the island chief, Mr. Donald McNeill, as to whether the Prince could depend upon his assistance'. Donald McNeill of Colonsay (an epileptic) politely but firmly replied that 'as he and his clan were loyal in their allegiance to the Clan Campbell and the British Crown, he could have nothing to do with the expedition'. The next chieftain, Colonel Archibald McNeill of Colonsay (who personally raised and commanded the 3rd Argyll Fencibles), married Lady Georgiana Forbes, daughter of the 5th Earl of Granard: of the branch of the highland Clan Forbes that had settled in Ireland. His successor, by a special family financial arrangement, afterwards typical of the Colonsay McNeill succession, was his first cousin John McNeill, 4th of Oransay (the neighbouring island), who was maternal grandson of Alexander MacDougall of Dunollie, Chief of Clan Dougall, and who lived 1767–1846. 'The forty years during which he was laird were the most prosperous that Colonsay and Oransay have ever known. He is still remembered with affection as the "Old Laird".' He established the crofting district of Kilchattan, and personally subsidised his tenants to build fireplaces and chimneys in their new houses. 'It seems the innovation was not popular at first. People objected that unless the fire was in its traditional place in the middle of the floor, the "wee things" or fairies would not be able to get around it.'

In 1847, the Old Laird's eldest son, Alexander McNeill of Colonsay (drowned in a shipwreck three years later), made another of the family financial arrangements whereby the island passed to his brother, afterwards Lord Colonsay, from whom it was similarly taken over by another brother, Sir John McNeill of Colonsay (who at the age of seventy-five married Lady Emma Campbell, daughter of the 7th Duke of Argyll), and then in the same way—but for the then crippling sum of £80,072—to his nephew, the actual head of the Colonsay family, Sir John McNeill of Colonsay, V.C., victor of the battle of Tophrik in the Sudan, who had always been the true heir. After his death the island, sold for debt, passed to Lord Strathcona.

and his other territories. In 1579 the Bishop of the Isles complained at being molested by Gilleonan Macneil of Barra, and some years later the Earl of Argyll was amused at the formality and state with which an ambassador from Macneil of Barra presented to him a letter offering aid 'as if he belonged to another kingdom'.

The chief at this time was a mighty sea-rover, Ruari Og Macneil of Barra, described as 'a Scot that usually maketh his summer's course to steal what he can', in the mode of his ancestors, the Viking sea-kings. As a young man, he had a romantic affair with Mary, heiress of the MacLeods of Dunvegan, who bore him a son and whom it is said he tried to rescue when she was given to a Campbell husband by her guardian Argyll. In 1591 Ruari Og, this fierce 'summer wanderer', led another foray into Ireland. The Burkes of Mayo resisted hotly under their chief, The MacWilliam Eighter, called the 'Blind Abbot', two of whose sons were slain in the fight, when Macneil of Barra's own son Ewen was also killed; and Graine Ni Maille, 'the redoubtable chieftainess of the Burkes, famous for her exploits at sea', doubtless supported by her ferocious son-in-law Richard Burke, 'the Devil's Hook', prepared twenty ships to pursue the Macneils and their Maclean allies.

Under the next chief, Ruari Macneil of Barra, 'an hereditary outlaw' known as Ruari the Tatar, the castle bay around Kisimul continued to be famous as a pirates' nest. Ruari might perhaps be called the Last of the Vikings, but his sons were chips off the old block. His first wife was Duart's sister, by whom he had several sons. The old corsair then disowned her and 'married' Clanranald's sister, by whom he had some more sons. The two groups of his sons fought each other for the succession even during Ruari's lifetime: except for one of them who was 'drowned in the sea'. The strife came to a head in 1610. Eventually Duart's Macneil nephews determined on a *coup d'état*, and surprised Kisimul Castle at the head of twenty picked men armed with 'swords, gauntlets, plate-sleeves, bows, darlochs, dirks, targes, Lochaber axes, two-handed swords and other weapons invasive'. They placed the Tatar and their half brothers in irons and kept them chained up in the castle, which they manned and provided with 'victual, powder, bullet and other warlike provision' against any siege. The reign of Ruari the Tatar thus came to an end, and his eldest son by Duart's sister, Neil Og Macneil of Barra, became chief in his stead.

It was Neil Og Macneil who re-established Catholicism in Barra. In his grandfather's time, the Barramen used to sail to Mayo, not only to loot and burn, but also to offer at the shrine in Knockpatrick; and in Neil Og's own time the ancient wooden image of St. Barr still stood clad in fine linen on the altar at Kilbarr. In 1652 the Catholic missionary Father Duggan reported:'MacNeill, Laird of the Island of Barra, having heard of me, sent a gentleman to beg me to do his island the same service as I had done for the Laird of Clanranald'. Eighteen months later he wrote of the Barra folk he had baptised, 'Amongst these were some troubled and annoyed by ghosts or evil spirits, who were completely delivered from them

after Baptism and never saw them again'. And when the first Vicar Apostolic for Scotland visited Barra at the close of the seventeenth century, he remarked that 'in this island many people are under the power of a kind of vision, called by the natives second sight, in virtue of which they foresee and predict unexpected and wonderful events. This power is quite beyond their control, and the effects actually correspond to the predictions. The bishop proposes certain spiritual remedies with a view to delivering these poor people'.

The authority of the central Government still scarcely reached Barra. In 1675 a Glasgow merchant, despairing of collecting a debt owed him by Gilleonan Macneil of Barra, assigned it to Iain Breac MacLeod of MacLeod, who sent a King's messenger at Arms to Kisimul with an escort of MacLeods to serve the writ on Macneil. When their boat approached the castle, it was received with shots from hagbuts and pistols, and great stones were dropped from the murder-hole above the great doorway so that they 'were in hazard of being brained'. The King's Messenger dared not affix his letter of service to the door, so he laid it down on the rocks and fled. James Macneil, the chief's brother, was in the castle and sallying out, pursued and caught the messenger and did 'rend and ryve' his writs. Such was still the 'hie and proud contempt' of the Macneils of Barra for the central authority. In 1688 nevertheless, the next chief, Black Ruari Macneil of Barra, received a Crown charter from King James VII erecting Barra into a feudal Barony, with a jurisdiction including the power of pit and gallows. When the Whig Revolution broke out that year, Black Ruari raised his clansmen for King James and sailed away to lead them in the fight under Bonnie Dundee at Killiecrankie. A devoted Jacobite, he raised his clan again for the 1715 Rising.

In 1750 a Jacobite secret agent reported to the exiled Prince Charles Edward that 'Macneil of Barra would bring 150 men to aid a new Rising in the Highlands'. By this time, the chief no longer lived at Kisimul Castle, but had moved to the main island of Barra. The local economy was changing fast, and many Barra folk began to emigrate to the New World, despite devoted efforts to dissuade them made by Colonel Roderick Macneil of Barra, whose father had fallen with Wolfe storming the Heights of Abraham at Quebec in the conquest of Canada and who himself died in 1822. His son, the irascible General Roderick Macneil of Barra, went bankrupt when the kelp industry failed as a result of the Government's Free Trade policy, and in 1838 the island of his forefathers was taken from him and sold to absentee proprietors.

As the general had no son, the chiefship passed to a cousin whose father had emigrated to the New World at the head of 370 Barramen in 1802, and whose great-grandson, the present chief, returned from America, and recovered Kisimul Castle with the greater part of the island of Barra in 1937. Himself a qualified architect, The Macneill of Barra has ever since been engaged in restoring the castle, although work was held up during the Second World War. First, he had to excavate the interior, filled with rubbish and rubble during the ninety-nine years the castle had been out of the family. He found the stone bollard to which the pirate galley of his forefathers used to be secured, and in the Chapel by contrast he unearthed the ancient stone font for holy water. When he cleared the Great Hall, he dug up the peat ashes of his ancestral hearth beneath the centre of the floor. Following an old Barra song that tells of two men who stole the lever that worked the portcullis windlass and hid it ashore, The Macneill searched for and discovered the site of the original portcullis entrance, walled-up when the present fortified doorway was made perhaps as long ago as the sixteenth century, and he made many other fascinating discoveries. Next, he repaired a great breach in the curtain walls, caused by nineteenth century herring fleets taking stones for ballast. The restoration of his living quarters has only just been completed, and once again Kisimul Castle has become the Hebridean home of Macneill of Barra, Chief of Clan Neill.

Robert Macneil of Barra, present Chief of Clan Neill, who has devoted his life to the restoration of Kisimul Castle. As a youth he studied at the Sorbonne, and became an architect in order to understand how to restore the castle. But it was a long time before the Lowland lady who was the absentee proprietress died, and he was enabled to buy back her share of the island. During a quarter of a century of inflation, and pressed for money for his building, the chief (unlike the State with its rising taxes) has struggled to avoid raising the rents of his islanders, although he had to tie up much of his own capital in the purchase. Although an American citizen, he also kept British nationality and so was able to serve as a volunteer with the Canadian Engineers in the First World War. During the Second World War he was Chairman of the Inventions Board of the British Purchasing Commission in the United States. It is often complained that some Chiefs have sold their old clan territory and emigrated. Here is an outstanding example of the reverse: of a chief who has devoted his whole life and fortune to returning from the New World to rebuild the ruined home of his forefathers.

Lamont

The Lamonts take their name from Ladman, a chief who was living in Cowall in 1238. He belonged to the dynastic family of Cowall and Knapdale: descended from the Irish prince Anrothan (son of Aodh O'Neill, King of the North of Ireland 1030–1033) who had crossed the Irish Sea to Argyll and married a daughter of the local king. Other clans descended from Anrothan are the Maclachlans, Macneils, and MacEwens, who all inherited estates in the same district, which was originally named Cowall because it was the appanage of the descendants of King Comhgall (slain in 537).

The Clan Lamont descended from Ladman were the greatest power in Cowall, and their chief was described as the 'great MacLamont of all Cowall' (*Mac Laomain mor Chomhail uile*). Their strength was much diminished by Campbell aggression, and especially by the apalling massacre of unarmed Lamonts at Dunoon in 1646, when girls and children were murdered and many gentlemen of the clan were half-hanged and then buried alive. But, although their castles of Toward and Ascog were burnt at the time of the massacre, the chiefs of the clan continued to live at Ardlamont until the last of their old homeland was sold in 1893 by John Henry Lamont of Lamont, the 21st Chief. The present Chief of Clan Lamont lives in Australia.

Their history is beautifully set out and fully illustrated in Hector McKechnie's *The Lamont Clan* (Edinburgh 1938), a fine example of such a work being specially commissioned by a Clan Society.

Glamis Castle in Strathmore. There is an old tradition that Sir John Lyon, to whom the thanage of Glamis was given as a barony in 1372 (and who soon afterwards married King Robert II's daughter), was a scion of the Chiefs of the Clan Lamont. His descendants' Arms were a *blue lyon on silver*, while the Lamonts bore a *silver lyon on blue*: and he was known as 'the White Lyon'.

Grim rumours tell of the Monster of Glamis, though his existence was supposed to be known only to the Earl, his heir and his factor. The Monster is said to have lived for many years in a secret room at Glamis. If there ever was such a monster, he could only have been the son, born to Lady Glamis on 21 October 1821, who officially died the same day, and who, of course, if he really survived, became the 12th Earl in 1846. Nobody would have bothered (anyway after his parents' deaths) to conceal anyone but the rightful heir, since any other child could have been sent to an asylum or committed to the care of a trusted retainer. If the story were true, it is dreadful to imagine the burden of horror that must have been placed on each heir when the secret was revealed to him at his coming of age, for he could not speak out without betraying his own parent, and by the time he himself succeeded he was too deeply implicated.

The Dunoon memorial stone, set up by the Clan Lamont Society in 1906 to mark the site of the ghastly massacre on 'the day the Lamonts got their bellyful' from the Campbells in 1646. Sir James Lamont of that Ilk, married to a daughter of Sir Colin Campbell of Ardkinglas, Crowner of Cowall, was a talented chief who in 1643 had established a schoolmaster at Toward, the only grammar school in Argyll being at Inveraray. In 1634, Sir James had represented the Barons of Argyll in Parliament. Two years later he had been gaily plotting in the Royalist interest with Macdonald of Sleat, MacLeod of Dunvegan, Maclean of Duart, Stuart of Bute and Stewart of Ardgowan: meeting boozily in the Edinburgh taverns called 'Euphame Wilsones in the Chanongaite, and Dixones in the Potteraw'. Seaforth and Clanranald were also involved, but *Mac Chailein Mor* found out about it all, and the Laird of Lamont was forced to steady-up and recant rapidly. In the Civil Wars that followed, King Charles I sent him a commission to act against the rebels, who of course in his neighbourhood were the mighty and terrifying Campbells of Argyll. At first, not only dared he not use it, but in fact found himself obliged to raise his clansmen for Argyll, on whose side he was nominally fighting when (doubtless with relief) he was taken prisoner in the Campbell defeat at Inverlochy. He was, however, soon released by the victor, Montrose, who gave him a new royal commission.

When Argyll was temporarily down, Sir James and the Lamonts saw the opportunity to revenge centuries of worry: also perhaps, to retrieve the whole ancient lordship of Cowall and pay off his pressing debts. In alliance with Sir Alasdair mac 'Colkitto' and his wild Antrim McDonnells, the Lamonts invaded the Campbell country. His Irish allies committed many atrocities, and his own men seized his unfortunate neighbour the Baron McGibbon of Auchnagarran, in Glendaruel, who was on his way to the Lowlands with thirteen cattle in a boat. When the Tower of Kilmun (belonging to the Campbell boy who had been entrusted by will to his care as his own 'pupill the Provost of Kilmun, to whom he was Tutor Testamentar') was surrendered to him on promise of quarter, the garrison being assured of life and liberty: 'they were all taken thrie myles from the place and most cruelly put to Death, except one who was in the hot fever'. In short, as he was afterwards forced to admit, he had joined in a band with the reasonably vengeful Clan Donald South 'for the ruin of the name of Campbell'.

When the Campbells came up again, which for him was all too soon, they were hopping mad. They invaded the Lamont country in 1646 under the then Ardkinglas himself, and besieged the Lamont castles of Toward and Ascog. Sir James surrendered Toward Castle, and persuaded Ascog Castle to surrender, after carefully negotiating a written peace treaty with the Campbells, including the express terms that 'it is agreed that the said Sir James Lamont shall overgive his house at Toward and shall have libertie to goe himself, his brethren, souldiers, wives and children, towards Sir Alexander Mack Donnald or anie of his quarters, who for that effect shall have a safe conduct, and boates sent along, who shall deliver them without anie harm of any person to bee done to them, under the said James's command, without prejudice to such women as intend to go to the east side or the Isle of Boote to be safely conducted there with boats.'

When the surrenders were actually completed, Sir James Lamont of that Ilk was cast into a dungeon at Dunstaffnage, 'grilled' by the Campbell chieftains, and kept a prisoner for five years without being allowed to change his clothes. But his chieftains and clansmen fared worse. The Campbells kept the other Lamonts prisoners for eight days, doubtless to ensure doing nothing rash to them in hot blood. During this week only Lamont girls (perhaps a few boys) and women were murdered, 'for obvious reasons', and all the Lamont country laid waste and burnt.

Then (one of the surviving witnesses was a boy of fifteen who hid 'wnder ane brea') the Campbells fixed the Lamonts, thinking of the way they themselves had been fixed after the surrender of Kilmun. They took their prisoners to Dunoon, and 'there in the churchyard they most cruelly murthered, without assyse or order of law, by shotts, by durks, by cutting their throats, as they doe with beasts, above ane hundreth, and lastly they hanged on one tree thirty and six at one tyme of the cheifs and speciall gentlemen of that name, and before they were half hanged they cutt them downe and threw them in by dozens in pitts prepared for the same; and many of them striveing to ryse upon their feet were violently holden downe untill that by throwing the earth in great quantity upon them they were stifled to death.' The dule tree, upon which thirty-six Lamonts were half-hanged before being buried alive, soon afterwards mysteriously shrivelled up; and for years a red substance like blood exuded from its roots, which would be incredible were it not that there exists a contemporary 'Declaratione . . . anent the tree wch. grew at the east end of the kirk of Dunoone upon wch. . . . the gentlemen of the name of Lamont were hanged', made in 1661, immediately after the Restoration, by the Minister of Dunoon and the Provost of Rothesay, supported by one of the burgesses. In this great punitive expedition, the Campbells carried off three thousand head of cattle from the Clan Lamont, adding insult to injury.

Toward Castle, stronghold of the Lamont chiefs from the fifteenth century until it was destroyed by the Campbells in 1646.

FORTIS ET FIDUS

Maclachlan

The Maclachlans take their name from Lachlan *Mor*, a great chief who lived by Loch Fyne in the thirteenth century. After him is named the barony of Strathlachlan with its village of Stralachlan, and Castle Lachlan where the Maclachlans of Maclachlan live, near where the Lachlan water flows into Lachlan Bay.

Lachlan Mor himself belonged to the great dynastic family that held most of Cowall and Knapdale in the days before surnames, and which descended from a daughter of the local king in the eleventh century, who brought the district to her husband Anrothan, son of Aodh O'Neill, King of the North of Ireland (1030–1033), whose royal ancestry is known as far back as the pagan sacral kings of Tara in the fourth century A.D. The district of Cowall was originally so named because it was the appanage of the descendants of King Comhgall, who was slain in 537.

For a history of the vigorous Irish dynasty from which the Maclachlans sprang, see Burke's *Peerage* under Lord O'Neill: the Ui Néill are 'the oldest traceable family left in Europe'. The name Maclachlan means of course Son of Lachlan, and Lachlan itself is from the older Gaelic name *Lochlann* which, literally, means 'Norway'. It was a favourite Christian name in a powerful branch of the O'Neill royal house of Northern Ireland; a branch that took the surname of MacLochlainn and were dangerous rivals to the senior line of O'Neill for the kingship itself from the eleventh to the thirteenth century, until King Brian O'Neill slew the last King Domnall MacLochlainn with ten of his *derbhfine* or immediate family in battle. The first of this branch, Lochlann, may have been the son of a Norse princess and hence got his name. He was a cousin of King Aodh O'Neill, whose elder son King Domnall 'the Young Ox' (slain by MacLochlainn) was ancestor of the later O'Neill kings in Ireland, while the younger son Anrothan was ancestor of the Maclachlans in Scotland.

Anrothan is said to have married a daughter of the King of Scots (probably the local King of Argyll or even the sub-king of Cowall) and to have received wide lands after campaigning there. Her inheritance appears to have been Cowall and Knapdale, as the chiefs of all the later clans there claimed descent from him. According to the mediaeval Irish and Scottish MS. genealogies, Anrothan was ancestor of the Maclachlans of Strathlachlan, the Lamonts of that Ilk (of whom the Lyons of Glamis, Earls of Strathmore, are possibly cadets), the MacSorleys of Monydrain, the McEwens of Otter, the Clan Neill in Scotland (i.e. the Macneils of Barra and the McNeills of Gigha and Colonsay), the MacSwins of Castle Swin (the ancient key to Knapdale) and the MacSweeneys in Donegal (who were great leaders of 'galloglasses' or mercenary battle-axe men). The Macmillans of Knap and the Scrymgeours of Glassary (now Earls of Dundee) seem to have inherited their Argyll lands from heiresses of his family.

The old MS. genealogies give Lachlan Mor's descent from the O'Neill kings as Lachlan, son of Gilpatrick, son of Gilchrist, son of Aodh, son of Anrothan, son of King Aodh 'Athlone' (who predeceased his father in 1033), son of Flaithbertach 'of the Pilgrim's Staff', the King of Ailech who died in 1036. This number of generations would place Lachlan Mor's lifetime in the mid-thirteenth century. And in fact, in about 1238, his father Gilpatrick mac Gilchrist witnessed the important charter whereby his cousin Sir Ladman (name-father of the Lamont clan) gave to Paisley Abbey the churches of Kilmun and Kilfinan and the chapel of Kilmory on Lochgilp, together with the fishings and lands attached to them. There is an old and improbable but charming legend that the reason why the Maclachlan chiefs' coat-of-arms is supported by two roebucks is that, when King Alexander II made his great shew of strength in Argyll in 1249, he ordered the local chiefs to send their tribute 'by the fastest messenger', and Lachlan Mor tied the money-bags to the horns of a roebuck.

In 1292, Gileskil Maclachlan, the then Chief, was one of the twelve great barons whose lands were formed into the newly-erected Sheriffdom of Argyll. 'Gileskil' is obviously a scribal error for Gillescop, 'Devotee of the Bishop', usually translated into Scots as 'Archibald'. In 1296 Ewen Maclachlan was among the Scottish landowners obliged to swear fealty to the victorious King Edward I, of whom in about 1305 Gillescop Maclachlan the younger requested 'the barony of Molbride, which was called Strat': presumably Kilbride in Strathlachlan. But young Gillescop Maclachlan, like his neighbour the Campbell chief, adhered to King Robert Bruce, from whom he received a charter; and as one of the Barons of Argyll, his name appears on a seal-tag of the letter to King Philip IV of France from the Scottish barons assembled in Bruce's first Parliament, held at St. Andrews in 1308.

In 1314, by a charter dated at 'Castellachlan', Gillescop Maclachlan granted to the Friars Preachers at Glasgow 'forty shillings sterling yearly from the ferms of his penny lands of Kylbryd, beside Castellachlan'. Kilbride indicates an ancient dedication to St. Brigid, venerated by the Kindred of St. Columba; into which great stock the Maclachlans had presumably inter-married, since the chief's Arms include (with the Dalriadic royal lyon, the Hebridean royal galley and the O'Neill salmon) a quartering of their Hand holding the Cross. Later Maclachlan cadets held the local benefices (the original mother church of Glassary, Kilneure near Ford on Lochawe, was dedicated to St. Columba) so much that modern writers sometimes refer to them as an 'ecclesiastical clan'. We are told that 'it was long the custom, when either the Laird of Strathlachlan or the Laird of Strachur died, that the survivor laid his late neighbour's head in the grave. This observance is traditionally connected with the time of the Crusades, when it is said that the heads of these two families accompanied each other to the Holy War, each solemnly engaging with the other to lay him in his family burying-place if he should fall in battle.'

An interesting Maclachlan genealogy, apparently covering the period from the thirteenth to the fifteenth centuries, and giving their marriages, is printed in Professor W. F. Skene's *Celtic Scotland* from an old Gaelic MS. It omits, however, elder and younger brothers except in the last generation. A Lamont charter of 1410 was witnessed by Iain Maclachlan, lord of Strathlachlan (*Johanne Lachlani domino de Straithlaon*). In 1436, Iain Maclachlan, lord of Strathlachlan, granted an interesting charter to his beloved cousin Allan, son of Iain *Riabhach* 'the Grizzled' Maclachlan, of 'All & Haill the Office of Seneschall and with the office commonly called Thoisseachdeowra of our land of Glassary lying in the Barony of Glassary in the Sheriffdom of Argyll'. This strange word corresponds either to 'Law-Thane' or else 'Chief Dewar', but the office is now known to have been the equivalent of that of Crowner and indeed the Manx form *Toshiaght-Joarrey* is translated 'Coroner'. According to the late Duke of Argyll's notes, this Allan Maclachlan was forefather of the Maclachlan chieftains of Dunadd. In 1456 Donald Maclachlan, lord of Castellachlan, confirmed the old grant to Paisley Abbey of an annual payment from his lands of Kilbride. Iain Maclachlan, the next Chief on record, was one of the many to marry a Campbell lady. But the present chief tells the writer that the 'Brounie', the good fairy that has watched over the Maclachlan family throughout the centuries, was so annoyed the first time a Maclachlan chief's heir married a Campbell, that he spirited away the wedding feast from Castle Lachlan.

Iain Maclachlan of Strathlachlan witnessed in 1485 a bond by Dougall Stewart of Appin to Colin Campbell, first Earl of Argyll, and in 1490 was one of the Constable of Dundee's bailies for putting his brother John Scrymgeour in possession of the Barony of Glassary. He was dead by 1509; and his son, Gillescop or Archibald Maclachlan of that Ilk, married a daughter and co-heiress of Iain Lamont of Inveryne, Chief of the Clan Lamont. Their son, Lachlan Maclachlan of that Ilk, appears high on the list of two hundred of the Earl of Argyll's kin, friends and followers, who

Lachlan Bay.

had a safe conduct in 1536 to pass with the Earl and the King to France, where King James V married Madeleine de Valois, the eldest daughter of King Francis I of France in the Cathedral of Nôtre Dame in Paris. Ten years later, the same Maclachlan chief forcibly ejected Mr. Archibald Lamont of Stroilog from certain lands; but soon afterwards he had to appear before the Privy Council, who decided that although on the death of his maternal grandfather (the Lamont chief) he had claimed the Lamont estates, the right of the Lamont heir male was preferable. He died between 1557 and 1559; and as his eldest son Donald, who is mentioned in 1553 as son and heir of 'the Lord of Maklachlane', had died before him, he was succeeded as chief by his second son, Archibald, who in 1540 had witnessed a deed at Dunoon when the fourth Earl of Argyll was holding a Justice Court there on the Castle Hill. This chief Archibald obtained a charter from the Regent Morton settling the succession of the estates on himself and (failing any heirs male of his own body) on 'Lauchlane oig Maklauchlane his brothers sone'; and died before 1581, leaving two daughters, but was succeeded in Strathlachlan under this charter by his nephew Lachlan *Og*, whose father Lachlan was already dead.

Soon after his succession to the Maclachlan chiefship, Lachlan *Og* was obliged to resign certain lands to the Lamont chief (afterwards his father-in-law) in part satisfaction for the slaughter of Robert Lamont of Silver-craigs by Lachlan Maclachlan of Dunnamuck: the 'Fort of the Swine'. He led the Clan Lachlan in the seventh Earl of Argyll's campaign in 1615 against the unfortunate Sir James Macdonald of Islay. In 1591/2 Lachlan *Og* had had a charter from King James VI, confirming him in his lands; and he obtained under King Charles I a special Act of Parliament 'in favour of the Laird of Macklachin', the Statute of 1633 cap. 141, confirming the Regent Morton's charter to the previous chief—his lands then comprised some thirty-four farms, a dozen lying in Strathlachlan and the rest in Over Loch Fyne, together with mills, fishing, and the advowson and patronage of the Kirk of Kilmory. But in 1634, being old, he resigned his

lands to his eldest son, Lachlan, and died about ten years later.

In the Civil Wars, when the Campbells took the opportunity to massacre the Lamonts in 1646, the Rev. Colin Maclachlan took a leading part in the butchery of the Lamonts, children and women being murdered at his instigation: Sheriff Macphail observed, ' the difference between an honest fanatic and a criminal lunatic is difficult to define and is of little interest to the victim '. After the Cromwellian English had conquered Scotland, ' L. Lachlane ' (presumably the then chief) was one of the signatories in 1652 of the ' Instruccons from the shire of Argyle to James Campbell of Ardkinglas, ther Comission^r . . for settling in Name of this shire wth the Comission^{rs} of the Parliam^t of the Comonwealth of England '—and in 1656 Oliver Cromwell appointed ' Lauchlane Mac Lauchlane of the same ' to be a Justice of the Peace for Argyllshire, during the Protectorate.

Lachlan Maclachlan of that Ilk was succeeded by his son Archibald, reckoned the fifteenth Chief of Clan Lachlan, who in 1680 received a Crown Charter erecting his whole lands into one Free Barony called the Barony of Strathlachlan, the manor place of Castle Lachlan at Kilbride to be the principal messuage of the Barony. The Maclachlan chiefs had of course already been immemorially Barons since such a rank first came into being in Argyll, but this new grant officially confirmed them in their powers of life and death throughout the whole of their territory. A misfortune for Clan Lachlan had recently occurred when the Scrymgeours of Glassary were unjustly deprived of all their lands and lordships, after the death of their chief the Earl of Dundee, in favour of the dictatorial Duke of Lauderdale's brother, Charles Maitland. The Scrymgeours had been kindly neighbours, and had feued out a great part of Glassary to local highlanders, among them some twenty Maclachlans including Archibald Maclachlan of that Ilk himself, and had not pressed them over-much about arrears of rent, feu-duties, teinds and like. In 1672, the grasping lowlander Maitland had got a decreet in the Court of Session against them all, ordering payment of all arrears, together with every possible fine that could be wrung out of their feu-charters.

In 1666, Archibald Maclachlan of that Ilk had signed the great band at Inveraray, whereby ten shillings were to be paid out of each merkland in Argyll for maintaining an armed Watch; and in 1679, as Laird of Maclachlan, he raised 50 men for his Company in Sir Colin Campbell of Ardkinglas's Regiment of 854 men to pursue the Macleans with Fire & Sword, but the expedition against Duart failed through the intervention of Lord MacDonell (Glengarry) and Cameron of Lochiel on the Macleans' side. The fifteenth Chief of Clan Lachlan died in 1687.

The Maclachlans were loyal Jacobites, and are said to have been with Bonnie Dundee in 1689 at the battle of Killiecrankie; while in the 1715 Rising, Lachlan Maclachlan of that Ilk signed the Address of Welcome to the Old Chevalier, the rightful King James VIII Stuart, on his landing in Scotland. According to Archibald Brown, *The History of Cowal* (Greenock 1908): ' The chief of MacLachlan appeared with the Earl of Mar at

Sheriffmoor as Colonel in the Pretender's army, and for this act it is said Campbell of Ardkinglas followed MacLachlan like a sleuthhound for five years and shot him dead in 1720 '. Certainly the sixteenth Chief died in March 1719, which is near enough to this date.

Under his son Lachlan Maclachlan of Maclachlan, the seventeenth Chief, Clan Lachlan played a gallant part as Jacobites in the 1745 Rising with Prince Charles Edward Stuart. When the Prince had reached Carlisle, according to Murray of Broughton: ' The recruits that he expected from Scotland not being able to get up so soon as was expected, he detached McLachlan of Castle Lachlan with a few horse to Perth to give them intelligence of his designs and to hasten their march to Carlisle '. After the failure of the Rising, the Rev. John Maclachlan of Kilchoan, who had been ' Chaplain-General to all the loyal Clans ' with the Jacobite Army, and had been in all the fighting from Gladsmuir (Prestonpans) to Culloden, wrote to his friend Bishop Forbes in 1748: ' I hope you'll take notice of Collonel MacLachlan of that Ilk, whom the newspapers and magazines neglected. 'Tis true he got but few of his clan rais'd, because most of them are situated amidst the Campbells. However he attended the Prince at Gladsmuir, and march'd with him to Carlyle, from whence he was detach'd by the Prince with an ample commission and 16 horses to lead on to England the 3000 men that lay then at Perth '. (He adds that the Governor of Perth refused to comply). ' The Collonel join'd us again at Stirlin, and when we retir'd to Inverness, the Prince made him Commissary of the army. At the battle of Culloden he had a regiment of 300 men, whereof 115 were his own people and 182 were Mackleans, who chose to be under his command, seeing their chief was not there. The said Collonel being the last that received orders from the Prince on the field of battle, he was shot by a canon ball as he was advancing on horseback to lead on his regiment, which was drawn up between the Macintoshes and the Stewarts of Appin '.

The Rev. John Maclachlan added, to the Bishop: ' I live for the most part now like a hermite, because all my late charge almost were kill'd in battle, scatter'd abroad, or are cow'd at home '. An eye-witness account (disguised, but by one of the ex-prisoners) of the treatment by the victorious

The ruins of old Castle Lachlan, overlooking Lachlan Bay in Loch Fyne. The original wooden stronghold of the Maclachlan chiefs was on a nearby island in the loch, but they moved to this site in the Middle Ages. The castle was abandoned forever when it was bombarded from the loch in 1746. ' The neck of land which connects the castle with the mainland is low and marshy, and may at an earlier period have been covered with water, while traces of a moat can be seen running across it.'

Government of the Jacobite prisoners at Inverness after Culloden (Prince Charles Edward had always been especially chivalrous to his own captives) tells us of the sufferings of Major Alexander Maclachlan from Ladhill in Argyllshire (who later escaped in 1748): 'When we had filled all the goalls, kirks and ships at Inverness with these rebell prisoners, wounded and naked as they were, we ordered that non should have any access to them either with meat or drink for two days. By this means no doubt we thought at least the wounded would starve either for want of food or cloaths, the weather then being very cold. The two days being passed there was a corum of officers pitched upon to goe and visit them in order to take down their names and numbers which was diminished pretty weell. . . . That night it was determined in the privy counsell that each prisoner should have half a pound oat meall per day (but Haly thought it too much) and accordingly they sent some of their commissarys to distribute the meall. I could not help laughing in the time of the distribution when the poor things had nothing left them to hold their meall but the fore skirt of their shirts, rather exposing their nakedness to the world than want their meall. They made very odd figures everyon with his half pound meall tied up in his shirt lap, and all below naked. Some were handcuffed, especially Major Stewart and Major McLachlan. Their handcuffs were so tight that their hands swelld and at last broke the skin so that the irons could not be seen. I can compare their case to nothing better than a horse sore sadle-spoild which runs a great deal of thick matter and blood. In this excessiff agony were they keep ten days notwithstanding all the application they made only to get wider handcuffs, or their being changed and put upon their other hands. Amongst the rest I seed a Frenchman in the agonies of death lying in nastiness up to his stomack, and I myself put a great stone under his head that he might not be choked with which he ly in. We allways took care not to bury their dead untill such time as we had a least a dozen of them. Only imagine yourself what for an agreeable smell was there—their own excraments with the stink of the dead bodyis that seldom were taken away befor they began naturaly to melt by the heat of the weather.'

A Government ship came up Loch Fyne and bombarded old Castle Lachlan, which the bereaved family were forced to abandon. It is said that as the Maclachlan clansmen straggled back from Culloden, their dead chief's riderless horse broke away and swam home across Loch Fyne, bringing the first news of the catastrophe—and that the horse thereafter took up residence in a ground-floor cellar of the ruinous castle. At first it was thought that the Strathlachlan estates had been forfeited. But the old chief had been killed before he could be attainted, and *Mac Chailein Mor*, then the most powerful magnate in Scotland, had always been a good friend to his Maclachlan neighbours. So, as early as 12 February 1747, the old chief's son Donald Maclachlan, now eighteenth of Maclachlan, got a charter of his lands 'at the intercession of the Duke of Argyll'. However, he still met with considerable opposition from the authorities, and under 'estates surveyed but afterwards found not to be forfeited', the Forfeited Estates Papers enter after 'McLauchlane' £10.12.1d. for 'Expenses of Surveying the Different Estates' and a further £5.6.7d. for 'Expenses of contesting claims before the Court of Session'.

The later history of the Chiefs of Clan Lachlan is to be found in Burke's *Landed Gentry*. Although the mediaeval castle had to be abandoned after Culloden, a new Castle Lachlan was built early in the last century, and is still the home of the lady who is the present twenty-fourth Chief of Clan Lachlan: Marjorie Maclachlan of Maclachlan, lady of the barony of Strathlachlan, who succeeded her father John (last of the original male line) in 1942. Through her mother, a daughter of the late Cluny Macpherson, she also descends from the Macpherson chief who hid in 'Cluny's Cage' after the '45, from Simon, Lord Lovat, the 'Old Fox' beheaded in 1747, and from Sir Euan Cameron, the 'Great Lochiel'. So her Jacobite blood fairly bubbles. She is married, and has six children, of whom the eldest son is Euan Maclachlan, yr. of Maclachlan.

Kilmorich Church by Loch Fyne, at the mouth of Glen Kinglas. This was the country of the Campbells of Ardkinglas, descended from Colin Campbell of Ardkinglas, living in 1428, brother of the first Lord Campbell. In 1692, Sir Colin Campbell of Ardkinglas, Sheriff Depute of Argyll, administered the belated oath of allegiance to *Mac Iain*, chieftain of the Macdonalds of Glencoe, and did his best to save him from the massacre which (unknown to either of them) the Master of Stair was already plotting in Whitehall, and for which the Campbells in general have received a disproportionate share of the blame.

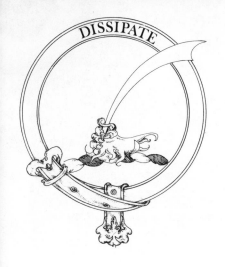

Scrymgeour

The Scrymgeours held some 100,000 acres in the highlands at Glassary in Argyll, until they were unjustly deprived of them by Lauderdale in 1668. This great territory had come to them as a result of the marriage in about 1370 of Alexander Scrymgeour of Dudhope, Constable of Dundee and Bannerman of Scotland, to Agnes of Glassary, heiress of Gilbert of Glassary.

Gilbert himself was the son of Sir John Glassary of that Ilk, otherwise known in the highlands as ' Iain MacMaster ', who was an adherent of King Robert Bruce, went mad, and was dead by 1341. Sir John's father was Master Ralf of Dundee, lord of Glassary and a Knight, who was one of the twelve great barons whose lands were formed into the sheriffdom of Argyll in 1292. He appears to have inherited Glassary from the family of Gillascop MacGilchrist, either by descent or through marriage to an heiress.

Gillascop MacGilchrist was a chief of especial interest, as a charter given to him by King Alexander II on 1 August 1240 is ' the earliest extant Crown grant of lands in Argyll, and dates from the time when that province was being finally incorporated in the Scottish realm '. It is also

The Cath-Buaidh or Battle-Victory reliquary of St. Columba, known as the ' Brecbennoch ', borne before the ancient Scottish royal armies in battle. It was the Scottish equivalent of the French kings' *oriflamme*, the reliquary containing the cape that St. Martin divided with a beggar, succeeded in heraldic times by the gonfanon of the Abbey of St. Denis. By the time of King William the Lyon, who was himself of the kindred of St. Columba, heraldry had also become established in Scotland, and his personal *vexillum* or royal battle-ensign was now the consecrated Lyon Rampant banner; while the old Celtic hereditary abbacies were becoming temporal lordships. Accordingly, before 1211, William the Lyon gave custody of the old *vexillum* or battle-ensign, the sacred reliquary of St. Columba, to the monks of his newly founded monastery at Arbroath: ' I have given and granted, with the Brecbennoch, the lands of Forglen given to God and to St. Columba and to the Brecbennoch, they making therefore the service in the army with the Brecbennoch which is due to me from the said lands '. A century later, soon after returning from his experiences at the battle of Bannockburn (where he had presumably borne the Brecbennoch as was his duty), the Abbot of Arbroath hurriedly unloaded the dangerous duty on to a local laird, bearing the significant Christian name of Malcolm and coming out of country that had long been held by the Royal kindred of St. Columba. With consent of his chapter, and looking to the welfare of the monastery, the Abbot granted to Malcolm of Monymusk the whole lands of Forglen pertaining to the Brecbennoch, ' to be held by the said Malcolm and his heirs on condition that he and they shall perform in our name the service in the king's army which pertains to the Brecbennoch, as often as occasion shall arise.' But by this time the Scrymgeour chiefs had long been accustomed to bearing the consecrated heraldic flag instead, if ever they had borne the Brecbennoch in pre-heraldic times. Indeed, as the Scrymgeours long held Balbeuchlie (the township of the Bachuil) in the Columban barony of Dunkeld, their original *vexillum* was more probably St. Columba's crozier, which is known to have been carried in battle locally against the Norsemen as late as 918, probably with a scarf wrapped round it in the usual manner of that period.

Glen Etive, in the Campbell country.

' believed to be the oldest writ in existence dealing with lands in Argyll '. This charter includes the lands of Fincharn near the south-west end of Lochawe, where the family had their stronghold.

The MacGilchrists of Glassary evidently belonged to the dynastic family of Cowall and Knapdale, whose other branches included the Maclachlans and Lamonts. They descended from the marriage of the local king's daughter to the Irish prince Anrothan, son of Aodh O'Neill, King of the North of Ireland (1030–1033): and from the dawn of heraldry they all bore the Dalriadic *lyon* in their Arms. So it is interesting that when Sir John Scrymgeour was thinking of exchanging Glassary with the Campbell chief for other lands in 1431, he expressly provided that it should not affect the bearing of the *lyon* in his Arms. On the other hand, there are reasons for supposing that the original Scrymgeours had also had a separate right to the *lyon*, although one cadet branch only bore *crossed scimitars*.

Gillascop MacGilchrist had a brother Ewen MacGilchrist, whose son

Charter of 29 March 1298, from the epic hero Sir William Wallace, as Guardian of Scotland, to Sir Alexander Scrymgeour, confirming him in certain lands and the hereditary office of Constable of the Castle of Dundee, ' for faithful service and succour given to the . . . kingdom in carrying the royal banner in the army of Scotland '.

Looking from the hall at Birkhill into the dining-room. Above the doorway are the *lyon rampant* Royal Banners of Scotland carried by their hereditary bearers at the Coronations of (right) King George V and (left) King George VI.

Charter of 5 December 1298, from our other epic hero Robert Bruce, Earl of Carrick (afterwards King Robert I), as one of the Guardians of Scotland, to the same Sir Alexander Scrymgeour, confirming to him ' the grant of Sir William Wallace ' referred to above. This is the only contemporary Scottish document in which the names of Wallace and Bruce are associated together. Sir Alexander Scrymgeour was later captured and hanged by King Edward I, still fighting for Scotland's Cause, in 1306.

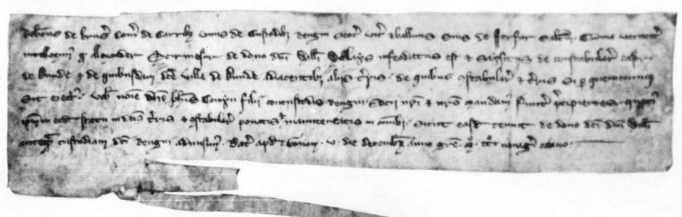

Iain MacGilchrist was another of the twelve great barons of Argyll whose lands were formed into the newly erected shire in 1292. In the reign of King David Bruce, this branch forfeited their lands, which were granted by the king in 1346 to Gilbert of Glassary; and ' it seems probable that by this grant Gilbert of Glassary became possessed of the whole estates of Gilchrist—the father of Gillascop and Ewen—which had been divided between his two sons '.

It was Gilbert of Glassary's daughter Agnes who brought this ancient Highland inheritance to the Scrymgeours. The surname Scrymgeour means a skirmisher, from the Old French word *eskermisor*, a fencer with the sword: and the Scrymgeour *lyon* bears a *scimitar*. The form ' William de scrameture ', in a Coupar Angus charter of 1242, may result from the common scribal error of ' de ' for ' le '. Agnes of Glassary's husband, Alexander Scrymgeour of Dudhope, Constable of Dundee and Bannerman of Scotland, was a cousin of King Robert II.

His family had already held the office of hereditary standard-bearer or Bannerman of Scotland since the days of King Alexander III. His grandfather, ' Alexander, called Schyrmeschur, son of Colyn, son of Carun of Cupar ' held lands in Cupar of Fife in 1293; was Constable of the royal castle of Dundee and royal Banner-Bearer under Balliol and Wallace; and was hanged by King Edward I in 1306, while a prisoner-of-war, for having carried Bruce's royal banner at the battle of Methven. The Scrymgeours

James, 11th Earl of Dundee, P.C., present *Mac Mhic Iain* and Royal Bannerman of Scotland. A former President of the Union at Oxford, and Member of Parliament, he was successively Under-Secretary of State for Scotland and Minister of State in the Foreign Office, before becoming Deputy Leader of the House of Lords. He is one of the Highlands' keenest foresters. He is seen here with his dog Mons.

Birkhill, in the kingdom of Fife, is the home of the Earl of Dundee, who is also Lord Glassary in Argyll. It looks across the Tay estuary to the city of Dundee, and lies north of Cupar, capital of Fife, in both of which areas the Scrymgeours already held lands in the thirteenth century. But Birkhill itself was acquired in the eighteenth century by David Scrymgeour, Sheriff Depute of Inverness and rightful 5th Earl of Dundee, whose grandmother was heiress of the Wedderburns of Wedderburn. The present house has considerable nineteenth-century additions, but the tower still flies the Bannerman's personal banner.

Finncharn Castle, ruined mediaeval Highland stronghold of the Scrymgeours of Glassary on Loch Awe. It now belongs once again to the Scrymgeour chief, the 11th Earl of Dundee, who was created Lord Glassary in 1954.

indeed have the unique distinction of charters from both Wallace and Bruce—in each case being confirmed in their hereditary offices of Constable of Dundee and of bearing the *vexillum regium* or Royal Banner of Scotland.

The armies of the old Gaels used to be led into battle by an abbot carrying a sacred reliquary or *vexillum*. Hereditary abbots sometimes delegated the custody and duty of carrying relics to cadet branches, such guardians being called dewars. The right of leading the Scottish host was vested in the Earls of Fife, Chiefs of the Clan Macduff (probably because the first earl of Fife was also the last hereditary abbot of Dunkeld), whose original demesne was at Cupar and whose Arms were a *red lyon on gold*. It seems probable that their rights were derived from that of bearing the royal *vexillum* (originally a reliquary of St. Columba and later a consecrated heraldic banner) and that they delegated this duty to a branch of their own clan. The Scrymgeours came from the Macduff homeland of Cupar in Fife, and their Arms were those of the Earls of Fife with the colours

reversed (a *golden lyon on red*) and the lyon holding a scimitar (though one cadet branch simply bore crossed scimitars). So it seems possible that the *vexillum* they bore was a reliquary (probably St. Columba's pastoral staff) before it was a consecrated heraldic banner, and most likely that they were themselves a branch of the Clan Macduff.

The mother church of Glassary had been founded by St. Columba himself, which is of interest because the Clan Macduff were probably the principal branch of the Kindred of St. Columba in Scotland. 'Glassarie seems to have been treated as a family living. Among others who held it, sometimes with other preferment, were, in 1423, James Scrymgeour, afterwards the ambassador from Charles VII to Martin V; in 1431 Robert Scrymgeour; in 1438 Hercules Scrymgeour; in 1454 Alexander Scrymgeour; in 1500 James Scrymgeour; and Henry Scrymgeour who died in 1572.' Glassary itself was given by his elder brother to John Scrymgeour o Glassary, who was thus firmly settled at Fincharn in the Highlands but was mortally wounded at Flodden in 1513 carrying the Royal Banner as depute for his infant nephew, the then Chief. The Gaelic title of the Scrymgeour chiefs was *Mac Mhic Iain*.

Glassary remained in Scrymgeour possession until the death in 1668 of John Scrymgeour, Earl of Dundee and Royal Bannerman of Scotland; when all his castles, estates and hereditary offices were unjustly seized by the all-powerful Duke of Lauderdale for the benefit of his own family. The Scrymgeour heirs male were unable to prove anything, as Lauderdale had sent a troop of dragoons to carry off all the Dundee papers from Dudhope Castle.

In modern times, the Scrymgeour heirs male have at last managed to prove their case, and have been restored by the House of Lords both to the office of hereditary Royal Standard Bearer of Scotland and also to the earldom of Dundee, though it was too late to recover the lands. In 1954 the present 11th Earl of Dundee, who carried the *lyon rampant* banner at the last two Coronations as Royal Standard Bearer of Scotland, was created also a Peer of the United Kingdom as Baron Glassary, becoming later Minister of State in the Foreign Office and then Deputy Leader of the House of Lords. A keen forester, he has reacquired part of the old Glassary lands for afforestation, together with the ruins of the Scrymgeours' ancestral stronghold, Fincharn Castle on Loch Awe.

Front and back views of Macmillan's Cross at Kilmorie in Knapdale. Erected by Alasdair Macmillan in the days when the Macmillan chiefs held Knap, it shows his claymore beneath a crucifix, and on the reverse he is dressed in his quilted saffron warcoat, with a hunting horn slung at his side and swinging a battle-axe, while hounds bring a stag to bay.

Two Celtic chiefs bearing the Royal Banners of two Celtic countries at the Coronation of King Edward VII: the present Earl of Dundee's grandfather with The O'Conor Don, heir of the ancient Kings of Connaught, bearing the banners of Scotland and Ireland.

Macmillan

The surname Macmillan is derived from the Gaelic *Mac Mhaolain*: 'Son of the Tonsured'. Since Highland surnames were in pre-Reformation times limited to those of ancient birth, it necessarily implies descent from one of the old Celtic monastic families, who were usually derived from the local dynastic houses and who were allowed to marry. The Celtic tonsure was not a bald circle on the top of the head, in the Roman manner, but meant shaving the whole front of the pate from ear to ear, leaving everything behind to grow long: to modern eyes, rather a redskin effect. The Macmillan keenness on hair-cuts is perhaps reflected in the Lord High Treasurer's accounts for 1473, where there is an entry for payment to 'McMwlane the barbour for the leichcraft done be him to the litil boys of the chalmire'—except that this Macmillan had been bleeding the lads rather than shearing them.

During the Middle Ages, the Macmillan chiefs acquired the extensive territory of Knapdale through an heiress of the MacNeills, a branch of the great Cowall group of clans descended from the Irish prince Anrothan (son of Aodh O'Neill, King of Northern Ireland 1030–1033) who had himself married the daughter of the local Scottish king. Thus the Macmillans have the royal *lyon* in their Arms. The beautiful Celtic carving of Macmillan's Cross commemorates their tenure of Knap. But long since gone (some say through Campbell chisels) is the famous inscription on a sea-rock by Loch Suibhne in Knap: *Coir Mhic Mhaoilein air a Chnap, Fhad's a bhuaileas tonn air creig*—'Macmillan's right holds good to Knap, So long as wave beats on the rock'.

And the old lands are also long since gone. However, the present chief, Lt-General Sir Gordon Macmillan of Macmillan and Knap, K.C.B., K.C.V.O., D.S.O., M.C., ruled another Rock from 1952 to 1955 as Governor and Commander-in-Chief of Gibraltar.

MacEwen

MacEwen is from the Gaelic *Mac Eoghain*, 'Son of Eoghan', a Gaelic personal name meaning 'born of the yew-tree' and Englished as Ewen. The principal clan of the name in the Highlands were the MacEwens of Otter on Loch Fyne, where their castle was on a rocky point about a mile south of Kilfinan, not far from Otter Ferry. These MacEwen chiefs belonged, like the Maclachlans and Lamonts, to the mediaeval dynastic house of Cowall and Knapdale, sprung from the marriage of the local king's daughter to the Irish prince Anrothan, son of Aodh O'Neill, King of the North of Ireland (1030–1033). But in 1431–2 Suibne (Swene) MacEwen of Otter resigned the destination of the Barony of Otter in favour of the Campbell chief's eldest son, and after his death it passed to the Campbells. Since then the MacEwens have been landless in the Highlands, and the line of their chiefs untraced.

However, the crest of the present McEwen baronet of Bardrochat in Ayrshire is the stump of a cut-down oak-tree still sprouting forth young branches—together with the significant motto REVIRESCO: I grow again. His father, the late Sir John McEwen of Bardrochat, who was also Laird of Marchmont (one of the most beautiful houses in Scotland), was one of the finest and most talented Scottish gentlemen of our day. These McEwens have held lands in Bardrochat since at least the time of James McEwen, who was born in 1695 and was drowned in the river Stinchar in 1737; there was a place called McEwinstoun in Ayrshire by 1622; and an Ayrshire McEwen (George Makewin, follower of the earl of Cassillis, uncrowned 'king of Carrick') was respited for murder as early as 1526. And although Ayrshire is separated from Cowall by the broadest part of the Firth of Clyde, the sphere of influence of the earls of Cassillis bordered on that of the Campbells of Loudoun, whose fourteenth-century ancestors had been near neighbours of the MacEwens of Otter on Loch Fyne. On the other hand, Bardrochat is in the south of Carrick (originally the northern province of the principality of Galloway), and Patrick McEwyn was Provost of Wigtoun (the capital of Galloway) as early as 1331; so the family may have taken their name from a completely different Ewen, and the *crowned lyon* in their Arms most probably alludes to that of the ancient Princes of Galloway.

Bardrochat, Galloway home of Sir James MacEwen of Bardrochat, 2nd Baronet, that looks across the river Stinchar. His sister Christian McEwen, Lady Hesketh, is the author of *Tartan* (London 1961), probably the best existing summary of this controversial subject.

The site of the McEwen castle on Loch Fyne.

Fergusson

Fergusson means what it says: a 'Son of Fergus'. The different family groups of the Name may well descend from completely separate men who happened to be given the Christian name of Fergus at their baptism. The main groups are the Fergussons of Dunfallandy (whose chieftain was styled Baron Fergusson) and of Baledmund in the Perthshire highlands; the Fergusons of Kinmundy and of Pitfour in Aberdeenshire; the Fergusons of Raith in Fife; the Fergussons of Craigdarroch in Dumfries-shire (whose coat-of-arms may indicate some relationship to the ancient Princes of Galloway, and whose head married the celebrated 'Annie Laurie' of the old song); and above all, the Fergussons of Kilkerran in Ayrshire.

However, the different families of the surname have long tended to keep in touch with one another under Kilkerran's aegis, and Fergusson of Kilkerran is officially recognised as Chief of the whole Name of Fergusson. The original coat-of-arms of Kilkerran had a chevron, and it seems most likely that they belonged to the Carrick branch of the old princely house of Galloway. The present chief's brother, the 'Chindit' jungle leader Sir Bernard Fergusson, recently Governor-General of New Zealand, is remarkable in that his father and *both* his grandfathers also governed New Zealand. The chief himself, Sir James Fergusson of Kilkerran, 8th Baronet, is the historian and broadcaster who was Keeper of the Records of Scotland.

Some tombstones of Fergussons at Strachur bear a winged human head, a normal emblem of the soul to be found on various other old tombstones (e.g. that of a Malcolm of Poltalloch at Kilmartin, and see the illustration under ROBERTSON). But the Clan Fergus believe it to depict the *brideag*, a bat with a human face that flutters eerily at the window when a Glenshellish Fergusson is about to die, to warn him of his impending doom. This spook's name is interesting, because the Fergussons link the *brideag* to the spirit of St. Brigid (specially venerated by the Kindred of St. Columba), and thence to the pagan goddess Brigid. The present writer believes that the Pictish royal throne-name of Bruide

was given to each successive king as well as his own name, and that in pagan times it represented the male manifestation of this mighty British goddess.

Pictish stone at Dunfallandy in Atholl. The Fergussons of Dunfallandy were styled Barons Fergusson from at least 1585 until 1746, because they had local powers of life and death under the Atholl family. A cadet of this family was Finlay Fergusson of Baledmund, who in 1611 obtained a feu charter of Baledmund, which still belongs to his present descendant, the active forester James Fergusson, 11th of Baledmund.

I HOPE IN GOD

Macnachtan

MacNachtan means 'Son of Nechtan', an old Pictish royal name that also appears (doubtless through a Pictish mother) in the male line of the Cenel Loarn—the royal house of Lorn during the Dark Ages. According to Skene's old Gaelic MS. genealogies, the Macnachtans were traditionally chiefs of a cadet branch of the Cenel Loarn, of the house of Ferchar *fada*, King of Argyll (died 697). The original Nechtan from whom the present surname is taken was probably a chief (i.e. *toisech* or thane) who held an appanage in Lorn in about 1200, a very early period for a patronymic to have become established as a surname: perhaps at first it designated only 'Himself', the late chief's actual successor in each generation.

The first chief to appear on contemporary record is Malcolm MacNachtan whose son Gillechrist MacNachtan, clearly of baronial rank, gave a church at the head of Loch Fyne to Inchaffray Abbey in about 1246; Gillechrist's brothers later granting to the same abbey another church on an island in Loch Awe, in the old district of Lorn. Gillechrist MacNachtan himself received from King Alexander III in 1267 a charter of the hereditary keepership of the royal Castle of Fraoch Eilean, the 'heathery isle' in

Loch Awe. When the Scottish Crown was establishing its authority more firmly in the west highlands, Gilbert Mac[Nachtan] was one of the twelve great barons whose lands were formed by Act of Parliament in 1292 into the newly constituted Sheriffdom of Argyll.

Holding a baronial jurisdiction of life and death, the mediaeval chiefs of the clan used the typically west and central highland style of Baron MacNachtan. Their homeland was between Loch Awe and Loch Fyne,

Entrance doorway and a sculptured window at Dundarave Castle, with the initials of the then chief and his wife, and the date 1596.

Charter with seal of Gillechrist MacNachtan in 1247. His coat-of-arms may indicate a relationship—across the narrow Irish Channel—with the then powerful Scoto-Norman barons from Moray, the Bissets of the Glens of Antrim in Ireland (whose heirs, the McDonnells, are still Earls of Antrim). His brother Ath (*Aedh*) sealed with a wyvern, not on a shield, in a charter of about 1257 which mentions a third MacNachtan brother, Sir Gilbert.

and especially in Glenshira. But through debt, they lost the last of their old lands by the eighteenth century; and the present chief, Sir Antony Macnaghten, 10th Baronet, belongs to a branch which had emigrated in about 1580 to the Glens of Antrim in Ireland. However, Donald Mac-Nachtan (son of 'an unmarried nobleman' of the family by a bishop's sister) was Bishop of Dunkeld (1436–1439) and thereafter the clan also appear in Perthshire: by 1480 another Donald MacNachtan held the lands since called Balmacnaughton on Loch Tayside, where a branch of the Macnaughtons have continued into modern times.

Fraoch Eilean, the 'Heathery Isle', the original stronghold of the MacNachtan chiefs on Loch Awe. It is the island on the left.

McCorquodale

The Barons of Argyll were those local chiefs and chieftains, of mixed Norse and Irish-Gaelic or even in some cases of ancient British stock, who held lands (whether of King or Bishop or Earl) ' with pit and gallows ', and thus had the ' high justice ' with powers of imprisonment and death within their territories. The West Coast was brought firmly under the Scottish Crown during the thirteenth century, and the ' Barons of all Argyll and the Foreigners' Isles' appear in the record of the Parliament held at St. Andrews in 1309.

The surname McCorquodale (still spelt Mactorquedil by a scribe of 1430) means Son of Thorketill, itself an old Norse pagan name meaning ' Cauldron of the Thunder Spirit '. From the earliest local records the family held sway over many thousands of wild mountainous acres to the west of Lochawe, exercising their baronial jurisdiction from Phantelane, the ' White Island '. Eilean-a-Bharain was the ' Baron's Island ' in Loch Tromlie. The loch has been much reduced by drainage, and the site of their ruined castle is no longer always an island.

Buchanan of Auchmar, writing before 1723 about ' MacOrquodaill of Faint Islands ', says of Baron McCorquodale's then much diminished estate: ' he is accounted one of the most ancient gentlemen, of his own station, in that shire, or probably of any other in this kingdom '. In the highland manner (like the Barons MacNachtan, Reid, Fergusson, etc.) they were more usually styled Barons McCorquodale than Lairds of Phantelane; and as chiefs of their baronial Name their Gaelic designation was *Mac-a-Bharain*, ' Son of the Baron '.

Eoghan or Euan McCorquodale of Phantelane was one of the Barons in Argyll at the close of the fourteenth century. In 1428 his son Euan, the next chief, was summoned as *baro de makcorkidal* together with the Campbell chief to appear before the King or his Council, bringing their muniments, in connection with their territorial claims in Argyll against Sir John Scrymgeour, Constable of Dundee and laird of Glassary. The Baron's claim was to Ederline, perhaps because of some descent from Iain, son of Euan (brother of the Scrymgeours' female-line ancestor Gillascop mac Gilchrist of Glassary, one of the Barons of Argyll in 1240, and a descendant of the O'Neill royal house of Ireland) whose heirs had apparently forfeited Ederline before it was granted to the Constable's then ancestor in 1346. Certainly Euan was a name much favoured by the successive McCorquodales. The dispute was ended in 1436 by the marriage of the Constable of Dundee's daughter to Malcolm McCorquodale of Phantelane, the next Baron, and Ederline was inherited by the McCorquodales.

This chief was called ' our well loved cousin ' by Colin Campbell, Earl

The present descendant of the mediaeval Barons McCorquodale of Phantelane: Brigadier Norman McCorquodale, M.C., late Royal Scots Greys, a member of the Queen's Body Guard for Scotland (the Royal Company of Archers). The elder brother of Lord McCorquodale of Newton, he was mentioned in despatches in the Second World War. The brigadier is wearing a smoking-jacket of the McCorquodale tartan.

Loch Tromlie in the barony of Phantelane, with the overgrown ruins of the island castle of the McCorquodale chiefs. In 1645 this castle was sacked by Alasdair *Colkitto*, as the then Baron McCorquodale was a Covenanter.

of Argyll, in a deed of 1470. His own seal accompanies that of the earl, a shield charged with *a stag's head* surrounded by the legend s MALCOLMI DNI DE FAUNTELAN: seal of Malcolm laird of Phantelane. His successor, Euan McCorquodale of Phantelane who was of age in 1470 and died in 1509, is said to have attempted to wed the wife of the Knight of Glenorchy who was away on a seven year's pilgrimage to Rome and the Holy Places. But it seems more likely to have been the ploy of an earlier Baron McCorquodale, as the Knight must be Sir Colin Campbell, laird of Glenorchy from 1432 to 1475, who went thrice to Rome and fought against the Turks as a Knight of St. John in Rhodes. The famous book of mediaeval Gaelic poetry collected by the Dean of Lismore (1514–1551) contains verses by the clan's poetess Effric neyn Corgitill: *nighean' Thorcaidaill*.

In 1542 all their lands were incorporated by a royal charter of *novodamus* into a new free Barony. The seal of Duncan McCorquodale of Phantelane, the Baron in 1556, bore the legend ' S.duncan.mak.corkatill ' around a shield charged with *a stag trippant couped halfway paleways*. He was dead by 1612, when his younger sons Iain and Lachlan McCorquodale were charged before the Privy Council with befriending the MacGregors in many crimes and with having stolen a brown mare from ' umquhile Duncane McCorcodell of Phantelands '. Duncan, the next Baron McCorquodale, apparently had sons by two separate unions, and their legitimacy was evidently hotly disputed between the two litters. As a result, the clan's history during the seventeenth century is rather tangled: but they supported the Campbells in the Civil Wars, and Alasdair *Colkitto* sacked their castle on Loch Tromlie in 1645. ' Duncan Mackarquodill of Phantellans ' was one of the Justices of the Peace for Argyllshire appointed by Cromwell in 1656, during the Protectorate. When Lyon Register was established in 1672, ' Duncan Macorquodaill of that Ilk ', the then baron, recorded his arms as *Argent a stag Gules attired Or, issuing from a fess wreathed of the Second and of the Third*, with the crest of *a stag standing at gaze Proper attired Gules*, and the motto VIVAT REX.

Since the death in the eighteenth century of the last Baron McCorquodale to hold the ancient clan lands around Loch Tromlie, the succession to the chiefship has not yet been clearly ascertained. But among the known descendants of the old baronial family today are Raine McCorquodale, Countess of Dartmouth (daughter of the novelist Barbara Cartland) and her cousin the Right Honble. Malcolm McCorquodale, who in 1955 was created Lord McCorquodale of Newton.

Livingstone

The great Lowland house of Livingston, called after their lands of Leving's-ton in West Lothian, and afterwards Earls of Linlithgow and Callendar, held the thanage of Callendar in the highland Trossachs (as well as Callendar by Falkirk) from the fourteenth until the eighteenth centuries. There they kept up the old Beltane fires, despite the local ministers. They had married the heiress of the ancient Thanes of Callendar, who were connected with the old dynastic Earls of the Lennox and who had been forfeited by King David II. Their heir female is today the Countess of Erroll, and their heir male probably one of the Livingstons of Livingston Manor in New York State of America.

But a small sacred Highland clan in the Argyllshire district of Lorn and especially in Appin have long tended to English as ' Livingstone ' their Gaelic name of Macleay, i.e. *Mac Dhunnshleibhe* or ' Son of Dunsleve '. The late Duke of Argyll, a great Gaelic genealogist, wrote of the Macleays or M^conleas that ' there is little doubt that their eponymic ancestor was Dunsleve, the son of Aedh Alain ', who belonged to that group of clans in the south of Argyllshire—including the Maclachlans, Lamonts, McEwens, MacSwenes and MacNeills—descended from the marriage of a local

Alastair Livingstone, Baron of the Bachuil, holding the Pastoral Staff of St. Moluag, with his son Niall and three daughters. Taken at Bachuil on the Isle of Lismore. In the background is *Cnoc Aingeil*: the ' Fire Knoll ' that gave their slogan to the Macleays or Livingstones. It appears to be an ancient artificial mound, perhaps connected with fire-worship, since Lismore was a sacred island and Christian holy places were usually sited on pagan religious sites. The Barons of the Bachuil were known as *muinntir a chnuic*, the people of the knoll, but this more probably alludes to the *Cnoc a Bhreith*, the ' Judgement Knoll ': for in Scotland in the old days the style of baron necessarily implied powers of life and death, and so the Macleays once upon a time long ago had presumably been the temporal arm locally of the ecclesiastics who originally held the island. The old Gallows Hill or *Tom a Chrochaidh* is near the Church.

Scottish princess to the Irish prince Anrothan, son of Aodh O'Neill, King of the North of Ireland (1030–1033). This group centred on Cowall, where McLea of Linsaig in the parish of Kilfinnan seems to have been the principal of the Name: ' the designation of the Family being Barron McLea, and it was one of the Barrons of Lindsaig the last that was buried within the Kirk of Kilfinan under their own seat within the Kirk there.' But Macleays spread southwards to Kintyre and northwards to Appin.

Before 1309, James mac Dunsleph held lands in Kintyre for his forinsec service to King Robert Bruce of a fully manned and victualled ship of twenty-six oars. Dunslaue McNeill joined in a Macdonleavie bond in 1518. In Benderloch, John McDunslaif of Achnacre appears in 1557: and the Macleays of Achnacree are said to have been almost annihilated supporting the MacDougalls of Lorn against the Campbells of Inverawe in a clan battle about the reign of King James VI. Ordinarily, of course, men did not always use their clan surname, but only the names of their father and grandfather. Thus among the MacDougall garrison at Dunavertie, treacherously massacred (after surrender) in 1647 by the Covenanters— egged on by their reverend minister's Old Testament blood-lust to ' smite the Amalekites '—there were three Macleays: Iain M^{c}ein V^{c}ein dui alias M^{c}onlea (John son of John son of Black John), Dunsla M^{c}ein V^{c}onlea (Dunsleve son of John) and his brother Iain Mconlea.

At this difficult period, when it was becoming convenient for Highlanders to have fixed surnames, often that of a powerful lord taken for protection, the ruler of Lismore was James Livingston of Skirling, of the branch of the Lowland Livingstons who became Earls of Newburgh. He was baron of Biel, also Keeper of the Privy Purse to King Charles I, who in 1641 granted him a nineteen-year lease of the lands and teinds of the bishoprics of Argyll and the Isles, followed in 1642 by a grant of the spiritualities and temporalities of the bishoprics for life, and to his heirs for nineteen years after his death. In 1648, when the King was a prisoner in England, they both found it wise to assign the lease to the victorious Marquis of Argyll who had been present at the Dunavertie massacre.

Before 1648, however, James Livingston of Skirling apparently resided for a while at Achandun Castle on Lismore; and it was probably at this time that the Macleays adopted his surname. Since he was their then overlord, this was perfectly proper by Highland practice, and it had the advantage of being a neutral but powerful Lowland name that tactfully prevented them from having to choose otherwise between the three great Lorn surnames of Campbell, Stewart and MacDougall. So the little sacred clan of Macleays on Lismore became Livingstones. However, as they spell it with an ' e ', it is not so much Leving's Town as Living Stone: which makes at least a modern though artificial difference.

The present head of this sanctified clan is Alastair Livingstone of Bachuil, whose Arms and insignia as ' *Baron of the Bachuil* in the isle of Lismore, lordship of Lorne and county of Argyll, *Heritable Keeper of the Bachuil or Pastoral Staff of St. Moluag* ' are recorded in Lyon Register. The Gaelic *bachuil* (from Latin *baculum*) was a crozier or pastoral staff, and many a saint's bachuil was held by hereditary keepers (usually called dewars) in mediaeval Scotland: but only two or three have survived the Reformation.

Saint Lughaidh, ' the founder of one hundred monasteries ', better known by his pet name of Moluag, was ' the pure and brilliant, the gracious and decorous '. An Irish Pict of high birth, from the monastery of Bangor, he founded an abbey on the isle of Lismore off the coast of what is now Appin (the *abthania* or ' abbey-lands ' of Lismore), to be the headquarters of his missionary journeys to the Northern Picts. He died in Pictland on 25 June 592. His name meant ' Gleaming Light ' and in this year there was a great eclipse of the sun.

St. Moluag's bachuil was eventually entrusted to a line of hereditary dewars, ancestors of these Macleays or Livingstones, who held a tiny ecclesiastical barony on the Isle of Lismore (where there is a *Tigh-nan-deora* or ' dewar's house '), as the bachuil's hereditary guardians on behalf of the lords of Lorn: now Dukes of Argyll. An ecclesiastic of the clan is said to have founded the castle of Achandun on Lismore, long the bishops' residence. In view of the quasi-sacerdotal character both of dewars and of heralds, it may be noted that the present Baron of the Bachuil's ancestor, Iain McMolmore Vic Kevir (i.e. John son of Maolmoire son of Ivar), Heritable Keeper of the Bachuil in 1544, is also described as *signifer* (normally 'pursuivant', but in this case perhaps literally 'ensign-bearer') to Archibald, Earl of Argyll. Of course, he may also have been one of Argyll's officers-of-arms as well, possibly called Lorne Pursuivant. The charter of 1544 confirming him in his lands on Lismore 'with the keeping of the great staff of the blessed Moloc, as freely as the father, grandfather and great-grandfather and other predecessors of the said Iain, held the lands of our predecessors, Lords of Lorn, with the keeping of the said staff', is especially interesting, as it was granted by *Mac Chailein Mor*'s heir while staying with Lachlan Maclachlan of that Ilk at Castle Lachlan, and Iain MacDougall of Dunollie (Chief of the old royal Clan Dougall of Lorn) was a witness to it. The lands included half of Peynabachuile (Penny-Bachuil).

Dewars were usually heads of cadet branches of the abbatial family. Celtic abbey-lands were held either by the *fine erluma*, the kin of the founder saint, or else by the *fine grin*, the kin of the dynastic granter of the land. As Picts, St. Moluag's kindred would in any case have been reckoned in the female line, and may well have been related in the male line to the kin of the granter, who was presumably the King of Lorn. Certainly the abbey-lands belonged in later times to the local kings who became the lords of Lorn, and whose representative is the Duke of Argyll. In the fifteenth century, a female-line branch of this dynastic stock retained these lands and became the Stewarts of Appin, which means 'abbey-lands'. The Macleays or Livingstones of Bachuil adhered to the Stewarts of Appin locally, and as keepers of the bachuil to Argyll as lord of Lorn.

Far away in Easter Ross, another group of Macleays or 'Sons of Dunsleve' appear in Strathconan before the close of the Middle Ages. But it may be no coincidence that Strathconan neighbours on Strathpeffer, where St. Moluag founded another abbey.

The full history of the Macleays or Livingstones in Lismore has yet to be traced. But there is the example of Luss in the Lennox, where the hereditary dewar of St. Kessog's *bachuil* was at least on occasion Dean of the Lennox. So it may be significant that in 1251 the then Dean of Lismore was named Gillemeluoc or 'Devotee of St. Moluag'. In his *Lismore in Alba*, the Rev. Ian Carmichael gives an interesting account of the sixteenth-century Baron of the Bachuil's quarrel with Maclean of Duart. The family spread throughout the isles and mainland around Lismore. One of these Macdonleavys or Macleays fell with the Stewarts of Appin fighting for the Jacobite cause at Culloden in 1746. His son farmed on the isle of Ulva, on the other side of Mull from Lismore, and was great-grandfather of the famous missionary, Stanley's 'Dr. Livingstone, I presume?'.

Dr. David Livingstone travelled through Africa with his walking stick (a nineteenth century *bachuil*). He put Darkest Africa on the map, and brought civilisation to the jungle. After him, the town of Livingstone in Nyasaland (now Malawi) was named. But Livingstone Avenue, in the capital of new Zambia, has recently been renamed in 'honour' of the two convicted murderers of a woman whom they had killed publicly in front of her family. Dr. Livingstone, most famous of all the Macleays and a missionary like St. Moluag, was buried in 1874 under a black slab in the nave of Westminster Abbey.

In more modern times, Sir Joseph Maclay was a Member of the War Cabinet as Minister of Shipping during the First World War, and was created 1st Lord Maclay in 1922. His younger son, the Right Honble. John Maclay, was Secretary of State for Scotland (1957-1962) and has now himself been created Viscount Muirshiel.

Bell shrine from Kilmichael Glassary, containing 'a small iron bell, probably that of St. Moluag of Lismore, which he made miraculously, according to the ecclesiastical tradition, with a bundle of rushes for fuel, the smith having declined to make him a bell because he had no coals. The Aberdeen Breviary relates that this bell was held in high honour in the Church of Lismore, which afterwards became the Cathedral of the diocese, of which Glassary was one of the rural deaneries. The shrine . . . has a round hole pierced in the bottom, sufficient to allow the insertion of a finger to touch the bell, an indication that the relic has been used . . . to swear oaths upon, so that there is no improbability in its having been brought to the deanery for that purpose.'

Linlithgow Palace, of which the Hereditary Keepers were the Livingstons, Earls of Linlithgow and Callendar, until the last earl was forfeited as a Jacobite in the 1715 Rising. Here Mary Queen of Scots was born. Her granddaughter, the 'Winter Queen', was fostered here by the then Livingston earl and his countess (sister of the Earl of Erroll), as fosterage continued as late as the reign of King James VI. It was from a kinsman of these Livingston earls that the Highland Livingstones took their new surname in substitution for Macleay.

IN ARDUA TENDIT

MacCallum

The name MacCallum means 'Son of Columba', and is often Englished as Malcolm, from the Gaelic personal name *Maol Chaluim* or 'Devotee of Saint Columba'. We are told that in 1414 the Campbell chief made Ranald MacCallum of Corbarron hereditary Constable of Craignish Castle, and that the last of these MacCallums left Corbarron to Zachary Mac-Callum, 5th of Poltalloch, who died in about 1688.

The chiefs of the clan were called MacCallum of Poltalloch from the time of 'Donald McGillespie vich O'Challum' (Donald son of Archibald son of the descendant of Calum) who had a charter of Poltalloch from Duncan Campbell of Duntrune in 1562—until their name was changed 'for aesthetic reasons' by Alexander Malcolm, 9th of Poltalloch 1758–1787, who probably died a centenarian. The MacCallums or Malcolms of Poltalloch were interrelated with the local dynastic Campbells, and eventually acquired Duntrune Castle itself.

John Malcolm, 15th of Poltalloch, was made a peer as Lord Malcolm of Poltalloch in 1896, having distinguished himself as M.P. for Argyll. He had also earned the V.D. and been awarded the C.B. while in command of the local volunteer battalion of the Argyll and Sutherland Highlanders. Unfortunately, he died childless and the peerage became extinct.

His nephew, Sir Ian Zachary Malcolm, 17th of Poltalloch, K.C.M.G., was one of the Directors of the Suez Canal Company, and married the daughter of the famous Edwardian beauty, Mrs. Langtry, 'the Jersey Lily'. Their son, Colonel George Malcolm of Poltalloch, the present chief, has abandoned the enormous mansion house of Poltalloch, and lives nearby in the charming old castle of Duntrune.

Duntrune Castle. Note the mediaeval lavatory chute on the facing corner of the tower. This castle, with its beautiful gardens, is the home of the present chief, Colonel George Malcolm of Poltalloch, Vice-Lieutenant of Argyll, the original organiser of the annual Edinburgh Tattoo, now a national institution and the martial culmination of each Edinburgh Festival.

Campbell

The crest of the Campbell chiefs is a boar's head. The boar was originally an emblem of the Mother Goddess, like the Galley, and may have come to the Campbells when they inherited Lorne through heiresses who descended from the Old Norse sea-kings of the House of the spirit Freya. But a boar is carved on the ancient rock of Dunadd, in the inauguration place of the early Kings of Argyll. And the Chief of Clan Campbell is also Duke of Argyll and Marquis of Lorne ultimately because of his royal descent in the female line from the ancient Kings of Argyll.

The Kingdom of Argyll was colonised by Gaels from Ireland by the fifth century, and came to be known as *Earr a' Ghaideal* (pronounced 'Argyll') or the Border of the Gaels. For a long time it formed part of the little Irish kingdom of Dalriada, which straddled the narrow channel between Antrim and the Mull of Kintyre, where the Atlantic meets the Irish Sea. Even after Argyll and Lorne, the adjoining sub-kingdom called after the Dalriadic king Lorn, became completely separated from Ireland, the population continued to speak Gaelic and to be called 'Scots' (which

The hawthorn tree in the vault at Cawdor Castle: more than half a thousand years old. In 1454 the then Thane of Cawdor decided to build a new stronghold. He dreamt that he should fasten a coffer of gold on the back of a donkey, and build his castle wherever the ass first stopped to rest. The donkey halted under the hawthorn tree, around which Cawdor Castle was therefore built.

Innischonaill Castle, on an island in Loch Awe. This was the original stronghold of the Campbell chiefs, as Barons of Lochawe, from the thirteenth century. But after they became Earls of Argyll and moved from the freshwater of Loch Awe to Inveraray on the seawater of Loch Fyne, Innischonaill was maintained by them as the stark State Prison for their Regality. In about 1484 the infant Donald *Dubh*, rightful heir to the Lordship of the Isles, was kidnapped from Islay and sent here for safe-keeping by his maternal grandfather Colin Campbell, 1st Earl of Argyll. The poor child was kept a prisoner in the island castle until he was nineteen; when, in 1503, a picked commando of Glencoe Macdonalds made their way unobserved through the heart of the Campbell country, rowed silently across to the island, rushed the castle, and freed their High Chief, who had never known any other life than prison. He was at once proclaimed King of the Isles, and the Hebrides rose in his support. But by 1506 the Rising had been suppressed by the Government, and poor Donald *Dubh* was warded in Edinburgh Castle for another thirty-eight years of imprisonment, until he escaped again in 1543. The Hebrides immediately rose once more in his support, and entered into a treaty with King Henry VIII of England, Donald *Dubh* acting (the spelling has been modernised for convenience) 'with advice and consent of our Barons and Council of the Isles: that is to say Hector Maclean, Lord of Duart; John mac Alasdair, Captain of Clanranald; Rorie MacLeod of Lewis; Alexander MacLeod of Dunvegan; Murdoch MacLaine of Lochbuie; Angus MacDonell, brother german to James MacDonell [i.e. Islay]; Allan Maclean of Torloisk, brother german to the Lord Maclean; Archibald Macdonald, Captain of Clan Uisdean [i.e. Sleat]; Alexander MacIain of Ardnamurchan; John Maclean of Coll; Gilleonan Macneil of Barra; Ewen Mackinnon of Strathairdale; John Macquarie of Ulva; John Maclean of Ardgour; Alexander Ranaldson of Glengarry; Angus Ranaldson of Knoydart; Donald Maclean of Kingairloch': almost all the Hebridean chiefs and chieftains, united in a last effort to restore their ancient Home Rule. It is interesting to reflect that they were really acting out of loyalty, and love of their national way of life—for of course each individual chief was personally far more powerful and independent under distant Edinburgh rule than under the immediate control of a Lord of the Isles, who could be no absentee from everyday local administration. However, although the English sent the exiled Earl of Lennox with supplies to support them, the Rising failed, and the gallantly tenacious Donald *Dubh* died after 'a fever of five nights' in Ireland, where Lennox saw to it that this last white hope of the Hebrides had the state funeral due to him as *Macdonald* himself. He had less than five years liberty in a lifetime of over sixty years, but had made his mark on history whenever he got the least chance. It had been a sort of Jacobite Cause, two hundred years before the '45. Thenceforward, Campbell rule of the West Coast inched forward remorselessly, using statecraft, legal cunning and moral courage to combine the Parchment with the Sword.

The fortified garden wall at Cawdor Castle, with a small bastion incorporated in it, loopholed for musketry defence against Fraser, Cameron or Clan Chattan marauders.

Cawdor Castle, with its great mediaeval tower built by the then Thane of Cawdor in the fifteenth century. It is the only privately inhabited castle in Scotland with its old drawbridge.

Campbells have always been noted for their moral courage (ignoring the opinion of the world, whether it be to risk death on the scaffold for what they believe a worthy Cause, or to order a massacre of those they consider superfluous), but even for them, the martial intrepidity of the Cawdor Campbells is remarkable. Decorations for valour have only been awarded to the British armed forces for little over a century, and except for the Victoria Cross itself, there was no such decoration until nearly the beginning of this century. Yet, in the last hundred years, out of only about fifty male descendants of the Campbell thanes of Cawdor who were of military age in time of war (and this figure includes clergy, politicians and other non-combatants) they have been awarded no less than twelve mentions in despatches, three brevets, three French *Croix de Guerre* (one with Palm and Star), the Legion of Honour four times, one A.F.C., one D.F.C., the M.C. twice, the D.S.O. sixteen times, and above all, three Victoria Crosses. It would be amazing if anything approaching these figures for steadfast gallantry ever applied to the first fifty people stopped in any street in Britain.

Sir Hugh Campbell, Thane of Cawdor (1642–1716), built most of the additions to the Tower. He also set up an elaborately-carved fireplace to commemorate the marriage in 1510 of Muriel of Cawdor, posthumous daughter and heiress of Iain, Thane of Cawdor, to Sir John Campbell, younger son of the 2nd Earl of Argyll. Having obtained a grant of the child's wardship and marriage from the Crown, Argyll had sent sixty clansmen under Campbell of Inverliver in 1499 to kidnap the four-year-old infant from her family. There are grisly tales of her mother (a Rose of Kilravock) branding her with a red-hot key and of her nurse biting off the joint of one little finger, as recognition marks. Inverliver's sons are said to have dressed up a corn-stook as the child, and lost their lives defending it from the pursuers while the main party got away with the tiny heiress. When it was suggested that the child might die, and all the Campbell loss of life be wasted, the firm reply was that Muriel of Cawdor would never die as long as there was a red-headed lass on the banks of Loch Fyne (or as some have it, Loch Awe).

in those days meant 'Irishmen'). They continued, too, to be ruled by Kings of Argyll or Lorne who sprang from the ancient Dalriadic royal house: traced back to the pagan god-king Conaire Mor of the Érainn. Professor O'Rahilly, in his *Early Irish History & Mythology* (Dublin 1957) regards the Dalriadic royal family as being *Fir Bolg*, an offshoot of the Belgae from the Continent (after whom Belgium is named) who settled in Ireland during the Iron Age, and whose kings derived themselves from the ancient Celtic god-spirit of lightning, Bolg or Bulga. He adds that 'the impairment of their power' (in the North of Ireland, by the Ui Néill conquests during the fifth century) 'was doubtless one of the reasons why a section of the Dál Riata crossed the sea and colonised Argyll'.

Sometimes the Kings of Argyll were independent, but more often they reigned as under-kings acknowledging the paramountcy of their kinsmen, the Picto-Scottish high-kings at Scone. By the eleventh century, the local throne of Argyll and Lorne appears to have already passed through the female line. Then in 1140 Somerled, the *regulus* or under-king of Argyll, greatly increased his power by marriage to the Hebridean king Olaf Morsel's daughter; and his descendants tended to prefer the Norse dynastic Galley to the Dalriadic Scottish dynastic Lyon as their family emblem.

Somerled's son, King Dougall, held Argyll and Lorne and founded the great Clan Dougall. In the thirteenth century the King of Scots (now ruling almost the whole of modern Scotland) brought the local dynasty under his power and made Argyll a sheriffdom, but the Clan Dougall of Argyll, lords of Lorne, continued to hold their former kingdom as a lordship under him. By 1407 the lordship of Lorne had passed through MacDougall co-heiresses (and a family arrangement) to the Stewarts, and three generations later a Stewart co-heiress married Colin Campbell, Earl of Argyll, who secured Lorne by another family arrangement (backed with cash and a bit of force). Since then the Campbells have quartered the Galley in their coat-of-arms.

The name of Campbell is thought to derive from some ancestor's Gaelic nickname of *Cam-beul*, ' Crooked-Mouth '. The Clan Campbell are known in Gaelic as the *Clann ua Duibhne*, and they descended from Duncan mac Duibhne, a chieftain by Lochawe who appears to have lived about the beginning of the thirteenth century and who is referred to in a Campbell confirmation charter of the following century. Some say he was of the Siol Diarmaid, descended from the Fingalian hero who slew the fierce wild boar at Ben an Tuirc in Kintyre and died from standing barefoot on its poisoned bristles: Diarmaid, significantly son of Fergus *Cerr-bel*, ' Wry-Mouth '.

But other old Gaelic MSS. genealogies represent the Campbells' pre-surname forefather as marrying the Ua Duibhne heiress in the thirteenth century and himself as descending (through many omitted generations) from the British legendary hero-king Arthur, son of Uther Pendragon. Certainly the family were of high standing when they first appear, and had an old connection with the British name of Arthur. The MacArthurs from Loch Awe to Loch Fyne were an important mediaeval branch of the same stock, until in 1427 their chief Iain MacArthur, *princeps magnus apud suos et dux mille hominum* (' a great prince among his own people and leader of a thousand men '), was beheaded by King James I and most of his lands were forfeited. So it is not impossible that the Campbells did in fact get Lochawe (and perhaps their nickname) with an Ua Duibhne heiress, and that they were themselves connected with some branch of the Ancient British royal house of Strathclyde, who had reigned not so far away at Dunbarton throughout the Dark Ages and on into the dawn of the Middle Ages. Indeed, a Campbell knight still held lands in Dunbartonshire in 1296, and about the same time the key post in Strathclyde, as Governor of Dunbarton Castle, was also in Campbell hands.

The then Campbell of Lochawe was one of the twelve great barons whose lands were joined together to form the newly-erected Sheriffdom of Argyll in 1292, when the Scottish Crown was taking control of the province.

John Campbell, 5th Earl Cawdor, whose wife was formerly Lady Gordon-Cumming and is mother of the present Cummin chief. Lord Cawdor is also the present Thane of Cawdor; and Thanage Courts (instead of Baron Courts) were held at Cawdor up to 1747.

Lady Cawdor's bedroom.

Looking up the Firth of Lorne towards the old Connel Ferry at the mouth of Loch Etive. The double-track railway bridge is now single-track, the other track having been converted to make it also a road-bridge, as motor transport gradually edges the railways out of the Highlands. This was successively Mac-Dougall, Stewart and Campbell country, as the Lordship of Lorne passed down through successive heiresses, their husbands backed by cash and a bit of force.

Highland cattle between Cladich and Inistrynich by Loch Awe, in the heart of the northern MacArthur country.

Glenmoriston, held by the Grants of Glenmoriston. Iain *Mor* Grant, first chieftain of Glenmoriston (died 1548), was a natural son of Iain Grant of Freuchie, Chief of Clan Grant, who already held Glenmoriston in 1488. Here the faithful 'Seven Men of Glenmoriston' sheltered Prince Charles Edward for a week when they were all in hiding after Culloden, calling him Dougall MacGillonie, and initiating him into the life of their outlaw band.

He was called Colin, and it is from this Sir Colin Campbell of Lochawe (afterwards slain in a private battle) that the present Campbell chief, the Duke of Argyll, takes his famous Gaelic title of *Mac Chailein Mor*, ' the Great Son of Colin ': as opposed to that of the greatest of Campbell younger-branch chieftains head of the Glenorchy branch and Earl of Breadalbane, who is called in Gaelic *Mac Chailein mhic Dhonnachaidh*, ' the Son of Colin Duncan's-Son '.

The Campbells of Lochawe originally lived on the island castle at Innischonaill in Loch Awe. They were distinguished by their loyalty to King Robert Bruce, whose sister married their then Chief, during the Scottish War of Independence. Throughout the Middle Ages they continued in their policy of loyalty to the Crown. When they moved from Loch Awe and the 1st Earl of Argyll founded the burgh of Inveraray by Loch Fyne in 1474, they continued this policy on a grander scale. For the move of their headquarters from the fresh-water of Loch Awe to the seawater of Loch Fyne opened up the whole coastline and all the Isles to their expansion at a time when the Scottish Crown was bent on overthrowing the rule of their distant Macdonald kinsmen in the Hebrides.

The Campbells also played a great part in national affairs. Colin, 1st Earl of Argyll, was Master of the Royal Household in 1464 (this office eventually became hereditary in the family, and is still held by the present Duke of Argyll), served as joint Ambassador to France, and became Lord Chancellor of Scotland. Archibald, 2nd Earl, was slain while commanding

Inveraray Castle, home of the present Ian Campbell, 11th Duke of Argyll and 25th *Mac Chailein Mor*, was built from 1746 to replace the older castle nearby. Here lived Queen Victoria's daughter, Princess Louise (sister of the German Empress), as Duchess of Argyll.

his highlanders against the English at the battle of Flodden. Colin, 3rd Earl, held the Border against England as Lord Warden of the Marches, and in 1528 was made Lord Justice General of Scotland (which office also became for a long time hereditary in the family, and greatly increased their power). Archibald, 4th Earl, distinguished himself against the English at the battle of Pinkie. Archibald, 5th Earl, afterwards Lord Chancellor, unfortunately was attacked by a swooning fit while acting as Mary Queen of Scots's general against her enemies at Langside: the Countess of Argyll was herself Queen Mary's natural half-sister. Colin, 6th Earl, was also Lord Chancellor. Archibald the Grim, 7th Earl (who was nearly poisoned by his heir), was defeated by the Catholic rebel Earls of Erroll and Huntly in 1594 at the battle of Glenlivat, where he was commanding the Government forces against them; but afterwards became a Catholic himself and entered the Spanish king's service.

But above all, the successive Earls of Argyll supported the Government and acted as its agents in the long struggle to bring the whole Western highlands and islands under its writ, just as the Gordon Earls and Marquises of Huntly normally acted for the Government in the Eastern highlands. Also, *Mac Chailein Mor* was almost invariably as canny as he was brave. The Earls never forgot they were also Chiefs, and were careful to look after

Kilchurn Castle on Loch Awe, dominating Glen Orchy, the original stronghold of the expanding Campbells of Glenorchy, later Earls and Marquesses of Breadalbane. In 1900 Gavin Campbell, Marquess of Breadalbane, Knight of the Garter, *Mac Chailein mhic Dhonnachaidh*, could ride a hundred miles in a straight line from east to west without leaving his own land. (*See also p. 30.*)

the interests of their clansmen. They took care to secure legal titles to lands into which the Clan Campbell was expanding. Sometimes they obtained Crown charters of forfeited lands, as when Earl Archibald the Grim got a grant of Kintyre after the Government had unjustly taken that district from the persecuted Macdonalds of Islay. Sometimes they carried off heiresses by force and married them to their own sons, as when the Thane of Cawdor's daughter was seized for the 2nd Earl's younger son, Sir John, ancestor of the present Earl Cawdor. Sometimes they bought up other chiefs' or chieftains' debts and mortgages, and then used their

The modern home of the Captain of Dunstaffnage, replacing the older house that was burnt some years ago.

Dunstaffnage Castle, kept for the Dukes of Argyll by a branch of the Campbells whose chieftain bears the hereditary title of 'The Captain of Dunstaffnage' and is called in Gaelic *Mac Aonghais an Duin*. The 1st Captain was a great-uncle of the 1st Earl of Argyll in the fifteenth century. The present 21st

Captain lives in a house nearby, but still has to sleep from time to time in a special flat at the top of the ruined keep in order to fulfil his duties. On occasions such as the Oban Ball, he wears over his lace *jabot* a key, insignia of his office as castellan.

own overwhelming power in the Argyllshire law courts to obtain a legal decree giving them possession, as when they overthrew the Macleans of Duart for a while.

But always they had the courage, the ability and the numerical strength to back up their legally-acquired rights with the sword. Only when they came up against a power equal to their own, that of the Earls or Dukes of Atholl to the east, was their expansion brought up short after a series of wars, mostly cloaked as national politics. The physical courage of the Campbells has brought them much glory: the Cawdor Campbell branch alone have won three Victoria Crosses. But their moral courage sometimes led them into acts of great brutality, as when they massacred the Lamonts, or even of treachery, as when Earl Archibald the Grim tricked the MacGregor chief to his doom. Since the Campbells were in the end the winning side, this has brought them a certain amount of romantic unpopularity: especially with the clans they had worsted. After the downfall of the Lordship of the Isles, the Earls of Argyll played off the declining Macdonalds against the rising Macleans, and then, when both were exhausted, the Campbells were ready to fill the vacuum of Hebridean power and to secure for themselves the valuable trade-routes with Ireland.

During the Civil Wars of the seventeenth century the squint-eyed Archibald, Marquis of Argyll, abandoned the traditional loyalty of his family to the Stewart kings as successors of the Bruces. He led the extremist Covenanting party that sought to impose religious control on the State, and after being defeated by Montrose, whose men ravaged Argyll, he was ultimately victorious. When the English beheaded King Charles I, the Marquis of Argyll personally crowned King Charles II at Scone, but nevertheless was beheaded himself at the Restoration for having collaborated with Cromwell. His son Archibald, 9th Earl of Argyll, first Colonel of the Scots Guards, was unfairly driven into continuing the policy of opposition to the Stewart kings, and was also executed after an unsuccessful rebellion in 1685, when the Athollmen occupied the old castle at Inveraray (later demolished when the present castle was built). Archibald, the next *Mac Chailein Mor*, came over from exile in Holland to take part in the Revolution of 1688 with William of Orange, who created him Duke of Argyll in 1701. His successors continued to play a great part in national affairs: the 2nd Duke was one of the first two Field-Marshals ever appointed in the British Army, the 5th Duke was also a Field-Marshal, the 8th Duke was a Liberal cabinet minister and the 9th Duke (who married Queen Victoria's daughter, Princess Louise) was Governor-General of Canada. Most of them were also talented Gaelic scholars.

From the Whig Revolution onwards the family had returned to their traditional policy of loyalty to the central Government, and the Dukes of Argyll had the leading role in Scotland in overthrowing the Jacobite movement. As a result, the Clan Campbell was, at the moment of the eclipse of the clans in the eighteenth century, the most powerful clan in Scotland.

Among *Mac Chailein Mor's* feudatories were the Barons MacPhunn of Dripp, who lived near Strachur. Gilneff Mcphun witnessed a Campbell sasine in 1494. Mary Queen of Scots spent a night as Argyll's guest at Dripp. Tradition has it that a MacPhunn of Dripp was hanged at Inveraray, but his wife begged for his body and managed to revive him with brandy and mother's milk as they were being rowed back across Loch Fyne, and he lived to enjoy a ripe old age. The name MacPhunn, sometimes written M'Funie, is of course a form of *Mac Gille Mhunna* or MacMunn, and is not to be confused with the old Galloway name of Maclumpha. Other feudatories of *Mac Chailein Mor* were the MacTavishes of that Ilk at Dunardry in north Knapdale, who equally must not be confused with the Ross-shire name of MacVanish, which has now almost vanished from the Black Isle.

BUAIDH NO BAS

MacDougall

The Gaelic words *Dubh-Gall*, literally 'Black Foreigner', were originally applied to one of the two groups of Northmen who raided Ireland and the Hebrides (the other group got called Finn-Gall or 'White Foreigner'). In time, however, like Finngall (of the Cave), it came to be used as a Christian name in Gaelic: and is the modern Dougall or Dugald. The surname MacDougall simply means 'Son of Dougall', and the chief of the clan is called MacDougall of MacDougall.

Curiously enough, the Dubhgall from whom the clan take their name may well have been a Norse dynast in the male line, although of course the old Gaelic seanachies made him out a Gaelic dynast. Certainly he was of mixed Celtic-Norse royal blood. For he was Dougall, King in the South Isles and Lord of Lorn, the son of King Somerled (who was slain campaigning against the King of Scots in 1164) by the daughter of King Olaf of Man.

For King Somerled's probable ancestry, see MACDONALD. But the probability is that Somerled descended from an heiress of the royal house of Lorn, for he first appears as the *regulus* or sub-king of Argyll under Scotland before he also established himself as a *rex* or king in the South Isles under Norway. The MacDougall coat-of-arms quarters the Dalriadic royal *lyon* with the Hebridean royal *galley*.

Somerled's son, the King Dougall from whom the MacDougalls take their name, held after 1164 Argyll and Lorn, together with the Hebridean islands of Mull, Lismore, Kerrera, Scarba, Jura, Tiree and Coll. His sons were all three of them recognised by the high King of Norway as themselves kings in the 'West beyond the Sea'—the South Isles or Hebrides. It is significant that the Old Norse word for king is *konungr*, meaning 'son of *the* (sacral royal) kindred', and that the Norse held that kings and jarls had to be of sacred royal descent: though they would accord the style to several (if not all) of the effective members of a royal family within the same kingdom. The son from whom the MacDougalls sprang was King Duncan mac Dugall, lord of Lorn.

At this time the principal castles of the Clan Dougall were Dunstaffnage (which afterwards passed to the Campbells) and Dunollie, still in their chief's possession. Dunollie Castle in Oban Bay is of the same proportions, style and dimensions as the castle of Bergen in Norway (badly damaged when a German munitions ship was blown up in Bergen harbour during the Second World War). For in the Middle Ages, sea communications between Oban and the Norwegian Court far away in Norway were easier than were land communications between Oban and the Scottish Court bogged down far beyond the mountains, at Scone or Dunfermline. It was not then so odd as it now seems that Mull, for instance, was part of Norway and not of Scotland. Indeed, the MacDougall possessions in the Hebrides formed part of the Norwegian Archbishopric of Trondheim until after 1266.

The 3rd MacDougall chief was Eoghan or Ewen of Argyll, King in the Hebrides and Lord of Lorn, 'the most prominent Highlander in Scotland in his day', who tried hard to remain loyal to both the expanding over-kingdom of Scotland and the declining over-kingdom of Norway. In 1249 Alexander II, King of Scots, died on the MacDougall island of Kerrera while on a campaign against him. In 1263 poor King Ewen MacDougall was forced to choose between the two paramountcies, and opted for Scotland with great dignity after asking the King of Norway's permission to do so and surrendering his islands back to him. When Argyll was first made into a shire in 1292, Alasdair of Argyll, lord of Lorn, the 4th MacDougall chief, was the most powerful of the dozen great barons whose estates were formed into the sheriffdom, and was himself appointed its first Sheriff to govern it on behalf of the Crown.

Alasdair of Argyll's seal in 1296 bears the Hebridean royal *galley* with dragon heads at stern and prow and a cross at the mast-head, unconsciously summing-up the superimposition of Christian heraldry on the very ancient symbolism of pagan times. His Norse connections were still very close, for his sister Mary was Queen of the Isle of Man. But after the death of her husband, King Magnus, the MacDougalls looked eastwards to Scotland; and her two subsequent marriages were to the Earl of Strathearn (one of the Seven Earls of Scotland) and to the Lord of Abernethy, head of the abbotly branch of the premier Clan Macduff.

Although then as now the Gaelic title of the chief was of course simply *Mac Dhùghaill*, the family themselves at that period used the surname ' of Argyll ', and the chiefs after 1263 were styled Kings no longer, but ' Lords of Lorn '. Argyll was written *Ergadia* in charter-Latin, just as for example the Christian name Gill was written *Egidia*: but it would be as absurd to refer to Gill of Argyll as *Egidia de Ergadia* as to refer to Mungo of Murray as *Quintigernus de Moravia*. Incidentally, King Ewen MacDougall's sister *was* Gill of Argyll, queen of Brian O'Neill, last King of Ireland, whose severed head was sent to London after the decisive English victory at Downpatrick in 1260.

Alasdair of Argyll, lord of Lorn, the 4th MacDougall chief, married a sister of the ' Black Cummin ', whose son the ' Red Cummin ' was slain in church by Robert Bruce, his rival claimant to the Scottish throne. The MacDougalls therefore joined in the blood-feud that followed, and threw their whole weight against King Robert Bruce, whom they nearly captured. After Bruce's triumph, the MacDougalls were forfeited, and never recovered their great island possessions. But the 7th Chief married a granddaughter of King Robert Bruce, whose son David II restored to the MacDougalls the lordship of Lorn on the mainland. Yet by 1388, after the death of Eoin MacDougall, lord of Lorn, the great lordship was carried away by his daughter to the Stewarts, who became lords of Lorn (1388–

The Pass of Brander, which was successfully forced by King Robert Bruce in 1309 against an ambush of 2,000 MacDougalls. Their leader, the chief's eldest son *Eoin Bacach* or ' Lame John ' MacDougall of Lorn, escaped in his war-galley; and in 1315 made himself for a while King of the Isle of Man; but he was eventually captured by Bruce and died a prisoner on Lochleven. The Clan Dougall never fully recovered from their defeat in the narrow Pass of Brander.

1470) and were ancestors of the Stewarts of Appin (and, in the female-line, of the Campbell dukes of Argyll and marquises of Lorne), all of whom duly quartered the *galley* in their Arms.

However, the male line of the MacDougalls was continued by the descendants of the 4th Chief's brother Duncan, who had supported Robert Bruce and had been given custody of Dunollie Castle by him. In 1451 the then Stewart lord of Lorn confirmed the MacDougall chief, Iain, in wide lands around Dunollie and Oban and in the island of Kerrera: he is surnamed 'McCowle' (i.e. MacDougall) and no longer 'of Argyll'. The later chiefs have been styled MacDougall of Dunollie or MacDougall of MacDougall.

But, in memory of the great lordship that once was theirs in the days when they were kings, MacDougall chiefs as late as the seventeenth century were sometimes referred to in official documents as MacDougall of Lorn. For a moment in 1686, after the forfeiture and execution of the Campbell chief (Earl of Argyll and Lord Lorne), it seemed as though the clan would recover its ancient territory: when Allan MacDougall, 20th of Dunollie, was granted a charter of the greater part of Lorn by King James VII. But the Campbells came about soon enough, and the next MacDougall chief nearly lost Dunollie itself when he in turn was forfeited for leading his clan as a Jacobite in the 1715 Rising, during which Dunollie Castle was besieged—but defended successfully by Lady MacDougall.

The ruins of Dunollie Castle still belong to the present chief, Coline MacDougall of MacDougall, who lives with her husband in the old family house nearby. Here in Lorn the MacDougalls have lived since long before their surname came into being. It is the old Scots custom to call an heiress the Maid of her inheritance. And so before her marriage, the present chief was quite firmly and appropriately known, not as the Maid of Dunollie, but as the Maid of Lorn.

Dunollie Castle, dominating Oban Bay in Lorn. This was the stronghold of King Dougall, who inherited it in 1164 and whose ancestors had held it from time immemorial. It still belongs to his descendants, the Mac-Dougalls of MacDougall, who live in an old family house nearby. The castle was besieged in 1646 and 1715, the MacDougalls being Royalists and Jacobites.

Cumming

The name Cumming is more properly Cummin, often spelt Comyn. It is a typical Norman nickname, taken no doubt from the herb called cummin, which the Concise Oxford English Dictionary describes as an 'umbelliferous plant like fennel, with aromatic seed'—and then proceeds to relate happily to kümmel. The three bundles of plants in the Cummin coat-of-arms, usually blazoned as *garbs* or wheatsheaves, were doubtless originally bundles of cummin.

The first Cummin to settle in Scotland was a powerful Anglo-Norman churchman, a close confidant of King David I, under whom he became Chancellor of Scotland. William Cummin the Chancellor also held the Bishopric of Durham by force (against the consent of the chapter) for some three years, but after his nephew William Cummin was killed in the dispute, he gave up the bishopric in 1144 in return for the castle and Honour of Northallerton being given to another nephew, Richard Cummin, ancestor of the Scottish clan.

Richard Cummin, lord of Northallerton, married the granddaughter and eventual heiress of King Donald III *Ban* (Shakespeare's 'Donald-bane'), the King of Scots who had been deposed and blinded in 1097. King Donald III's family seem to have been appanaged in Lochaber and Badenoch at the expense of the MacWilliams, whose progenitor King Duncan II had been slain by King Donald. After the overthrow of the MacWilliams in 1230, the Cummins became undisputed Lords of Badenoch, holding also much of Lochaber and the 'Great Glen'. Richard Cummin himself was dead by 1182, and his widow married the Earl of Atholl—by whom she was maternal grandmother of *Kelehathonin*, probably the local chief called Gillechattan whose descendants, the Clan Chattan of Lochaber and Badenoch, were long at feud over rival land claims with the Cummins.

During the thirteenth century, the Cummins became the most powerful and patriotic noble family in all Scotland. At this period, the highest rank in Scotland was that of earl, held only by the mightiest cousins of the king or by the heirs of former local kings, and there were only thirteen earldoms altogether. In 1242 Alexander Cummin was Earl of Buchan, Walter Cummin was Earl of Menteith and John Cummin was Earl of Angus, all as the result of further marriages to Celtic dynastic heiresses. So nearly a quarter of the Scottish earls were Cummins, and the Cummins themselves had come to have as much Celtic as Norman blood (which scientists now prefer to call genes). From 1270 to 1308 the Cummins also held the great military office of hereditary Constable of Scotland, whose duties included the guarding of the king's own person. A Cummin endowed the rebuilding of Glasgow Cathedral in those halcyon days.

Their chief, 'the Black Cummin', was one of the Competitors for the Crown of Scotland in 1291—claiming as heir of King Donald III. He

The ruins of Dunphail Castle, once a Cumming stronghold. Legend has it that the 'old knight' of Dunphail and his five younger sons were beheaded here by an Earl of Moray, and that their skulls were dug up accidentally in 1712 (when the castle belonged to the Dunbars) and given decent burial. The 'old knight's' eldest son, Alasdair *Ban* Cummin, is said to have been smoked out of a cave and dirked before Dunphail was captured, and his head thrown over to his father in the castle. But this tale, if true, would seem to belong to an earlier period than the present ruins.

married the sister of King John Balliol, who won the competition, and (after the much-maligned King John's forced abdication) this greatly strengthened the royal claims of his son, 'the Red Cummin'. These claims led to the downfall of the Cummins. Their rival, Robert Bruce, stabbed the Red Cummin during a conference within the precincts of a church—and believed himself to have been punished with leprosy as a result.

During the long wars that followed, King Robert destroyed the Cummins. The Red Cummin's only son, rightful Lord of Badenoch and chief of the name, was killed in action against his father's slayer on the field of Bannockburn. His heiresses carried abroad the family claim to the Scottish throne; and it is ironical to reflect that when the exiled Stuarts (heirs of Bruce) fled to refuge in France, the then heir of Balliol and of the Red Cummin was their host King Louis XIV himself: today it is the Duke of Parma. The junior co-heir of the Red Cummin, curiously enough, is the Premier Baron of England (Lord Mowbray and Stourton), who quarters the Arms of Cummin and has returned to live in Scotland.

The Buchan branch of the Cummins were also destroyed. After harrying Buchan with fire and sword, Bruce gave the Cummin castle of Slains—together with their hereditary office of Constable of Scotland—to his own friend and supporter the Hay lord of Erroll, whose grandmother had been a Cummin. As the present Lord High Constable is a woman (the Countess of Erroll) it is interesting to reflect that, had the Cummins triumphed over Bruce, their present heir as Constable of Scotland would equally have been a woman: Baroness Beaumont, whose son (Major-General the Honble. Miles Fitzalan-Howard) is also eventual heir to the premier dukedom and the office of Earl Marshal of England. However, a few Cummins survived in Buchan into modern times.

Far to the north, on the borders of Badenoch, between the Spey and the Findhorn, a branch of the Cummins continued and became a clan. Their chiefs, the Cummings of Altyre, claim descent from the Red Cummin's uncle Sir Robert Cummin, who was slain by Bruce's friends while trying to save his murdered nephew in that fatal church in 1306. They received various grants from King David II and King Robert II, and by the end of the fourteenth century were once again a power to reckon with in Moray.

Their feuds with the Shaws or Mackintoshes of Clan Chattan are remembered in many a Highland legend. There is the tale of the black bull's head, and the tradition of their damming up Loch Moy to flood out the Mackintoshes' island castle. This story could even possibly have got transferred from Loch-an-eilean castle in Rothiemurchus, which is said to have been long disputed between the two clans. But the main cause of the feud was the two clans' rival claims to Rait Castle in Strathnairn, which doubtless arose (together with the Rothiemurchus trouble) in the usual way from some family relationship between their two chiefs (or the chieftains of two of their branches) and a resulting inheritance dispute.

It may therefore not be unreasonable to suggest that these very Cummins were the brave Clan *Qwhewyl* (pronounced ' wheel ') whom the chronicler Wyntoun tells us fought the famous duel in 1396 with the Clan *ha* (usually and probably correctly identified with the Shaws or Mackintoshes of Clan Chattan). Since the Cummin chiefs had originated in the South, and now had their principal residence at Altyre in the Laigh of Moray (' where all men taken their prey ', as a later Lochiel wrote to the Laird of Grant), it may perhaps also be suggested that Wyntoun's ' Clahynnhe Qwhewyl ' should be read *Clann a' Ghaill* in its sense of ' Children of the Low country-man ': a name quite separately applied to the Makgills in Galloway and the MacGills in Jura.

The Clan Qwhewyl had the honour of being almost the first clan ever noticed *as a clan* in surviving Scottish contemporary record, when they took part four years earlier in the historic raid on Sir David Lindsay of Glenesk in Angus—made by a group of wild Highlandmen, some of whom were Roses and their adherents from Strathnairn, of which Sir David Lindsay was the then overlord. The fifteenth century *Book of Pluscarden* implies that the famous duel was connected with this raid. So it may further be suggested that, in the dispute over Rait Castle in Strathnairn, the Earl of Moray had encouraged his friends the Cummins, while Sir David Lindsay as overlord of Strathnairn had supported the Mackintoshes.

Certainly, the chroniclers tell us that the duel was specially arranged between them by the Earl of Moray and the Lindsay chief, as a means of bringing peace to the Highlands. The great duel, since known as the Battle of the Clans and immortalised by Sir Walter Scott, was hacked out horribly in a fenced enclosure, thirty men a side, armed with cross-bows— three arrows each, what archers call a ' pair '—and battle-axes, dirks and two-handed swords, in front of the King himself, and under the responsibility of the Lord High Constable, on the North Inch of Perth: the marshy ' island ' nearest to Scone that was the special place for important Trials by Combat in mediaeval Scotland.

The largest rhinoceros horns ever shot and (for obvious reasons) of great value. This trophy was slain by the famous African explorer and Big Game hunter Roualeyn Gordon Cumming (1820–1866), brother of the then Chief.

The present House of Altyre, formerly the dower house and now the home of the Chief of the Cummin clan.

The Clan Qwhewyl chieftain engaged in the combat, if Wyntoun gives the ' chifftanys twa ' in the same order as he names the clans, was either Sir Farquhar's son or else Shaw Farquhar's-son: ' Schir Ferqwharis sone ' according to the standard edition, but ' Sha Fercharson ' according to Professor Skene; and Wyntoun's continuator Bower (who reverses the two leaderships) calls him *Scheabeg* or ' Little Shaw '. Farquhar and Shaw were both favoured Clan Chattan names, but if the dispute arose because of a family row, both clans probably favoured the same Christian names. So it may not be a coincidence that the duel was fought in the lifetime of Farquhar Cummin of Altyre: indeed a later branch of the Cummins took the surname of Farquharson after a descendant of the same name. Moreover, the Irish Gaels often render John as Shane—and Farquhar Cummin of Altyre had a younger son John, a name often rendered locally as Shaw.

Farquhar's eldest son, Sir Alexander Cummin of Altyre, married the same Earl of Moray's sister in 1408. The ' Clanchewill ' still appear as such in 1594, immediately after the ' Clanchattane ' and before the ' Clanchamron ' (to which clans they clearly therefore did not belong) in the official Parliamentary list of thieving clans, which includes such other neighbours as the Grants but which very curiously omits all reference to the Cummins (if they were not the Clanchewill) despite their continuing tradition of lawlessness on the fringes of the Highlands.

As late as 1664, Robert Cumming of Altyre was summoned by the Privy Council, as chief of his clan, to find caution (security guaranteed in cash) for the good behaviour of his whole Name and Clan. The other clans had a rhyme: *fhad's bhios maide anns a' choill cha bhi Cuimeanach gun fhoill*, ' so long as there is a stick in the wood there will be treachery in a Cumming '. The Cummings prefer the form: *fhad's bhios maide anns a' choill cha bhi foill an Cuimeanach*, ' so long as there is a stick in the wood there will be no treachery in a Cumming '—but alas, it doesn't rhyme.

The chiefs have held the Barony of Altyre near Forres ever since the Middle Ages. The present chief, Sir William Gordon Cumming of Altyre (whose coat-of-arms has the *three garbs* of Cummin, gold on blue), still lives there—although he recently blew up their vast Victorian mansion and replaced it with a splendid cowshed, as all the modern conveniences of water, drainage and electricity were already connected to the site.

A combine harvester at Altyre, carrying Sir William Gordon Cumming of Altyre, 6th Baronet, present Chief of the Cummins, who in the thirteenth century were the most powerful Name in all Scotland. A former Regular officer in the Royal Scots Greys, Sir William is now a highly-mechanised farmer in the Laigh of Moray, on land which the Cummings have held against all comers since the Middle Ages.

Grant

The surname of Grant is simply from the Norman-French nickname *le Grand*, meaning 'Big'. In 1246 William le Grant was lord of a Nottinghamshire manor in right of his wife, a Bisset heiress. The Bissets also held great estates in the Aird (two-thirds of which descended eventually through heiresses to the Frasers of Lovat), and also apparently in Stratherrick, where the Grants first appear in the Highlands. Sir Laurence le Grant was Sheriff of Inverness as early as 1258. It is interesting therefore that the coat-of-arms adopted by the Grant chiefs, *three golden antique crowns* (now on red, formerly on blue), is the same as that quartered by the Frasers of Lovat for their Highland inheritance.

The Grants gradually became the ruling clan in Glenmoriston and Glenurquhart to the west of Stratherrick (which the Frasers came to dominate), and in Strathspey to its east. Their then chief, Sir Iain Grant, Sheriff of Inverness in 1434, acquired what has ever since been their principal holding in Strathspey by his marriage to Maud, daughter and heiress of Gilbert of Glencarnie. The Glencarnies were a younger branch of the Celtic dynasts who had held these Strathspey lands at the dawn of local recorded history: the Earls of Strathearn. Gilbert mac Ferteth, Earl of Strathearn ' by the Indulgence of God ' (1171–1223), held Kinveachy in the twelfth century: and today Kinveachy is the home of his descendant Nina Ogilvie Grant, Countess of Seafield—having never in its whole recorded history passed by purchase.

Until recently, however, Kinveachy was a favourite family shooting lodge and the chiefs' principal stronghold was at Castle Grant, formerly called Ballachastle or *Balachaisteal*. They were styled Grant of Freuchie

The hill of Craigellachie, gathering-place and slogan of the Clan Grant.

Scottish-born reindeer, descendants of those imported from Swedish Lappland by Mr. M. N. P. Utsi and first released in 1952 on land leased from Lt.-Colonel J. P. Grant, 15th of Rothiemurchus.

Nina Ogilvie-Grant, Countess of Seafield, in her own right, in her home at Kinveachy in the Grant country of Strathspey. The panelled room is surrounded with stag's heads. Kinveachy belonged to her ancestor Gilbert mac Ferteth, Earl of Strathearn (1171–1223), and descended through a fifteenth-century heiress to the Grants of Grant. In 1718 the future Laird of Grant inherited the original baronetcy of Colquhoun of Luss from his father-in-law (Sir Humphrey Colquhoun of Luss) and on his accession to the Grant chiefship it became the baronetcy of Grant of Grant. In 1811 Sir Lewis Grant of Grant further inherited the Ogilvie earldom of Seafield (created in 1701) from his grandmother's family; and in 1858 the 7th Earl of Seafield was made a Peer of the United Kingdom as Lord Strathspey. On the death of the 11th Earl in 1915, of wounds received in action against the Germans, he was succeeded in the earldom by his daughter, the present Countess; but the baronetcy of Grant of Grant passed to his brother, who became also 4th Lord Strathspey, and was father of the present Patrick Grant of Grant, 5th Lord Strathspey. Lady Seafield's son and heir in the Grant estates is Ian Grant, Viscount Reidhaven. (*See also pp. 113 & 129.*)

until, in the sixteenth century, they became known as the Lairds of Grant; and in 1694 their old Barony of Freuchie was erected into the Regality of Grant, while the Castletown of Freuchie became Grantown-on-Spey, replanned and rebuilt in 1766 by the then Chief as a modern burgh.

This regality was almost a semi-independent State: in which the Grant chiefs had to build prisons, appoint judges and executive officers, maintain a municipal system in the burgh, regulate weights and measures and issue brieves from their own Chancery to their bailies and other officers, enforce laws with the power of life and death, and hold a Council or petty parliament of their principal vassals, mainly the chieftains and gentlemen of the Clan Grant. This was in fact local Home Rule for the Clan Grant, as, although their chief had this 'almost royal jurisdiction', he was as bound by the customary law as was the Sovereign, and just as dependent upon the advice of his Council. Indeed, we are told that on one occasion, sometime between 1719 and 1732, the Grant Council firmly imprisoned the Young Laird of Grant (i.e. the heir) lest his generous prodigality imperil the Grant country and estates.

Although the Regality of Grant was erected as a reward for their support of William III and the Whig Cause, and although it was the Grants who retook Inverness for the Whigs after its capture by the Jacobites in 1715, the British Parliament (despite the contrary vote of a majority of the Scottish members of Parliament) broke the Treaty of Union and in 1747 abolished regalities, and thus did away with Home Rule in the Grant country. It is hard to understand why a closely-negotiated treaty should be binding and legal, whose terms can be abolished the very next day by the one of the two contracting parties who always had the majority. But the spirit of Clan Grant went on. 'Came the Grants of Rothiemurchus, ilka ane as proud as Turk is, every man a sword and dirk has': well expresses their feeling.

Latterly, the Clan Grant in war wore a more or less uniform tartan. In 1704 they were ordered to be at forty-eight hours notice to parade in tartan of red and green sett, broad-springed, and also with gun, sword and dirk: and the Grants raised to support the Government in 1715 wore 'ane livery of tartan'. In peace-time they wore, of course, whatever tartan pattern took their fancy, just as today Scots Guardsmen don't always wear Scots Guards tweed every day. This is clear from the remarkable set of ten Grant portraits (now brought from Castle Grant to Kinveachy) painted by Richard Waitt in the first quarter of the eighteenth century: in which no two tartans are alike, even when a sitter is himself wearing two different pieces of tartan. But it was in plaids of the red and green war tartan that the clansmen were gathered in 1710 for that historic occasion when the old chief, Ludovic Grant of Grant, retired in favour of his son Alexander. 'My dear Sandy,' he said in front of the whole gathering, 'I make you this day a very great present, namely the honour of commanding the Clan Grant . . . God bless you all'. In the sad times a century later, there were no infamous 'clearances' on the Grant estates, whose chiefs planned the local economy very wisely.

Probably the doyen of historians today about Highland economy and social life in the old clan days is Dr. I. F. Grant. In her concise book on 'The Clan Grant' (Edinburgh 1955), she tells us a splendid story written down by a prominent participant, her grandfather Field-Marshal Sir Patrick Grant, a cadet of wild Tullochgorm. He was only fifteen in 1820, when the Grant Chief's brother was Tory candidate for the 'Elgin Burghs'. The Whig candidate was Lord Fife's brother, Colonel Duff, and the Elgin townsfolk who supported him blockaded Grant Lodge in Elgin where the Chief and his sisters were in residence. *The Fiery Cross was promptly sent round, for the last time in Highland history*, and 800 Grant clansmen immediately rose and marched on Elgin. 'The townspeople barricading Grant Lodge fled at their coming and their Chief and Lady Anne came out to welcome and thank them. The authorities of Elgin promised that there should be no further molestation, and the men marched home without doing any damage whatever to the town'. Well is the Grant motto STAND FAST.

Mackintosh

Mackintosh, more properly Macintosh, is from the Gaelic *Mac an Toisich*, Son of the Toisech. The word *toisech*, literally 'leader' (and applied by the modern Irish to de Valera), can be translated equally as *Captain*, in the sense of Chief, or as *Thane*. 'Captain' is simply an old word for 'headman' (from Latin *caput*, a head) or 'chief'. The ancient Scottish thanages originated in the territories allotted as appanages to the principal branches of the dynastic kindred ruling in each province: though the system can be more readily studied among the better-recorded Gaels or Scots of Ireland. The thane of the land was the captain or chief of the clan: so that he may equally be found called *toisech* of the territory or *toisech* of the clan.

Different chiefs or thanes gave their style to different families called Macintosh or Tosh. Thus the Macintoshes of Tirinie in Atholl descended from the Thanes of Glentilt, themselves a branch of the royal house of MacRuari in the Isles; while the Toshes of Monzievaird in Strathearn sprang from the Thanes of Strowan, evidently a branch of the dynastic house who were Earls of Strathearn 'by the Indulgence of God'. But the principal Mackintoshes in Highland history were the Captains of Clan Chattan in Badenoch and Lochaber. The chief of this great Clan Mackintosh is known as The Mackintosh.

The Mackintosh tradition is that their ancestor was a cadet of the celebrated Clan Macduff of Fife, who married the heiress of the ancient Captains of Clan Chattan. There seems no reason to doubt the tradition—the more especially as from the rise of the Macphersons within Clan Chattan, it would have been better for Mackintosh to have claimed (what would anyway have seemed more probable) to descend from Gillechattan in the male line. Gillechattan, name-father of the Clan Chattan, may perhaps reasonably be identified with the *Kelehathonin* who was maternally cousin of the first Cummin to be lord of Badenoch (1230–1258). Badenoch borders on Strathavon and on lower Strathspey, much of which during the thirteenth century was held by the Earls of Fife, chiefs of the Clan Macduff —whose great stretch of Highland territory in that area lay on both sides of the thanage of Rothiemurchus, which the Mackintoshes later held under the bishopric of Moray and believe to have been 'their earliest possession'.

The Mackintosh himself still quarters the *red lyon on gold* of the old chiefs of the Clan Macduff on his armorial shield and on the flag that blows above Moy. And the *lyon* appears so quartered in 1481 on the earliest surviving Mackintosh seal: that of Alexander Mackintosh, Thane of Rothiemurchus, who was ancestor of the Shaws of Rothiemurchus in Strathspey and the Shaws of Tordarroch in Strathnairn, also of the Farquharsons of Invercauld on Deeside, all of whom quarter the same *red lyon on gold*. The thanage of Rothiemurchus is said to have been ceded to

Stone at Culloden, marking the site where the Mackintoshes fell and lie buried.

The present Moy Hall, home of The Mackintosh. It was built in 1957 by the late Vice-Admiral Lachlan Mackintosh of Mackintosh, C.B., D.S.O., D.S.C. (who went down with the aircraft carrier H.M.S. *Eagle* when she was sunk by the Germans in the Second World War, but was rescued), to replace the famous and vast Scots baronial Moy Hall, that was unfortunately riddled with dry rot.

The bed in which Prince Charles Edward slept at Moy as Lady Mackintosh's guest in 1746. A Government force of 1,500 men was sent to capture him, but was ambushed and put to flight by half-a-dozen of Lady Mackintosh's men. Unfortunately, Donald *Ban* MacCrimmon, paragon of pipers, was with the MacLeods in the Government forces and was killed.

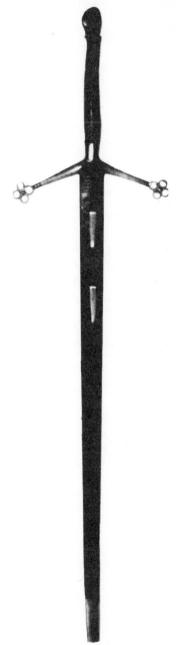

The great mediaeval two-handed claymore of the Mackintosh chiefs. Note the characteristically Highland quatrefoil ends of the cross-guard. (*See also pp. 32 & 148.*)

Alexander by his cousin, the Mackintosh chief (who was called Malcolm, a characteristically Clan Macduff name like that of his son Duncan); and in 1464 Alexander had got a feudal charter of the lands from their technical superior, the Bishop of Moray. In 1472 he strengthened his position, presumably in dealing with his expanding neighbour the Earl of Huntly, by giving a 'bond of manrent' to Huntly's son-in-law Erroll: 'me Alexander Mackintoche Thane of Rathamurcus to be ridin man to my Lorde William Erll of Eroll Lord the Hay and Constable of Scotland for all dayis of my lyffe'.

The Shaws of Rothiemurchus fell into debt by 1536, and their lands passed into the hands of the Gordons, who were then lords of Badenoch. In spite of protests by the Mackintosh chief, who as head of the whole clan offered to buy in the lands himself, the Gordons allowed Rothiemurchus to be acquired by the Grants. The Laird of Mackintosh then entreated Grant to let him save his family's most ancient possession, writing on 26 February 1568: 'And for all these causes above written, and perpetuity of friendship, alliance, and blood, the Laird of Grant whom I esteem my greatest friend, to let me have my own native country of Rothiemurchus for such sums of money as he gave for the same, or as he and I may goodly agree, and that because it is not unknown to the Laird and his wise Council that it is my native country as said is'. Entreaties proving vain, Mackintosh tried force, but also without success.

The Mackintoshes were certainly a force to be reckoned with from Strathnairn through Badenoch to Deeside before the end of the Middle Ages. Farquhar son of Shaw, who appears in the Mackintosh genealogies as their then chief, witnessed a charter of the Bishop of Moray in 1234 and held the key office of Seneschal of Badenoch under its first Cummin lord. In 1382 the king himself ordered his son and heir (who was also Earl of Atholl, immediately south of Deeside) and the Lord of Badenoch to try and stop Farquhar Mackintosh ('Farchard Mctoschy', the first time the name Mackintosh appears in a contemporary record) and his adherents

from persecuting and troubling the Bishop of Aberdeen and his men on the bishop's lands in the Forest of Birse on Deeside: these lands later formed the inheritance of the Farquharsons of Finzean, a branch of Invercauld.

Many tales have come down to us of a long feud in the fourteenth and fifteenth centuries between the Mackintosh Captains of Clan Chattan and the Cummins, both of whom claimed the lands of Meikle Geddes and the castle of Rait in Strathnairn. The present writer suggests that the Cummins were the mysterious Clan Qwhewyl who fought in the historic duel called the 'Battle of the Clans' before the King himself in 1396, and that the Mackintoshes were their rival duellists of the Clan 'ha'. *Ha* would indeed give us the Gaelic pronunciation of the genitive of the name 'Shaw', then apparently an alternative clan name for the Mackintoshes and still nowadays the surname of that branch of whom Shaw of Tordarroch (Chief of Clan Ay) is the leading chieftain. 'Shaw' itself is derived from the Old Gaelic name *Seaghdha*, meaning Happy or Lucky. That the combat concerned Rait is the more likely, in that the duel was arranged by the local earl, the Earl of Moray, together with Sir David Lindsay, who was then the overlord of Strathnairn. Whoever triumphed in 1396, the earliest document among The Mackintosh's muniments is a charter of 1442, putting or confirming 'Malcolm M'Kyntosh' (referred to in later charters as 'Lord of Moye' and 'Captain of Clanchatane') in possession of Meikle [Geddes] and Rait Castle.

From this time, the Mackintosh chiefs, as Captains of Clan Chattan, had their principal strongholds at Rait and in Strathdearn on the island in Loch Moy: where in the next century they became Barons of Moy under the bishopric of Moray. However, they were often styled 'Mackintosh of Dunachton', where they had a home, and which they did not hold of the bishopric of Moray. Since the island castle on Loch Moy was abandoned, the chiefs have had several successive houses on the shore nearby, but Moy is still The Mackintosh's home.

TOUCH NOT THE CAT BOT A GLOVE

Macpherson

Macpherson is *Mac a Phearsoin*, 'Son of the Parson'. Clerical celibacy was very late in being enforced by the Roman Catholic Church in the Highlands, where it was often popularly ignored despite the canon law, for the old Celtic Church had had married clergy and the innovation was especially unpopular among the ancient families who were accustomed to filling particular sacred offices in their own districts. Of course many people called Macpherson may take their surname from completely different parsons who lived in widely separated parts of Scotland. Thus perhaps the first to appear on record, Donald M'Inpersuyn in 1335, belonged to a family of Macphersons connected with the Argyllshire church of St. Columba in Glassary, where a later Donald Macpherson was rector in 1420, in the territory inherited from its old Celtic dynasts by the Scrymgeours, Constables of Dundee. But the principal kindred of the name of Macpherson are the famous Clan Mhuirich in Strathnairn, Strathdearn and Badenoch. Their chief is called Macpherson of Cluny—or Cluny Macpherson, to distinguish his designation from other places called Cluny held by other families.

These Macphersons belong to the great Clan Chattan, a strong confederation of some sixteen clans descended in the male or female line from a chief called Gillechattan, whom the old Gaelic genealogists trace from Ferchar the Long, King of Lorn (died 697), ancestor also of the last Kings of Moray, of which local kingdom Badenoch, Strathdearn and Strathnairn were part. Gillechattan was probably the *Kelehathonin* who appears on record in the thirteenth century and was maternally a first cousin of the Lord of Badenoch (1230–1258). The Mackintosh, 'Son of the Chief', was the chief of the whole kindred and therefore styled the Captain of Clan Chattan. The Mackintoshes claim to descend from Gillechattan through an heiress, and there are reasons to support this, though it is not impossible that in fact they descend from him in the male line. The Macphersons claim to descend from him in the male line, though again it is not impossible that they are actually a branch of the Mackintoshes. Further research may one day resolve these questions.

Professor Skene wrote of the religious office of lector in Celtic abbeys, where the offices were usually held by members of the Gaelic dynastic families, and added: 'Diarmada, the grandfather of Gillachattan, the *eponymus* of the Clan Chattan, is said in the old Irish genealogy to have been called the *Ferleighinn*, or lector. Tradition ascribes to Gillachattan the epithet of *Clerech* or Cleric, and he and his descendants the Clan Vuireach are said to have been hereditary lay parsons of Kingussie, one of whom, Duncan the son of Kenneth, appears in 1438 as Duncan parson. From him the chief of the Clan Vuireach takes his name of Macpherson.' The Macphersons themselves believe their name-father to have been this Duncan's great-grandfather Muredach, from whom they certainly derive their other name of Clan Mhuirich: 'the Children of Muredach'.

Duncan the Parson must have been a person of importance, for we are told that he was imprisoned with the Lord of the Isles himself. A generation or so later, the Macphersons first appear on record, holding lands in Strathdearn (the Mackintosh centre) and at Brin in Strathnairn. 'Bean Makinpersone', who appears from 1481 to 1508, witnessed a bond of 'Duncan Makintosche, captain of Clancattane' in 1490. In The Mackintosh's charter chest there is also a deed signed in 1534/5 by Bean's son 'Donald Makferson, wᵗ my hand on the pen' (the usual formula when a signatory could not write himself, as was common among the Scottish gentlemen of those days). His seal bears a fine *lyon rampant* and the legend s. DONALD MACFERSONE. This looks like a Mackintosh or Clan Macduff coat-of-arms: later Macpherson coats-of-arms have the *galley* normally used by the Clan Chattan (probably from some heiress in Lochaber of the

Peat-hags on the high ground in the Forest of Rothiemurchus, with a fine Scottish reindeer from the herd which is being built up by the Reindeer Company under the management of Mr. Utsi.

Eroded raised bog in the Cairngorms, the 'Blue Stone' mountains, where the Grant and Clan Chattan countries met under Gordon suzerainty.

royal house of the Isles). So it is interesting that a tradition existed among the two oldest branches of the Macphersons (Pitmean and Invereshie) that the Parson himself was a Mackintosh: in 1672 their own chieftains complained to the Privy Council that Cluny ' nayther is nor ever was Cheiffe nor did any of his predicessors claim right thairto; but upon the contrair it is notter and manifest without the least doubt that the complainers are descendit of Macintosh '.

Be that as it may, the chieftains of the Cluny branch eventually came to be recognised, both by the Crown and the clan, as the Chiefs of Clan Macpherson. They first appear in Badenoch in the sixteenth century, and came to hold the great mountainous district from Kingussie to Ben Alder and Loch Laggan: with a long stretch of the Spey. They lived for some generations at Cluny before they managed to get a charter of their lands. The overlord of Badenoch was Huntly, to whom a number of the clan, headed by ' Andrew Makfersone in Cluny ', gave a bond of manrent in 1591. Huntly formed a wily scheme for setting up Cluny Macpherson against Mackintosh, who as Captain of the whole Clan Chattan was too powerful to please Huntly. The policy was to be ' divide and rule '—as so often, the division remained long after the rule had waned and perished.

Cluny Castle, former home of the Macpherson chiefs. Built to replace the older castle burnt by the Government troops in 1746, it had to be sold for debt in 1943. Modern taxation is specially designed by paid experts to complete the work begun at Culloden: the severance of all links between the continuing past and the passing present.

The Macpherson Museum, established at Newtonmore in Badenoch by the Clan Macpherson Association. Here is Landseer's painting of ' The Young Chief's First Ride ', also notable relics of the clan, including their famous ' Black Chanter ' (which, we are told, ' fell from heaven and was caught by the piper ' of the clan, to whom it always brought victory when played in battle) and the chiefs' Green Banner or *Bratach Uaine*.

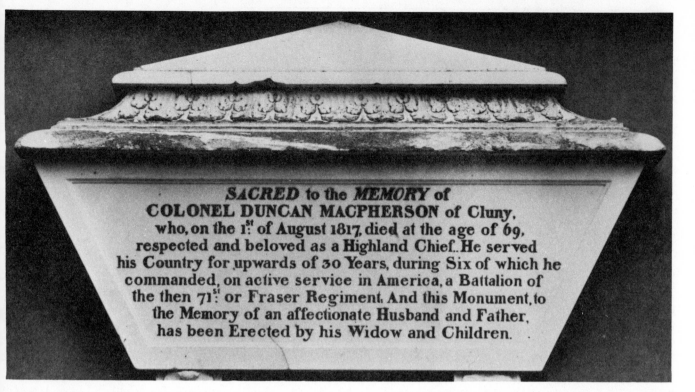

SACRED to the MEMORY of
COLONEL DUNCAN MACPHERSON of Cluny,
who, on the 1ˢᵗ of August 1817, died at the age of 69,
respected and beloved as a Highland Chief. He served
his Country for upwards of 30 Years, during Six of which he
commanded, on active service in America, a Battalion of
the then 71ˢᵗ or Fraser Regiment. And this Monument, to
the Memory of an affectionate Husband and Father,
has been Erected by his Widow and Children.

Tomb of Duncan Macpherson of Cluny (1748–1817), known as 'Duncan of the Kiln' because he was born in a corn-kiln convenient to shelter his mother while his father, the Jacobite chief, was skulking in secret in 'Cluny's Cage,' a special hideout constructed for him on the precipice of Ben Alder by the loyal Macpherson clansmen. Duncan's mother was daughter of 'the Old Fox' Simon Fraser, 11th Lord Lovat (beheaded in 1747); and so he joined the Fraser Highlanders in 1775 for the war against the revolting colonials in America. Late in life, he wrote: 'The men were . . . chiefly from the Highlands—not surprising, when I inform you there were no less than seven Chiefs in the regiment: Lovat, Lochiel, Macleod, Mackintosh, Chisolm, Lamont, and your humble servant'. But the hardy American settlers gave a good account of themselves, for Cluny Macpherson continues: 'Out of 2,200 men, only 175 men came home alive, and I got the out-pension for most of them, being at that time a Colonel in the 3rd Regiment of Guards.' This means that Cluny Macpherson saw to it that those of the survivors for whom he was responsible received their proper retired pension from the Army, but recalls the Highland distrust of Government promises, so often broken to the men.

It was suggested that as the Macphersons in Cluny claimed descent in the male line from Gillechattan, whereas the Mackintoshes claimed to have inherited the chiefship of Clan Chattan through an heiress, Cluny Macpherson ought to be regarded as rightful chief of 'the Old Clan Chattan' (a newly-invented body). This was a fairly cynical trick, as Huntly himself had only inherited the Gordon chiefship through an heiress. But the row that ensued lasted for centuries, and on several occasions disunited the Macphersons and others of the Cattanach from supporting the Mackintosh chiefs of Clan Chattan in war—although in 1688, after the last clan battle ever fought, when Mackintosh had been defeated and captured by the Macdonells of Keppoch, Cluny Macpherson brought his own clansmen up and ironically rescued Mackintosh. As late as 1744 the row was fanned anew in a bond between Cluny and Lord Lovat (whose own dicey position depended on his having overturned the heiress of his own clan), together with Lochiel, whose lands had mostly been taken by the sword from the Mackintoshes and Clan Chattan during centuries of feud. However, on a number of occasions from 1609 onwards the Cluny of the time acknowledged Mackintosh as his 'Captain and Chief', and the matter was officially settled in Mackintosh's favour in 1672 by the Privy Council and the Lord Lyon King of Arms.

The exploits of Cluny Macpherson and his clansmen in the '45 Rising are well known, and how they loyally hid him for nine long years in a specially designed cave in his own country. His cousin William Macpherson, 'the Purser' of the clan, was killed fighting for the Jacobite Cause at Falkirk in 1746, and was ancestor of the present chief, whose home is Newton Castle at Blairgowrie and who became Cluny Macpherson in November 1966. 'The Purser's' nephew, James Macpherson of Balavil, gave to the world the controversial but marvellously beautiful 'translation' of Ossian, which moved even Napoleon. Balavil became a Member of Parliament, and in 1784 the Government offered him the forfeited Cluny estates, 'but he refused them in favour of the rightful heir'.

The Macphersons have continued to the fore, and number three peers—Lord Strathcarron, Lord Drumalbyn and Lord Macpherson of Drumochter—among their distinguished clansmen. And although today the Macphersons are scattered far afield from Badenoch, the active Clan Macpherson Association, under the guiding drive of William Cheyne-Macpherson of Dalchully (a chieftain who is the clan historian), has acquired part of the old Cluny lands and some of the treasured clan relics.

Clan Chattan

The Clan Chattan is a confederation of clans in Lochaber, Strathnairn and Badenoch, under Mackintosh hegemony. The original clan were the descendants of a thirteenth-century chief called Gillechattan *Mor*, and as other clans established or settling in the district intermarried with them, they too joined in the confederation.

Besides Mackintosh and his own principal branches—Farquharson of Invercauld, Shaw of Tordarroch, MacThomas (McCombie) of Glenshee—there were the Macphersons and Cattanachs, also the MacGillivrays of Dunmaglas (whose chief commanded the whole Clan Chattan for Lady Mackintosh at Culloden), Macleans of Dochgarroch ('Macleans of the North'), McBains of Kinchyle (whose present chief, Hughston McBain of McBain, lives in America but has established a memorial park at Kinchyle), Macqueens of Corribrough, as well as the other clansmen bearing such names as Davidson, Macphail, MacAndrew, Gow, Clark, Macintyre, Crerar, Gillespie, Gillies, Noble, Ritchie, MacHardy, and Mackilligin.

The confederation was led by a high chief called the Captain of Clan Chattan, descended from the heiress of the original line of chiefs who took

Dunmaglas in Strathnairn, former home of the MacGillivray chiefs. Alexander MacGillivray of Dunmaglas was killed commanding the Clan Chattan regiment in the Jacobite army at Culloden in 1746. 'The brunt of the battle fell upon Clan Chattan', wrote a contemporary bailie of Inverness. The MacGillivray chief was the first man to reach the enemy line in the Jacobite charge, cutting his way through past the second line as well.

Loch-an-Eilean Castle at Rothiemurchus, original stronghold of the Mackintoshes and later of their cadets the Shaws. Since the sixteenth century it has been held by the Grants of Rothiemurchus, at first having to back their parchment with the sword against the aggrieved Clan Chattan.

In the Farquharson country. The Farquharson clan had their gathering-place at Carn-ma-cuin, which therefore became their slogan.

Heraldic ironwork shewing the coat-of-arms of Pye impaling that of Thom, a cadet of the Clan MacThomas of Glenshee, who place a chevron over the old *red lyon* of Macduff. The Clan McThomas or McComies held a wadset of the barony of Forter in Glenisla, and in 1571 'John McComy-Muir' (i.e. *Mac Thomaidh Mhoir*) was confirmed in the lands of Finzegand in Glenshee, of which his family had been '*ab antiquo* tenants and possessors'. Under Cromwell's Protectorate, the Mac-Thomas chieftain supported the Roundheads, and after the Restoration was described as 'haveing great power with the late Vsurpers as their intelligencer and favourite'. He had a feud with his neighbours, the Farquharsons of Brochdarg (also of the Clan Chattan), and it culminated in an affray near the Muir of Forfar in 1673, when two of the McComies were killed. Tales of the MacThomas feuding at this period are told by Jervise in his *Memorials of Angus and the Mearns* (Edinburgh 1885, 2nd edition).

Dalcross Castle, home of Arabella Mackintosh of Mackintosh (later Mrs. Anthony Warre and now Mrs. John Montagu-Douglas-Scott) who was herself 30th Captain of Clan Chattan 1938–1942 in succession to her grandfather, The Mackintosh.

their name from their ancestor Gillechattan Mor. Gillechattan means ' St. Cattan's gillie ', i.e. that at his baptism he was placed under the special protection of the saint. The old Gaelic MS. genealogies attach Gillechattan to the family of King Loarn Mor (indeed to the branch of King Ferchar the Long of Loarn, died 697, from whom also sprang the old royal house of Moray), and it may therefore be worth noting that ' the saint specially venerated by, or specially connected with, the rulers of Cinel Loarn, was St. Cattan. From Dunolly they built him a shrine at Ard-chattan '. St. Cattan's name means ' little cat ', and the wild cat is the heraldic ' beast ' of the Clan Chattan.

These old genealogies give two chiefs also called Gillechattan in the immediate line of descent from Gillechattan Mor, both of whom may be ascribed to the thirteenth century and one of whom may reasonably be identified with the 'Kelehathonin' who appears in the *Liber Vitae Ecclesia Dunelmensis* as the son of Bethoc, daughter of Malcolm mac Madadh, Earl of Atholl, by the heiress of the line of King Donald *Ban* (deposed and blinded 1097), which was appanaged in Badenoch and Lochaber. She was half-sister of William Cummin, Earl of Buchan, whose son became in 1230 Lord of Badenoch: the territory in which the Clan Chattan became the rivals of the Cummins, who were perhaps the mysterious 'Clan Quhele'.

Their differences culminated in an affair remembered in clan tradition as having taken place in about 1424. The leading family of Clan Chattan (the Mackintoshes) were invited to a feast by the Cummins, but were secretly warned beforehand of treachery, for which the signal was to be the entry of a black bull's head (a very ancient symbol in many countries of the proposed killing of an enemy chief). The result was that when the

McBain crest in the clan memorial park at Kinchyle.

Corrybrough in Strathdearn. Here the Mac-Queen chiefs had their home until the second half of the eighteenth century.

Kinchyle, heart of the McBain country. These lands had to be sold for debt in 1760 (by Donald McBain of Kinchyle's attorneys, while he was away fighting as an officer of the Fraser Highlanders against the French in America), but have been recovered in part by the present chief, who is an American citizen.

Invercauld, home of Captain Alwyne Farquharson of Invercauld, M.C., whose Gaelic style as Chief of the Farquharson clan is *Mac Fhionnlaidh*. He also owns Braemar Castle, once a stronghold of the Erskine earls of Mar, and he and his wife organise the annual Braemar Festival. By 1745 the Farquharsons (like the Macphersons) operated as a separate clan from the main Clan Chattan, although the famous Lady Mackintosh who raised Clan Chattan for Prince Charles was herself a Farquharson of Invercauld.

Tulloch Castle, near Dingwall, former home of the Davidsons of Tulloch, eighteenth century successors of the Bains of Tulloch. The Bains of Tulloch and the Dingwalls of Kildun were allies of the Clan Munro 'in their rare but sanguinary conflicts with their Mackenzie neighbours'. By 1900, Davidson of Tulloch could ride from coast to coast in Ross-shire without leaving his own ground.

black bull's head was brought in, the Mackintoshes forestalled the Cummins and massacred them instead.

But although the Clan Chattan strength has long lain in Strathnairn and Strathdearn and Badenoch, around the Monadhliath mountains, their original chiefs' homeland was Glenloy and Loch Arkaig in Lochaber, with their stronghold at Torcastle, near modern Spean Bridge, possibly inherited (with the Galley in their Arms) through a daughter of the royal house of the Isles, long overlords of Lochaber: and although after centuries of blood-feud they were obliged to cede these actual lands in 1665 (in return for 72,000 merks) to Cameron of Lochiel, who had long held them by the sword, the agreement specially provided that the Captains of Clan Chattan should retain the designation 'of Torcastle'.

According to the genealogies, the then Captain of Clan Chattan's daughter and heiress, Eva, brought the high chiefship to her husband Angus, Chief of the Mackintoshes towards the close of the thirteenth century. It seems perhaps more likely that it was a little later. The Mackintosh chiefs continued to be Captains of Clan Chattan until The Mackintosh's death in 1938, when the chiefship of Mackintosh passed with the Moy estates to the present Mackintosh of Mackintosh's father, while the high chiefship of Clan Chattan passed first to the old chief's grand-daughter and then in 1942 to his cousin and present heir male, Duncan Alexander Mackintosh of Torcastle, present and 31st Captain of Clan Chattan.

Tordarroch farmhouse, in Strathdearn. It belongs to Major Ian Shaw of Tordarroch, M.B.E., T.D., D.L., Chief of Clan Ay; but the old House of Tordarroch has long been demolished. Tordarroch served on the North-West frontier of India and in Palestine, was mentioned in despatches while serving against the Germans as an officer of the Highland Division in 1940, and has been Falkland Pursuivant Extraordinary. Cadets of the Mackintosh chiefs of Clan Chattan, the Shaws descend from Shaw 'Buck-tooth' (said to have d.1405). The Tordarroch line derive from Aodh (Englished as Adam), brother of Alasdair *Ciar*, Thane of Rothiemurchus in 1469. The Clan Ay take their name from this Aodh, whose grandson held Tordarroch of The Mackintosh by 1543. In 1609 the then Tordarroch signed the Band of Union of the Clan Chattan 'for himself and taking the full burden of his race of Clan Ay'. The clan were staunch Jacobites in the 1715 Rising, when the future chief was taken prisoner as an officer of the Clan Chattan Regiment. His son, Alexander Shaw of Tordarroch, Lt-Governor of the Isle of Man (1790–1804), commanded the Royal American Regiment of Foot against the French, and was severely wounded at the capture of Quebec in 1759. Unfortunately, Tordarroch was only held on a wadset, which was redeemed by Sir Aeneas Mackintosh of Mackintosh at this period. The Governor was, however, succeeded as Chief of Clan Ay by his son, Major-General John Shaw, who fought against Tippoo Sahib in India, and was one of the first to enter the city walls in the assault on Seringa-patam. In the nineteenth century, the then chief inherited the Mackenzie estate of New-hall in Ross-shire, but the family have also now re-acquired their old lands of Tordarroch.

In Glenshee, the 'Fairy Glen', homeland of the McCombies (Clan MacThomas) of Glenshee.

Cameron

Colonel Donald Cameron of Lochiel, *Mac Dhomnuill Duibh*, present Chief of Clan Cameron and Vice-Lieutenant of Inverness-shire. His father was the first Knight of the Thistle ever to be nominated, who was not either a peer or a baronet; and he himself is the largest landowner in Britain not to be officially a peer, holding over 100,000 acres (he is of course, Jacobite titular 9th Lord Lochiel). A scholar at Balliol, most learned of Oxford Colleges, Lochiel became a Chartered Accountant, and has been a member of the British Transport Commission and Chairman of the Scottish Area Board, also a member of the British Railways Board and then of the Scottish Railway Board; and is still a Crown Estates Commissioner. During the Second World War he served with the Lovat Scouts, becoming their Colonel, and in 1958 was appointed Honorary Colonel of the 4th/5th Territorial battalion of the Cameron Highlanders. (*See also pp. 22, 25 & 26.*)

Cameron is a place-name in the ancient 'kingdom of Fife', meaning 'Crooked Hill', from the Old Gaelic words *cam brun*. It gave its name to a knightly family who were prominent in the counties around the Tay estuary in the Middle Ages. There are reasons for supposing them to have been a branch of the famous Clan Macduff, who were the premier and most privileged clan among the Gaels of mediaeval Scotland and who were therefore certainly of royal and probably also of sacred origin (possibly through a marriage between the existing royal house, who were the Kindred of St. Columba, and the heirs of King Duff, slain in 967, who were 'peculiarly connected with Fife').

By the thirteenth century a custom existed among some great houses of having two coats-of-arms (perhaps originally a shield and flag, or else a banner and a standard): one having a 'charge' or device and the other an 'ordinary' or partition, but each coat being of the same 'colours' (metal and tincture) as the other. The Macduff chiefs, Earls of Fife 'by the Grace of God', had both a red lyon on gold, and a *paly* coat (vertical stripes) presumably of the same colours: perhaps eventually a 'War Coat' and a 'Peace Coat', a fashion the Black Prince made famous. Now, the Cameron coat is simply the old Fife paly coat 'differenced' by turning it on its side—a well-known method of differencing by cadets throughout Christendom in the twelfth and thirteenth centuries—so that it became gold *bars* on red, horizontal stripes of the same colours. So it is perhaps significant that the parish of Cameron itself originally formed part of the demesne land specially reserved for the family use of the Earls of Fife, Chiefs of the Clan Macduff, whose capital was at Cupar.

The name Adam was popular in the Clan Macduff. Adam of Ceres (Syras)—which lies between Cupar and Cameron—is thought to have been a younger son of Gillemichael Macduff, Earl of Fife *c.* 1133; and Duncan, Earl of Fife (1154–1204), had a younger brother Adam. A charter of Tay fishings in the Carse of Gowrie was witnessed by Adam of Cameron (Kamerum) early in the thirteenth century. Robert of Cameron (Cambrun) was granted the lands of Ballegarno in the Carse of Gowrie by King William the Lyon (1165–1214). A branch of the Clan Macduff, sprung from a younger son of the Earls of Fife, became Earls of Atholl in the second half of that century; and in 1296 Sir Robert Cameron (Cambron) was Sheriff of Atholl, the great highland district bordering on Lochaber. He was doubtless the Sir Robert Cameron (Cambroun) of the county of Perth, whose red castle was at Ballegarno near Dunsinane in the Carse of Gowrie, near the Earl of Fife's barony of Kinnoull, and whose seal in 1292 bore a shield with the same *three bars* borne later on their armorial shields by the Camerons of Lochiel in Lochaber.

King Edward I, the 'Hammer of the Scots', quartered himself in the Cameron castle of Ballegarno on 7 August 1296, during his conquest of our country. But the family supported King Robert Bruce, and in 1320 Sir John of Cameron (Cambrun) was one of the Scottish barons who sealed the Declaration of Independence at Arbroath. By 1388, Cameron itself and the Ballegarno estates had passed through Sir John Cameron's co-heiresses to the Haliburton lords of Dirleton and the Erskine lairds of Kinnoull, and the great Ruthven earls of Gowrie who eventually succeeded as Lords Dirleton were proud to quarter the *three bars* of Cameron with their own Arms. However, about the end of the century, marriage to an Inverness-shire heiress had brought the Camerons—like the Frasers and Chisholms about the same time—to what became their clan lands around the Great Glen.

By the beginning of the fifteenth century, if not earlier, the Camerons appear as chiefs of a highland clan west of the Lochy in Lochaber,

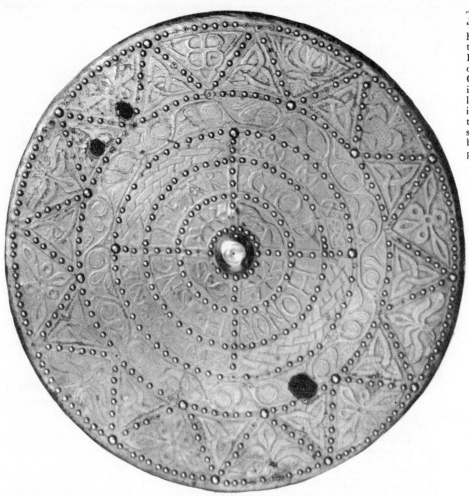

Targe or shield of Sir Ewen Cameron, the 'Great Lochiel', c. 1670, shewing three bullet-holes received in battle. It is embossed in the leather: FEAR GOD – HONOR THE KING. Sir Ewen was the last chief to hold out against Cromwell, biting through a Cromwellian officer's windpipe while locked in mortal combat on the ground near Inverlochy, and only made a peace treaty with them in 1658, the Camerons keeping their arms and taking no oaths—while in 1689, at the age of sixty, he led the victorious Jacobite charge barefoot at the battle of Killiecrankie. His portrait in armour is at Achnacarry.

Achnacarry Castle, home of Cameron of Lochiel. Only two stone gable-ends survive nearby of the chiefs' old wooden house, 'an immense pile of timber', burnt by Government troops in 1746. John Prebble, *Culloden* (London 1961), adds, 'Some time later, two platoons of Munro's regiment arrived at Achnacarry, and picked over the smoke-blackened stones. In a mean hut was found the Chief's gardener, and then Lochiel's cook was also dragged from hiding. They were ordered to tell the soldiers where the gold and the silver and the jewels had been buried, but the frightened old men would not say or did not know, though they were flogged again and again by the drummers. With their backs cruelly flayed, they were finally sent in irons to Inverness.' The present castle was rebuilt early in the nineteenth century by the Gentle Lochiel's grandson Donald, to whom the estates had been restored in 1784; and was completed in 1837 by his son Donald Cameron of Lochiel, who had fought as an ensign in the First Foot Guards at the battle of Waterloo.

Beautifully balanced two-handed 'Andrea Ferrara' battle-sword of Allan Cameron of Lochiel, who led his clan for Huntly and Erroll against Argyll at the battle of Glenlivat in 1594. The blade is inscribed ALLAN CAMRON OF LOCHELL and the date 1585.

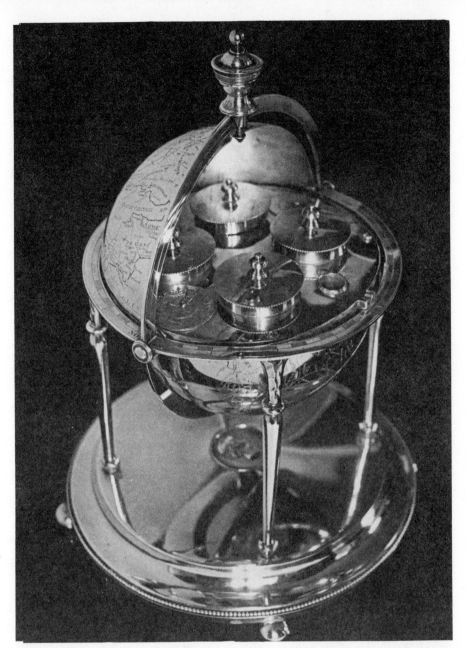

Silver globe that opens to reveal an inkstand, presented by Prince Charles Edward to the 'Gentle Lochiel' in exile in France after Culloden. Lochiel commanded the Regiment d'Albanie in the French Service until his death soon after that of his father, John (exiled since the 1715 Rising), in 1748.

apparently through descent from an heiress of the local dynastic MacGillonies—the *Clan Mael-anfaidh* or 'Children of He who was Dedicated to the Storm'—of whom the MacMartins of Letterfinlay, on the east shore of Loch Lochy, were an early sept. These MacMartins often took their new chiefs' name of Cameron, and it is interesting that the letter *b* of the old Fife place-name spelling sometimes survived into Lochaber as late as the seventeenth century: thus in 1617 three clansmen were described as 'Cambroun *alias* M'Martene'. Like the Clan Chattan of Lochaber and Badenoch, the MacGillonies themselves were traced by the old Gaelic genealogists back to Ferchar the Long, King of Lorn (died 697), another branch of whose descendants were the last Kings of Moray, which then included Lochaber.

The MacGillonies' name-father Mael-anfaidh was son of Gilleroth mac GillaMartain, whom Professor Skene reasonably identified as the chief called by that name who was a sort of thirteenth-century Jacobite. He appears to have been one of the leading supporters of the last gallant but hopeless Rising led by the MacWilliam claimant to the throne in about 1228–1230. The MacWilliam claimants were princes appanaged in Lochaber and Badenoch (provinces of the former kingdom of Moray), and belonged to a disinherited senior branch of the Scottish royal house, being the family of King Duncan II (killed 1094). The loyal Lochaber men had risen for them several times, for by the old laws of the Gaels their claim to the Scottish throne was just, but each claimant had been slain. On the previous occasion, the MacWilliam claimant had been defeated and beheaded by his own northern neighbour in Moray, *Maccintsacairt*, afterwards first Earl of Ross, who was a supporter of King Alexander II's government. In 1230, when the new Rising had also failed, Gilleroth mac GillaMartain fled to Galloway with the unhappy MacWilliam claimant, who was however captured and killed by Alexander II's men. The whole family of the Lochaber claimants to the throne were then ruthlessly stamped out by the Government; and even ' the same MacWilliam's daughter, who had not long left her mother's womb, innocent as she was, was put to death in the burgh of Forfar, in view of the market-place, after a proclamation by the public crier: her head was struck against the column of the market Cross, and her brains dashed out ', as the monkish chronicler of Lanercost tells us.

The famous Commando Memorial erected near Achnacarry, which was the tough Commando training centre during the Second World War.

Skulking in Galloway, Gilleroth took part in the 1235 Rising of the Gallowegians against his former rightful king's old foe Alexander II, but it was once again bloodily suppressed by *Maccintsacairt*, now Earl of Ross, and Gilleroth escaped to Ireland in search of reinforcements. ' And after the aforesaid Gilleroth had returned from Ireland ', writes the chronicler of Melrose, ' as soon as he touched the land, he broke up all his ships; employing this trick, so that those whom he had brought with him should not be able to return to their own country in any way.' He was however outnumbered, forced to surrender, and taken captive: after which we hear no more of this spirited chief. He was certainly a fitting ancestor for the heroic Jacobite Camerons of Lochiel, and for their devoted MacGillonie and MacMartin clansmen.

By the fifteenth century, when the MacGillonie chiefship had passed to the Camerons, Lochaber formed part of the semi-independent realm of the

great Macdonald, Lord of the Isles and Earl of Ross. The MacGillonies, or their Cameron successors, evidently intermarried with the Clan Donald; and the 'sons of Somerled' or MacSorleys of Glen Nevis, cadets of the royal Clan Donald of the Isles, joined the Clan Cameron. As late as 1678, Sir Ewen Cameron of Lochiel placed a *galley* (the device of the royal house of the Isles) in the first quarter of his coat-of-arms: the Cameron *three bars* appearing in the third quarter. Although (according to *Lays of the Deer Forest*) the sixteenth and seventeenth century Chiefs of Clan Cameron were apparently still sometimes styled 'MacGillonay', their usual Gaelic title since the fifteenth century has been *Mac Dhòmnuill Duibh*, 'Son of Black Donald', after the first chief from whom the succession can be traced in contemporary records from generation to generation. Black Donald was a mighty warrior chief who led his Lochaber men on Macdonald's side at the famous battle in 1411 between the Lord of the Isles and the government forces at Harlaw.

For centuries the Camerons held *by the sword* the lands, from Loch Oich through Loch Arkaig to Glen Loy, that had once been Clan Chattan's heritage in Lochaber. Their ferocious war-cry was a promise to feed their enemies' flesh to dogs: *Chlanna nan con thigibh a so's gheibh sibh fèoil*, 'Sons of the hounds, come here and get flesh'. Indeed, the Cameron chiefs long lived at Torcastle, originally the chief place of Clan Chattan, until they moved to their present home at Achnacarry. At last, in 1665, Mackintosh invaded Lochiel's country at the head of a large force. But Breadalbane (related to both chiefs) arrived with his Campbells and said that if either attacked the other, he would join in against the aggressor. And Argyll himself gave the Cameron chief a great sum to buy out the claims of Mackintosh, the then Captain of Clan Chattan, who retained in future only the right to use the designation 'of Torcastle'. Argyll did this as a part of his long struggle with Huntly (an earlier Huntly had beheaded Ewen Cameron of Lochiel in 1547) to gain control over the Inverness-shire clans. Neither succeeded in the end.

In 1528 the lands of the Captain of Clan Cameron (this is the older style for a chief) were erected into the Barony of Lochiel, which has ever since been the chief's designation. A long line of very remarkable chiefs up to the present day have made *Lochiel* one of the most famous chiefly titles in the world: just as the valiant fighting men of the clan were a *corps d'élite* in the '45 Rising and later made the Cameron Highlanders the same in the days when our country stood in danger from Napoleon or Hitler. After Culloden, the future General Wolfe (conqueror of Quebec), who was present on the Government side, wrote of his old regiment and the Jacobite charge that ' They were attacked by the Camerons (the bravest clan amongst them) '.

The exiled ' King over the Water ' made the then chief Lord Lochiel in 1717, in the Jacobite Peerage—for, like their remote Lochaber forefather Gilleroth mac GillaMartain, the brave and chivalrous Camerons were ever loyal to what they could not honourably but regard as their rightful royal house: the Stuart Cause then, where once there had been the MacWilliam Cause so long ago. Sir Ewen, the ' Great Lochiel ', last of the wolf-hunters, held out longer than anybody else in all Britain for King Charles II against the English invader Cromwell: biting out a Roundhead officer's throat as they grappled in combat by Loch Arkaig. His grandson Donald, the ' Gentle Lochiel ', was perhaps the finest highland chief there will ever have been: and his brothers, who became a doctor and a priest to tend their clansmen in peace, both died horribly for the White Cockade, equally the noblest and best of highland gentlemen.

Camerons should read the late Charles Ian Fraser of Reelig's brief history, *The Clan Cameron* (Edinburgh 1953), and the books he recommends: J. Drummond's *Memoirs of Sir Ewen Cameron of Lochiel* (Edinburgh 1842) and D. K. Broster's moving novels, *The Flight of the Heron* (which first gave the present writer as a boy his interest in highland lore), *The Dark Mile* and *The Gleam in the North*.

Broadsword with silver basket hilt, used in the 1745 Rising by Donald Cameron, the ' Gentle Lochiel ', who was shot in both ankles at the battle of Culloden but was carried home by his clansmen and escaped to die in exile in France in 1748. He had not wished to commit his clan to so desperate a venture, and had initially sent his kindly brother, Dr. Archibald Cameron (the last Jacobite to be hanged, drawn and quartered, eight years later), to ask Prince Charles Edward to hide in the Highlands until the promised French munitions of war arrived. The Prince observed that Lochiel, whom he had always understood to be his father's foremost and firmest friend, could stay at home and learn his Prince's fate from his newspapers. Lochiel's reply was immediate: ' I will share the fate of my Prince, and so shall every man over whom nature or fortune has given me power.' His decision altered the whole course of Highland life for ever, as (apart from Clanranald) the other chiefs were waiting for Lochiel to declare himself; and the hush of relief when the Cameron pipes were heard approaching the Prince's gathering-place at Glenfinnan was one of the dramatic moments of history.

In 1746, during the Jacobite retreat, the Gentle Lochiel intervened personally to save the City of Glasgow from damage, and the City Council resolved that whenever Cameron of Lochiel came to Glasgow in all time coming, the church bells would welcome him. Still today, if Lochiel pays an official visit to Glasgow, the bells ring out to do him honour.

Loch Eil in the Cameron Country. From this loch the Cameron chief derives his famous style of *Lochiel*.

Fraser

Fraser, originally Fresel, appears to be a French nickname, though its meaning is uncertain. It could be connected in some way with the pun on the name, whereby the Fraser coat-of-arms came to have strawberry-flowers or *fraises*. In the eleventh century there was a knightly family in Anjou called Frezel, who gave their name to the seigneurie of La Fréze-lière. During the following century many younger sons of Norman, Breton and Frankish lords were invited to settle in the newly-consolidated realm of Scotland by our energetic kings, who had found them to be good administrators and who needed mailed knights to subdue the outlying principalities and local kingdoms that so often supported rival claimants to their throne. Accordingly, Simon Fraser appears holding lands at Keith in East Lothian in 1160. These lands were called after him, Keith Simon; and although they passed through his granddaughter to the Keiths, Marischals of Scotland, the name Simon has been the favourite among the Frasers in Scotland ever since.

One branch of the family became Sheriffs of Peebles and acquired Tweed-dale through an heiress. Their stronghold was Oliver Castle on the Tweed. Their head, Sir Simon Fraser, was a famous Scottish patriot. He fought for Wallace, personally defeated the English three times in one day at Rosslyn in 1302, and was captured fighting for King Robert Bruce. The English took him to London, and executed him ' with great cruelty '. He was hanged stark naked in public, cut down choking but still alive, had his private parts cut off and was disembowelled and saw his own entrails burnt in front of him; next his arms and legs were hacked off, and only then was he finally beheaded. This was the English way of ' hanging,

Tombstone in Beauly Priory shewing effigy in armour of Hugh, 3rd Lord Fraser of Lovat, who was slain in battle against the Clanranald in 1544, in the greatest disaster the Frasers ever sustained. This is the earliest known likeness of a highland Fraser to survive.

Contemporary illumination of a noble being publicly hanged, drawn and quartered in fourteenth-century England.

Tomnahurich, 'the Knoll of the Yew-wood', near Inverness. Here Lord Lovat held his Court, and the Frasers held horse-races, as early as 1500. As horse-racing was a pagan religious festival, the custom may have been very ancient, for Tomnahurich was magic ground in the old days. Burt, an English officer writing *c.* 1730, tells us that 'the Fairies within it are innumerable, and witches find it the most convenient Place for their Frolics and Gambols in the night-time.' Here, too, the Aird Frasers gathered to cut their lucky sprigs of yew when *Mac Shimi* mobilised his clan for war. The Stratherrick Frasers took their sprigs from an ancient yew tree on Beinn a' Bhacaidh in Stratherrick. (*See also pp. 39, 128 & 129.*)

drawing and quartering', which they first devised for the last native Prince of Wales and for Sir Simon's friend Wallace, and last used on Jacobite gentlemen in the eighteenth century. Sir Simon's eldest daughter carried his great estates in Tweeddale to the Hays, now Marquises of Tweeddale, who still quarter the Fraser *fraises* in their coat-of-arms.

Sir Simon's kinsman and chief, Sir Alexander Fraser, Chamberlain of Scotland, one of the heroes of Bannockburn, married King Robert Bruce's sister: she had been a prisoner of the English, who kept her in a cage in public. They were the ancestors of the Frasers of Philorth, now Lords Saltoun, to whom King James VI by royal charters of 1592 and 1601 granted and confirmed the unique right to have their *own* University at Fraserburgh. The right still continues, but nearby Aberdeen University was so jealous that Fraserburgh University was deliberately undermined during the first few years of its existence. Alexander Fraser, 19th Lord Saltoun, M.C., is the present head of the whole Name of Fraser.

Curiously enough, the Frasers are connected with another university: this time in the New World. For the new university founded in British Columbia in 1964 has been named Simon Fraser University, after the intrepid Canadian explorer. He was a Fraser of Culbokie, of the branch whose chieftains were styled *Mac Huisdean*, and was descended from a younger son of the 2nd Lord Lovat.

The Clan Fraser of Lovat call their chief in Gaelic *Mac Shimi*, the 'Son of Simon'. There is little doubt that the forefather called Simon from whom he derives this style was the Chamberlain's brother, Sir Simon Fraser, who (according to Froissart) 'chased the Englishmen three days' after the battle of Bannockburn. By marriage to heiresses, these Frasers acquired a vast territory around Lovat in the Aird, and later also Stratherrick and part of Glenelg. Simon Fraser, 11th Lord Lovat, was created Duke of Fraser by 'the King over the Water', but was beheaded as a Jacobite on Tower Hill in 1747: the last peer of the realm to be axed. His elder son, General Simon Fraser of Lovat, raised the Fraser Highlanders and commanded them at the capture of Quebec, when they scaled the Heights of Abraham.

The 11th Lord Lovat's younger son, Colonel Archibald Fraser of Lovat, M.P., who raised the Fraser Fencibles when invasion from France was expected, took the lead (with the Marquis of Graham) in Parliament in obtaining the repeal of the laws banning the Highland dress: and was thus responsible for the restoration of the kilt. Major-General Simon Fraser, 16th Lord Lovat (if the two forfeited chiefs be counted), K.T., G.C.V.O., K.C.M.G., C.B., D.S.O., carried on the Fraser tradition by raising the Lovat Scouts, which he commanded with distinction in the field in the Boer War. His son, the present Simon Fraser, 17th Lord Lovat and 22nd *Mac Shimi*, D.S.O., M.C., LL.D., was the brilliant Commando leader who carried out so many successful raids in the Second World War, treating the Germans as his ancestors did the English.

Brigadier Simon Fraser, Lord Lovat, the 22nd *Mac Shimi* and wartime Commando leader.

Colour plate
Farm near the river Foyers in the old Fraser country of Stratherrick, south of Loch Ness: a typical highland strath. Glens are narrow valleys, while straths are broad river vales.

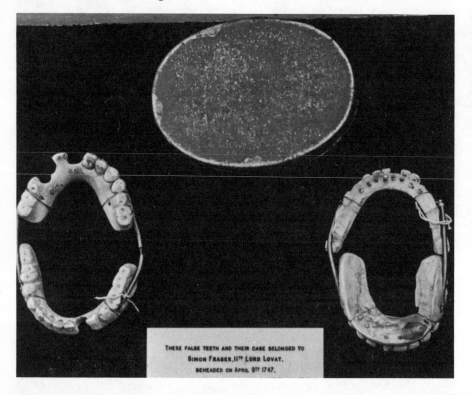

These false teeth and their case belonged to Simon Fraser, 11th Lord Lovat, beheaded on April 9th 1747.

False teeth of Simon Fraser, 11th Lord Lovat (beheaded 1747), with their travelling case.

Section of a silver snuff-box in the possession of the present Master of Lovat shewing Castle Dounie ablaze in 1746. It is said to have been presented by a clansman to the 11th Lord Lovat during his trial. This is the only known picture of Castle Dounie to survive. The only remains of the old castle are a rockery beside the modern Beaufort Castle.

Lord Lovat (seated spinning, with pipe in mouth) disguised as a woman while Grenadiers search for him after the failure of the 1745 Rising.

Castle Leod, in Strathpeffer, home of Rorie Mackenzie, Earl of Cromartie. Much of it was added in 1616, to an older castle of the family, by his forefather Sir Rorie Mackenzie, the dreaded Tutor of Kintail.

Early nineteenth-century tartan pattern-book in the possession of The Mackintosh at Moy, shewing among others the Mackintosh tartan and an early form of the Clan Chattan tartan.

PRESENTED TO
Lt.Col.LORD LOVAT. C.V.O.,CB.,D.S.O
BY THE OFFICERS OF THE
FIRST BATTALION THE CONNAUGHT RANGERS
IN MEMORY OF THE CLOSE FRIENDSHIP
FORMED WITH THE LOVAT SCOUTS
DURING THE SOUTH AFRICAN WAR

Silver presentation statuette of Simon Fraser, 16th Lord Lovat, commanding Lovat's Scouts in the Boer War. He raised the Regiment himself, and led it in action.

Mackenzie

The surname Mackenzie comes from the Old Gaelic *Mac Cainnigh*, 'Son of Cainnech' (in modern Gaelic spelt Coinneach), a personal name meaning 'Fair One' or 'Bright One' that has long been Englished as Kenneth: though really in origin quite another name. Mackenzie was always pronounced 'Mackaingye' until it became smart in the Anglicised eighteenth century and later to pronounce the old Scots guttural *y* (written *z*, as in Menzies, zett, etc.) as though it were the same as the English *z* (as in zebra). Hence the famous seventeenth-century Lord Advocate, Sir George Mackenzie of Rosehaugh, was still known in his own time as 'Bluidy Mackingie'.

The Mackenzies form one of a group of clans in Ross who held lands between the Aird on the east coast and Kintail ('the head of the salt water') on the west coast. Others in the same group were Clan Anrias and the Mathesons. Matheson is an Anglicisation of the Gaelic *Mac-Mhathain*. All three clans are traced by the old Gaelic genealogists back to a local dynast called Gilleoin of the Aird, who appears to have lived about the beginning of the twelfth century. He himself is said to have belonged to a branch of the ancient royal house of Lorn, another branch of whom became the last Kings of Moray, which then included Ross.

The last Chief of Clan Anrias was Paul the Wolf, whose heiress carried their appanage to her husband Walter Ross of Balnagowan, 8th Chief of Clan Ross from about 1398 to 1412. As for the other two clans, Mackenzie and Matheson, they also held their lands under the mediaeval Earls of Ross. Cormac Mac Mhathain, the second Matheson chief, was rewarded in 1264 for having supported the then Earl of Ross in the campaigns against the Norsemen during the two previous years: when expanding Scotland

Tomb in Beauly Priory with effigy in armour of Kenneth Mackenzie of Kintail, who died on 7 February 1491/2. This is the earliest known likeness of a Mackenzie to survive.

conquered the Isles from Norway. This worthy chief is mentioned thus in the Saga of King Haakon of Norway (*Frisbok's Hakon Hakon's son's Saga*): '. . . the dispeace that the Earl of Ross, and Kiarnak Makamal's son [Cormac Mac Mhathain], and other Scots had made in the Hebrides, when they went out to Skye and burned a town and churches, and slew very many men and women. And . . . the Scots had taken the little children and laid them on their spear-points, and shook their spears until they brought the children down to their hands; and so threw them away, dead.' Of the early history of the Mackenzies, less is known as yet. We are told by Bower of the two related clans, Mackenzie and Matheson, that in 1427 their two chiefs—'Great Kenneth' or *Cainnech Mor* and *Mac Mhathain*, 'Bear's Son'—could each raise two thousand men.

But, after the overthrow in 1476 of the mighty Macdonald, who was the last semi-independent Earl of Ross, the fortunes of the two clans differed completely. The Mathesons held in Lochalsh, west beyond Kintail, under the last Earl of Ross's nephew, whose grand-daughter carried the superiority to her descendants, the haughty Macdonells of Glengarry. As the Mathesons remained loyal to Clan Donald in adversity, and later adhered to their Mackenzie kinsfolk in their prime, they never came into direct contact with the Crown until modern times. In 1851 Sir Alexander Matheson, ancestor of the present Baronet of Lochalsh, was at last rich enough to buy back the ancient Matheson lands and indeed acquire the barony of Lochalsh itself. Unfortunately, through an heraldic error, the family recorded as their Arms about this time the three red hands of the Galloway McMickings (a coat akin to that of Adair of Kinhilt in Galloway) instead of the lyon which is apparently appropriate to the highland Mathesons.

The Mackenzies, on the other hand, rose in Ross on the ruins of Clan Donald. Alasdair 'the Upright' Mackenzie of Kintail, the then chief, saw his opportunity, and raised his clan against the last Earl of Ross in the moment of the earl's peril. On the Macdonald earl's successful downfall, a grateful King James III in 1477 rewarded the Mackenzie chief by

Looking across the Cromarty Firth to the Black Isle.

Dining room at Castle Leod. (*See also the coloured illustration of Castle Leod at p. 148.*)

granting or confirming him in wide lands, including Strathconan, the superiority of which had been 'resigned' by the fallen earl. His son, Kenneth Mackenzie of Kintail (who died in 1491 and whose tomb effigy in full armour can still be seen at Beauly Priory in the Aird) continued the work of expansion and consolidation and yet more expansion.

In 1508 Kintail was erected into a Barony for the then Chief. The *reddendo* for Kintail was a stag to be rendered to the King: hence no doubt the old motto *Cuidiche an Righ*, 'tribute to the King', and the stag's head in the Mackenzie chiefs' coat-of-arms, from which he derived his Gaelic title of *Caberféidh* or 'Deer's Antlers'. The sixteenth-century seals of the chiefs show a Moray star between the antlers on their shield. The use by the clan of deer-grass—and sometimes staghorn moss, worn by the MacRaes —also alludes to the Mackenzie Arms. The Mackenzie slogan was Tulloch Ard, from the mountain at whose foot was their gathering-place in Kintail.

Royal portrait snuff-box given by the King of Sweden to his colonel aide-de-camp, John Mackenzie, Count Cromartie. The count was eldest son of the 3rd Earl of Cromartie, who had been condemned to death as a Jacobite after the 1745 Rising; though reprieved. As the family estates (the whole county of Cromarty) had been forfeited, the son entered the Swedish Service—the cost of his equipment being paid by the Old Chevalier (the Jacobite King James VIII)—and distinguished himself as a soldier, being created a Swedish count. He returned to Scotland in 1777, raised a Highland regiment and commanded it in action against Hyder Ali in India, becoming a British major-general and M.P.; and the Cromartie estates were restored to him in 1784. While in exile, the Jacobites were very kindly treated by the Swedish king, whom they hoped perhaps might make war on Hanover. They had a drinking-song about the further Rising they forlornly looked for. It was sung to the oldest known Scots tune *Hey Tooty Tetty*, which dates from at least the fourteenth century and is now attached to Burns's famous anthem *Scots Wha Hae*. One verse of the exiled Jacobites' song ran:

> Here's tae the King o' Swede,
>   May fresh laurels croun his heid!
> Foul fa' every sneaking blade
>   That winna do't again.

And the wistful chorus was:

> Fill, fill a bumper high!
>   Drain, drain your glasses dry!
> Out upon him, fie oh fie,
>   That winna do't again.

The drinking-song concluded:

> When you hear the pipe sounds
>   'Tooty tetty' to the drums,
> Up your swords—and doun your guns—
>   And at the loons again!

This last stanza refers to the old Highland tactic of throwing firearms away in the charge, that had caused such havoc when the Jacobites were unable to close with the enemy at Culloden and had been reduced to throwing random stones against controlled volleys of musketry.

Rorie Mackenzie, Earl of Cromartie, M.C., at Castle Leod, wearing a rare pine-marten sporran. He is a County Councillor and honorary Sheriff Substitute of Ross & Cromarty, and was a Major in the Seaforth Highlanders (the regiment raised in 1778 by Kenneth Mackenzie, Earl of Seaforth, then chief of the clan). Lord Cromartie served in Nigeria and in operations on the North-West Frontier of India, but was taken prisoner by the Germans with the rest of the Highland Division on the fall of France in 1940.

The Mackenzies produced shrewd lawyers with crafty reasons to back their skillful use of armed might, and so by the seventeenth century their territory extended from coast to coast in Ross, from the Black Isle to the Gairloch, and from Kintail to Coigeach; and then across the stormy Minch to the Outer Hebrides. Lochalsh was finally conquered from the Macdonells of Glengarry by 1609; the great island of Lewis with its castle of Stornoway was finally wrested from the unfortunate MacLeods a few years later; and the Gairloch was gradually 'acquired' from other MacLeods between the fifteenth and seventeenth centuries.

The Mackenzie chiefs had their western stronghold on Loch Duich in Kintail, at Eileandonan Castle. This was sometimes given in keeping to their kinsfolk the Mathesons. But it was usually held for them by the MacRaes, who became almost hereditary Constables of the Castle and were known as 'Mackenzie's Shirt of Mail'. MacRae means 'Son of grace', and their arms shew Moray stars and a lyon. The MacRaes had their own clan gathering-place beneath Sgùr Urain in Kintail. Eileandonan Castle was blown up by English sailors after the exiled Mackenzie chief had landed with Spanish troops in 1719 in an unsuccessful Rising for the Jacobite Cause. It has been romantically restored, and now belongs to a descendant of the Mackenzies' Constables, John MacRae of Conchra. The Mackenzie chiefs' eastern residence was in Strathconan until in the seventeenth century they built Brahan Castle near Dingwall, so well known from the remarkable prophecies of the 'Brahan Seer'.

The then chief was made a peer as Lord Mackenzie of Kintail in 1609, and his son became Earl of Seaforth—a sea-fjord or loch on the coast of the island of Lewis—in 1623. The clan were staunch Jacobites, and the 4th Earl (one of the eight Founder Knights of the famous Order of the Thistle) was created a Jacobite Marquis by the exiled King James VII, the 'King over the Water' at St. Germain. The 5th Earl was attainted as a Jacobite, so that the old family peerages were forfeited. Although his grandson (who raised the celebrated Seaforth Highlanders) was made Earl of Seaforth again, and a cousin who had later succeeded was made Lord Seaforth, Baron Mackenzie of Kintail, their immediate male line came to an end in 1815, and the vast estates have passed through successive heiresses, dwindling sadly ever since. The Brahan Seer's last prophecy has been fulfilled.

The 1st Lord Mackenzie of Kintail's alarming and vigorous younger brother was the present writer's own ancestor Sir Rorie Mackenzie of Tarbat, Tutor of Kintail, who lived at Castle Leod and who got such a move on the more lawless clans in the reign of James VI that there is still a Gaelic proverb: 'There are two things worse than the Tutor of Kintail—frost in Spring, and mist in the dogdays'. Sir Rorie's heir today is Rorie Mackenzie, Earl of Cromartie, who won the Military Cross in the Second World War and still lives at Castle Leod in Strathconan, one of the straths granted or confirmed to the Mackenzie chief in 1477. The estates of the Mackenzies of Cromartie were disjoined from the shire of Ross and erected by Act of Parliament into a special County of Cromartie: although the two counties are nowadays joined together again for practical purposes. Both the present Earl of Cromartie and the present Mackenzie of Gairloch have inherited the clan name and their Mackenzie lands through the female line. But Lord Cromartie and Mackenzie of Gairloch are the only two Mackenzie chieftains holding parts of the old clan territory today.

Brahan Castle, that was long the main residence of the Mackenzies of Seaforth, chiefs of the clan. Their doom was predicted in a remarkably detailed prophecy by 'Sallow' Kenneth or *Coinneach Odhar*, the 'Brahan Seer', which was literally and accurately fulfilled in the nineteenth century. The Seer is usually said to have been put to death (rolled downhill in a burning tar-barrel lined with rather prickly spikes) by a Countess of Seaforth, for telling her what his second-sight told him her husband the chief was up to in France, or (according to other accounts) for being rude about some young ladies. Seaforth is said to have arrived home just too late to save him and prevent him cursing the family with his dying breath. But the Seer appears to have lived long before the creation of the Earldom of Seaforth, and to have been executed at the instance of the Government: for in January 1577/8, a royal commission was issued from Holyroodhouse commanding various Ross-shire justiciaries to 'apprehend, imprison, and try Kenneth *alias* Kennoch Owir, principal or leader in the art of magic'. (See also p. 165.)

ROSS

The Clan Ross take their surname from the county of Ross, of which their chiefs' forefathers were the earls from about 1226. Their first chief, Ferchar, styled *Macc in t'sacairt* (' the Son of the Priest '), already held by inheritance the vast district of Applecross in Wester Ross as heir of the O'Beolain hereditary abbots of Applecross. They probably came of the same stock as the O'Beolain hereditary abbots of Drumcliff in Ireland, who descended from Cairbre, son of King Niall of the Nine Hostages. Applecross abbey was founded in 673 by Saint Maelrubha, abbot of Bangor, who descended from Eoghan, another son of King Niall. As St. Maelrubha was himself connected on his mother's side with St. Comgall, founder and first abbot of ' Bangor of the Irish Picts in the Ards of Ulster ', the right to the abbey-lands may at first have passed in the Pictish mode, and the O'Beollans perhaps have acquired the abbacy by a female descent in the transitional ninth century.

In 1215, Ferchar ' the Son of the Priest ' brought his numerous warriors to assist the new king, Alexander II, against rival claimants to the throne who were powerful in the North of Scotland. The *Chronicle of Melrose* records his prowess on this occasion: ' Maccintsacairt attacked them, and mightily overthrew the king's enemies; and he cut off their heads, and presented them as new gifts to the new king; on the seventeenth day before the Kalends of July. And because of this, the lord king appointed him a new knight '. A decade or so later, the same king entrusted him with the whole Earldom of Ross: so called after the Ancient British word *ros*, meaning a moor—or possibly from the Gaelic word *ros*, a headland, after the huge promontory formed by Easter Ross.

The first five chiefs were Earls of Ross. But on the death of William, Earl of Ross and Lord of Skye, in 1372, the earldom passed to his daughter; while the chiefship devolved on his younger half-brother Hugh Ross, 1st of Balnagown and 6th Chief of Clan Ross, whose inheritance in Easter Ross was so great that by 1632 the Rosses could raise 1,000 men. After the death in 1711 of David Ross, 13th of Balnagown, Sheriff of Ross, the chiefship of the clan passed to Malcolm Ross, 5th of Pitcalnie; but the great estate of Balnagown had been burdened with debt and passed to

Old St. Duthus Church in Tain. In this sanctuary was kept the sacred shirt of St. Duthac, worn in battle by the mediaeval Earls of Ross. The hereditary guardians of this sanctuary were the MacCullochs of Nigg: from their heiress descended the Gairs of Nigg, whose Arms were recorded in Lyon Register in 1672 and of whom the present Lt.-Colonel Robert Gayre of Gayre and Nigg has been officially recognised as the representative. The sanctuary was unwillingly violated by the 3rd chief, William, Earl of Ross, in 1306, when he dragged out King Robert Bruce's queen and daughter and handed them over to be caged by the English. He had been released by Edward I of England after seven years as a prisoner-of-war in the Tower of London, and presumably had no wish hopelessly to renew the experience. But as soon as possible, he was reconciled in 1307 to King Robert (who gave his sister Lady Maud Bruce in marriage to the chief's son Hugh) and he led the men of the North for Bruce at Bannockburn. Hugh, 4th Earl of Ross, was killed wearing St. Duthac's shirt in battle against the English and King Edward Balliol at Halidon Hill in 1333. Balliol found the holy shirt on his body and restored it to the sanctuary at Tain.

strangers, whose descendants evicted many of the clansmen in the 'progressive' days of the Clearances. The Rosses of Pitcalnie, however, continued to function as chiefs of the clan in Ross, and the celebrated Simon, Lord Lovat (beheaded in 1747) wrote to the then Pitcalnie in 1740 as 'My Dear Brother Chief'. The late 34th chief was ninety-nine-year old Miss Ross of Ross, who lived on the outskirts of the old royal burgh of Tain in Ross. Her appointed heir, David Ross of Ross, the new Chief, belonged to the Shandwick branch of the clan, and is heir male of *Macc in t'sacairt* who became Earl of Ross seven and a half centuries ago.

Balnagowan Castle, long the stronghold of the Chiefs of Ross. But after the death in 1711 of David Ross, 13th of Balnagowan and 18th Chief, a Lowland family who happened also to be called Ross (but from the Norman name *de Roos*) managed by financial intrigue to get possession of the castle and the vast clan territory. 'In all the annals of Scotland there is, perhaps, no greater case of fraud and wrong than the unscrupulous but ultimately successful attempts of Lord Ross and General Charles Ross, strangers to the family, to possess themselves of the estates of Balnagowan'. The usurping line have come to an end, and the castle now belongs to English ladies.

Betsy Ross, widow of John Ross who was killed in the American War of Independence and whose brother Colonel George Ross was one of the signatories of the Declaration of Independence itself, made the first 'Stars and Stripes' flag for the United States' Congress. They were Rosses of Balblair, descended from a younger son of Hugh Ross of Balnagowan, 9th Chief of Clan Ross from about 1412.

DREAD GOD

Munro

'Munro' appears to have been a place-name, now unidentified. In Gaelic the clan were called *Rothach*. Their chiefs are the Munros of Foulis, and their territory was Ferindonald beneath lofty Ben Wyvis, extending from high Loch Morie down to the fertile coastland of the Cromarty Firth opposite the Black Isle. Ferindonald means 'the Land of Donald', which the Munros understand to have been the name of their first chief, who presumably received the appanage as a cadet of some Ross dynastic house. In time of clan warfare, a signal beacon was lit on the highest tower of Foulis Castle to gather the clan under arms, so the Munro slogan or gathering-cry was *Caisteal Fòlais na theine* : 'Castle Foulis ablaze'.

A Munro sealed with a lyon rampant in 1453, but by the sixteenth century the chief's Arms were a *red eagle's head* on a golden shield. These arms probably derive from the marriage which the old genealogies tell us took place in the fourteenth century between Robert of Munro, chief of Foulis, and a niece of Queen Euphame Ross, consort of King Robert II and half-sister of William, 5th Earl of Ross. For Earl William was the last of the mediaeval Celtic earls of Ross, of whom the Munros originally held their lands, and whose arms in the fourteenth century were three lyons on a shield which was charged on the breast of a *red eagle*. (This eagle was adopted by the Ross earls to mark the Buchan lands they had inherited from the Cummins, and later added to the heraldic Galley of the Isles by the Macdonald chiefs when they in turn inherited the earldom of Ross).

Certainly the then Munro chief, Robert of Munro, was killed in 1369 fighting in defence of this William, Earl of Ross and Lord of Skye, who had confirmed him in possession of the family lands of Easter Foulis and the Tower of Strath Skiach, in Ferindonald. The earl's daughter confirmed Hugh of Munro, the next chief, in the Tower of Strath Skiach (predecessor of the present Foulis Castle) and also in the lands of Wester Foulis in 1394. But after the downfall of the Macdonald earls of Ross in 1476, the Munros came to hold the Barony of Foulis directly of the Crown.

How Hector Munro of Foulis, the then chief of the clan, taken ill in 1589, generously employed witchcraft to offer up the life of his younger half-brother George Munro of Obsdale as a Substitute Victim for himself, has been told in the Introduction to this book. This Hector Munro of Foulis was father of the 1st Baronet (so created in the Order of Nova Scotia in 1634). But the 2nd Baronet (Hector's grandson) died at Durness at the age of sixteen in 1651; and by an irony of fate, the Baronetcy passed together with the chiefship and the old baronial estates of Foulis to the Substitute Victim's grandson, Robert Munro of Obsdale, who thus became 3rd Baronet of Foulis.

In the seventeenth century, the Munros were fine professional soldiers. An Obsdale's brother, General Robert Monro, in his *Expedition* (London 1637), tells us of his own training as a young recruit in the King of France's Scots Guard, how he was punished for some breach of discipline by being made to do sentry duty all day in hot armour under a blazing Paris sun. He also tells us of the splendour of his own clan chief's entourage and hospitable table, when the Black Baron of Foulis arrived to join the Swedish Service as an ordinary volunteer, bringing with him a Company of his Munro clansmen. Above all, he makes us realise that the Protestants among the Highland mercenaries genuinely felt that they were fighting (under the 'Lion of the North') in the righteous cause of the Winter Queen's husband, their own Stuart king's brother-in-law whom they wanted indeed to make Emperor—which reminds us that the tune of their dreaded *Scots March* (now known as 'Dunbarton's Drums') was originally set to the words 'I serve a worthy Lady-o'.

From the gallant General's elder brother, there descended Sir Robert Munro of Foulis, 6th Baronet, first Commanding Officer of the Black

Captain Patrick Munro of Foulis, Chief of the Clan Munro. His maternal grandfather, Sir Hector Munro of Foulis, 11th Baronet, died in 1935. The present laird, who was taken prisoner as an officer of the Seaforth Highlanders with the rest of the Highland Division on the fall of France in 1940, is one of the most energetic and efficiently modernised farmers in the whole of the Highlands: as is indeed in keeping with the far-sighted Munro tradition.

Watch, which he commanded at Fontenoy in 1745. Instead of making his men stand rigidly to receive and return the French volleys, in the usual military mode then in fashion, Sir Robert ordered them to 'clap the ground' at the moment the French officers gave the order to fire, and then to fire themselves and charge in upon the enemy before the French could reload. This tactic was a great success. The Munro chief himself, 'being old and corpulent, was unable to "clap the ground" with his men, but although he alone of the regiment remained erect, with the Colours behind him, he escaped nonetheless'. However, he was killed in the next year at the battle of Falkirk, fighting against the Jacobites for George II, who was great-grandson of the Munros' beloved Winter Queen. Sir Robert was slain in close combat with six Camerons, killing two and breaking his broadsword on the others, before a seventh Cameron shot him with a pistol. The enemy gave him a military funeral, which all the 'rebel' Jacobite chiefs attended.

James Monroe, twice President of the United States (1817–1825) and author of the celebrated 'Monroe Doctrine' banning outside intervention on the American Continent, probably descended from the mediaeval Munro chiefs of Foulis.

Foulis Castle, built in the Dutch mode by the 'Scholar Chief', Sir Harry Munro of Foulis, 7th Baronet, to replace the older 'castle gaunt-peaked, the eagle's nest' of the Gaelic poem, burnt down accidentally in 1750. Sir Harry was son of Sir Robert Munro of Foulis, a Whig Member of Parliament. At the Parliamentary election of 1721, Sir Robert's clansmen knocked on the doors of all Dingwall burgh councillors suspected of being likely to vote against him, dragging them forth (to the indignation of their wives) and holding them prisoners all next day until the election was over. He was duly re-elected, despite a certain amount of protest afterwards, which was naturally disregarded. At the battle of Fontenoy, Sir Robert commanded The Black Watch, and he was killed on the Government side at the battle of Falkirk in 1746.

In the next century, General Sir Charles Munro of Foulis, 9th Baronet, commanded a Division of the Colombian revolutionary army, in South America, under the great Bolivar at the decisive battle in which South America was liberated from Spanish control. Sir Charles's brother was ancestor of the present Baronet of Foulis-Obsdale. But Sir Charles's grandson, Sir Hector Munro of Foulis, 11th Baronet, Lord Lieutenant of Ross and Aide-de-Camp to King George V, was maternal grandfather of the present baron and chief: Captain Patrick Munro of Foulis, Deputy Lieutenant of the County of Ross.

Novar House, home of the Munros of Novar, now represented by Arthur Munro-Ferguson. Behind Novar is Fyrish Hill, crowned by a replica of the Gates of Negapatam in India, a Madras town captured by General Sir Hector Munro of Novar in 1781. He caused this 'folly' to be built in order to provide work for the unemployed (at a time when the Government made no provision for them) as they were too proud to accept money for nothing. Many lairds provided similar relief out of their own resources by commissioning such 'romantick' building work at this time.

Gunn

The chief of Clan Gunn was Gunn of Killearnan, whose Gaelic title was *Mac Sheumais Chataich*. The family derived their name from their Norse Orcadian ancestor Gunni, whose wife Ragnhild (widow of Lifolf 'Baldpate') inherited great estates on the Scottish mainland in Caithness and Sutherland after the death in battle in 1198 of her brother Harald Ungi, Jarl in Orkney and Earl in Caithness. Her father descended from Moddan 'in Dale', probably son of Moddan, mormaer of Caithness (slain 1040); and her grandfather was Saint Ragnvald (St. Ronald), Jarl in Orkney, who built Kirkwall Cathedral in honour of his own uncle St. Magnus: the bones of both saints still sanctify the building. These Orkney jarls descended from 'Turf' Einar, Jarl of Orkney from 894, who taught the Orcadians to burn turf or peat in their fireplaces and was half-brother of Rolf the Ganger, founder of Normandy. It was Turf Einar who avenged the murder of their father Ragnvald the Wise, Jarl of Möre, son of Eystein Glumra, Jarl of the Upplanders: descended through the Norse sea-kings of Vestfold and Raumariké from the ancient pagan sacral 'Peace-Kings of Uppsala' in Sweden. Their emblem was the *galley*, the boat that symbolised their ancestral mother-goddess Freya.

Gunni himself was son of Anders by Frida, sister of Bishop Bjarni and daughter of the famous Kolbein Hruga (her mother was also descended from the Norse jarls of Orkney). Gunni's father Anders (just possibly the Gillanders who was with the six earls who besieged King Malcolm IV at Perth in 1160 on behalf of the whole North of the realm) was son of the daring but wily Sweyn Asleif's-son, famed in the Sagas, whose stirring life as 'The Ultimate Viking' has given its name to a book by Eric Linklater, and the outlines of whose vanished long-hall can still be discerned on the little island of Gairsay in the Orkneys. The Orkney *roithman* family of Rendall probably also descended from the piratical Sweyn. His mainland home in Caithness was at Freswick, a few miles south of Duncansby Head.

Sweyn Aleif's-son had two brothers—Valthiof, drowned at sea on his way from his island of Stronsay to attend Jarl Paul of Orkney's Yule feast, and an earlier Gunni, outlawed for having a child by the widowed Margaret, Countess of Atholl—also a sister Ingirid, who married Thorbiorn 'Clerk', murderer of Saint Ragnvald (St. Ronald), the Crusader Jarl of Orkney. Sweyn himself (the Gunn ancestor) was called Asleif's-son from his mother Asleif, after the death of his father Olaf Hrolf's-son, who had been burnt alive in his house at Duncansby (near the modern John o' Groats) in Caithness by Olvir 'the Riotous' at the instigation of Olvir's ambitious grandmother Frakok, aunt of Jarl Paul 'the Silent' of Orkney. Jarl Paul rashly outlawed Sweyn Asleif's-son for murdering Sweyn 'Breast-rope', one of the Jarl's bodyguard, but had earlier made him his own warden (Crowner, in a sense) in Caithness. However, in 1137, Sweyn Asleif's-son kidnapped the Jarl while he was otter-hunting, and carried him off to Atholl. Poor Jarl Paul the Silent was never heard of again. Later, Sweyn avenged his father by defeating Olvir 'the Riotous' in Helmsdale and burning Frakok in her own house. Sweyn Asleif's-son was eventually killed in Ireland in 1171, after capturing the city of Dublin in a successful raid from his long-ships.

His grandson Gunni, the name-father of the clan, was thus a power to reckon with in Caithness. Snaekoll Gunni's-son, the 2nd Chief, was forfeited and fled to Norway in 1231 after slaying the then Jarl of Orkney: John, who was Paul the Silent's great-nephew and eventual heir. This murder was on account of a considerable land-claim dispute between Jarl John and Snaekoll, arising out of their mutual descent from the ancient Jarls. This feud was to continue between their descendants for centuries. Snaekoll Gunni's-son retained his great estates in Caithness, and from his son Ottar, living in 1280, there sprang the later chiefs of the Clan Gunn. The traditional genealogy from the thirteenth to fifteenth centuries runs:

The coat-of-arms of the Gunn chiefs has not yet been recorded in Lyon Register. In 1800, Gun-Munro of Braemore recorded a coat with a three-masted ship on the sea, and on a red 'chief' (i.e. the top third of the shield) the Three Legs of Man between two golden stars. The Manx Legs reflected a late and erroneous tradition that the name-father of the clan, Gunni, was the son of a Norse king of the Isle of Man: whose royal house in fact probably sprang from the same Ynglingar stock as the jarls of Orkney to whom the real historic Gunni was related. The three-masted ship is simply a differenced version of the old *galley* of the Orkney jarls, thought up by the heralds to disentangle Caithness from Orkney symbolically. Burke's *General Armory*, which lists a number of officially unrecorded coats-of-arms, attributes to Gunn (Sutherland) a three-masted galley, and on a red 'chief' a bear's head between two stars; while for Gunne (Caithness) it has a ship under sail on the sea, and three stars on a red 'chief' above the ship. Basically, therefore, the Gunn coat is obviously the Ship of Caithness (derived from the Galley of Orkney) with a 'chief' of Sutherland (golden stars on red) on which another device is usually also incorporated. This device in the Braemore coat is the Three Legs of Man, a late misconception, and on the other attributed coat it is a Mackay bear's head (from so many key Gunn–Mackay marriages in the sixteenth and seventeenth centuries) that was only adopted in error by the Mackays in the seventeenth century. It therefore falls to be considered what was the earlier device borne by the Gunns in their 'chief': and the obvious answer is, their famous silver brooch (heraldically a 'buckle') as Crowners of Caithness.

Startlingly enough, the earliest surviving example of the Gunn chiefs' coat-of-arms appears to have been punch-marked by a mediaeval armourer-smith on a rock in Massachusetts in or about 1395 (see SINCLAIR). Obviously it is impossible to attain certainty in such a matter, especially from photographs, but the heater-shaped shield there, borne by what seems to be the effigy of a fourteenth century knight, appears to shew arms of a distinctively Norse-Scottish character: a galley, and in chief a star between two large buckles. As with many Scandinavian heraldic boats, no mast appears to be shewn: but the oars are crossed in saltire at the blades, as in some Highland coats. The dexter (left-hand) buckle is badly eroded, but part of its outer curve remains, and heraldically the star would always be placed between two similar objects. The rest of the shield seems too clear to be a mistracing of any natural rock formation or of some redskin inscription, the more especially considering the circumstances attending its discovery by someone without specialist and mediaevalist heraldic knowledge. The conventional style of the ship has a flavour of Scandinavian heraldry, and nearly ten per cent of old Scottish coats are marshalled with objects in chief. The earliest surviving Scottish armorial roll, painted on parchment, shews the shield in 1332 of the then Earl of Caithness as a *golden galley on red*; and no line on the Westford rock suggests that the shield there had a separately-coloured chief, so that it may not be too unreasonable to suggest its blazon, in heraldic jargon, as *Gules a lymphad, sails furled, oars in saltire, and in chief a mullet Gold between two large buckles Silver*. Moreover, the mode in which the Galley of Caithness is depicted on the roll (see illustration under GRAHAM, first row of shields) makes it possible that it is not oars but mast-ropes that are punchmarked on the Westford rock. The illustrations here shew a drawing of the shield as punch-marked on the rock, together with a rough sketch by the writer shewing the dexter buckle restored and the dotted lines connected.

The effigy at Westford in Massachusetts may therefore possibly mark the grave of a Gunn companion-of-arms of Henry Sinclair, Jarl of Orkney, on his celebrated voyage of exploration in the far West.

George, Crowner of Caithness in 1464, son of James (i.e. *Seumas*), son of Donald, son of Ingram, son of James (i.e. *Jakop*), son of Ottar, son of Snaekoll Gunni's-son. Ingram is so unusual a name so far North (being the same as the Frankish Enguerrand) that it is perhaps worth observing that Malcolm, Earl of Caithness and Angus in 1232, had a daughter and heiress Maud, whose husband Sir Gilbert de Umfraville belonged to a great Norman baronial house which favoured the distinctive Christian name of Ingram: and the generations shew that Ingram Gunn must have been born about the beginning of the fourteenth century, when Maud's Umfraville descendants still had influence in Caithness; and indeed he is said as 'Ingram Guyn' to have witnessed a charter in the reign of King David II, who succeeded to the throne in 1329.

The eventual homeland of the Gunn chiefs was in the highland tracts of Caithness, and especially throughout the thirty miles-long *Gleann na Guineach* or 'Gunn's Glen' in the wide parish of Kildonan on the Sutherland border, around the upper reaches of the river Helmsdale dominated by Ben Grainmore and in Strath Ullie: in a sort of 'buffer state' between the territories of the rival earls of Sutherland and Caithness. But we are told that in 1464 the tower of Dirlot, 'occupying a very picturesque position on the top of an isolated crag close to the River Thurso', was forcibly held by George Gunn, chief of the clan and hereditary Crowner of Caithness, who also had another castle of his own at Hallburg or Halberry in Mid Clyth, north of Lybster, on a promontory jutting out to sea, with a trench cut in the rock for a drawbridge on the landward side. For these were still the days before the Gunns were driven back into the mountains on the Caithness border. In modern times, there was still a place called the 'Crouner's Garden' at Strath farm near Watten; and the Gunn family burial place was long in St. Magnus' Chapel at Spital, about five miles from Dirlot Castle. George Gunn was nicknamed *am Bràisdeach Mor*, 'Big Broochy', for the insignia worn by the Gunn chiefs as Crowners of Caithness was a large silver brooch, still remembered in local legend as *am Bràisd Mor*.

Since at least 1426, the Gunn chiefs had been locked in conflict with the Keiths of Ackergill, who had inherited through a Cheyne heiress important rival Caithness land-claims derived from her remote ancestor John, Jarl of Orkney (murdered by Snaekoll, 2nd Gunn chief, in 1231). The Clan Gunn had been defeated in 1438 in a battle on Tannach Moor near Wick, by the combined forces of the Keiths and the Mackays. There is a distinctively Norse flavour about the tale that in another battle, near Halberry Castle itself, a huge Keith was attended by the devil in the shape of a raven sitting on his shoulder and assisting him 'by tearing the eyes out of the sockets of some of the Gunns'. For the Raven is the bird that symbolises the spirit of Woden, whose Raven-Banner the old Orkney jarls (ancestors of the Keiths and Gunns alike) had displayed in many a battle: there was a prophecy that it would always have the victory, but its standard-bearer would always be killed. The Gunns were again defeated by the Keiths in 1464 in Strathmore near Dirlot. 'Soon thereafter Crowner Gunn and some of his sons were massacred by the Keiths in the chapel of St. Tyer, near Wick.' Four of his sons were slain that day, which other accounts place in 1478. There is a well-known tale that it had been agreed to hold a reconciliation meeting of twelve horsemen from each side. Twenty-four Keiths came, two on each horse, and slew the Gunns, who had sought sanctuary in the chapel.

In 1517, the Clan Gunn played a decisive part in the battle of Torran Dubh in Rogart, when the Sutherland Murrays, supported by the Rosses of Balnagowan, defeated the Mackays and their allies. An old Gaelic song has the stanza:

> *Thainig na Guinich 's gu'n tainig iad,*
> *'S ann an deagh am a thainig iad.*
> *Thair iad as Macaoidh 's siol Mhothan,*
> *Mharbhadh leo siol Phail gun acain.*

'The Gunns came and came they did, It was in an hour of need they came,

The Mackays and Mathesons fled, But the Polsons were mercilessly slain '.

The famous Crowner of Caithness's son James Gunn, the next Chief, was probably the Seumas from whom the later Gunn chiefs derived their Gaelic title of *Mac Sheumais Chataich*, ' Son of James of Caithness '. His son ' William MacKames ', the 1st *Mac Sheumais*, was the Chief who avenged the Crowner by killing George Keith of Ackergill and his son, with ten of their men, at Drummoy. Famed in Gaelic song, he was father of David Gunn, whose son *Alasdair mac Dhaidh* (Alexander son of David) the 2nd *Mac Sheumais*, married Barbara, sister of Uisdean *Dubh*, Chief of the Mackays, whom he supported with his clan in an unsuccessful attack on the Earl of Caithness's stronghold of Girnigoe in 1589, after which they sacked the town of Wick. The leaden casket containing the 4th Earl of Caithness's hard heart was opened in a vain search for treasure, and its grim dust and ashes scattered to the wind. At Whitsunday in the same year, ' MacHamish Gunn of Killearnan again wasted Caithness with great ferocity . . . and this was called Creach ne Kamish ' (i.e. *Mac Sheumais's* cattle raid). This great raid was made by Alasdair Gunn of Killearnan, chief of the whole clan, because the ancient friendship between the Clan Gunn and the Sinclair earls of Caithness had some time since begun to turn into enmity as the result of the late policies of the ferocious 4th Earl of Caithness, who had slowly done his own son to death and who in 1556 had had to get a Government remission for his excesses in carrying Fire & Sword into the country of the ' Clan-Gun and Clan-Morgun ' (i.e. Gunns and Mackays).

But the nearest enemy (with pressing land-claims) to the Gunns were a fanatically self-sufficient branch of the Mackays known as the Aberach Mackays, who often acted in opposition to their own chief, Alasdair Gunn of Killearnan's brother-in-law Uisdean *Dubh* Mackay of Strathnaver. Ian Grimble, the leading modern historian of the far North, writes: ' It appears . . . that the conspiracy to liquidate the Clan Gunn originated in about 1582, that the Gunns were supported by the Earl of Caithness and Mackay, and that five years of bungling and brutality achieved little. In 1585 the Earl of Sutherland took over the protection of the Abrach Mackays, leaving Uisdean . . . the Chief of a fragmented clan.' The young 5th Earl of Caithness agreed to an alliance with the Earl of Sutherland against the Clan Gunn in 1586. By chance, a raiding party of true Mackays came upon the retreating Gunns, and joined them in defeating the Sinclairs on the ' Day of the Heather-Knoll ' on the slopes of Ben Grian; but the Gunns were later defeated in their turn by the Sutherland forces (including the dissident Aberach Mackays) near Lochbroom. It was therefore natural that in 1589 Alasdair Gunn of Killearnan made his great raid on the Sinclair lands in Caithness.

His son, William *Mor* mac Alasdair Gunn, the 3rd *Mac Sheumais* to be Chief of Gunn, succeeded to Killearnan in 1614. He was father of Alasdair Gunn of Killearnan, 4th *Mac Sheumais*, husband of Mary Mackay, widow of Sir Hector Munro of Foulis (Chief of the Clan Munro) and sister of Donald, 1st Lord Reay (Chief of the Clan Mackay). His son, Iain Gunn of Navidale, yr. of Killearnan, was father of Alasdair Gunn of Killearnan, the 5th *Mac Sheumais*, who in about 1650 married Christina Mackay, daughter of Donald, 1st Lord Reay. Their son was Donald *Crottach* ' the Hunch-Backed ' Gunn of Killearnan, usually reckoned as the 6th *Mac Sheumais*, whose mansion house at Killearnan was accidentally burnt down in 1690: ' it is said that the chief and another of the clan were preparing for a hunting expedition, when some powder ignited, with the result that the whole buildings were destroyed by fire '. Later, ' Gordon of Kilgour obtained Killernan from the Earl of Sutherland, probably on a writ of apprising for debts, and Donald, the McHamish of that time, was threatened with ejection. He assembled 250 of the clan in and around his home, and refused to leave. His father-in-law, Major Sutherland of Torbo, interfered in his favour, and Badenloch was obtained for him. He had sent his family to Caithness previously, to prevent their being asked as hostages to ratify a settlement of the quarrel.'

The rock at Westford in Massachusetts, punch-marked with what appears to be the effigy of a fourteenth-century knight, bearing a shield with what may possibly be the earliest surviving example of the Arms of Gunn. Note the heater-shaped armorial shield to the right of the typically fourteenth-century sword.

Aerial view, looking southwards, of Halberry Head at Mid Clyth on the coast of Caithness. Here was the long-vanished stronghold of the Gunns, on the headland jutting into the sea in the foreground. As late as 1890, we are told that ' the isthmus has a trench across it, cut in the solid rock, 150 feet long, 18 feet broad, and from 9 to 12 feet deep. Over this was the drawbridge, with external and internal guard-houses. No castle exists, but the marks of three buildings can be discerned, and there are indications of other constructions.' The stronghold was apparently abandoned by the Gunns after George Gunn, Crowner of Caithness, was slain in the fifteenth century.

Further up the coast of Caithness is Duncansby Head, in the extreme north-east of Britain. At Duncansby Olaf, Hrolf's son, had his wooden long-hall, where he was holding his Yule-tide feast early in the twelfth century when it was surrounded and set afire by his enemies, and he was burnt to death with his men. His widow was Asleif, from whom his famous Viking son, Sweyn the pirate Chief, took the name of Sweyn Asleif's-son. From Sweyn's grandson, Gunni Ottar's-son, the Clan Gunn take their name. The Gunn chiefs in later times bore the Gaelic title of *Mac Sheumais* (pronounced Mac Hamish). ' So devoted were his followers that their common saying was *Toill Dhea's McHamish*, "Let the will of God and that of McHamish be done".'

The Strath of Kildonan, homeland of the Clan Gunn. Contemporary sketch by an Inverness architect of vain prospecting for gold-mines there in the nineteenth century.

Donald the Hunch-Backed was succeeded in 1723 by his elder son Captain Alexander Gunn of Badenloch, the 7th *Mac Sheumais*, who was known as *Alasdair Mor* and ' was one of the celebrated and ancient stock who kept up the reputation of the chiefs in the Highlands. He had a piper, band, armour-bearer, an armoury and the fiery cross. When he built his new mill he put the whole machinery to work by whisky, and called it *muilliann a clabharr* '. In 1736 his brother George Gunn in Corrish was in danger of his life from a charge of claiming payment on a forged bill, whereupon the chief attended the Sutherland Regality Court at Dornoch, asked to see the bill and then fought off the whole court with a chair while he swallowed the dangerous document. In the 1745 Rising he supported the Government, like all his neighbours; and accordingly the Campbell Earl of Loudoun was joined by ' 120 Gunns under their chief MacKemish '. At his death in 1763, he was succeeded by his young son William Gunn, the 8th *Mac Sheumais*, who fell in battle as a Highland officer against Hyder Ali at Conjeveram in India, in 1780.

Thereafter, the chiefship passed lawfully to their cousin Hector Gunn, in Thurso, who in 1803 was served heir to his great-great-grandfather *quondam Alexander Gunn MacHamish de Navidale et Kilearnan, communiter vocatus MacHamish quintus, princeps tribus de Gunn*, i.e. Alasdair the 5th *Mac Sheumais*. Hector Gunn thus established his right to be the 9th *Mac Sheumais*, ' for aught yet seen ', and was succeeded as Chief of Gunn by his son George Gunn in Rhives, Lieutenant Royal Marines, afterwards Factor at Dunrobin.

The line of chiefs of the whole Clan Gunn was of course always that of ' MacHamish ' of Killearnan, but there were two important branches with chieftains of note: the ' Robson ' Gunns of Braemore and the Bregaul Gunns in Dale. The ancestor of the ' Robson ' Gunns was Robert, a younger son of the Crowner slain in the fifteenth century. From John, the Crowner's third son, ' are descended the Gunns of Dalmore and Dale, and others; Henry, the fourth son, is the traditional ancestor of the Caithness Hendersons; and William, the fifth son, of the Williamsons and Wilsons '. One of the Crowner's other four sons (also slain in 1464) appears to have been called Alasdair, for an inventory in 1456 of the goods of the Earl of Caithness's late father-in-law mentions ' Alexander the Crowner's son ' as owing for ' the teinds of Dale, Thurso and the River, with uther geeds that he tuk of myn ', while ' Henry the Crounars son ' also owed for teinds and cattle that he had taken. Nevertheless the will, to which the inventory of 1456 relates, has an item: ' I leave to the Crowner a horse '.

In the sixteenth century, Iain Gunn, the chieftain of the Robson branch of the clan, married a natural daughter of Adam Gordon, Earl of Sutherland. His son Alasdair Gunn, the next Robson chieftain, was executed at Inverness in 1565 by the Regent Moray (whose wife, incidentally, was a Keith). In the seventeenth century, Sir William Gunn, Keeper of Dirlot Castle (younger son and brother of the then Robson chieftains, both called Iain), distinguished himself as a soldier of fortune on the Continent. He was wounded commanding two regiments of horse and 1,000 musketeers at the battle of Witstock in Germany, in the Swedish Service, but the Swedish Chancellor mistrusted him because he was a Catholic. He fought as a Cavalier under Lord Aboyne at the Bridge of Dee, for King Charles I, who knighted him in 1639. Sir William Gunn then transferred into the service of the Holy Roman Emperor, marrying Baroness Anna Margaretha von Freiburg at Ulm in 1640 (the town councillors were invited to the wedding banquet in the ' White Ox ' inn), afterwards becoming an imperial Generalwachtmeister and being created a Baron of the Empire in 1649. About the same time, Colonel Iain Gunn (' Johann Gunn ') from Golspie was Governor of Ohlau in Silesia, which he re-fortified between 1638 and 1649 in the Swedish Service: the citizens genuinely lamented his death, and preserved his mail-armour into the present century, ' hung up in the High School '.

The Robson chieftainship was continued by John Gunn of Braemore, who held Braemore in 1664 and whose son George Gunn, yr. of Braemore, had a tack of Dirlot in 1689. These Gunns of Braemore ended in an heiress, Janet Gunn, married to the Rev. John Munro and ancestress of the Gun-Munros, who were obliged to sell Braemore for debt in 1793, but recorded Arms in Lyon Register as Gun-Munro of Braemore in 1800.

In September 1821, George Gunn, the 10th *Mac Sheumais*, was invited to preside over a special gathering to form a clan society. The letter of invitation says, ' There are none to be admitted but those that can spell Gunn as their name. . . . We expect to muster about 200 men to form the society, who will, it is proposed, wear the clan tartan at the yearly meeting '. Accordingly, three months later, the Loyal & United Benevolent Society of the Clan Gunn was instituted at Thurso. By its rules and regulations, ' Rebels, swearers, thieves and Sabbath-breakers ' were rigidly excluded; and every member was to appear on the yearly meeting in a coat of tartan belonging to the clan, under a fine of one shilling. But provision was made for Gunn widows and orphans, and for Sick Allowance, also funeral expenses. The old patriarchate of the Chiefs was gone, and the Welfare State had not yet arrived, but the Clan Gunn understood very well the obligations of collective pride.

Since the death of George Gunn, the 10th *Mac Sheumais*, the heir to the chiefship is as yet unascertained, although other descendants of the 5th *Mac Sheumais* appear to exist. Meanwhile, under the stimulating guidance of its Secretary, Iain A. Gunn, LL.B. (Edinburgh), the revived Clan Gunn Society maintains the age-old links between Gunn clansmen, so long scattered throughout the world from their homeland in Sutherland and Caithness.

Eilean Donan Castle on Loch Duich, in Kintail, the great westerly stronghold of the Mackenzie chiefs from the Middle Ages. There is reason to suppose that a vitrified fort may already have occupied the island site from prehistoric times, and the original curtain walls are probably of the thirteenth century. An unusual feature of the Mackenzie castle is the cistern tower, on the east side, connected to the main castle by a long, sloping, walled passage. This tower was always open to the sky, and provided much needed fresh water for the garrison.

Eoin Mackenzie of Kintail had some difficulty in gaining occupation of the castle after his half-brother, the previous chief, was murdered in 1498: as his uncle (who held the castle) tried to maintain that he was illegitimate. In 1511, the Lords of the Privy Council ordered this uncle, Hector Mackenzie of the Gairloch, to give him free entry into the castle.

From 1520 onwards Eilean Donan was held for the Mackenzie chiefs by the MacRaes, their hereditary Constables of the Castle, who were known as ' Mackenzie's Shirt of Mail '. In 1539, Donald ' the Grim ' Macdonald of Sleat arrived with fifty galleys to attack the castle, held by only three men. One of them was Duncan son of Gilchrist son of Finlay MacRae, who mortally wounded the Macdonald chief with a brilliant bow-shot. The Macdonalds burnt Eilean Donan Castle and Mackenzie's beached fleet of galleys, and harried the countryside in revenge.

William Mackenzie, 5th Earl of Seaforth, raised his clansmen for the Jacobite Cause in 1715, and fought at the Battle of Sheriffmuir. The Government forces occupied Eilean Donan, but Seaforth escaped to France, where King James made him a marquis. His people continued to send their rents to him in exile, and attacked the Government Factor and his escort whenever rents were demanded by King George's administrators of the estates. In 1719 the Jacobite Marquis of Seaforth returned to take part in another Jacobite Rising. His clansmen rallied to him, and a garrison of 45 Spaniards were placed by him in Eilean Donan Castle, while the Mackenzies advanced up Glen Shiel with the other Jacobite forces. They were defeated. Seaforth escaped severely wounded and with a price on his head of £2,000, and the English troops took ' a tour through all the difficult parts of Seaforth's country to terrify the rebels by burning the houses of the Guilty '. Meanwhile, the Spaniards had held out in Eilean Donan Castle against the Royal Navy, until shelling from the frigates had forced them to surrender. The English sailors then blew up the castle, and it became a ruin.

In the twentieth century, however, the Castle was restored by a descendant of the MacRaes who had been its hereditary Constables for the Mackenzie chiefs. The restoration was carried out under the guidance of Mackie Watson, the Edinburgh architect, and a causeway built for convenient access to the island from the mainland. Today it still belongs to John MacRae of Conchra, who at Highland Balls wears a Key, insignia of a castellan, in memory of his descent from the MacRaes who held Eilean Donan so loyally for the Mackenzies centuries ago.

The Castle of Mey, otherwise known as Barrogill, a former stronghold of the Earls of Caithness. It is now the Scottish home of Queen Elizabeth the Queen Mother.

Dunrobin Castle, from the beach. The castle looks out across the North Sea.

Dunrobin Castle, seat of the Earldom of Sutherland since it was the *dun* of *Robin*, 6th Earl of Sutherland (c.1370–c.1427). Earl Robin married a daughter of the 'Wolf of Badenoch', King Robert III's ferocious brother. Their son John, Master of Sutherland (afterwards 7th Earl) rode out from Dunrobin in 1408 to win his spurs adventuring abroad, when he accompanied his uncle the Earl of Mar on an expedition to help 'John the Fearless' Duke of Burgundy to establish the Elect of Liège in his bishopric: where the young Master was knighted by his uncle on the morning of the battle of Othée in which the burghers under Hendrik van Hoorn were routed. Half a millennium later, the late Duke of Sutherland (who was also 23rd Earl) journeyed similarly from Dunrobin to pursue Big Game in distant Continents.

Sinclair

The surname of Sinclair or St. Clair is derived from Saint-Clair-sur-Elle near St. Lô in the Cotentin peninsula of Normandy. In 1162 Henry de St. Clair received a charter of the lands of Herdmanston in Haddingtonshire from the Constable of Scotland, whose Sheriff he was. A St. Clair of Herdmanston was at the battle of Bannockburn, and another was with the dead Douglas when he won the moonlight fight against the Percies at Otterburn. The lands of Herdmanston remained in the family into modern times, and the present head of this branch is Lord Sinclair, whose Arms are a *blue Cross engrailed on silver*.

But the principal line of the Sinclairs bore a *black Cross engrailed on silver*. Their chief, Sir William Sinclair, Sheriff of Edinburgh, Haddington, Linlithgow and Dumfries, also Justiciar of Galloway, was guardian (that is, foster-father) of the heir to the throne, and was granted the Barony of Rosslyn in 1280. His son, Sir Henry Sinclair of Rosslyn, Pantler of Scotland, fought for Bruce at Bannockburn. Sir William Sinclair of Rosslyn was slain with the Douglas, carrying Robert Bruce's heart on Crusade against the Saracens in Andalusia. The next baron of Rosslyn married Lady Isabel, co-heiress of Orkney and Caithness; and their son, Henry Sinclair, was recognised as Jarl of Orkney in 1379 by the King of Norway. As Jarl of Orkney, Henry 'the Holy' Sinclair was the premier noble of Norway.

Through Lady Isabel, the later Sinclair chiefs descend from the pagan Norse and ancient Pictish dynasts who were already ruling in Orkney and Caithness at the time of the earliest surviving historical records, a thousand years ago. These primitive ancestors of the northern Sinclairs were often distinguished by comic nicknames. In the ninth century, conquests were made on the mainland of Pictish Caithness by the Norse jarl Thorstein the Red: son of Olaf the White, 'the greatest war-king in the West-beyond-Sea', by Aud the Deep-Minded, daughter of Ketill Flat-Nose, first Norse ruler of the Hebrides. Thorstein the Red's daughter Groa married the local Picto-Scottish dynast Duncan, mormaer of Caithness, and so their daughter Grelod inherited a mixed claim to the loyalty of the local Picts and Scots and also of the Norse settlers in Caithness. She married Thorfinn Skull-Cleaver, Jarl of Orkney (nephew of Rolf the Ganger, conqueror of Normandy), who belonged to the great Ynglingar dynasty descended through King Halfdan the Stingy and King Eystein the Fart from King Ingiald Ill-Ruler, last of the pagan sacral 'Peace-Kings' of Uppsala.

Their remote Ynglingar ancestors had incarnated the spirit of Mother Earth, the goddess Nerthus or Freya after whom Friday is named. So their emblem was her sacred Galley, shaped like the moon that influences women and also like the horns of the cow that gives milk to mankind. But they had intermarried with the rival Skiöldung house of Woden and their battle-standard was the Black Raven of Woden.

Thorfinn Skull-Cleaver and Countess Grelod were grandparents of the mighty Sigurd, Jarl of Orkney and Caithness (which then also included Sutherland), who fell at the historic battle of Clontarf in 1014 while attempting the conquest of all Ireland. Sigurd's descendants were Jarls of Orkney under the Kings of Norway and Earls of Caithness under the Kings of Scots—although Sutherland was later detached from their domain and given by the Scottish kings to the present Sutherland family, with whom the Earls of Caithness therefore had a feud until the seventeenth century. Sigurd's male line ended in 1156, but his female line has continued ever since, and through the Lady Isabel brought his dynastic claims to the Sinclairs in the fourteenth century. Since then, the Sinclairs have quartered the *golden galley* in their Arms.

While conquering the Faroes in 1391, Henry Sinclair, Jarl of Orkney enlisted a shipwrecked Venetian as captain of his fleet, and later sailed on

Rosslyn Castle, mediaeval stronghold of the Sinclair chiefs, who were Barons of Rosslyn in Scotland and Jarls of Orkney in Norway. In 1395 Henry Sinclair, Jarl of Orkney, made a great naval expedition to seek new lands reported in the far West across the Atlantic Ocean, and he wintered there after he had made a successful landfall, in order to continue his explorations. The initial voyage is described by Antonio Zeno, the Venetian patrician who was Captain of his Fleet, but whom he sent home with the main fleet before winter set in. Although long a matter of controversy among scholars, it is argued that the Jarl's westerly course brought him first to Nova Scotia, where Zeno observed burning pitch running into the sea at the foot of a mountain: possibly at Stellarton, where there are exposed seams of bituminous pitch which have from time to time gone on fire. The Sinclair jarl may well have stayed awhile in Massachusetts, where what is apparently the effigy of a fourteenth century knight in bascinet, camail and surcoat is still discernable on a rock at Westford. If it is not a clever hoax by some truly learned heraldic scholar, the figure would seem to have been punch-marked by a mediaeval lord's armourer-smith to mark the grave of a companion-in-arms.

Charles M. Boland, the enthusiastic writer of *They All Discovered America* (New York 1961), describes its discovery: ' The original evidence on the rock was thought to be a picture, graven in the stone by Indians. It was what appeared to be the drawing of a sword, but people in the vicinity regarded it not as a sword, but as a smallish drawing of an actual Indian. It was first brought to light by William Goodwin, who ran two pictures of it in one of his books, without any caption. Goodwin didn't profess to know what it was, nor did anyone else who saw the photographs. Frank Glynn pondered over it for a long time, and leaned toward the idea that it might be viking. The hilt of the sword was plainly visible as such, but not much more of its character was revealed.

On a hunch, Glynn sent a copy of the book, with the pictures specially noted, to Thomas Lethbridge, then curator of the Museum of Archaeology and Ethnology at Cambridge University in England. He hoped Lethbridge could either confirm his suspicions that the sword was viking, or offer some concrete opinion on its origin. A few weeks later Lethbridge wrote Glynn that the sword was of fourteenth-century origin, and would Glynn please get more details on it? Lethbridge was excited over the find. With this encouragement, Glynn set out for Westford and found the rock with the sword upon it. . . . . He felt there was more engraving in the rock, but since the upper portion of it was over-grown with bushes, he couldn't be sure.

He went to work with a sickle and axe and cleared away the growth obscuring the remainder of the rock. Then he carefully washed its surface down. When he had finished, he gazed upon a six-foot portrait of a knight in full armour, complete with shield bearing heraldry!

Because the faintness of the figure prevented a good photograph, he made a drawing of the outline and sent it off immediately to Lethbridge.' Tom Lethbridge sent the sketch to the present writer, then Unicorn Pursuivant, whose opinion was that the effigy's heater-shaped shield bore Arms of a Norse-Scottish character such as might have been expected of a knight in Jarl Henry Sinclair's entourage. On mature reflection, indeed, this would appear to be possibly the earliest surviving example of the coat-of-arms of Gunn, at that time perhaps the next most important family on the Pentland Firth after the Sinclairs themselves (see GUNN), to whom they were related. There is of course, nothing remarkable in the idea of the Jarl of Orkney, premier noble of Norway, sailing to America in the fourteenth century: for the Norsemen had certainly been crossing the Atlantic since at least four centuries before, and the great Scandinavian houses were all inter-related.

a long voyage of exploration, possibly to America. His grandson, William Sinclair, last Jarl of Orkney, was granted the old family earldom of Caithness in 1455. He is was who built beautiful Rosslyn Chapel: so famous in the world of Freemasonry, in which the Sinclairs came to occupy a very special position. This gem of a chapel, with the picturesque ruins of Rosslyn Castle, still belongs to Anthony St. Clair-Erskine, 6th Earl of Rosslyn, descended in the female line from William St. Clair or Sinclair, last Jarl of Orkney and first Earl of Caithness.

The 1st Earl of Caithness disinherited his mentally deficient eldest son William ' the Waster ', 2nd Lord Sinclair; leaving the barony of Rosslyn to his second son and the earldom of Caithness to his third son, William Sinclair, 2nd Earl of Caithness, who fell in battle at Flodden. John Sinclair, 3rd Earl of Caithness, was slain in Orkney helping his cousin, Lord Sinclair, to put down a rising led by other Sinclairs in the Orkneys in 1529: ' great cruelties were practised on both sides '.

George Sinclair, 4th Earl of Caithness was as tough and ferocious as his Viking forefathers. After an attack on the Murrays in 1570, he imprisoned his own eldest son, the kindly Master of Caithness, for concluding a peace treaty with the Murrays without his leave. The unfortunate Master was chained up in a dungeon in Girnigoe Castle and ' wes keiped in miserable captivitie for the space of seaven yeirs, and died at last in prissone by famine and vermine '. It was rumoured that the Master was so hardy that his gaolers, at the instigation of his brother William Sinclair of Mey, had to finish him off by giving him salt beef but withholding all drink until he died raving.

One day, while William Sinclair was taunting his captive brother, the frenzied Master leapt upon him and tried to strangle him with his chains. William got away with some difficulty but died from the bruising within a fortnight. The upshot of this interview was that the present Viscount Thurso is not Earl of Caithness, although that peerage is held by a younger branch of the family. For William Sinclair of Mey's untimely death

Sir John Sinclair of Ulbster, 1st Baronet, P.C., M.P., first President of the Board of Agriculture, which he persuaded Pitt to found in 1793. Descended from the 4th Earl of Caithness, he was himself the ancestor of the present Viscount Thurso, K.T., P.C.

Girnigoe Castle, ruined stronghold of the Earls of Caithness, overlooking Sinclair's Bay north of Wick in Caithness. Here the unfortunate Master of Caithness was kept chained up by his own father from 1571 to 1578, and strangled his mocking brother with these chains before dying mad with thirst in his grim dungeon.

His brutal gaolers, David Sinclair and Ingram Sinclair, were slain in revenge some years later by his son George Sinclair, 5th Earl of Caithness, who kept a coining den in the castle, run by a forger called Smith. This earl was at feud with the Earl of Orkney (a Stewart royal bastard), and played a rough practical joke on some servants of Orkney's, ' who had been forced to touch at Caithness through stress of weather. After making them drunk with whisky he shaved one side of their heads and beards, and sent them to sea, although the storm had not abated. On 3 March 1609, the king wrote to the council about the outrage', and Caithness received a sharp rebuke.

The ruins of Girnigoe belong to the present chief, Malcolm Sinclair, 20th Earl of Caithness, whose father was the first Commander-in-Chief of the Army of newly-independent Ceylon and then the Queen's personal Factor at Balmoral.

prevented him from legitimating ' by subsequent marriage ', in the usual Scottish manner, the two sons of the exquisite lady of his choice; and so the earldom of Caithness and chiefship of the Sinclair clan passed eventually to the descendants of his younger brother.

However, the two natural sons were given estates out of the old family inheritance in Caithness. The elder died unmarried; while from the younger there descended the Sinclair baronets of Ulbster, now represented by Archibald Sinclair, 1st Viscount Thurso, K.T., who declined the Viceroyalty of India, offered him by Winston Churchill, but was Leader of the Liberal Party and Secretary of State for Air throughout the Second World War. Lord Thurso has great estates in Caithness, of which county he was the Lord Lieutenant for many years until he retired from ill-health. But Malcolm Ian Sinclair, 20th Earl of Caithness, who owns the ruins of grim Girnigoe Castle on the rocky Caithness coast, is the present Chief of the Sinclair clan.

Sutherland

The Sutherland clan take their name from the highlands of the far north of Scotland, which is known as 'Sutherland' because to the Norsemen it was the *sudrland* that lay to the south of their settlements in Orkney and the dales of Caithness. Sutherland was originally the southern part of the ancient earldom of Caithness, but after it was detached from the Norsemen, it was given by the King of Scots, about the beginning of the thirteenth century, to a great lord called Hugh of Moray. Hugh's grandfather Freskin, probably son of Ollec, was a Flemish noble with lands in various parts of Scotland and apparently as far afield as the Welsh border. During the twelfth century Freskin's family seem to have intermarried with the old Picto-Scottish royal house of Moray from whom the Mackay chiefs (who bore the Three Stars of Moray until the seventeenth century) are believed to spring in the male line.

Certainly the great lords of Freskin's line called themselves 'of Moray', and they still bear the Three Stars in their Arms: the Sutherlands have the Three Stars *gold on red*, surrounded by a royal tressure. Hugh of Moray, who thus became Lord of Sutherland before 1211, had a younger brother, William of Moray or Murray, ancestor of the historic name that are today Dukes of Atholl, Earls of Dunmore and Mansfield and Viscounts Elibank. Hugh of Moray, lord of Sutherland, was father of William of Sutherland, who took his surname from his territory, and in about 1235 became first Earl of Sutherland (earldoms in those days were accorded to the near kin of royalty). He was forefather to all the Earls and Dukes of Sutherland ever since. Although cotton-sedge (very common in Sutherland) is the Sutherland clan plant-badge, it is interesting that the Sutherlands as late as the nineteenth century sometimes also wore butcher's broom, plant of the Murrays.

Kenneth, 4th Earl of Sutherland, was killed with the Regent of Scotland and three other earls while leading his men against the English invaders at the battle of Halidon Hill in 1333. The chronicler of chivalry, Froissart, tells us that William, 5th Earl of Sutherland, was the first to join his brother-in-law King David Bruce with 'many men-at-arms' for the campaign that ended so disastrously at Nevill's Cross in 1346. Earl William's grandmother had been a daughter of Llewellyn, Prince of Wales, and his first wife was Princess Margaret, daughter of King Robert Bruce. His son by her was about to be made heir to the throne, instead of the ancestor of the Stewarts, when he died of the plague in 1361. The later earls descended from Earl William's second wife. He himself died in 1370, possibly as the result of revenge for his brother's treacherous murder of the Mackay chief at a conference that year. Thenceforward for nearly four centuries and ten generations or more, there was a feud between the Mackay clan and the Sutherlands.

Dunrobin, which means 'Robin's Castle', was named after Robert, 6th Earl of Sutherland, who married in 1389 a daughter of the 'Wolf of Badenoch', King Robert III's ferocious brother: and it has ever since remained the chief stronghold of the earldom of Sutherland. There may have been an earlier castle on the same site, and not far away are the remains of a Pictish broch or dry-stone tower.

John, 8th Earl of Sutherland, went mad in 1494. His son John, 9th Earl, was also weak-minded and was placed under the care of his sister Elizabeth, wife of Huntly's brother Adam Gordon, who held Dunrobin and took possession of the earldom of Sutherland at his death. Elizabeth thus became Countess of Sutherland in her own right, despite a gallant struggle by her half-brother Alexander Sutherland, the rightful heir, who captured Dunrobin Castle obviously with considerable local support, but was soon forced to surrender it to the Gordons. Desultory fighting continued, however, for a year or so until he was killed in a skirmish elsewhere in Sutherland. 'His head wes careid to Dunrobin on a spear, and wes

The mediaeval two-handed Justiciary Sword of the Earldom of Sutherland, still at Dunrobin. This sword was borne before the earls or their deputes when they held their Courts of Regality, to symbolise their power of life and death.

placed vpon the height of the great tour'. Elizabeth, Countess of Sutherland in her own right, 'full of spirite and witt . . . of good judgement, and great modestie', was succeeded by her grandson John Gordon, 11th Earl of Sutherland, known as the 'Good Earl John', who was poisoned in 1567.

In 1598, the 13th Earl of Sutherland caused the first coal pits to be sunk at Brora (near Dunrobin) where he also established saltpans. In his time, too, the earldom of Sutherland was erected in 1601 into a Regality, making it well-nigh an autonomous principality 'with a high and almost royal jurisdiction'. The little royal authority that was retained was in the hands of the sheriff, and the Earl was also Hereditary Sheriff of Sutherlandshire. Inverbrora (later Dornoch) was the capital burgh of the sheriffdom, but the chief place of the earldom remained the castle of ' Dwnrobene '.

In the time of John, 16th Earl of Sutherland, K.T., a wolf was killed within twelve miles of Dunrobin. It was he who, as Chief of the Sutherlands, resumed the ancient surname of Sutherland instead of Gordon. In 1715, as Lord Lieutenant of all the eight northern counties, he raised his men for King George and garrisoned Inverness against the Jacobites. William, 17th Earl of Sutherland, a Fellow of the Royal Society, continued the Hanoverian tradition of his line. In 1745, on rumours of a Jacobite Rising, he reconciled himself to Lord Reay in spite of the ancient feud between the Sutherlands and Mackays. When the Rising began, Earl William raised his own clansmen for the Government. In 1746, the Earl of Cromartie had been left in command of the Jacobite invaders occupying Dunrobin Castle, when his men were surprised and defeated by the Earl of Sutherland's militia who surrounded the castle, killed a number of the Jacobites and captured the Earl of Cromartie in ' an apartment which was afterwards called the Cromartie Room '. Dunrobin was thus the last castle in Britain to be captured with bloodshed in time of war, and it seems fitting that its final captors were the Sutherlands themselves.

William, 17th Earl of Sutherland, was succeeded in 1766 by his infant daughter and heiress Elizabeth, Countess of Sutherland in her own right.

Uppat House, the Countess of Sutherland's home near Brora.

At this time, the love and loyalty of the Sutherland clansmen for their chiefs the Earls was a byword, and was particularly remarked by Lord President Forbes of Culloden in his important memorial about the highland clans. It was therefore all the more sad that their old happy way of life, poor and hardy though it was, should have been destroyed by the good intentions of the Countess's conscientious English husband, the Marquess of Stafford. He was a keen reformer and progressive 'planner' who was horrified to be faced with a 'population explosion' and to find her people still living the old feudal and Gaelic way of life in their 'black houses'. Like so many reformers he was willing to dedicate his life and fortune to making other folk do something they found desperately disagreeable for the sake of what he believed to be their future good. He therefore used his great English funds to move the Sutherland people from their barren glens to new industries that he set up on the coast. He also eliminated the tacksmen, the gentlemen of the clan who were its natural local leaders and whom the native Earls had always felt the usual Celtic moral obligation to provide with a certain holding of land.

All this was only achieved by a ruthless abandonment of the customary obligations that had bound a chief to his clan, and by the relentless Clearances that shocked reactionary old-fashioned chiefs like Robertson of Struan. It is perhaps typical of a zealous reformer's inhumanity towards folk who prefer old ways, that he sought no personal benefit but assumed

In the inner courtyard of the old part of Dunrobin Castle. Above a window are the initials IES for John, 14th Earl of Sutherland, and ICS for his first wife Jean, Countess of Sutherland (only child of the first Earl of Perth), whom he married in 1631 and who died of consumption in 1637. This grim old part of the castle was encased in a fairy-tale new building, designed between 1835 and 1850 by Sir Charles Barry (the architect of the Houses of Parliament), and altered again after the fire of 1915 by Sir Robert Lorimer. But in this courtyard, the hard core of the old earls' stronghold still survives. (See also p. 166.)

Some of the heads shot by the 6th Duke of Sutherland (died 1963); in the building in the gardens of Dunrobin that houses his Big Game hunting trophies.

Elizabeth Sutherland, 24th Countess of Sutherland in her own right, *Ban Mhorair Chataibh* and Chief of the Clan Sutherland. The attractive and talented Chairman of Dunrobin, the School which she has founded in her ancestral castle on the ideals of Gordonstoun. Lady Sutherland is married and has four children; of whom the eldest is Alastair Sutherland, Lord Strathnaver. 'Dunrobin does not wish to force boys into a religious way of life, but it will seek to create an atmosphere in which faith will be accepted without mockery as the foundation of the life of man.'

his own infallibility. The plans in fact went astray when the kelp industry failed and inshore fisheries declined, and the misery was wasted.

However, even at the end of these tough Clearances, the population of Sutherland was larger than it was before they were begun. In 1801, before the Clearances, it was 23,117, in 1831 it was 25,518, and by 1851 it had risen to 25,793: the highest point ever reached in the history of the county. 'So far were the clearances from being merely selfish improvements, that from 1811 to 1833 the country yielded him no rent, and resulted in a loss of £60,000 in all. In these efforts he spent the best years of his life, In politics he was a liberal, and supported . . . the Reform Bill '. In 1833 he was created Duke of Sutherland shortly before his death.

George Granville William, 3rd Duke of Sutherland, K.G., a Fellow of the Royal Society, contributed nearly a quarter of a million pounds towards the construction of the Highland Railway. His wife was the Countess of Cromartie in her own right, whose family had sheltered many of the refugees from the Strathconan Clearances, settling them around Castle Leod, and who descended from the Jacobite earl who was captured in Dunrobin Castle in 1746. Their son, Cromartie, 4th Duke of Sutherland, K.G., succeeded to well over a million acres in Sutherland. He was grandfather of the present chief of the clan, Elizabeth Sutherland, 26th Countess of Sutherland in her own right. Although she has organised the newer and grander parts of Dunrobin Castle as a modern boarding school, she still keeps a flat of her own to be her home in the older part of the castle.

Mackay

Mackay is the Gaelic name *Mac Aoidh*, Son of Aodh. More anciently the name was spelt Aed (later Aedh), and is an ancient Gaelic name meaning ' Fire '. The old Scots chroniclers sometimes wrote the name Ed, Eth or Heth, and put it into charter-Latin as Odo. As late as the seventeenth century, it was often spelt simply Y (' Y Mackay ' for *Aodh Mac Aoidh*), but from the sixteenth century it tended to be Englished as ' Hugh '; just as from the seventeenth century the Mackays tended to English another of their favoured Christian names, Angus, as ' Aeneas '. There should really be no ' k ' in Mackay, but they have written Mac (son) as ' Mack ' for centuries; however, it is misleading to write the name ' MacKay ', as this should imply not son of Aodh but son of Kay.

Long before surnames came generally to the Gaels of the highlands, a few branches of the royal house used such names to indicate the source of their rival claims to the hotly-disputed throne in the twelfth and thirteenth centuries. The chief of these were the houses of MacWilliam and MacAedh (Macheth or Mackay). Both had their great strength in Moray, the northern highlands that included Inverness and Ross. Both were suppressed by the house of King David I, whose line have been Kings of Scots ever since.

There is some reason to suppose that the MacAedh claimants to the Scottish throne descended from a marriage of the heiress of Moray to Aethelred (rendered into Gaelic as Aedh), last Abbot of Dunkeld and first Earl of Fife, elder brother of King Alexander I and King David I; that as abbot he was debarred from the throne; and that he died in about 1128. She was sister of Maelsnechtai, who died in 1085, last King of Moray of the house of Lorn, and who was also Chief of Clan Duff through their grandmother Queen Gruoch (the ' Lady Macbeth ' of Shakespeare), heiress of the Fife royal line of King Duff (slain 967). In 1130, soon after the abbot-earl Aedh's death, the Moraymen rose under ' Maelsnechtai's sister's son ' Angus, King of Moray, together with Malcolm MacAedh (called David I's nephew), probably Angus's brother, in an attempt to gain the Scottish throne from King David I. But they were defeated by Norman mercenaries, and King Angus was killed.

The Sons of Aedh, however, were by no means finished. Gillecoimded

Painting of Kasteel Ophemert in the Netherlands, as it was in the nineteenth century when Baron Aeneas Mackay was Prime Minister of Holland. The moated towerhouse was built by one of the knightly family of Van Werdenburg in about 1420, and passed through an heiress to the Barons Van Haeften. In 1672 the *kasteel* was damaged by invading French troops, and restored at this period, when the pavilions with ogee roofs (one is a dovecote, the other a stairway to the moatside) and the stables were added. In the late eighteenth century, Colonel Aeneas Mackay, of the Scots-Dutch Brigade, married Baroness Ursulina Phillipina Van Haeften, and their son Barthold Mackay (created a Baron of the Netherlands in 1822) afterwards succeeded to Ophemert. The late Lord Reay converted a room in the stables (now the garage) into a Head Hall for his Big Game trophies, a task of interior decoration accomplished with remarkable good taste. In 1966, an unexploded Allied shell was found in the moat and a German Nazi steel helmet was dug up in excavations for a swimming-pool.

MacAedh, who was a highly-placed witness to a charter *c.* 1131–44, was probably one of them. Malcolm MacAedh himself, called 'Jarl of Moray' by the Norsemen, married a sister of King Somerled of the Isles and is known to have had more than one son. He carried on the struggle until his eldest son Donald MacAedh was captured in 1156; when he was nominally reconciled to the King of Scots, and became Earl of Ross (northern Moray) until his death in 1168. His grandson Kenneth MacAedh made a final attempt in 1215, after Alexander II's accession, but was defeated and beheaded by his neighbour *Maccintsacairt*, who afterwards himself became Earl of Ross.

It was during these struggles, in about 1163 (during an attempt by King Malcolm IV to deprive Malcolm MacAedh of the earldom of Ross in order to give it to his own foreign brother-in-law, the Count of Holland: many knightly Flemings being already settled in southern Moray), that King Malcolm IV 'transported' many of the Moraymen *extramontanas Scociae*, 'beyond the mountains of Scotland'. This would appear to be the far North, certainly to a Morayman. Earl Malcolm MacAedh's son-in-law Harald, Jarl of Orkney (1158–1206), was also Earl of Caithness, to which at that time both Sutherland and Strathnaver belonged. It is in Strathnaver, the farthest North of all, that the MacAedh chiefs appear early in the thirteenth century.

The great district of Strathnaver, which became known as the Mackay country or *Duthaich Mhic Aoidh*, was the whole north-western corner of the mainland of Scotland, measuring eighty miles by eighteen and culminating in Cape Wrath itself. The Mackay clan who held it were sometimes also known as the Clan Morgund, and Morgund was a favourite Christian name in the old royal house of Moray. Moreover, although (from a tradition of kinship with the Forbes clan) they adopted the Forbes *bear's heads* in the seventeenth century, the Mackay chiefs at late as 1503 bore for arms *three blue stars on silver, with a hand in chief*: the colours and stars of the arms of Moray, charged with the Hand that among the Gaels signified the 'true family'. And, like the Morays or Murrays (including the Sutherlands), 'butcher's broom' was one of their two plant-badges.

The importance of the Mackays in the world of the Gael can be gauged

The House of Tongue, former home of the Lords Reay, Chiefs of the Clan Mackay, on the coast of their ancient province of Strathnaver. It was burnt in 1656 by the Cromwellian English invaders, but rebuilt by the Master of Reay in 1678, and added to in the eighteenth century. But in 1829 it had to be sold by the 7th Lord Reay, together with the vast Mackay estates (the whole north-western corner of Britain) for debt to the Sutherland family.

from the marriage before 1415 of their then chief, Angus *Dubh* Mackay of Strathnaver, to Elisabeth, sister of the greatest of highland potentates, Donald Macdonald, Lord of the Isles, and grand-daughter of Robert II, the first Stewart king of Scots. Angus is described by Bower as 'the leader of 4,000 Strathnaver men' in 1427. But from at least the fourteenth century until 1829, the history of the Mackays was one of desperate struggle to prevent their beloved *Duthaich Mhic Aoidh* from being absorbed by the Earls of Sutherland: the line of the twelfth-century Flemish lords of Moray who had been brought to the North by King David I and had perhaps then married a MacAedh princess, for they too bore the *three stars* in their Arms. A moving account of much of this long struggle is given in Ian Grimble's *Chief of Mackay* (London 1965).

In the end, the power of gold prevailed in one solitary generation of weakness, where the power of the sword had never prevailed over many generations of strong and sensible chiefs. The Sutherland lawyers found a flaw in the entail that protected the lands at the time of the Mackays' weakest chief, to whom they then lent money to encourage his gambling until (despite his brother's protests) all had to be sold—to the Sutherlands, who promptly evicted his clansmen. What little remained, he left to a bastard daughter. Fortunately, in 1875 the chiefship passed to another and very able branch.

Donald, Chief of Mackay, had been created Lord Reay in 1628. He was a fine soldier, and raised the famous 'Mackay's Regiment' in the Danish and Swedish Services that did so much to advance the Protestant Cause in Germany during the Thirty Years War. A younger son of the 2nd Lord Reay, being maternally a nephew of the famous Scots-Dutch General Hugh Mackay of Scourie (who commanded William of Orange's army at Killiecrankie), entered the Scots-Dutch Service himself in the seventeenth century and became a Brigadier-General. His branch remained in that Service; his son fell as a Colonel at Tournay in 1745; and his grandson, Colonel Aeneas Mackay, married the eventual heiress of the Barons van Haeften, whose moated *kasteel* of Ophemert (built by a female-line ancestor in the fourteen hundreds) was inherited in the nineteenth century by the Mackays, already themselves Dutch Barons. In 1875, Baron Mackay van Ophemert succeeded his distant kinsman as 10th Lord Reay and as Chief of the Clan Mackay. His nephew, Baron Aeneas Mackay, who was Prime Minister of the Netherlands, was great-grandfather of the present Chief.

Mackay's Highlanders, from a contemporary German woodcut in 1631. This is probably the earliest surviving likeness of highlandmen in tartan.

GRACE ME GUIDE

Forbes

The Chief of the Clan Forbes is Lord Forbes (former Minister of State for Scotland), who is the premier of his own degree in the whole Peerage of Scotland. He and his clansmen take their name from the lands and barony of Forbes on Donside, that in turn derives its name from the Old Gaelic *forba*, a 'field' or 'district', coupled with the Pictish ending of place *-ais*. King Alexander III (1249–1286) confirmed Duncan of Forbes in these lands by a charter of which the original has been missing since 1730, but which was quoted by the famous Sir John Skene in 1593. In 1582 King James VI confirmed his 'trusty and well beloved cousin' Lord Forbes in the 'barony and lands which have been in continued possession

Brother Archangel (1570–1606), who gave up the world to become a friar, but would otherwise have been John, 9th Lord Forbes. The Forbes chiefs were strongly Protestant; but his mother (divorced in 1574 on grounds of a conflict in religion) was their enemy Huntly's daughter, the saintly Lady Margaret Gordon, who was a devout Catholic. Despite Lord Forbes's natural wishes, some of her children yearned for their mother's Faith. The eldest son William, Master of Forbes, served under the Duke of Parma on the battlefields of Flanders, and received a pension from King Philip II of Spain; but eventually became a Capuchin friar at Ghent as the first Brother Archangel. He had written in 1589 to his father, renouncing all his rights in the Lordship of Forbes to his brother John, here portrayed. But John, the new Master of Forbes, secretly 'left his father's house early one morning, changing clothes with a shepherd boy, and so made his way (by devious paths, covering his tracks skilfully) to the sea, and eventually to Antwerp. Arrived in Antwerp, John, a friendless stranger, was arrested as a suspicious person who wore silk stockings under a poor habit, and he suffered a long and painful imprisonment, narrowly escaping hanging by the Spanish authorities'. In 1594, he took his final vows and entered the Capuchin friary of Antwerp, like his late brother before him, as the second Brother Archangel. As he had formally renounced all claim to the peerage and clan estates, and this resignation was recognised by King James VI, Brother Archangel never became Chief of the Clan Forbes, the peerage passing instead to his equally sincere Protestant younger half-brother, Arthur, 9th Lord Forbes, ancestor of the present Chief.

of his family in times past the memory of man'.

The early lairds of Forbes were closely connected with (it has even been suggested identical with) the noble family, usually called 'of the Aird', who were powerful around Castle Urquhart in 1297. A charter by King Robert Bruce to Sir Christin of the Aird, who had been present at the siege of Castle Urquhart in 1305 and who was one of the leaders at Halidon Hill, is still in Lord Forbes's possession. In the same reign, William of Urquhart became hereditary Sheriff of Cromarty; and it is perhaps significant that the later Urquhart chiefs believed themselves to be of the same stock as Forbes.

The Forbes arms are *three bear's heads muzzled*, and we are told a strange but not unique folk legend of a bear that slew nine maidens by the Nine Maidens well in the parish of Forbes, and was himself slain by the forefather of the Forbes chiefs. The Bear certainly had a sacred significance among the ancient Celts; and 'King Arthur' (whom some scholars think to have been a god-spirit) was identified sometimes with the constellation of the Great Bear, for his name was derived from the Old Celtic *arth*, a bear. So it is interesting that, long after such derivations were forgotten, Arthur was a popular Forbes name. Perhaps the most celebrated was the 6th Lord Forbes's youngest son, 'Black Arthur Forbes', slain in battle against the Gordons at Tullieangus in 1571, as 'he stooped down to quench his thirst and one of the Gordons gave him his death blow through an open joint in his armour'.

In 1445 Sir Alexander Forbes of that Ilk, who had married a grand-daughter of King Robert III, was created Lord Forbes. The history of the Clan Forbes for the next three centuries was that of a long struggle with the Gordons. To the writers of *1066 And All That*, the Gordons would have seemed Wrong but Romantic, and the Forbes chiefs Right but Repulsive. This would not have been quite fair. Certainly the Gordons held to the Old Faith, were loyal to Mary Queen of Scots, were Cavaliers and Jacobites; while the Forbes chiefs were Protestants, Covenanters and Whigs. But the 'Gey Gordons' were not so called because of their gaiety, for *gey* was used in the sense of 'a bit too much'. The Forbes clan were sturdy soldiers, staunch friends and, although Whig by tradition, were so faithful to their leading Jacobite fellow-clansman Alexander Forbes, 4th Lord Pitsligo, that he was able to hide in his own country from 1746 until his death there in 1762. Lord Pitsligo's sister married the then Lord Forbes (also of Jacobite sympathies, unlike his predecessors) and was ancestress of the present Chief.

Today, Lord Forbes still lives on Donside at Balforbes. Not far away is the beautiful Castle of Craigievar, long the home of the Forbes chieftains who became Lords Sempill. Higher up the Don lives Sir Charles Forbes of Newe, whose branch of the clan have been for generations associated with the March of the Forbes Men at the annual Lonach Gathering.

The original Castle Forbes, home of the Lords Forbes until the new Castle Forbes was built in 1815. However, the present chief lives in the more convenient house of Balforbes.

Lonach is the Forbes slogan, and at Lonach on Donside the Forbes still hold their Annual Gathering. They are joined by the men of Wallace of Candacraig, seen here with pikes.

MEANE, SPEAK AND DOE WEIL

Urquhart

The surname of Urquhart is taken from Castle Urquhart, the great royal stronghold by Loch Ness, long in ruins but dominating Glen Urquhart and the eastern mouth of the Great Glen. The Constable of Castle Urquhart was usually also Sheriff of Inverness. Gaelic scholars differ about the meaning of the name. Some say 'on a rapid torrent'—others 'upon a rowan wood'. Perhaps the most sensible are those who translate it 'the fort on the knoll', which is exactly what Castle Urquhart is.

The Urquhart tradition is that they were closely connected with the original Forbes chiefs, who in turn claim kinship with the great local

Castle Urquhart and the Loch Ness Monster, thought to be most probably one of a family of plesiosaurs. Similar creatures have been sighted both in Loch Ness and in other Northern European lakes, as also at sea, for the last 1,400 years. This photograph was taken by Mr. P. A. MacNab in 1955. The Loch Ness Phenomenon has been seen in recent years, for instance, by Lord Lovat, by Lady Erskine of Cambo and by Lady Maud Baillie, sister of the late Duke of Devonshire and mother of Michael Baillie of Dochfour, Lord Burton.

Castle Urquhart on Loch Ness, a royal fortress in the North: in a sense the predecessor of Fort George in Government control of the north-eastern end of the Great Glen. Urquhart is the 'fort on the knoll' from which the Clan Urquhart take their name.

family, called 'of the Aird', who were powerful around Castle Urquhart in 1297. So the Urquhart *boar's heads* may just possibly be a corruption of the Forbes *bear's heads*.

In the reign of King Robert Bruce, William of Urquhart became Sheriff of Cromarty, having married a daughter of the Earl of Ross; and in 1358 his son Adam of Urquhart had a grant from King David II of the same Sheriffdom, which became hereditary in the family.

Perhaps the most famous chief of the Name was Sir Thomas Urquhart of Cromarty, the rumbustiously colourful Cavalier and seventeenth-century translator of Rabelais. The principal branch surviving in Scotland today is that of which the well-known forester-laird Bruce Urquhart of Craigston is the head (Craigston Castle is an architectural gem built by his ancestor the famous Tutor of Cromarty in 1607). But the chief of the clan is an American citizen, Wilkins F. Urquhart of that Ilk, who lives in Louisiana.

Chisholm

Chisholm means in old Beornician the 'waterside meadow good for producing cheese'. It's a place in the Roxburghshire parish of Roberton, and became a feudal barony. The family who held Chisholm took their surname from it, and Alexander of Chisholm witnessed a charter as early as 1248/9. The Chisholm coat-of-arms has borne a boar's head since at least 1292, and shews the family to have been connected at the dawn of heraldry with that great group of Border families, including the Gordons, Elphinstones, Nisbets, Rollos and Trotters, who also bore boar's heads. This group centred on the Swintons of that Ilk, who bore the Boar *par excellence*, and who were almost certainly the leading branch, to survive the Norman Conquest, of the male line of the old Anglo-Saxon dynasts who had held Bamburgh and Edinburgh and had ruled all Beornicia from the Tyne to the Forth from 878 until 1018. Certainly the mediaeval Chisholm lairds' lands of Paxton in Berwickshire lie very near Swinton itself.

The Chisholms came to the Highlands, where they became known as *an Siosalach*, when Robert Chisholm of that Ilk succeeded his maternal grandfather, Sir Robert Lauder of the Bass, as royal Constable of Castle Urquhart on Loch Ness in 1359. This castle is the key to Inverness and the Great Glen, and the laird of Chisholm soon also became Sheriff of Inverness and Justiciar of the North. He inherited from his Lauder grandfather lands in Moray near Elgin and Nairn, and the Chisholm focus of interest shifted to the North. The estate near Elgin was called Quarrelwood, doubtless from having hardwoods that provided the crossbow arrows called quarrels. The estate near Nairn was Cantray, which passed with his daughter to the Roses of Kilravock and thence (doubtless through another lady) to the old local family of Dallas (descended from William de Rypely): who incorporated the Chisholm boar's head with the Moray stars in their own arms. It is perhaps interesting to note that the heads of the two allied families appear as The Chisholm and as The Dallas of Cantray in the Inverness burgh records of the seventeenth century.

Robert Chisholm of that Ilk, Justiciar of the North, had a younger son who continued the line of the Chisholms on the Border, and who was also ancestor of the Chisholms of Cromlix in Perthshire, the branch to which belonged three strongly anti-Reformation bishops in the sixteenth century.

It was Robert Chisholm of that Ilk's eldest son Alexander, however, who established the Chisholms in what was to become the clan country. He acquired estates in five counties, including Erchless and part of Strathglass in Inverness-shire, through his marriage to Margaret, daughter of Wiland of the Aird. It isn't known how she came to inherit the Inverness-shire lands, but it was presumably through a descent from the family called du Bois or Wood who in turn had got them with an heiress of the great Scoto-Norman house of Bisset, the founders of Beauly Priory: from whom the Chisholms' neighbours in the Aird, the Frasers of Lovat, had also inherited the wide lands on which they still live.

The Chisholms nearly came into the vast earldom of Caithness as well, for Margaret of the Aird's brother claimed it but then resigned it in 1375: their mother Maud had been eldest daughter and co-heiress of Malise, last of the ancient Celtic dynasts who were Earls of Strathearn ' by the Indulgence of God ' and who was also (through a Norse heiress descended from the pagan god-kings in Scandinavia) Earl of Caithness and Jarl of Orkney. Earl Malise's wife had been a daughter of the fifth Earl of Ross (by a sister of the heroic King Robert Bruce), and this may perhaps account for the Chisholms also coming into possession of Comar in the earldom of Ross, which established them thoroughly in Strathglass. These lands were erected into the Barony of Comar-more for the then Chisholm in 1538, but had to be sold together with Erchless Castle and the other Chisholm lands in 1937. The Clan Chisholm Society, however, has recovered the chiefs' modest house of Comar in Strathglass.

By the seventeenth century, the chief had come to be known as The Chisholm. In fact, a number of chiefs of other names have also been styled ' The ' at various periods, and some still are, but the Chisholms managed in a way that reflects much credit on their one-upmanship to get it put around in Edwardian Catholic circles that ' there were but three persons in the world entitled to be called *The*—The King, The Pope and The Chisholm '. In modern Protestant circles the saying is sometimes varied to ' The Queen, The Devil and The Chisholm '.

Erchless Castle, a seat of The Chisholm until 1887.

Loch Mullardoch, where *An Siosalach*, The Chisholm, used to gather his people when the Fiery Cross went out for war. There is a plaque on the north shore of the loch commemorating the site of the Chisholm Stone. Today it has a different function, no longer for war, but important in the Highlands' struggle for survival in peace. The Mullardoch dam—2,385 feet long and 116 feet high—is the longest dam so far constructed by the North of Scotland Hydro-Electric Board, and is the main storage reservoir for the Glen Affric scheme.

Gordon

The Gordons first appear under that name in the twelfth century, when surnames were first being adopted in Scotland and the family were already holding the lands of Gordon in Berwickshire. The place-name would appear to be local, from the Ancient British *gor din*, 'great hill-fort'. The family also held Huntly nearby, famed for its links with the prophet Thomas the Rhymer and the Queen of Elfland: 'True Thomas lay on Huntly bank . . .' They were obviously closely connected at the dawn of heraldry with their neighbours, the Swintons of that Ilk, and like them bore *three boar's heads* on their battle-shield. Like many kinsmen who quarrel over inheritances, the Gordons were long at feud with the Swintons, until in 1407 Sir John Swinton of that Ilk knighted his fellow baron Sir Adam Gordon of that Ilk on the battlefield at Homildon Hill, where both fell gallantly charging the English host.

Indeed, it has been reasonably suggested that perhaps the Gordons were actually a branch of the same *Edulfingar* stock as the Swintons, and that they took their present surname from their own lands of Gordon when surnames first began in Scotland. The difficulty is that Adam was a peculiarly favoured name among the Gordons of Huntly from the time of Adam of Gordon, who witnessed a charter *c.* 1189–1199, and that this Christian name was equally popular with a family in Hampshire called *de Gurdon* or 'of Gurdon' in the thirteenth century: one of whom, Sir Adam de Gurdon, was wounded in a chivalrous personal combat with the future King Edward I in 1266. From this it has been supposed that the two families derived their surname from the same place, somewhere else, and that our Gordons were perhaps Anglo-Norman settlers in Scotland who gave their name to their new home. On the other hand, the Swintons sprang from the great Beornician dynastic family (called *le Vicomte* by the Normans) who were still Sheriffs of the Northumbrians after the Norman Conquest, and who still held lands in England as well as in Scotland. Though it is a far cry from Berwickshire or even from Northumberland to Hampshire, an heiress could possibly have lured a younger son there, and for once reversed the northwards trend of emigration at that period. Other such instances are known, about this time: for example, the family

Glen Fruin, in the Colquhoun country. Here the MacGregors lost their name for slaughtering the Colquhoun forces, during the great raid in 1603.

Huntly Castle in Strathbogie, ruined stronghold of the Gordon chiefs. Burnt in 1595 after the Counter-Reformation Rising led in the previous year by the Earls of Huntly and Erroll, it was restored in 1602 by the 'Cock of the North'; below the windows of the upper floor he caused to be carved the inscription GEORGE GORDOVN FIRST MARQVIS OF HV[NTLY], HENRIETTE STEVART MARQVISSE OF HV[NTLY]. (*See also p.15.*)

Dochfour House near Inverness, home of Michael Baillie, 3rd Lord Burton and 15th Baillie of Dochfour, which was granted to their forefather Alexander Baillie, Constable of Inverness Castle, by his cousin the 1st Earl of Huntly as a reward for his valour in Huntly's victory at Brechin over the Earl of Crawford in 1452.

The 'Two Noble Friends', a cartoon by Kay. Both came to a tragic end. The tallest is George Hay, 16th Earl of Erroll, who committed suicide on a point of honour in 1798, because he had inadvertently disclosed a secret confided to him by Mr. Pitt, the Prime Minister. His friend is George Gordon, Lord Haddo (father of the 4th Earl of Aberdeen, Prime Minister), whose death in a riding accident when he fell from his horse near Gight fulfilled an old prophecy.

Loch Lomond, from the South. The left bank was held by the Colquhouns and Macfarlanes, the right bank by the MacGregors, Grahams and Buchanans, while the Cunninghams held part of the South bank. Their overlords, the Stuart earls of the whole Lennox (in which Loch Lomond lies), kept most of the South bank in their own hands.

of St. Andrews in Northamptonshire took their name from St. Andrews in Fife, and held land in England as well as Scotland through their connection with the Quincy earls of Winchester who were also Constables of Scotland.

The Scottish War of Independence brought the Gordons to the Highlands. Sir Adam of Gordon, the then chief, had been a close supporter of the Lord of Badenoch, the 'Red Cummin' who was fatally stabbed by Robert Bruce. At first, Sir Adam joined Edward I in trying to avenge his friend, but after Edward's death the foolish English commander on the Borders harried the Gordon lands indiscriminately and even dared to imprison the chief himself. Sir Adam thereupon joined King Robert Bruce in 1313, and supported him loyally thereafter. In 1320 he was the Scottish Ambassador to the Pope, to bring him the historic Declaration of Independence sealed at Arbroath.

King Robert Bruce rewarded Sir Adam of Gordon with such large tracts of former Clan Macduff territory in the North, that it seems most unlikely he had no family connection with them already. For Bruce was usually careful to give out forfeited lands to supporters of his own who were related to the former owners, in order to secure local loyalty. Perhaps Sir Adam's wife Amabelle or else his mother Marjorie was related to the Clan Macduff earls of Fife or Atholl, as the Clan Macduff chiefs bore a *red lyon on gold* and the later Gordons of Huntly quartered *three red lyon's heads on gold* with their *boar's heads*. In particular, Sir Adam of Gordon got Atholl's great lordship of Strathbogie (120 square miles in extent), whose capital was renamed Huntly by the Gordons, and also perhaps the Cairngorm territories of the earls of Fife, which were certainly held by the later Gordon chiefs, who in the fifteenth century also acquired the lordship of Badenoch.

The later Gordons of Huntly also quartered the *fraises* or strawberry-flowers that pun on Fraser, as their Highland territories were greatly increased through the marriage of the then chief (Sir Adam Gordon of that Ilk who fell at Homildon Hill) to a daughter of the Marischal of Scotland by the Fraser heiress of Aboyne on Deeside. She was Margaret Fraser: whose own grandmother had been kept publicly in a cage by the English because she was sister of King Robert Bruce, who afterwards gave Aboyne to her husband for his gallantry in the War of Independence. The Gordons soon became a mighty power on Deeside.

When Sir Adam Gordon of that Ilk was killed in action at Homildon Hill, the legitimate line of the old Gordon name was continued by the Gordons of Lochinvar in Galloway, later Viscounts of Kenmure, sprung from his grandfather's younger brother. However, his own elder brother, Sir John Gordon of that Ilk, left two natural sons 'Jock' and 'Tam' from whom various chieftains of the Gordons in Buchan descended. These included the Earl of Aberdeen who was Prime Minister during the Crimean War and also the Marquess of Aberdeen who was Governor-General of Canada. This branch of the Gordons is still very firmly rooted in Aberdeenshire.

But the chiefship itself passed through Sir Adam Gordon of that Ilk's daughter, whose son was belted Earl of Huntly in 1445. Her husband, Sir Alexander Seton, appears as Lord Gordon in 1429, in the first known list of Lords of Parliament after that dignity came into being in Scotland as a result of the 1428 Act that led to the distinction between 'lords' and 'lairds': though modern peerage writers, who know nothing either of Scotland or the subject, have got it into their heads that the entire Scottish peerage was somehow invented by a schoolboy king in 1445, just because a charter of that year undoubtedly refers to lords.

Sir Alexander Seton's father had himself been son of the heiress of the Setons of that Ilk by an adventurous youth called Alan of Wyntoun, probably her kinsman, who had abducted her (with powerful backing) in 1347. The chronicler tells us that the King's Court left her to settle his fate, giving her a sword—and a ring. She chose the ring. So they were married. But her family went on at him, until eventually he went off on Crusade and perished in the Holy Land. Yet the history of Scotland was changed. From this dashing Alan of Wyntoun there came to descend in the direct male line the Seton earls of Winton and Dunfermline, the Seton viscounts of Kingston, the present Montgomerie earls of Eglinton, the Gordon earls of Huntly, Sutherland and Aboyne, the dukes of Gordon and the present Marquis of Huntly, Premier Marquis of Scotland, Chief of the *Gey* Gordons and 'Cock of the North'.

Gordon Castle, originally known as the Bog o' Gight. Here the Marquises of Huntly, later Dukes of Gordon, long had their principal residence. At first they didn't hold it directly from the Crown, unlike their other vast territories, and so it was a well-known joke to refer to the 'Cock of the North' as the 'Gudeman of the Bog' instead (a gudeman was a tenant-farmer). Gordon Castle passed through an heiress to the Lennox dukes of Richmond (really royal Stuarts, descended from a natural son of King Charles II), who are now also Dukes of Gordon. Given with the estates to the Government in settlement of Death Duties, they were of course all grossly neglected by absentee officialdom over the years, and much of it is now ruinous. However, it has been bought back by the Grenadier Lt-General Sir George Gordon Lennox, grandson of the late Duke of Richmond & Gordon, and what remains is being put in order by him.

SERVA JUGUM

Hay

The surname of Hay is derived from La Haye in the Cotentin peninsula of Normandy. A *haie* is a stockade, such as surrounded Norman castle motte-hills. The surname is written *de Haya* in charter-Latin, to indicate that it is *de la Haye* and not de Haye: it was rendered into English as Hay and eventually into Gaelic as *Garadh*, which is from the same linguistic root and has ultimately the same meaning. 'Hedge' comes from the same root: it all might really be called a zareba, like the thorn hedges Africans made to keep out wild beasts.

The first Hay in Scotland was William de la Haye, Butler of Scotland and first baron of Erroll, who appears at the Scottish Court from about 1160 and was an Ambassador to England in 1199. He was a nephew of Ranulf de Soules, lord of Liddesdale and also Butler of Scotland (whose family became Hereditary Butlers of Scotland but were forfeited for plotting to seize the throne itself during the Wars of Independence). Soules was the manor bordering on the Hay fiefs of La Haye-Hue (now

The painted ceiling at Delgatie Castle, put up in 1597 by Alexander Hay, 10th baron of Delgatie, to commemorate his double bigamy. He had married Lord Altrie's daughter, Elizabeth Keith, but had settled down with another married lady, Barbara (one of whose two husbands was still living), daughter of Lord Forbes. In 1599 the Laird of Delgatie was charged with this bigamy and with having misconducted himself with three other ladies. To quote Sir Thomas Innes of Learny, present Lord Lyon King of Arms: 'The Laird's first defence was a novel one. He had along with his Chief, the Earl of Erroll, and Lord Huntly, fought against Argyll, the King's Lieutenant, at the Battle of Glenlivat when the "Popish Earls" received the benison of James VI for sending back the crest-fallen Argyll with a mien "sae like a subject". For his share in the Glenlivet campaign Delgatie received a remission and general whitewashing, including "all other crimes except Treason and Witch-craft", and therefore he claimed exoneration from a charge of adultery'. But he died before the case was concluded. His tempera-painted ceiling, however, has the arms of Hay of Delgatie 'impaling' as if in marriage those of Forbes, together with his initials AH and her initials BF.

Tomb effigy in plate armour of Sir William Hay of Lochloy (died 1421) in Elgin Cathedral. He married Janet, daughter of William Mackintosh, 8th Captain of Clan Chattan, and his son married a daughter of the Thane of Cawdor. The Hay barons of Lochloy were early cadets of Erroll; and had their stronghold at Inschoch Castle near the Moray Firth until the eighteenth century. Their cadets, the Hays of Woodcockdale, married the heiress of the Bruces of Kinnaird and took that name: so that Sir William Hay of Lochloy was forefather in the direct male line of the celebrated James Bruce of Kinnaird, who explored Abyssinia and the sources of the Nile in 1768, and whose interesting tartan suit is still preserved by Lord Bruce at Broomhall. Other cadets of Lochloy, descended from Sir William, were the Hays of Mayne; one of whom, Colonel Alexander Hay—the 'Saunders Hay' whose gallantry was described in Monro's *Expedition*—went to Denmark in Mackay's Highlanders in 1626, and afterwards transferred to the Swedish service, being killed as a Colonel of Dragoons in battle with the German Imperialists. He is claimed as ancestor of the Barons Haij in Sweden.

called La Haye-Bellefond), La Haye-Belouze, Villebaudon and Beaucoudray, near St-Lô in Normandy—whose La Haye seigneurs bore for Arms the same *three red shields on silver* as have always been borne by the Hays of Erroll in Scotland. The motte, or artificial mound on which the first baron built his wooden tower at Errol in the twelfth century, still belongs to his descendant Diana Hay, Countess of Erroll, as 31st Chief of the Hays in Scotland.

The *three shields* appear on the seal of David de la Haye, 2nd baron of Erroll, Sheriff of Forfar, who with his successors was so great a benefactor of Coupar Angus Abbey that their Arms appear beside those of its royal founder on the abbey seal. His mother Eva had been the Celtic heiress of Pitmilly and possibly of other lands near the Tay estuary, and the old legend that the lands of Erroll were acquired by a falcon's flight, in reward for an ancient victory with ox-yokes over Viking invaders, may have been derived from the clan of which she was heiress. David de la Haye himself married Ethna, daughter of the local dynast Gilbert mac Ferteth, Earl of Strathearn 'by the Indulgence of God'. So the second and third chiefs of the Hays in Scotland were already both half Gael by birth.

The 2nd Chief's younger brother, Robert, was probably ancestor of the Lords Hay of Yester, now Marquises of Tweeddale, who bore *three blue shields on silver*. To this branch belonged Lord Charles Hay, the courteous Grenadier hero commanding the King's Company of the First Guards, who drank to the French Guards before receiving and returning their fire at Fontenoy. The 2nd Chief's younger son, William, Ambassador to England in 1258, was ancestor of the Hays of Leys, who bore *three red shields on ermine*. His descendants included the Hays of Megginch; Father Edmund Hay, Provincial of the French Jesuits in 1574; James Hay, 1st Earl of Carlisle, K.G., who was also first Hereditary Proprietor of Barbados (then called the Carlisle Islands); John Hay, Jacobite Duke of Inverness and Secretary of State to the 'King over the Water'; and the Earls of Kinnoull, from whom the Barbadoes were unfortunately recovered by the Crown in the second half of the seventeenth century.

Gilbert de la Haye, 3rd baron of Erroll, Sheriff of Perth, was one of the co-Regents of Scotland in 1255 and 1258. He married Lady Idoine Cummin, sister of the Constable of Scotland and daughter of William, Earl of Buchan. She too was more than half Gael, and descended from the heiress of King Donald III's line. Their grandson Sir Gilbert de la Haye, 5th baron of Erroll, was one of the most loyal and effective sup-

John Hay, 12th Earl of Erroll, seated at the door of the Parliament House with his baton of command as Lord High Constable of Scotland, in front of his Doorward Guard of Partizans, to receive the peers and other members in the ceremonial opening called the Riding of the Parliament.

Sir Gilbert Hay, 5th baron of Erroll, the friend and companion-in-arms of King Robert Bruce, whose life he saved and who made him hereditary Constable of Scotland. He was ambassador to England after Bannockburn. Taken from his equestrian seal in about 1308, this is the earliest surviving likeness of a Hay, although of course his face is covered by a helmet.

porters of King Robert Bruce, who made him hereditary Constable of Scotland after Bannockburn in 1314.

The Lord High Constable was the commander of the royal bodyguard, responsible for the King's personal safety, as well as the martial judge within the Verge of the Royal Court and Household, and (after the Steward became King) the ceremonial Commander-in-Chief of the whole Scottish army—the military equivalent of the Lord High Admiral—also responsible for all Courts Martial and Trials by Combat. Later Hay chiefs fell as Constables of Scotland in battle against the English at Nevill's Cross and Flodden. They had their own private officer-of-arms, called Slains Pursuivant after their castle and regality of Slains on the coast of Buchan. Sir Thomas de la Haye, 7th baron of Erroll, married Elizabeth of Scotland, daughter of King Robert II; and their elder son William, the 'Lorde Constabill', regularly appears (after the 1428 Act distinguishing lords of parliament from the ordinary lairds in the Scots baronage) as first among the 'domini de parleamento' mentioned from 1429, and he thus became premier lord-baron of Scotland as Lord Hay. His younger brother, Sir Gilbert, was among the Scottish knights with Joan of Arc at the Dauphin's coronation as Charles VII of France at Rheims, and was ancestor of the Hays of Delgaty, including the great Montrose's chief of staff, Sir William Hay of Delgaty, Baronet, who was executed as a Royalist in 1650 but was given a State Funeral and buried with Montrose at the Restoration. To this branch belongs Sir Arthur Hay of Park, the present 10th Baronet of another creation, whose Arms are *three red shields beneath an ox-yoke, on silver*.

William, Lord Hay, the 9th Chief, was belted Earl of Erroll in 1452; and his wife, Lady Beatrix Douglas, daughter of the 7th Earl of Douglas, was ultimately co-heiress of her unfortunate brother the last 'Black Douglas'. William Hay, 4th Earl of Erroll, Hereditary Sheriff of Aberdeen, received a bond of manrent from the Provost, magistrates and town council of Edinburgh, who bound themselves faithfully to him in 1508, in return for which he made them his deputies in the office of Lord High Constable. In 1559, George Hay, 7th Earl of Erroll, was appointed by Francis and Mary, King and Queen of Scots, Dolphin and Dolphiness of Viennois, to be their Lord Lieutenant of all central Scotland, highland and lowland, 'from the Earn to the North Water', i.e. the Spey.

Francis Hay, 9th Earl of Erroll, was a leader of the Counter-Reformation, and with his allies Huntly, the 'Cock of the North', and Angus, the 'Red Douglas', he entered into a secret treaty with King Philip II of Spain to depose Queen Elizabeth I and put King James VI (who was to be converted) on the throne of an united Catholic Britain. In 1594, Huntly and Erroll defeated the Government forces under Argyll, although Erroll was wounded by a Maclean arrow as he led a cavalry charge with his personal war-cry of 'The Virgin Mary!'. Many of the clans fought on one side or the other in this battle.

Erroll and Huntly held out throughout the winter, sending Lord Balcarres as their envoy to get more help from Spain. But in 1595 King James VI felt obliged to make a demonstration against them; and they went into exile for a while, during which the King personally blew up their castles. Erroll's castle of Slains has been a ruin ever since, for on his return he built a new castle on to another tower of his further north.

The sixty-year-old Mary Hay, Countess of Erroll in her own right, raised her men for Prince Charles Edward in 1745, arming them under her Chamberlain's command. She was succeeded by her great-nephew James, Lord Boyd, son of the beheaded Jacobite earl of Kilmarnock by the daughter of her sister, Lady Margaret Hay, who had married James Livingston, last earl of Linlithgow and Callendar, also forfeited and exiled as a Jacobite. James, Lord Boyd, who had thus lost the lands of three earldoms through his family's loyalty to the White Cockade, then took the surname of Hay and became 15th Earl of Erroll. His descendant, Diana Hay, 23rd Countess of Erroll, present Chief of the Hays, also Lord

The Gathering of the Hays at Delgatie Castle in Aberdeenshire, shewing the procession starting from the castle to the games field and pavilion tent. Diana Hay, 23rd Countess of Erroll, Lord High Constable of Scotland and Chief of the Hays, is styled in Gaelic *Mac Garaidh Mor* and is the senior Great Officer of the Royal Household in Scotland, having precedence before dukes and before every other hereditary honour after the Blood Royal. As the direct descendant of the Jacobite leader, Lord Kilmarnock (who was beheaded in 1746), she is Honorary President of the 1745 Association and unveiled the cairn at Arisaig to mark Prince Charles Edward's landing and departure. Lady Erroll is seen here in a Hay tartan skirt, preceded by Captain John Hay of Hayfield bearing her justiciary sword. He is her Commissioner for the Clan Hay Society, and she gave him Delgatie Castle several years ago to be the international headquarters of

the Clan Hay society. Hayfield is wearing a Hay tartan kilt and a jacket of the Hay tweed. In front of him, leading the procession, is Slains Pursuivant, wearing a real cloth-of-silver tabard embroidered with the three red *scutcheons* of the Hays in red damask. Today, the only two Scottish mediaeval earldoms still to maintain their private officer-of-arms are the earldom of Crawford's *Endure Pursuivant* and the earldom of Erroll's *Slains Pursuivant*, both dating from the fourteenth century. The present Slains is Mr. Michael Maclagan, the Oxford don. Behind Lady Erroll is her banner, carried by Mr. George Hay, with the colour escort armed with ox-yokes, the Hay badge. Behind them is the Baron Bailie of Delgatie, followed by the banners of the various chieftains such as Sir Arthur Hay of Park, the Marquis of Tweeddale and the Earl of Kinnoull.

Gold, enamel and pearl mistletoe brooch given to the bridesmaids at the wedding in 1900 of Queen Victoria's godson Victor Hay, Lord Kilmarnock, afterwards 21st Earl of Erroll, K.C.M.G. In *The Golden Bough*, Sir James Frazer cites an old Hay custom: 'the badge of the Hays was the mistletoe. There was formerly in the neighbourhood of Erroll, and not far from the Falcon Stone, a vast oak of an unknown age, and upon which grew a profusion of the plant: many charms and legends were considered to be connected with the tree, and the duration of the family of Hay was said to be united with its existence. It was believed that a sprig of the mistletoe cut by a Hay on Allhallowmas eve, with a new dirk, and after surrounding the tree three times sunwise, and pronouncing a certain spell, was a sure charm against all glamour and witchery, and an infallible guard in the day of battle. A spray gathered in the same manner was placed in the cradle of infants, and thought to defend them from being changed for elf-bairns by the fairies.'

William Harry Hay, 19th Earl of Erroll, Lord High Constable of Scotland and maternal grandson of King William IV (by Mrs. Jordan the actress). Note his wounded hand; also the old custom of wearing the bonnet with a tweed suit. Chief of the Hays, he is still remembered in Buchan as a benevolent patriarch, and was the founder of the fishing village of Port Erroll. He gave his fisherfolk their cottages at an almost nominal rent; their widows remained in occupation for life rent free; and their sons thereafter had first refusal of taking on the family cottage at the old rent. The writer has been told by a descendant of one of the fishermen concerned, that Lord Erroll's first action on his return from being wounded at the battle of the Alma, in the Crimea, was furiously to take up with the Admiralty the question of some of his beloved fisherfolk who had been press-ganged into the Navy (although exempted under the 1835 Act), and to secure their immediate release. He gave only two annual balls in Slains Castle: one for the fisherfolk and the other for his many farm tenants. He personally controlled the rocket life-saving apparatus on the cliffs of his sea-girt territory, where many shipwrecks took place. Instead of a lodge, he built a Congregationalist chapel (still in use) at his front drive gates, for his fisherfolk were of that religion, and his wife taught in the Sunday school. He would allow no public-house and no poor-house on his land. Instead, he built a public reading-room, with a warm fire in winter; and gave chits to the needy to be supplied with necessities by the shops at his expense, knowing not to tempt them with the actual cash. He distributed among them, also, the produce of his home farm and gardens. He attended all three churches in Cruden Bay: and if the sermon was too long in the Episcopal Church (the entire stones for which were cut out of a single great rock, long ago associated with pagan fire-worship) he used to lower his gold watch on its chain over the edge of the 'laird's loft' (as it is customary to call such pews in Scotland). He was perhaps the last chief to keep a shrewdly 'simple' retainer called the Laird's Fool: Sandy Cruikshank, known locally as 'Sandy Sheep'—who used to go down to the sea every morning and pump away, up the cliffs to the oldest tower of the castle, the cold sea-water bath that Lord Erroll took every morning. But the maids often pulled the plug out for fun, and the Laird's Fool couldn't make out why it sometimes took so long in the pumping. The present writer has been told by the old Port Erroll folk how they loved and respected Lord Erroll as children. Curiously enough his most endearing quality to them was his gruff insistence on their good manners: if the boys didn't take their caps off, or the girls didn't curtsey, when he went past, his big dog used to pull them to him to be cuffed for want of proper respect. Lord Erroll died in 1891, but the welfare-state methods he had followed in looking after his people had prevented the accumulation of any liquid reserves to meet the deliberately vindictive taxation that was to follow. His son struggled on until 1926, when he had to sell all that was left of what had been entrusted to the Hay chiefs by Robert Bruce for helping to free Scotland.

High Constable of Scotland and as such the first subject *by birth* after the Blood Royal in Scotland, built in 1960 a remarkable wooden house to be the family home within the sea-girt ruins of Old Slains castle. Lady Erroll is Honorary President of the 1745 Association, and was a signatory to the Covenant in favour of Home Rule for Scotland.

The Hays held lands in the Highlands from the fifteenth to the seventeenth centuries, through the marriage of the 7th Earl of Erroll's father, George Hay of Logiealmond (killed at Flodden in 1513), to Margaret, daughter of Lyon Logie of that Ilk, baron of Logiealmond. Her family, the Thanes of Logie, were from the *chevrons* in their Arms probably a branch of the old Celtic dynastic house of Strathearn: and in 1363 the widow of Sir John Logie of that Ilk had become Queen of Scotland by marriage to David II, last of the Bruce dynasty.

As a result of their Logie inheritance, the Hay chiefs (who also held the barony of Caputh on the borders of Atholl and Gowrie) long had a sphere of influence in the Perthshire highlands. In the time of Francis Hay, 9th Earl of Erroll, who appears on the celebrated parliamentary roll of High-land landlords in 1587, 'Logie Tower a bumbies' byke' was the saying: as Catholic plotters made their way to his Tower of Logie, just as Jacobite agents were to make their way to the Hay castles of Delgaty and Slains during the eighteenth century.

In 1612, ' with all Atholl in chaos, the Robertsons in the earldom rallied to the authority of Struan. Apparently worried lest the worthless Earl of Atholl should object, they enlisted the aid of the Earl of Erroll, Lord High Constable of Scotland, as guarantor. Erroll had a castle nearby, at Logiealmond in the Perthshire highlands, and his grandmother had been a daughter of the 5th Chief of Clan Donnachaidh. Indeed, the winged head of Margaret Robertson, Countess of Erroll, crudely carved in stone at Delgaty Castle in Buchan, is probably the oldest surviving attempt at Robertson portraiture. Accordingly, in 1612 the Robertson chieftains of Faskally, Strathloch, Lude, Monzie, Dulcaben, Calvine and others signed a document headed " Band Clan Donachie to thair Cheiff ", in which they undertook to Erroll that they would, " by his lordship's advice, concur and assist the said Laird of Struan, maintain and help his house and estate so far as possibly we can be able ".'

Another branch of the Hays to impinge on the Highlands were the Hay barons of Lochloy, whose castle was at Inshóch on the Moray Firth. Sir William de la Haye, baron of Lochloy, was Sheriff of Inverness in 1296: the family intermarried with the local clans—daughters of Mackintosh, of the Thane of Cawdor and of Cummin of Altyre—and in the seventeenth century, for example, their cadet Alexander Hay (' Saunders Hay ') became an officer of Mackay's Highlanders in the Danish Service. He transferred into the Swedish Service, and was killed in action as a Colonel. From him the Barons Haij in Sweden claim descent.

Slains Castle, near Port Erroll, originally the Tower of Bowness. It was the home of the Hay chiefs, the Earls of Erroll, from the reign of King James VI until after the First World War; when it had to be sold by the fine old Boer War flying-column leader Major-General Charles Hay, 20th Earl of Erroll, K.T., C.B., former Commanding Officer of the Royal Horse Guards (the Blues) and Lord-in-Waiting to King Edward VII. His son Lord Kilmarnock (afterwards 21st Earl) was at the time serving abroad in the key position of British High Commissioner in the occupied Rhineland, with the local rank of Ambassador.

The original Slains Castle was also on the coast of Buchan but some miles further south; after it was blown up by King James VI in 1595, the 9th Earl (on his return from exile) came to occupy his more northerly strongpoint here at Bowness dominating Cruden Bay. At that time there was probably only part of the tower in the right foreground, perched above a deep inlet of the sea. A great deal was added after the Restoration by Gilbert Hay, 11th Earl of Erroll, who had raised a Regiment of Horse for King Charles II (at whose Scottish Coronation he officiated, although a minor, as his presence as Lord High Constable was regarded as a necessary part of the solemnity) and had been one of the very last to hold out against Cromwell in Scotland. He married Lady Katherine Carnegie, heroine of the rude ballad, ' the Countess of Erroll ', in which she

accuses him of impotency and he proves the contrary on a willing servant-maid in front of wise judges (' if it be the length of five barley-corns, Erroll's proved a man '): hence the saying ' Carnegie mares cannot live on Hay '. As a widow, she was arrested in 1689 for secretly smuggling correspondence and money to ' Bonnie Dundee ' in bags of oatmeal; and she eventually died in exile at the Court of St. Germain, where she was Lady Chief Governess to the little Jacobite Prince of Wales, afterwards the Old Chevalier. She was succeeded as Governor in charge of the boy, on whom all Jacobite hopes depended, by the Duke of Perth, whose sister, Lady Anne Drummond, had married the 12th Earl of Erroll.

The Jacobite correspondence between the exiled Duke and his sister, Lady Erroll, much of it written in milk as a secret ink, shows that she was one of the most active of Jacobite secret agents. Her son, Charles Hay, 13th Earl of Erroll (last of the male line of the earls), one of the very few Knights of the Jacobite Order of the Thistle, voted and protested against the Act of Union with England in 1707; and arranged for the Old Chevalier to be piloted up the Forth in the Jacobite attempt of 1708, but the plot failed when the proud pilot got drunk. Erroll was arrested and imprisoned in Edinburgh Castle, where he continued an ancient family row with his fellow-prisoner, the Earl Marischal of Scotland (the hereditary Lord High Constable's junior colleague and territorial neighbour), whom he wounded by throwing a bottle at him when exasperated. The 13th Earl was succeeded by his devoted sister Mary Hay, 14th Countess of Erroll in her own right, who made Slains Castle the chief centre for landing Jacobite secret agents (she had an implied understanding with the naval officer patrolling the coast of Buchan to let her know when his ship was passing off Slains). Once landed at Slains, they were hurried inland to another of her strongholds, Delgatie Castle, with its hidey-holes and secret passage.

Countess Mary was succeeded in 1758 by her great-nephew, the magnanimous and scholarly 15th Earl who entertained Dr. Johnson and Mr. Boswell at Slains. They were much impressed by the rugged splendour of its storm-lashed site. Dr. Johnson said that he would not wish for a storm at sea, but if one happened, he would like to see it from Slains; and Mr. Boswell observed, correctly, that Lord Erroll's nearest neighbour was the King of Denmark.

The castle was much altered, and encased in red Aberdeen granite, by William George Hay, 18th Earl of Erroll, K.T., who had officiated as Lord High Constable during King George IV's famous Royal Visit to Scotland in 1822, when Lord Erroll was attended by eight mounted Esquires, four Pages, ten Grooms, and 25 of the Lord High Constable's Doorward Guard of Partizans: the oldest royal bodyguard in Britain. The Highlanders, called out for the occasion by the Duke of Argyll, the Countess of Sutherland, the Earl of Breadalbane, Sir Evan MacGregor of MacGregor and MacDonell of Glengarry, were fitted into the royal procession ceremonially by being constituted the Lord High Constable's Highland Guard: the ceremonial duty of guarding the Sovereign having been Hay of Erroll's since the time of Bruce.

After the 20th Earl was obliged to sell Slains, attempts were made to demolish it entirely, but the Erroll mortar proved as strong as the Aberdeen granite, and its ruins still dominate the coastal sky-line of Cruden Bay.

Old Slains, home of the present Countess of Erroll, Chief of the Hays, on the coast of Buchan.

There has been a castle on this site since prehistoric times, from which the old outworks survive. Lady Erroll descends from its twelfth-century owners, the original Celtic earls of Buchan, through the marriage of Gilbert Hay, 3rd baron of Erroll, co-Regent of Scotland during the minority of King Alexander III in 1255, to Lady Idoine Cummin, daughter of the Earl of Buchan and sister of the Constable of Scotland. The shattered remains of the Great Tower, seen in this picture, were probably built by her father, who had married the Celtic heiress. Her grandson, Sir Gilbert Hay, 5th baron of Erroll, was given Slains and the office of Constable of Scotland, when his Cummin cousins were forfeited, by his friend King Robert Bruce.

In 1513 William Hay, 4th Earl of Erroll, hereditary Sheriff of Aberdeen, rode out from Slains with many Hays and Buchan men to die as Constable of Scotland with King James IV on Flodden Field, when the division he commanded was broken by the Percies. With him fell eighty-seven gentlemen of the surname of Hay, besides their followers. ' The Flowers of the Forest ', the lament for this lost battle, is still the most famous and the most melancholy of all Scots laments.

At this time old Slains Castle was almost the centre of a little principality. The Earls of Erroll not only had powers of life and death like ordinary barons (and the barons of Cowie, for instance, were their vassals), but the authority of the royal courts did not normally extend into their Regality and Lordship of Slains (except for high treason)—whereas the royal courts themselves were in Erroll's jurisdiction as hereditary Sheriff of Aberdeen. Until the fifteenth century they had levied taxes throughout all Scotland on goods brought to market, and some claimed for them a tax on every reeking chimney in the land.

At Slains they kept a typical mediaeval household—a Chamberlain, Bailie, Secretary, Steward, Standard-Bearer, Marischal, Master of the Horse, Pursuivant, Chaplain, Jester—besides esquires, pages, ladies-in-waiting, grooms of the chamber, and men-at-arms. They had of course their Falconers and Huntsmen, for hawking and the chase were the great outdoor sports of those days—in the

intervals of war, statecraft and the administration of justice. Periodically there were tournaments or banquets at the castle, and in the evening they listened while tales of chivalry were read aloud, or else listened to their harpers or their pipers or their other musicians, or played at chess or ' the tables ' (draughts or backgammon). A flat piece of ground above the Old Castle is still known as the Tilting Ground. Other lairds nearby, like Fraser of Philorth or Udny of that Ilk, took the Earl of Erroll's service for protection, binding themselves to follow him by ' bonds of manrent '.

The castle was captured from Andrew Hay, 8th Earl of Erroll, by rebellious Hays. His first wife had been his cousin, the 6th Earl's daughter, and by her he had three sons, the eldest and youngest both deaf and dumb and the other very able. After her death, the Earl married Lady Agnes Sinclair, daughter of the ferocious 4th Earl of Caithness, and had more children. He started giving her blank charters, and the Hays feared he might disinherit his Hay wife's sons. So in 1576 his own brothers and the Hays of Megginch surprised Slains Castle with scaling ladders by night, captured the Earl in his own keep, and held him prisoner in the dungeon-tower for a month. King James VI personally intervened, temporarily entrusting the whole Erroll fief to Alexander Hay, Lord Clerk Register; while a special Act of Parliament was passed fixing the succession on the earl's younger son Francis Hay, and the unfortunate Master of Erroll was placed in the custody of the Captain of Edinburgh Castle in 1584, being cognosced insane a dozen years later.

The 8th Earl's fetching wife, cause of the trouble, was still attractive as a widow: for in 1587 she had to be rescued by the Earl of Atholl from ' Mad Colin ' Campbell of Glenlyon, who wounded her men and burnt her house at night, carrying her off ' to use her according to his filthy lust and inclination '.

Slains Castle was blown up by King James VI in person in 1595, after the failure of the Counter-Reformation Rising led by Huntly and Francis Hay, 9th Earl of Erroll. When Earl Francis returned from exile, he tried a witch in the stables of the ruined Castle, but though she was convicted, he released her. However, he did not rebuild the Castle: and a fishing village sprang up awhile on the site.

In 1960, the present Countess of Erroll made her home there again: in a wooden house designed by Stanley Ross-Smith.

Graham

The surname of Graham has been notable in Scottish history for more than eight centuries. But the family belonged originally to the Anglo-Norman aristocracy, and derived their surname from the lordship of an English manor, the 'grey home' called Graegham in the Domesday Book. Research in England and perhaps in France might well uncover details of their history before their then ancestor came to Scotland in the twelfth century.

William de Graham was one of the Anglo-Norman baronial companions of King David I, and witnessed personally that king's important charter founding the Abbey of Holyroodhouse in 1128—for King David had made many friends in England while he was Earl of Huntingdon before his accession to the Scottish throne. The Scots often tended to translate 'de Graham' as 'the Graham' instead of as 'of Graham', when speaking English instead of Norman-French. Thus Blind Harry refers to the Graham cadet who was Wallace's closest friend and companion-in-arms, and who was slain at Falkirk in 1298, as 'Schir Jhone the Grayme'.

This worthy Sir John's gallant great-uncle, Sir Patrick de Graham, fell carrying the King of Scots's banner (presumably as depute for Sir Alexander Scrymgeour) against the English at Dunbar in 1296. Sir Patrick had married into the great Celtic dynastic house of the Earls of Strathearn 'by the Indulgence of Scotland'; and was the first of the family to get a foothold in the Highlands, being granted Loch Corriearklet and land on the banks of Loch Lomond. His son, already a Gael on his mother's side, exchanged a beautiful estate that King Robert Bruce wanted (and made his real home) for lands at Montrose in Angus.

By 1445 Patrick, the then Graham chief, became a peer as Lord Graham, during the formative period when lords were first being distinguished from lairds. It is interesting to note, however, that in a petition by Sir Colin Campbell of Glenorchy to Pope Paul II in 1465/6, he is mentioned as 'Patrick Graham of that Ilk, Knight'—although of course he never had any lands called Graham, so it was thus a very early example of the Highland use of such a designation to indicate chiefship of a Name alone. In 1460, he had exchanged with the Buchanan chief, for lands near Mugdock, the old Graham lands in the Highlands by Loch Arklet and Loch Lomond.

A branch of the Grahams received a much greater Highland territory in the fifteenth century, but to their sorrow. The chief's half-brother Patrick Graham, Earl Palatine of Strathearn, who had acquired that royal earldom by marriage to King Robert II's granddaughter, was slain by the Drummonds in 1413, leaving his infant son to the guardianship of his own younger brother, Sir Robert Graham of Kinpont. In 1427 King James I seized the boy's rich earldom, giving him instead the Highland parish of Aberfoyle and part of Port of Menteith, with the almost empty title of Earl of Menteith (Strathearn had once been a kingdom that included Menteith)—and at the same time he sent the poor boy as a hostage to England, where he was imprisoned in Pontefract Castle for nearly twenty-six years (more than three times as long as an average modern 'life' sentence in practice, and for no crime save his high birth). The boy's uncle and guardian, Sir Robert Graham, protested in vain, organised an opposition and tried to arrest the king in full Parliament, publicly renounced his allegiance to a tyrant, and finally raided Perth at the head of his Highlanders and slew the king himself: for which he was publicly tortured to death in the most revolting manner.

These Grahams continued to hold their Highland territory, through many feuds and wild affrays—until in 1680 William Graham, Earl of Menteith and Airth, being childless and in debt, made over the inheritance of all the lands of his earldom of Menteith to his chief James Graham,

The coat-of-arms of the 'Sr. de Graham' appears on the earliest known surviving roll of Scottish Arms. As yet unpublished, and unknown to Scottish heraldic writers, this 'Balliol Roll' of 1332 is painted on the back of the last membrane of *Cooke's Ordinary*, and is in the personal possession of Sir Anthony Wagner, Garter Principal King of Arms. It depicts the Royal Arms of King Edward Balliol during his short-lived reconquest of his father's throne, after he was crowned at Scone in 1332, together with those of thirty-five of the greatest Scottish lords of that time, Highland and Lowland, including many who were opposed to him. Besides those of the then Graham chief (Sir David de Graham), it has the Arms of the then chiefs of the Clan Macduff, Cummin, Ross, Sutherland, Stewart, Murray, Sinclair, Hay, Fraser, Gordon and MacDougall ('le Sr. Dargael' or lord of Argyll)—besides those of the Earls of Lennox, Mar, Moray, Menteith (a Stewart) and Caithness, together with two Clan Macduff cadets (the Earl of Atholl and the lord of Abernethy). The shield of Graham is second from the left in the last row. Its *scallop shells*, pilgrim's begging-bowls, indicate doubtless some pilgrimage to Santiago de Compostella in Spain by an earlier Graham chief. A scallop shell already appears on the earliest surviving Graham seal, in about 1230.

3rd Marquis of Montrose, who had already regained the original Graham lands on Loch Lomondside and also the whole of the insolvent Buchanan chiefs' estates. By this time, each Marquis was styled in Gaelic *An Greumach Mor*, 'the Great Graham '.

The third Duke of Montrose, as a Member of Parliament (while Marquis of Graham) joined Lovat's heir in securing the repeal of the statutes against Highland dress: thus restoring the tartan which today we take so for granted. The late Duke of Montrose, inventor and designer of the first aircraft carrier in the First World War, became the leader of the Home Rule movement in Scotland. The present Duke, although a Rhodesian Cabinet Minister, is a keen Gaelic-speaker who has competed and been runner-up in the *Mod*. His son, the Marquis of Graham, still lives at Auchmar near Loch Lomond in Dunbartonshire, whose Lord Lieutenant is Admiral Sir Angus Cunninghame Graham of Gartmore in Menteith.

Mungo Maxtone, 10th of Cultoquhey (1687–1763) used to assemble his household daily at a well near his house, as we are told, to intone the Cultoquhey Litany:

> ' From the greed of the Campbells,
> From the ire of the Drummonds,
> From the pride of the Grahams,
> From the wind of the Murrays,
>   Good Lord, deliver us '.

That the adage was applied anyway to the Grahams before Cultoquhey's Litany can be seen from a letter in 1690 to the Marquis of Atholl's son from Margaret Graham of Inchbrakie, Dowager Lady Nairne: ' My Lord I beg pardon for this long & I believe troublesum letter, but I am a proud Graeme & loves not to be slighted & not tell it '.

A proud Graham was Thomas Graham of Balgowan, M.P. for Perthshire, husband of ' The Beautiful Mrs. Graham ' immortalised by Gainsborough. She died young off the south of France, and while her husband was bringing her lovely corpse home for burial in Perthshire, the French Revolutionaries

Buchanan Castle, built by the Graham Dukes of Montrose on the site of the former stronghold of the Buchanan chiefs, but now a ruin. The present duke's son, the Marquis of Graham, still lives nearby, at Auchmar.

The ruins of Mugdock Castle, from a Victorian drawing. A Graham possession from the thirteenth century, Mugdock lies in Strathblane, in the Lennox, bordering on the original Colquhoun country. James Graham, 3rd Earl of Montrose, supported the future Regent Lennox against Mary Queen of Scots at the battle of Langside in 1568; and as a result, Argyll, the epileptic Campbell chief who was married to the Queen's natural sister, Lady Jean Stuart, laid waste the lands of Mugdock. In 1641, the castle's charter-room was searched repeatedly, but in vain, for evidence against the Great Montrose, then a political prisoner. But when his fortunes changed and he was created a Marquis in 1644, the ugly name of 'Mugdock' was changed to the more romantic 'Montdieu', and one of the subsidiary titles conferred on Montrose was that of Lord Montdieu (pronounced 'Montdew', as the spelling in a contemporary inventory of writs shews us). In the Civil Wars, Montdieu Castle was sacked and burnt by the squint-eyed *Mac Chailein Mor*, Marquis of Argyll; but James Graham, 2nd Marquis of Montrose restored and enlarged the castle, once more known as Mugdock, and it remained the principal home of the Graham chiefs until in 1680 they acquired Buchanan Castle on Loch Lomondside.

The beautiful Mrs. Graham, by Gainsborough. The Honble. Mary Cathcart (d. 1792), was wife of Thomas Graham of Balgowan, afterwards Lord Lynedoch, who raised 'Graham's Grey Breeks' and defeated the French at Barrosa to avenge the violation of her coffin by French revolutionaries. She was daughter of the 9th Lord Cathcart, Ambassador to Russia; and her sisters were the Duchess of Atholl and the Countess of Mansfield, both married to Murrays.

insisted on breaking open and searching her coffin. He promptly gained service against the French as a prominent civilian volunteer at Toulon, personally raised a regiment which became known as 'Graham's Grey Breeks', became a General and defeated the French Marshal Victor at the battle of Barrosa: ending up as Lord Lynedoch.

It is hardly necessary to remind anyone that two of the three greatest commanders of Highland clansmen in the Stuart Cause were Grahams: the Great Montrose and Bonnie Dundee. The whole gallant history of the Grahams shows that, to the enemies of what they believe to be right and true, a pride of Grahams is more dangerous than a pride of lions.

Buchanan

The lands of Buchanan lie on the shores of Loch Lomond, opposite the island of Clarinch where the clan had their gathering-place in time of war: boats being the most convenient vehicle of mobilisation in that mountainous country. Clarinch was granted in 1225 by the mighty Earl of Lennox to their chiefs' ancestor Absalon son of Macbeth, in return for a pound of wax to be rendered annually at Christmas. He took his name, however, from his lands on the shore, and appears as Sir Absalon of Buchanan before about 1224. Buchanan is Old Gaelic for the ' house of the canon ' (*buth chanain*), and Sir Absalon may have belonged to one of the sacred families of the old Celtic Church—the Earl of Lennox sometimes

In the Buchanan country on Loch Lomond-side.

The island of Clarinch in Loch Lomond, gathering-place of the water-borne Buchanan clan on the outset of war.

James Buchanan, President of the United States (1857–1861).

styles him *clericus meus*—like the original family of Luss on the other side of the loch. In 1238 he or his son was Steward of the Lennox.

His son Absalon *mac Absalon* was no doubt the first to be styled by this name, which became 'Macauslan' and was often used instead of 'Buchanan' by their descendants. In 1282 the then Earl of Lennox gave a charter to the chief of that time, Sir Maurice of Buchanan, confirming him in the lands of Buchanan and granting him the right to hold courts with the baronial powers of life and death. Here at Buchanan was the homeland of the clan until, after the death of John Buchanan of that Ilk in 1682, the ancient estate had to be sold: it is said for commitments deliberately incurred on the old chief's behalf by his doer, Buchanan of Arnprior, whom he had alienated by withdrawing a promise to make him the heir.

The early Buchanans were probably related to another Lennox clan, the Galbraiths, who were of ancient British origin and had bear's heads (Arthur means a bear) in their coat-of-arms. For the Buchanan chiefs also originally bore bear's heads on their shield, until they came gradually to adopt a very significant coat instead: the Royal Arms of Scotland differenced only by changing the lion and tressure from royal red to mourning black (the lion was sometimes shewn 'degraded', without tongue or claws, and sometimes splashed with tears), together with the crest of a hand holding up a ducal bonnet. Although there is some doubt from which of Sir Walter Buchanan of that Ilk's two wives the later chiefs actually descended, there seems little doubt that this change in the Buchanan arms alluded sadly, almost treasonably, to a belief in the descent of at least some of the Buchanan chiefly family from Sir Walter's second wife, Lady Isabel Stewart. Her rights in the Dukedom of Albany fell through the forfeiture of her beheaded father, the Regent Albany, in 1425, but her brothers left no (openly) legitimate descendants. The Lennox itself would have been but a part of her claim, as the Lennox Rose on top of the bonnet perhaps reminds us.

Galbraith

The name Galbraith is derived from the Gaelic words for 'Foreigner Briton'. When the Galbraith chiefs first appear on record, in the twelfth century, they were already noble Britons who had intermarried with the greatest family among the local Gaels and held lands in the Lennox (the earldom watered by the Leven) north of Dunbarton, 'the Fortress of the Britons', former capital of the kingdom of Strathclyde.

This had been established as a kingdom of the Ancient Britons after the withdrawal of the Roman legions from Britain in the fifth century, and was only finally united with Scotland in 1124. The early Scottish chiefs were heads of branches of dynastic houses; so the Galbraith chiefs may well have been remote cadets of the old royal house of Strathclyde.

Certainly, their first recorded Chief, Gilchrist *Bretnach* or 'the Briton', living in 1193, was married to a daughter of Alwyn *Og* mac Mureadhach, Earl of Lennox (and descendant of the ancient Mormaers of the district), at a time when earls' daughters were not accustomed to marry below the rank of thane or baron.

The Galbraiths had a stronghold on the island of Inchgalbraith in Loch Lomond, and were known as *Clann-'a-Bhreatannich* or 'Children of the Britons'. Their arms of *three bears' heads* may perhaps allude to the Ancient British heroic name Arthur, which was used in their family and means a bear.

Sir William Galbraith of Buthernock, the 4th Chief, married a sister of the 'Black Cummin', head of the greatest family in Scotland and later a Competitor for the Crown. All the same, Sir William sided against the Cummins, and took part in the daring plot whereby the boy-king Alexander III was 'rescued' from their control. This Galbraith chief then became so powerful as to become himself one of the co-Regents of Scotland in 1255. His son, the next Chief of the Galbraiths, married a sister of the famous 'Good Sir James of Douglas' who fell carrying the dead Bruce's heart on Crusade against the Saracens in Spain.

By 1320, a branch of the Galbraiths held Culcreuch in Strathendrick, and towards the end of that century the Galbraiths of Culcreuch inherited the chiefship of the clan. Thomas Galbraith of Culcreuch, 12th 'chieffe of the Galbraiths', was captured by King James IV in 1489 and hanged.

Inchgalbraith, where the early Galbraiths had their island stronghold in Loch Lomond.

Throughout the sixteenth century, the Galbraiths were involved in many a wild and lawless action, except during such periods as when the 16th Chief was appointed Sheriff-Depute of Dunbartonshire in 1578 to administer the Lennox on behalf of its absent statesman-duke.

In 1622, Robert Galbraith of Culcreuch, 17th Chief, in debt to his brother-in-law (whom he waylaid and fired upon, but in vain), was denounced as a rebel and forced to give up Culcreuch Castle to him. The Chief then emigrated to Ireland.

From a younger brother of the 13th Chief (who died in about 1512) there descended the Galbraiths in Balgair, which adjoins Culcreuch. This branch in modern times has produced the Honble. ' Tam ' Galbraith, M.P., Civil Lord of the Admiralty and Under Secretary of State for Scotland in Harold Macmillan's administration, and his father the Right Honble. Thomas Galbraith, P.C., Minister of State in the Scottish Office, who in 1955 was appropriately created 1st Lord Strathclyde.

Macfarlane

Macfarlane is from the Gaelic *Mac Pharlain* meaning ' Son of Parlan ', which comes from the Old Irish name Partholon, often translated ' Bartholomew '. The chiefs, and later the clan, took this name from their ancestor Parlan, whose great-grandfather Gilchrist of Arrochar was a younger son of Alwyn, Earl of Lennox from about 1180 to 1225. These ancient Celtic earls of the Lennox, the remote forefathers of the Macfarlanes, were themselves Gaels in origin, although they sometimes bore old Anglo-Saxon names because of their descent from an heiress of the line of the great Northumbrian thegn Arkil Ecgfrith's-son, who fled to Scotland from William the Conqueror in 1070.

A famous scholar of Celtic myth suggests of the use of the name Parlan by the Lennox family: ' that Parlan or Partholon had figured from time immemorial in the family legend of the Gaelic earls of Lennox as a great ancestor, and possibly as a divine personage '. For the ancient dynastic houses of the Gaels usually traced themselves back to sacred Spirits whom they may have incarnated in pagan times, and *Par-tholon* or ' Sea-Waves ' appears in Irish mythology as the first to take possession of Ireland after the Flood. According to the old Irish Gaelic MS. genealogies, these mormaers or earls of the Lennox sprang from the ancient royal house of Munster (though several generations are obviously omitted), and this is certainly supported by the family's continued use of the Munster royal family names Muireadhach, Maelduin and Corc as late as the thirteenth and fourteenth centuries.

The senior branches of the Lennox family came to a grisly end in 1425, when eighty-year-old Duncan, Earl of Lennox, had his grey head hacked off after being made to watch his own Stewart grandsons being put to death first, all to slake James I's hatred of the poor old nobleman's late son-in-law, the Regent Albany. Thenceforward the Macfarlane chiefs claimed to be chiefs of the whole Lennox clan, as heirs male of the old earls. But the earldom of Lennox was later regranted to the Stuarts of Darnley, descended from Earl Duncan's youngest daughter; and we are told that Macfarlane opposition to them was overcome by the marriage of the then chief, Andrew Macfarlane of Arrochar, to a daughter of the new earl.

Andrew's son, Sir Iain Macfarlane, who used the old-style chiefly title of ' Captain of Clan Pharlane ', is said to have fallen under the English arrows at Flodden in 1513, leading his clansmen in the rearguard commanded by the Earls of Lennox and Argyll. He was related to both earls, as the Macfarlanes had acquired lands in 1395 through Duncan Macfarlane of Arrochar's marriage to a sister of the 1st Lord Campbell, the then *Mac Chailein Mor*. Sir Iain's son, known as Andrew the Wizard, was father of

The ruins of Inveruglas Castle, an island stronghold of the Macfarlane chiefs in Loch Lomond. It was burnt by the Roundheads after the English invasion of Scotland under Oliver Cromwell. In the background is Ben Lomond; and in the foreground is Loch Sloy Power Station, which uses the water of Loch Sloy.

Duncan Macfarlane of that Ilk, who was killed fighting for Scotland at Pinkie in 1547. His clansmen were earlier described as ' men of the head of Lennox, that spake the Irish and the English-Scottish tongues, light footmen, well armed in shirts of mail, with bows and two-handed swords '. Buchanan of Auchmar wrote: ' This Duncan, laird of MacFarlane, was one of the first, of any account, who made open profession of the Christian religion in this kingdom '—but the *errata* in a later edition runs ' for *Christian* read *protestant* '. The next chief brought three hundred Macfarlane clansmen to fight against Mary Queen of Scots at the battle of Langside, since her assassinated husband had been the heir of Lennox.

The turn of the century saw lawless times, and the 1587 Act of Parliament that sought to bring order among the clans included ' the Laird of M'Farlane of the Arrochar ' among those lairds responsible for the good conduct of their clansmen, for the ' M'Ferlanis, Arroquhar ' are listed among the ' clannis that hes capitanes, cheiffis and chiftanes quhome on thay depend, oft tymes aganis the willis of thair landislordis '. In 1589, for instance, the Macfarlanes caught Sir Humphrey Colquhoun of Luss having an affair with their then chief's wife, hunted him to Bannachra, set fire to the castle, and brought home to the poor lady an unspeakable portion of the Colquhoun chief's corpse—serving it up to her on a wooden dish with the obscene jest ' That is your share. You will understand yourself what it is.' Again, in 1624 many Macfarlane clansmen were convicted of armed robbery. Hence the well-known Macfarlane pipe-tune is appropriately called *Thogail nam bò*, ' Lifting the cattle '—and the cattle-raiders' full moon became known as ' Macfarlane's Lantern '.

Walter Macfarlane of that Ilk was fined by the victorious Covenanters for having fought under Montrose for Charles I: and when the Cromwellian English invaded the still independent kingdom of Scotland, he held out against them—his island castle of Inveruglas in Loch Lomond being burnt to the ground by the Roundheads. The other Macfarlane stronghold was on Eilean-a-Vow in Loch Lomond, while the chiefs' primitive house was at Arrochar on the shore of Loch Long.

By the eighteenth century, their Arrochar home had been replaced by a comfortable house, the home of the celebrated antiquary Walter Macfarlane of that Ilk. Some years after this chief's death, a highlander with the second sight prophesied that a black swan would soon settle among Macfarlane's white swans and that when it did the chiefs would lose all their lands. The black swan duly appeared and remained for three months, after which in 1785 the whole lands of Arrochar had to be sold for debt, and the last Macfarlane chief emigrated to America.

Loch Sloy, gathering-place and slogan of the Macfarlane clan in the old days of war and cattle-raid. The dam, 177 feet high, was part of the first major hydro-electric project constructed in the Highlands by the North of Scotland Hydro-Electric Board.

Loch Long, in the Macfarlane country.

MacAulay

DULCE PERICULUM

MacAulay can mean 'Son of Olaf' or 'Son of Amalghaidh'—the one clan of Norse and the other of Gaelic origin. The Sons of Olaf appear to spring from Ullapool (the Old Norse 'Olaf's Place') on the mainland of Ross, and became the Macaulays in the island of Lewis, which was part of Norway until 1266. To this clan belonged the nineteenth-century historian and poet Thomas, Lord Macaulay.

The Sons of Amalghaidh became the MacAulays of Ardencaple in the Lennox. Their ancestor was probably Amalghaidh mac Amhalghaidh (pronounced Amleth mac Auleth), whose father was one of the younger sons of Alwin, Earl of the Lennox in the year 1200. These Lennox dynasts claimed descent from the ancient royal house of Munster in Ireland. Amalghaidh's eldest son Sir Duncan Macaulay was ancestor of the last native Earls of Lennox (after 1364), but Amalghaidh also appears to have had at least one younger son, Alwin Macaulay, who appears in 1271.

The MacAulays of Ardencaple believed themselves to have some connection with the MacGregors, as appears from a bond of manrent given by the MacAulay chief to the MacGregor in 1591: at a moment when the MacGregors were in great peril and needed every support. The MacAulays continued to hold Ardencaple Castle in the Lennox until the then MacAulay chief was obliged to sell it for debt in 1767.

Ardencaple Castle a hundred years ago. It was the home of the Macaulay chiefs, styled Ardencaple of that Ilk or later Macaulay of Ardencaple, until it became ruinous in the time of the last Macaulay of Ardencaple, who died in 1767. It was acquired by *Mac Chailein Mor*, and the Dukes of Argyll made various nineteenth-century additions before selling it to Sir James Colquhoun of Luss. It has now once again become a ruin.

SI JE PUIS

Colquhoun

Since the very earliest records that have come down to us, the deer-haunted hills and wooded glens and loch-side lands of Luss have belonged to the ancestors of the present Chief of the Clan Colquhoun: Sir Ivar Colquhoun, 32nd of Luss.

His remote forefathers who lived here more than seven hundred years ago were most likely a branch of the ancient rulers of the Lennox, and they used the surname of Luss, taken from the name of their lands. They were a sacred family, Celtic priests and hereditary guardians of the *bachuil* or crozier of St. Kessog: the martyr who dwelt in Glen Luss or on Inchtavannach, the ' monk's isle ' in Loch Lomond. So it is possible that they were also related to the saint himself, as was often the case with hereditary guardians of saintly relics in the old Celtic Church. Indeed, the place-name ' Luss ' itself is probably derived from an old word meaning the bounds of a sanctuary: for King Robert Bruce confirmed by royal charter that all the ground within a ' girth ' of three miles around the church of Luss was a holy place of refuge.

The present chief's forebear, Maelduin of Luss, was Dean of the Lennox in 1220, and three generations later his then ancestor, Sir Iain of Luss, appears on record as still guarding their family saint's *bachuil*. The heiress of this ancient Celtic line was the Fair Maid of Luss, who by 1368 had married Sir Robert Colquhoun of that Ilk, chief of a clan that had fought for King Robert Bruce in the War of Scottish Independence and whose strong castle of Dunglass lay some miles away to the south on the river Clyde at Colquhoun near Dunbarton. Colquhoun is in the parish of Old Kilpatrick, and had been granted to their ancestor Humphrey of Kilpatrick in about 1241: the family then taking their name from the lands. There is still a Loch Humphrey in the Kilpatrick Hills, between Milngavie and Dunbarton. Dunglass Castle remained in the possession of the Colquhoun chiefs until the eighteenth century.

The Fair Maid's grandson, Iain or John Colquhoun, 10th of Luss, had to be called upon in 1411 by Duncan, Earl of the Lennox, to implement his solemn contract and oath to marry the earl's daughter, Lady Margaret. In 1424, when King James I returned from his long captivity in England and destroyed the Lennox family whom he regarded as his personal enemies, this Colquhoun of Luss was chosen by the king for the key post of Governor of Dunbarton Castle, the royal fortress that dominated the Lennox. This was possibly the occasion of the traditional story explaining the Colquhoun heraldic supporters of two greyhounds, together with their crest of a stag's head and motto SI JE PUIS (their coat-of-arms, the black engrailed saltire on a silver shield, is obviously derived from the saltire of the Earls of the Lennox, itself probably related to the arms of a group of powerful Northumbrian families at the dawn of heraldry). The tale runs that the king asked the Colquhoun chief to recover Dunbarton Castle from his enemies; that Luss replied ' Si je puis ' (if I can), and then pursued a stag with hounds past the castle until the garrison joined in the chase, whereupon his clansmen rushed the castle and captured it for the king. Iain Colquhoun, 10th of Luss, who was Sheriff of Dunbarton in 1427, was later slain by a band of marauding Western Islesmen, led by the robber chief Lachlan Maclean of Duart, while making a gallant last stand on the Isle of Inchmurrin in Loch Lomond on 24 September, 1439.

His capable grandson Iain or Sir John Colquhoun of that Ilk, 11th of Luss, one of the greatest of his canny line, had his lands erected into the free Barony of Luss by King James II in 1457, with the right of ' pit and gallows ' which meant a local jurisdiction including the powers of life and death (held by the Colquhoun chiefs until 1747). The Gallowshill across the main road from Rossdhu still marks the site of the Colquhoun ' dule-tree '. In 1475 King Edward IV of England personally ordered his

The modern Ardencaple Castle, replacing the old stronghold of the Macaulay chiefs, sold in 1767.

Loch Lomond.

Ambassador in Scotland to give redress to the Laird of Luss for a ship of his captured by Lord Grey of England. Sir John, who was Great Chamberlain of Scotland and joint Ambassador to England, built the old castle on the 'black headland' of Rossdhu that forms a peninsula in Loch Lomond, and also the architecturally interesting private chapel of St. Mary of Rossdhu, dedicated in 1469 but now roofless. This mediaeval chapel's beautiful contemporary illuminated MS. Book of Hours has recently been identified among the public treasures of New Zealand, at the other end of the whole world: a place undreamt of by the holy man who wrote it. But Sir John's younger son Robert Colquhoun, Bishop of Argyll, had previously been rector of St. Kessog's Church in the village of Luss itself (the church of the family saint), and so his mediaeval tomb effigy is still to be seen there. Sir John himself, 11th Laird and 1st Baron of Luss, was killed in 1478, by a cannon ball (no longer a military novelty) which also killed two other distinguished knightly lairds, while taking part in the siege of Dunbar Castle. The family continued to have ancient Celtic church connections by inheritance from the remote past, and in 1497 Sir Iain Colquhoun, 13th of Luss sold a half merkland in the territory of Innerquhapill occupied by a certain procurator with the staff of St. Mund, called in Scots 'Deowray'. (For the functions of such a Dewar, see under MACNAB.)

A century later, in 1592, Sir Humphrey Colquhoun, 16th of Luss, had a love affair with the wife of the Macfarlane chief. The enraged Macfarlanes surprised him at his dalliance and pursued him past Rossdhu to another of his castles at Bannachra, where they tried to smoke him out. In the ensuing confusion Sir Humphrey was slain by an arrow, some say by his greedy younger brother Iain, his expectant heir, who was afterwards executed at the Mercat Cross in Edinburgh for the crime. Sir Humphrey's body was mutilated in a peculiarly revolting though appropriate manner and the result served up to poor Lady Macfarlane as a mocking dish, and 'so little regard did these savage freebooters pay to the laws of chivalry that they brutally violated the person of Jean Colquhoun, the fair and helpless daughter of Sir Humphrey'.

When the Colquhouns went to war, their Chief dipped a charred wooden cross in goat's blood, and sent this reminder of fire and sword by relays throughout the entire district of Luss: the bearer (usually mounted on a garron pony) shouting out the name of the mustering-place as he passed. Such was the Fiery Cross or *crois taraidh*, the Scots successor to the old pagan Norse 'fire arrow'. The Colquhoun mustering-place was most often at Cnoc Ealachainn, the 'armoury hillock' near Rossdhu. Here the clansmen paraded for war, wearing badges of hazel, the lucky plant of their Name.

In the time of Alasdair or Alexander Colquhoun, 17th of Luss, the wild Clan Gregor made a ferocious raid into Luss, when King James VI's sympathy was aroused by the frantic Colquhoun women bringing him the bloody shirts of their dead and wounded (some say a few extra shirts were added dyed in sheep's blood). Two months later, in 1603, the MacGregor chief himself raided Luss at the head of 400 clansmen, and defeated the Colquhouns (now invested with the royal authority) at the famous clan battle of Glenfruin: for which massacre a special Act of Council was passed outlawing the whole Clan Gregor and forbidding anyone on pain of death even to bear the dreaded surname of MacGregor.

A later chief of Clan Colquhoun was the sinister but clever Sir John Colquhoun, 19th of Luss, who was made a Baronet of Nova Scotia in 1625, when this title was first introduced into Scotland. He married the Great Marquis of Montrose's sister, but eloped with his pretty sister-in-law Lady

Tomb effigy of Robert Colquhoun, Bishop of Argyll (1473–1495) brother of Humphrey Colquhoun, 12th of Luss.

The ruined castle of Rossdhu, built by Sir Iain Colquhoun of Luss after the Barony of Luss was erected in 1457. Mary Queen of Scots stayed here with a later Sir Iain Colquhoun of Luss on two occasions. The castle was defended against the Cromwellian English in 1654, but was eventually captured by the Roundheads: the then chief being the Great Montrose's nephew. (See also p. 183.)

Katherine Graham, and was 'fugitated and excommunicated' for abducting her. Rumoured also to practise necromancy and witchcraft, he fled abroad and died in exile in Italy. His haughty successor Sir John Colquhoun, 20th of Luss, of whom there is an interesting portrait at Rossdhu in his red baronial robes edged with white fur, was known throughout Scotland as the 'Black-Cock of the West', just as the Gordon chief, Lord Huntly, is still known as the 'Cock of the North'.

In 1718 the vast Luss estates passed through Anne Colquhoun of Luss, whose husband inherited the Colquhoun baronetcy by a special arrangement with the Crown, but later became Chief of the Clan Grant in his own right. Their eldest son carried on the line of the Grants of Grant (now represented by Lord Strathspey and the Countess of Seafield), while their second son James became Colquhoun of Luss and was created a Baronet anew in 1786. This Sir James Colquhoun, 25th of Luss, was one of the earliest officers of the Black Watch and fought at the battle of Dettingen. Life in the Highlands had become more peaceful, and so he built the present elegant Georgian mansion house of Rossdhu between the old mediaeval castle (now a romantic ruin) and the world-famous banks of Loch Lomond. Sir James also founded the modern town of Helensburgh, which he named after his wife Lady Helen Colquhoun, sister of the 17th Earl of Sutherland.

A hundred years later, in 1873, Sir James Colquhoun, 28th of Luss, M.P., Lord Lieutenant of Dunbartonshire, was drowned in Loch Lomond within earshot of Rossdhu (everybody thought the cries were joyous boating cheers) with five of his gillies while sailing homewards from stalking red deer on the Island of Inchlonaig.

The late Chief was Sir Iain Colquhoun, 31st of Luss, Knight of the Thistle, Lt.-Colonel Scots Guards, who was Grand Master Mason of Scotland and also Lord High Commissioner to the General Assembly of the Church of Scotland: the nearest appointment Scotland has to a temporary Viceroy. A true Highland chief, he was lightweight boxing champion of the British Army, killed a Prussian officer with his revolver and five Bavarians with an improvised club (both weapons are preserved at Rossdhu), kept a fairly tame pet lion in the trenches, and won the D.S.O. and bar, though wounded more than once in the First World War: on the first occasion by a German bullet striking the hilt of his drawn sword at the First Battle of Ypres. But as a gentle lover of Highland scenery and the Gaelic way of life, Sir Iain was also Chairman of the National Trust for Scotland and was elected by the students as Lord Rector of Glasgow University.

His son, the present Chief, served in the Middle East and in Germany and was a Captain in the Grenadier Guards during the Second World War, being an officer of the élite 'King's Company' (now the 'Queen's Company'). He is a Deputy Lieutenant and Honorary Sheriff Substitute of Dunbartonshire, of which he is also the Hereditary Crowner. But before everything else he is the Chief of the Clan Colquhoun and the head of the thirty-second generation to care for Luss.

The Arms of the Burgh of Helensburgh, founded by Sir James Colquhoun of Luss, and named after his wife Lady Helen Colquhoun, sister of the Earl of Sutherland. The Burgh Arms combine the Sutherland stars with the Colquhoun saltire.

The Georgian mansion house of Rossdhu, which faces directly on to Loch Lomond. The central block was built by Sir James Colquhoun of Luss in 1774, while the portico and wings were added by the next Baronet. It is still the home of their descendant, the present Sir Ivar Colquhoun of Luss, on land which has been held by the family for at least thirty-two generations.)

MacGregor

The original homeland of the Clan Gregor was the 'three glens' of the rivers Orchy, Strae and Lochy on the opposite watershed to Strathfillan and Glendochart. From Glenstrae they afterwards branched out to Glengyle and Roro. They were probably connected with their neighbours the Macnabs, descended from the Celtic hereditary Abbots of Glendochart, of royal race—the MacGregor motto *S'rioghal mo dhream* means 'royal is my blood'.

The line of Iain of Glenorchy, captured by the English in 1296, ended in a childless heiress who carried the superiority of the glens to her husband's clan, the Campbells. But the male line of the old family, apparently descended from Iain of Glenorchy's nephew Gregor, would not submit to another clan and continued to hold their ancestral territory as long as they could by the sword.

This Gregor 'of golden bridles' was the name-father of the clan, and his son Iain 'the One-eyed' MacGregor of Glenorchy, who died in 1390, was thus the 2nd Chief of Clan Gregor. In 1519 the Campbells managed to establish as Chief of the whole Clan Gregor their own nominee, the MacGregor chieftain of the junior Clan Dughaill Ciar branch (who had ravished but then married Campbell of Glenorchy's daughter), although the Campbells' own *Black Book of Taymouth* tells us that he 'was not righteous heir to The MacGregor'. The disinherited line, known in Gaelic as the chieftains of the Children of the Mist (which could equally be translated heads of the Fog Folk: though some say the real name was 'Sons of the Wolf'), carried on the resistance with such success, involving the usurping chiefs in their brigandage, that in 1603 the whole Clan Gregor were outlawed and the Name of MacGregor proscribed on pain of death.

The scattered clansmen had to take other surnames, and some branches (such as are probably the Marquesses of Londonderry, to which Castlereagh belonged) have never yet resumed the name of MacGregor. A glance at the Burke's *Peerage & Baronetage* entry for the chiefs' immediate family alone shows twenty-two MacGregors as hanged, four as beheaded, three as murdered (two by arrows in the back), and five as killed in battle. To get away from it all, in the mid-seventeenth century one brother of the then chieftain of the Children of the Mist emigrated to America, where he was scalped by redskins.

In 1774, however, the penal laws against the Clan Gregor were finally repealed by Act of Parliament; and a few years later the head of the rightful but long-disinherited branch—the Children of the Mist—was officially recognised as chief of the whole clan. The present chief of the Children of the Mist is Sir Gregor MacGregor of MacGregor, 6th Baronet and 23rd Chief of Clan Gregor, who commands the 1st Battalion Scots Guards.

The present Chief of Clan Gregor's silver kilt pin, in the form of the MacGregor Arms: an uprooted oak tree surmounted by a sword bearing an antique crown on its point. These Arms appear in a MS. armorial of c.1565-6, now in Lyon Office, as those of 'Lord Makgregour of ould'. The *Black Book of Taymouth* gives Campbell of Glenorchy's opinion of this coat-of-arms, with special reference to the present chief's ancestor, Duncan *Ladasach* MacGregor (beheaded by Glenorchy in 1552):

    Off the Mc'Gregoris Armes.
The Sworde and firtree croceit beneath ane croun
Ar fatall signes appropriat to this race,
By sum foirseeing fellow weill set doun,
Meit for suche lymmaris spoilzeing euerie place.
The croun presentis the Kingis most royall grace,
Ane rychteous judge with skill quha dois decre
That thai and all such cutthirttis suld imbrace
His seueir censure for thair villanie,
To wit, gif ony fra his sworde goie frie
Onexecute, continewing in their wrang,
He will erect ane gallows of that trie
And thairopone thame in ane widdis hang.
Sa faris my wittis can serve, I can nocht ken
Ane better badge for such a sort of men.
        Postscriptum.
One thing yit restis that sould their armes befit,
If with Sanct Johnstounes rubenis thai war knit.
           Amen.
(St. Johnston's or Perth ribbons were gallows' ropes.)

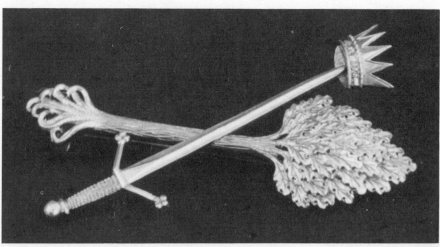

The outlawed Clan Gregor were frequently pursued with bloodhounds, known in Gaelic as *conn dubh* or 'black dogs'. This gun is inscribed 'This is the Fuzee with which the last of the Blood-Hounds used for tracking the MacGregors is said to have been killed'. The hound in question was shot by Malcolm *Og* MacGregor, chieftain of the *Clan Dubhghaill Ciar* in Glengyle, who in 1624 led 300 clansmen to help the Earl of Moray against the Clan Chattan in Petty. He shot it near Lochearnhead, on the slope of a hill still called *Meall a Mhadaidh*, the Hill of the Wild Dog. Of him, we are also told that 'it was Callum Oig who, whilst shut up with the Clan on the island on Loch Katrine in 1611, shot one of the Besiegers dead with a long barrelled gun'. In 1816, the 'bloodhound' gun belonged to Francis Macnab of Macnab, from whom it was obtained by the MacGregor chief, Sir John, 1st Baronet.

Sir Gregor MacGregor of MacGregor, 6th Baronet and 23rd Chief. Heir of a long line of outlaws, he is himself a professional soldier, having been Brigade Major of the Parachute Brigade, and is now Commanding Officer of the 1st Battalion Scots Guards.

His forefather Duncan *Ladasach* 'the lordly' MacGregor of Ardchoille, Tutor of Glenstrae, and really the rightful Chief, was ringleader of all the most recalcitrant Gregarach of his time (so that *Ardchoille* became the MacGregor slogan); but was captured, apparently by a treacherous trick, and beheaded by 'Grey Colin' Campbell of Glenorchy in 1552. Two of his sons were beheaded with him (the third being murdered by the usurping branch of the MacGregors), and his grandson was killed in a skirmish with the Campbells at Bintoig in 1604. (*See also p. 36.*)

The Chief of the Children of the Mist: Major-General Sir Evan MacGregor of MacGregor, 2nd Baronet and 19th Chief, G.C.H., K.C.B., Governor of Dominica and the Windward Islands (lived 1785–1841). Sir Evan married Lady Elizabeth Murray, daughter of the 4th Duke of Atholl.

He was wounded in seven places when treacherously attacked, his own sword sheathed, while receiving the surrender of Fort Talneir in India in 1818: receiving severe *kris* wounds in the left shoulder, left side, and in two places on his right side—not to mention 'a sabre wound across the mouth, a second right through his nose, and a third nearly cut off his right arm above the elbow joint'. The wicket gate had been slammed behind him, but his men, led by Captain Peter MacGregor, had thrust in a musket from outside to prevent the gate from closing completely. They rushed the fort and rescued him, although Captain MacGregor

was shot dead. The treacherous *killedar* commanding the fort was hanged on the following morning.

This picture was painted four years later, when Sir Evan at the head of a 'tail' of his clansmen guarded the Honours of Scotland: and at the great royal banquet in Edinburgh given by King George IV, the MacGregor chief personally proposed the loyal toast: 'The Chief of Chiefs – The King'. (*See also pp. 19, 20 & 183.*)

Edinchip, in Balquhidder, is the home of Sir Gregor MacGregor of MacGregor. His forefather, Duncan *Ladasach* 'the Lordly' MacGregor of Ardchoille, led the Clan Gregor on a great raid into Balquhidder in Easter Week 1543; and it was in the Kirk of Balquhidder that the clan gathered to take their grisly oath on Drummond-Ernoch's severed head in 1589. Another of the present Chief's forefathers, Iain *Og* or 'Young John' MacGregor of Glencarnock (1668–1744), acquired the lands of Glencarnock beyond Invercarnock at the head of Loch Doine in Balquhidder; and after the failure of the 1745 Rising, Robert MacGregor of Glencarnock, the Jacobite Chieftain of the Children of the Mist, marched his clan regiment home to Balquhidder. 'We marched ... straight to Rannoch, still with flying colours thro' Glenlyon into Breadalbane ... The Argyle Militia was in the Castle of Finlarig and they durst not move more than pussies. We came straight to the Kirk of Balquhidder. Then every man to his own house and did not know well where it was'. In 1795, the 18th Chief (nephew of the Jacobite Glencarnock) was created Baronet of Lanrick and Balquhidder. Edinchip was completed in 1830 by Sir Evan MacGregor of MacGregor, when he sold Lanrick Castle; and it has ever since been the home of the Chiefs of Clan Gregor.

Looking across Loch Lomond to the famous peak of Ben Lomond, in the MacGregor country.

Grave of 'Rob Roy' at Balquhidder. Rob *Ruadh* or Red Robert MacGregor used the *alias* of Campbell, for his mother was sister of the Campbell of Glenlyon who carried out the Massacre of Glencoe. He himself acted as Tutor of Glengyle during the minority of his nephew, the young chieftain of the *Clan Dughaill Ciar* branch, and he commanded a force of MacGregors in the 1715 Rising. A brigand, romanticised by Sir Walter Scott, 'he was one of the best swordsmen in the country, partly because his arms were so long that according to tradition he could tie his garters without stooping'. In 1734 he set out to bully the peaceful MacLarens, with whom the Clan Gregor had long been at feud in Balquhidder; and died as a result of an apparently slight wound received in single combat with Alasdair Stewart of Invernahyle, who had accepted his challenge in order to avert a clan battle between the Gregarach and the combined forces of the MacLarens and their hereditary allies the Stewarts of Appin. In 1736, his death was 'avenged' by his youngest son, Robin *Og* MacGregor, who shot John MacLaren of Wester Invernenty (Baron Stobchon) in the back while he was peacefully ploughing a field. The unsuccessful advertisement for Robin *Og's* arrest described him as 'a tall lad, aged about 20, thin, pale-coloured, squint-eyed, brown hair, pockpitted, ill-legged, in-kneed, and broadfooted'. Robin *Og* was eventually hanged in 1754 for abducting and raping a girl who died as a result of his brutality.

Macnab

Macnab means 'Son of the Abbot', and the Nacnab chiefs were the descendants and heirs of the Celtic hereditary Abbots of Glendochart, themselves the *coarbs* or heirs of St. Fillan mac Feradach, who was a prince of the Dalriadic royal house of Lorn and died in 703. He founded his principal abbey in Glendochart, the upper part of the glen becoming known as Strathfillan. It was the Celtic custom for abbots to be chosen from the Founder's Kin, and the old Gaelic MS. genealogies trace the mediaeval Macnab chiefs through some twenty generations from Saint Fillan's brother, Ferchar mac Feradach.

In the thirteenth century, the Abbot of Glenochart still ranked with the Earls of Atholl and Menteith, and after the discontinuance of the Celtic abbacies the Macnab chiefs retained the barony of Bòvain in Glendochart. But in 1828 an old prophecy was fulfilled, that 'when a great storm blew a branch of a pine tree against the trunk of another, and grafted itself on to the trunk, the Macnabs would lose their lands': and the old clan lands were sold up for debt. However, the offending pine branch has died since the present snowy-bearded chief bought back the last 7,000 acres of the clan country, and returned to live in the home of his forefathers as The Macnab.

The Macnab, 22nd Chief, C.I.E., with his wife Alice, daughter of Dame Flora MacLeod of MacLeod. The Macnab was Financial Commissioner of the Punjab in the Indian Civil Service, and his wife was awarded the Kaisar-i-Hind silver and gold medals. His elder brother, the 21st Chief, resigned the Chiefship to him when he recovered the old Macnab lands from the Campbells. His heir is his nephew, James Macnab of Macnab, yr. (son of the 21st Chief), who is married to Lord Kilmany's daughter and lives nearby, also in the ancient Macnab country.

Sir Allan MacNab, 1st Baronet, Prime Minister of Canada, who became heir male of the Macnabs on the death of the 17th Chief in 1860, but left an only daughter Sophia MacNab, Countess of Albemarle. On William Lyon Mackenzie's rebellion against what he called ' the Family Compact ', in Canada in 1837, ' MacNab turned out with his militia battalion—known by the rebels as " the Men of Gore "— defeated the rebels at Montgomery's tavern, cleared the neighbouring districts, and cut adrift the schooner Caroline, belonging to a body of American " sympathisers ", who had taken possession of Navy Island, a little above Niagara, and sent her in flames over the falls.' (Mackenzie, who also called his innocent sovereign ' Victoria Guelph, the bloody queen of England ', later died of softening of the brain.) The Iron Duke of Wellington declared that it was his conviction ' that owing to the loyalty, zeal and active intelligence of Sir Allan MacNab the Canadas had been preserved to the British Crown '.

The bronze crozier-head added in the Dark Ages to encase the wooden pastoral staff of St. Fillan (died 703). This bronze head was itself later in turn encased in a silver head during the Middle Ages.

The Bell of St. Fillan, known as the *Bearnan* or 'Little Capped One'. As late as 1488, it was carried in the sacred pageant at King James IV's Coronation. It was in the hereditary custody of a Dewar whose toft is referred to in 1640 as 'Dewar-Vernan's Croft', at Suie in Glendochart. The relics of the Founder Saint were the essential insignia of a Celtic abbacy, and were sometimes given in hereditary custody with a toft of land to younger branches of the abbatial family. Such hereditary custodians were styled 'dewars', which often became their surname. In Glendochart there were five separate hereditary Dewars, each with a separate relic of St. Fillan (the pastoral staff, the bell, the arm-bone, the 'meser' and the 'fearg'): they were presumably cadets of the hereditary Abbots of Glendochart, whose principal heirs were the Macnabs of Macnab. *Fearg* means 'Wrath', and it is uncertain what relic acquired this bye-name. Its hereditary Dewars had their toft at Dewar-na-fargs-croft, which is referred to as late as 1632, and was at Auchlyne in Glendochart, where the ruins of their *Caibel-na-Fairge* or Chapel of the Fearg can still be seen. It has been suggested that the 'meser' was a *meise* or portable altar, but it seems more likely that it was the saint's missal, miraculously written by night. In 1468 a MacGregor certified to the Bailie of Glendochart that he held the tack of the lands of Corehynan from the 'Deore of the Meser'. The saint's arm-bone was known as the *Main*, and his toft at Killin is referred to in 1640 as 'Dewar-na-Mans-croft' and in 1670 as 'Dewar-na-Maynes-croft'. King Robert Bruce prayed in the Priory of Strathfillan while a fugitive, and attributed his escape from the MacDougalls to the saint's intervention. Accordingly, the silver shrine of the saint's arm-bone was brought to spend the night in the king's tent on the eve of Bannockburn, and was borne to the battlefield by the Abbot of Inchaffray himself. This enshrined arm-bone must have been an especially interesting relic,

as we are told that once upon a time, 'when the saint was in his cell after sundown, a lay brother was sent to call him to supper. The messenger, curious to know what St. Fillan was doing, looked through a chink in the wall, and was astonished to see him writing by means of a light that streamed from his left arm. Next day a tame crane that was kept by the holy fraternity picked out the eye of the lay brother who was guilty of prying upon the saint, and rendered him quite blind. but at the request of the rest of the brethren St. Fillan restored his sight to the erring one'. In 1549, the Privy Council protected 'Malise Doir of Quickrich' (Malise Dewar of *Coigreach*, the saint's pastoral staff) 'Archibald Doir of Fargy' and 'Malcolm Doir of Bernane' (*Bearnan* was the saint's bell) from having to hand over their sacred relics to the Prior of Strathfillan. St. Fillan's bell and pastoral staff are now in the National Museum of Antiquities of Scotland, in Edinburgh. The most important family of Dewars today is that of which the millionaire peer Evelyn Dewar, 3rd Lord Forteviot, is the head. Coming from the Perthshire highlands, they are most probably sprung from one of the five hereditary Dewars of St. Fillan, and so ultimately akin to the Macnabs, the Sons of the Abbot of Glendochart.

The elaborate silver crozier-head added to encase St. Fillan's pastoral staff, probably in the fourteenth century. In 1336, the Menzies chief, as then overlord of Glendochart, confirmed Donald McSobrell, dewar Cogerach, in the lands of Ewich in Strathfillan. The saint's staff was known as the *Coigreach* or 'Stranger', because it was so often carried by its hereditary Dewar to far places: for if any inhabitant of the parish of Glendochart should have goods or cattle carried off from him and 'be unable' to follow them, whether from doubt of the culprit, or feud of his enemies, then he might send a messenger to the Dewar of the Coygerach, with fourpence, or a pair of shoes, and food for the first night, and the said Dewar should follow the goods, or cattle, wherever they might be found within the bounds of the Kingdom of Scotland'. The inquest that reported this to the Bailie of Glendochart in 1428 declared that 'the office of bearing the said relic was given to a certain

progenitor of Finlai Jore' (i.e. Finlay Dewar) 'the present hereditary bearer, by the coarb of St. Fillan' (i.e. an ancient Celtic hereditary Abbot of Glendochart); and that in return for his services, the Dewar was due certain specified quantities of meal from each inhabitant of the parish. In 1487 the then bearer of the 'Quegrich', Malise Doire (i.e. Dewar) was confirmed in possession by King James III. After a later 'Malise Doir of Quickrich' in 1549 got the Privy Council to prevent the Prior of Strathfillan from forcing him to surrender his hereditary charge, the 'annoyance of the Church at being defeated in its action against the Dewars may account for the fact that in the following year the Crown authorities stepped in and imposed certain charges upon the lands which Malise Dewar of the Quigrich and his ancestors had always held free'. As a result, in 1575, the next Dewar of the *Coigreach* was obliged to sell all his lands of Eyicht, Cryt-in-dewar in Auchincarne and the half merkland called Cragwokin, to Campbell of Glenorchy. In the reign of Charles II, the then Dewar was so poor that he had to sell the *Coigreach* itself to MacDonell of Glengarry, who venerated the relic as a Catholic. But the Dewars 'never rested until they regained possession of the Quigrich, and brought it back from Lochaber to Breadalbane'. In 1782 its then bearer, Malise Dewar, was a day labourer living in *Sraid Glas* (Grey Street) at Killin. As late as 1795, Presbyterian highlanders were wont to come 'over a hundred miles to Killin to procure water that had been passed through the interior of the crozier'. The succession of the family in the nineteenth century is set out in the Rev. William Gillies' invaluable *In Famed Breadalbane* (Perth 1938). In 1818 Archibald Dewar of the *Coigreach* emigrated to Canada, taking the relic with him; and Highlanders settled in Canada used to come to him to get water in which it had been dipped to cure their sick cattle. But in 1876, Alexander Dewar of the *Coigreach* (with the consent of his own son) was induced to transfer the saint's pastoral staff to the Society of Antiquities of Scotland, 'on trust to deposit the same in the National Museum of Antiquities at Edinburgh, there to remain in all time to come for the use, benefit, and enjoyment of the Scottish Nation'. However, the present representative of the Dewars or Keepers of St. Fillan's crozier, Robert St. Fillan Dewar, bears as heraldic insignia two such pastoral staves in saltire behind his arms.

The 'Neish Island' in Loch Earn, where the Macnabs massacred the MacNeishes in 1612. The MacNeishes had been defeated near Comrie at Boltachan and a few survivors had withdrawn to this artificial island, whence they continued raiding the Macnabs. The Macnab chief's eldest son, 'Smooth John' or Iain *Min* Macnab, fiar of Bovain, with three of his brothers, carried a boat from Loch Tay overland some eight miles over the hills and down Glen Tarken, and launched it at nightfall on Loch Earn. The next day the brothers returned to The Macnab's castle on Eilean Ran on the river Lochay, and brought their mother a sack from which they 'emptied out the gory heads of their victims'. (In 1965, The Black Watch territorials successfully carried a boat all the way from Loch Tay to Loch Earn over the same hills as an energetic military exercise, in memory of this historic operation). Eilean Ran Castle

was burnt by the Cromwellian English invaders, after Iain *Min* Macnab, now himself the Laird of Macnab, had been killed in an attack on their occupying forces in Bread-albane in 1653. The English commander in Scotland reported that: 'the Lord MacKnab, one of the great Montrossians, with his whole clan, did rise upon our partie; and coming to them, after some little parley (we having got some of their cattel together) they offered our partie free quarter, if they would lay downe arms and return in peace. But our men, not willing to be so affronted, stood upon their defence; which the Highlanders perceiving, sent a flight of arrows and a volley of shot among them; and ours letting fly again at them, killed MacKnab, the great chieftain of that wicked clan, with four more, and fell upon them and routed them all.'

Kinnell House, home of The Macnab. After Eilean Ran Castle was burnt by the Round-head English in 1654, the Macnab chiefs moved to Kinnell nearby. The walls of the older part of the building are from three to five feet thick. When an official came to serve a writ on Francis, 16th Chief, the laird went into hiding while the stranger was lavishly entertained overnight. Meanwhile a dummy was hanged on an elm-tree near the house. When the official 'woke with a splitting headache and bleary eyes the next morning and asked what was the grisly sight, she told him 'Oh that's just a wee bit baillie body that angered the Laird ': whereupon the bailiff fled without daring to serve the writ.' The next chief, Archibald, took over so burdened an inheritance that he was soon in danger of being arrested for debt. So one morning in 1823, he went out for a walk with his gun and a couple of dogs, as usual; and then just disappeared. He never returned to Kinnell. But his creditors tracked him in Scotland and thence to London; and he had to flee to Canada. The estates had to be sold to the main creditor, the 4th Earl of Bread-albane. and remained in Campbell hands until 1949, when Kinnell was recovered by another Archibald Macnab of Macnab, the present 22nd Chief. (*See also p. 14.*)

In the greenhouse on the left of the picture grows the famous Black Hamburgh vine. At one time it was 192 feet long and considered to be the largest vine in the world. Though its branches at both ends have been cut back, it still produces 600 bunches of grapes a year.

MacLaren

The MacLarens are the Sons of Laurence, and take their name from their ancestor Laurence, Abbot of Achtow in Balquhidder, who apparently lived in the thirteenth century. In those days, abbey-lands were held hereditarily by the Founder's Kin, often with the title of abbot, and of course the Celtic church permitted their ecclesiastical functionaries to marry just as the Protestant churches do nowadays. Achtow was doubtless dedicated to some religious foundation by the local dynasts of Strathearn.

Balquhidder is the highland part of Strathearn, around Loch Voil and Loch Earn, and the heraldic 'beast' of the lordship of Balquhidder is the mermaid—two of whom 'support' the MacLaren chief's shield, which is simply that of the ancient Celtic earls of Strathearn (*two red chevrons on a golden field*) differenced by the addition of the *black galley* of Lorn and the Isles. For it is a probably well-founded tradition of the clan that they were a younger branch of the powerful local dynasts—Strathearn was a kingdom in Pictish times—who as late as the thirteenth century styled themselves ' By the Indulgence of God, Earls of Strathearn ', and who were even uniquely the temporal superiors of their own Bishops of Dunblane. But when the last Celtic earl of Strathearn was deprived of the earldom in 1344, the MacLarens found themselves under alien overlords.

Achtow itself adjoins Achleskine and the Kirkton of Balquhidder at the foot of Loch Voil, and this was the heartland of the clan, which later spread to other parts of Strathearn and (the Murray dukes of Atholl being lords of Balquhidder) into Atholl as well. The dukes conferred baronial powers of life and death on some of the MacLaren chieftains who held under them, but unfortunately were never superiors of the original MacLaren homeland. However, although the MacLarens of Achleskine never got a royal or ducal charter of their lands, they were never dispossessed by the successive nominal superiors. But they were over-run and massacred in 1542 and again in 1558 by the ' Children of the Mist ', the wildest ' house and gang ' of the MacGregors, and became for a while a ' broken clan '. The landless MacGregors may have had some land-claim through a MacLaren heiress, for their chief's crest of a lyon's head crowned with an antique crown is differenced from that of the MacLaren chief only by its colour, and by the MacLaren addition of their laurel plant-badge. Indeed, the present

Creag an Tuirc, the ' Boar's Rock ' near Achtow and Achleskine in Balquhidder, was the gathering-place and slogan of the Clan Labhran.

MacGregor chief lives on what was once MacLaren land. Luckily, the MacLarens always had staunch allies in the Stewarts of Appin in Lorn, who never forgot their descent from a MacLaren lady.

A number of MacLaren gentlemen emigrated from the Middle Ages onwards. In 1498 Robin and Gilbert MacLaren joined the Scots Men-at-Arms in the service of the King of France, and Colin and Simon MacLaren accompanied them as mounted Archers. They took part in the invasion of Italy in 1499, when Bernard Stuart, Marshal of France (cousin of the Earl of Lennox) captured Genoa and conquered all Lombardy. They were a touchy lot, their Highland pride mingling with that of their other Scottish comrades. 'The men-at-arms were always of good lineage, as Chevalier Bayard affirmed to the Emperor Maximilian at the siege of Padua, which that sovereign and the French were then attacking.' Bayard said the Scots men-at-arms were too well-born to assault the city alongside the mere German lansquenets, and that they must be allowed to ' fight by the side

Standard of The MacLaren, supported by the fetching Mermaid of Loch Voil, heraldic ' beast ' of Balquhidder. The Mermaid, like the Crescent Moon and the Boat, is a very ancient sacral royal symbol in the matrilinear tradition of the Dawn Religion. Normally she carries a mirror and a comb, but the MacLaren fish-goddess has the laurel clan plant-badge instead of the comb, although her flowing hair has been let down all the same. As far afield as Japan, where the imperial dynasty claims descent from the goddess-spirit Amaterasu, the imperial regalia has always consisted (with the Sword, common to almost all dynasties) of a Sacred Mirror and a Moon-shaped jewel, both of which are said to have come to Japan with the first Emperor, in the hereditary custody of ancestors of great noble clans. Similarly, the matrilinear royal Picts included a Sacred Mirror and Comb (as well as a Flowering Crescent, and the Sun-and-Moon either as brother-and-sister or husband-and-wife) among the fourteen different symbols, perhaps totems or tattoo-marks, that occur (never singly) on the Pictish carved stone memorials. When the Murrays of Tullibardine (descended in the female line from the ancient Earls of Strathearn) became lords of Balquhidder in 1587, they adopted the Mermaid as a crest. The MacLaren's standard also displays, next to the national St. Andrew's Cross in the hoist, the MacLaren Arms (the Strathearn *chevrons* and Lorn *galley*), and beyond their Mermaid badge, the clan slogan CREAG-AN-TUIRC spreads across the fly.

The seal of Scone Abbey, depicting the King of Scots being inaugurated at Scone, and attended by seven dignitaries, possibly the Seven Earls of Scotland: his peers in the old sense (peer means ' equal ', and he was then *primus inter pares*). Beneath are the Royal Arms of Scotland, between the *gold and red paly* ' Peace Coat ' of the Earl of Fife, Chief of the Clan Macduff, and the *red chevrons on gold* of the Earl of Strathearn's shield: both earls using the Royal Colours of Scotland. In a charter before 1177, the Macduff chief was styled ' Duncan, by the Grace of God Earl of Fife '; and in 1200, the Strathearn dynast, when founding Inchaffray Abbey, was styled ' Gilbert mac Ferteth, by the Indulgence of God Earl of Strathearn '. The Highland part of the Earldom of Strathearn is the mountainous district of Balquhidder, where the MacLaren chiefs claimed descent from an early branch of the Strathearn dynasts, and were important enough in the Middle Ages to be included among the thirty-odd clans in the old Gaelic MS. genealogies of the Highland chiefs. The MacLarens ' differenced ' their own coat-of-arms by adding the *Black Galley of Lorn* below the *red chevrons on gold* of the ancient Earls of Strathearn.

of their equals '. These proud MacLarens took part with the other Scots men-at-arms in the magnificent (but too boisterously tough) military pageant in honour of the victorious King Louis XII at Milan in 1507, after which one of the Scottish gentlemen died of a fractured skull. Other McLarens later entered the Swedish service, where ' Johan Laurin ' was enrolled as a Noble of Sweden in 1647, with the name of Lagergren, and ' Magnus Laurin ' was also enrolled as a Noble in 1691, with the name of Lagerström. As Lagergren was born in about 1578, not so long after the disastrous massacres that disrupted MacLaren records, it is interesting that his Arms (recorded in Sweden) were a MacLaren laurel branch impaling the *two red chevrons on gold* of the old Earls of Strathearn; and that Lagerström, besides two chevrons, bore the MacLaren black lyon holding a laurel branch (clearly derived from the MacLaren chiefs' crest). The traditional MacLaren Arms eventually recorded by the late MacLaren of MacLaren and Achleskine are thus corroborated from an unusual source.

CREAG·AN·TUIRC

'The MacLarens of Achleskine were all grand, strong men. They buried inside the Kirk' of Balquhidder. 'When the Old Kirk was repaired in 1839 Donald dug up bones at that spot 23½ inches long!' The last of these Achleskine MacLarens to farm Achtow died in 1892, but his family continued at the Kirkton nearby until 1957. After careful investigation, his great-grandson Donald was officially recognised by the Lord Lyon King of Arms as MacLaren of Achleskine and chief of the clan as The MacLaren. He acquired part of the old clan territory once more, including *Creag an Tuirc*, the Boar's Rock, which was the MacLarens' rallying-place in the days of clan warfare. Dying in 1966, The MacLaren was buried with his ancestors in the Old Kirk of Balquhidder. His young son is the present MacLaren of MacLaren.

Balquhidder Church. The 'auld kirk' was the burial place of the MacLarens of Achleskine, principal line of the clan. In 1532, Sir Iain MacLaren, the then vicar of Balquhidder (priests were called 'Sir' like knights), was slain in a dispute with some other MacLarens, who were promptly outlawed.

Drummond

The early Drummonds were evidently closely related to the ancient Celtic earls of Menteith, whose Arms of *three wavy bars* they bore differenced only by colour, and in whose family burial place at least one Drummond—of age by 1248—was buried beneath a fine stone carved with his effigy in Celtic armour. In the early thirteenth century, when a few surnames were gradually coming into use in Scotland and cadets often adopted the name of their own estates, the earls of Menteith were themselves closely related to the earls of Lennox. It may therefore be significant that the Drummonds not only took their surname at this very period from the lands of Drymen in the Lennox (Gaelic *Dromainn*, a ridge), but also held the office of Seneschal of the Lennox, the most powerful the almost regal earl could bestow.

Their first undoubted ancestor to be so far traced for certain was *Maelcolum Beg* or 'Little Malcolm' of Drummond, who was obviously of high West Highland birth and appears in still extant charters as Seneschal of the Lennox from about 1225. He is not called Drummond in any of these charters, but his younger son Eoin of Drummond's tombstone near the high altar in the ruined priory church on the romantic island of Inchmahone in the beautiful Lake of Menteith is inscribed 'Johannes de Drvmod filius Molqalmi de Drvmod'. The elder son, Malcolm of Drummond, was captured by the English at Dunbar in 1296, and again ' to the great joy of King Edward I ' was taken prisoner by them in 1301. His son, also called Malcolm, is said to have strewn ' caltraps ' (spiked booby-traps that always fall in such a way as to penetrate horses' hooves in the nastiest manner) in front of the English heavy cavalry at Bannockburn: in memory of this feat of military fun, caltraps are still one of the Drummond badges and are strewn on the ' compartment ' of Lord Perth's heraldic achievement, while the Drummond motto is ' Gang Warily '.

At this time the chiefs of the family were also ' Tosachdiors ' of the Lennox: this apparently means ' Law-Thane ' or perhaps Itinerant Headman, but corresponded to the Scots ' Crowner '. They also kept up their connection with Menteith, and in the fourteenth century John Drummond, the then chief, had a blood-feud with the Menteiths—family quarrels are usually the most bitter—though he made peace with them in 1360. He became John Drummond of Stobhall, still the present chief's home in Perthshire, by his marriage in about 1345 to an heiress of the Montfichets, the family to whom Stobhall had been granted in about 1190 by King William the Lion.

The ladies of John Drummond of Stobhall's clan were famous for their charm and beauty. Indeed, his sister Margaret and his daughter Annabella both became Queens of Scotland. Queen Margaret Drummond married King David II, son of the national epic hero Robert Bruce. Queen Annabella Drummond was the wife of King Robert III, second of the ill-fated Stewart dynasty. A century later a third Drummond girl was murdered to prevent her from becoming the Queen of King James IV, whose secret wife she may already have been.

Queen Annabella's eldest brother, Sir Malcolm Drummond of Stobhall, ' a manful knicht baith wise and ware ', came to an unhappy end. He had become Lord of Mar through his marriage to the Countess of Mar in her own right, sister of that heroic Black Douglas who fell in the moonlight fight at Otterburn, in which battle Sir Malcolm Drummond had distinguished himself by aiding in the capture of Sir Ralph Percy. The Wolf of Badenoch's son coveted this rich Earldom of Mar, which included fair Deeside and Donside. So he caused Sir Malcolm Drummond to be kidnapped by a gang of Highlanders, who maltreated him in prison till he perished, and then the Wolf's son married the widowed Countess himself.

A caltrap, one of the heraldic badges of the Drummonds, and to which their motto GANG WARILY alludes. According to tradition, Sir Malcolm of Drummond, their then chief, organised the strewing of caltraps to impede the English cavalry at Bannockburn in 1314. A caltrap lands point upwards whichever way it falls, and is disagreeable to chargers' hooves.

Stobhall, which came to the then Drummond chief, John Drummond of Stobhall, baron of Cargill and *Tosachdior* of the Lennox, by marriage to the heiress of the Montfichets or Mushets, more than six hundred years ago. He was brother of Queen Margaret Drummond, and father of Queen Annabella Drummond. The main block was incorporated on to the older site by the second Lord Drummond, whose widow completed the new buildings in 1578. Their combined coat-of-arms—Drummond and Ruthven, for she was a daughter of Lord Ruthven—can still be seen on the gable of the beautiful chapel, with its pre-Reformation altar and its old 'confessional' (the Drummonds are Catholics), also its famous tempera-painted ceiling which was so adorned in the reign of Charles I. The attached buildings were once lent by the family to the artist Sir John Millais as a studio, but now contain quarters for the present Earl of Perth's guests. A mediaeval Scots poet wrote of Stobhall, whose castle walls overlook the banks of the river Tay:

> Joy was within and joy without
> Under that wlonkest waw,
> Quhair Tay run down with stremis stout
> Full strecht under Stobschaw.

Stobhall is now home of David Drummond, 17th Earl of Perth, P.C., *An Drumanach Mor*, Jacobite titular Duke of Perth and former Minister of State for Colonial Affairs. This part of the castle was built as a Dower House by John Drummond, 2nd Earl of Perth. It displays his arms and initials carved with those of his wife, Lady Jean Ker, through whom their younger son, William Drummond, inherited the valuable Border earldom of Roxburghe, taking the name of Ker and being forefather of the Dukes of Roxburghe. This Dower House seems to have been completed in 1671 by the 3rd Earl of Perth, a gallant Cavalier who had fought under Montrose for King Charles. 'Bonnie Dundee' stayed at Stobhall during the Whig revolution in 1689, on his way north to raise the Highlands for King James, whom Lord Perth and his brother Lord Melfort followed into exile. The Dowager Duchess of Perth, who had been imprisoned in 1746 for entertaining Prince Charles Edward at Drummond Castle, died at a great age in the Dower House at the castle of Stobhall in 1773. Thereafter, Stobhall lay derelict until 1953, when the present Earl of Perth restored it as his own home. He and Lady Perth live in the Dower House itself.

Stobhall passed to poor Sir Malcolm's brother, Sir John Drummond, Justiciar of Scotland, whose great-grandson was made a Peer in 1488 as Lord Drummond: a Peerage still held by the Earl of Perth. The 1st Lord Drummond was a peppery old gentleman who lived up to the reputation given his family in the old Perthshire litany: ' From the ire of the Drummonds, good Lord deliver us '. At the age of seventy-six he was imprisoned for striking the Lord Lyon King of Arms, whom he thought disrespectful to his grandson, the Red Douglas, second husband of Queen Margaret Tudor.

But old Lord Drummond was well accustomed to the violence of those times. Three of his daughters had been poisoned together by political enemies in order to prevent King James IV from making one of them his Queen: fair Margaret Drummond, ' the diamond of delight ' who was the King's true love. And the old Lord's younger son, David Drummond, had been executed in 1490 for burning a number of Murrays in the church

at Monzievaird—the two families had been at feud, and a Murray had foolishly provoked the ' ire of the Drummonds ' by shooting one of them with an arrow from the kirk window.

Lord Drummond had acquired the lands of Concraig near Crieff in Strathearn from a cousin, the forefather of John Drummond of Megginch, now 15th Lord Strange, and with those lands the offices of Steward, Crowner and Forester of Strathearn. The Drummonds thus also held these offices in Glenartney and Balquhidder. In order to function properly as Hereditary Steward of Strathearn, Lord Drummond built a new castle at Concraig and called it Drummond Castle. This castle still belongs to his female-line descendant James Drummond-Willoughby, 3rd Earl of Ancaster, former Lord Great Chamberlain of England.

The 2nd Lord Drummond, like all his house before and afterwards, was a loyal supporter of the Stewart dynasty. As a Privy Councillor, he was staunch to Mary Queen of Scots throughout the troubles of her fateful reign. His elder son Patrick, 3rd Lord Drummond, appointed as his deputy Royal Forester of Glenartny his unfortunate kinsman Drummond of Drummond-ernoch, whose severed head was placed by marauding MacGregors on his own sister's dining-table at Ardvorlich and was then taken to the altar in Balquhuidder church to be touched and sworn on by the ferocious Gregarach in a band of mutual support against his avengers. The 3rd Lord Drummond's younger brother was James Drummond, 1st Lord Maderty, created a Peer of Scotland in 1609. This branch (to which the present Chief belongs) founded Innerpeffray Library, the first public library in Scotland and still one of the gems of Perthshire. To this branch also belonged Andrew Drummond, founder of Drummond's Bank, whose descendant, Lt.-Commander Geoffrey Drummond, won the Victoria Cross in 1918.

The 4th Lord Drummond was created Earl of Perth in 1605. However, the Highlanders continued to call the Drummond chiefs by their Gaelic style: *An Drumanach Mor*, as we are told in a seventeenth-century MS. Among the eight founder Knights of the Thistle were the 4th Earl of Perth and his brother, who was created Earl of Melfort. ' The two brothers ruled Scotland under King James VII ', Lord Perth being the Lord Chancellor and Lord Melfort the Secretary of State. At the same time their martial cousin, General Sir William Drummond of Cromlix (brother of Lord Maderty), was Commander-in-Chief in Scotland. A scholarly Cavalier, he had been Governor of Smolensk in Muscovy while in exile, and later became the 1st Viscount of Strathallan. He married at midnight

Tombstone of Sir Iain of Drummond, near the high altar in the island Priory of Inchmaholmein the Lake of Menteith, family burial place of the mediaeval Earls of Menteith, whose coat-of-arms had also *three wavy bars*. Sir Iain, who was younger son of the then Drummond chief, first appears in 1248 and died soon after 1304. He was taken prisoner fighting against the English at Dunbar in 1296, but liberated on condition he served in France, the Earl of Menteith becoming surety for him. Sir Iain is wearing an unusual *clogaid*, the Celtic conical helm, as it tapers into a crest-like cross.

Glenartney, of which the Lords Drummond (afterwards Earls of Perth) were hereditary Royal Foresters. In 1589 the Forester Depute was John Drummond of Drummond-Ernoch, who had cut the ears off some MacGregor poachers. Accordingly, some Gregarach (of the branch called the ' Children of the Mist ') cut off his head.

Drummond Castle in Strathearn. Originally called Concraig, its site was acquired in 1487 from Drummond of Concraig (ancestor of the present John Drummond, 15th Lord Strange) by his cousin and chief John, afterwards 1st Lord Drummond, who built the old tower and called it Drummond Castle. It was much added to by the Earls of Perth in the seventeenth century, and again by their successors in the nineteenth century, and is still the Scottish home of their descendant in the female line: James Drummond-Willoughby, 3rd Earl of Ancaster.

in the old Abbey Kirk of Holyroodhouse the daughter of his old political enemy Lord Warristoun, hanged leader of the Covenanters; and with his sinister colleague Tam Dalyell of the Binns he is credited with having introduced the torture of the ' thumbscrew' into Scotland from Russia. The present writer descends from this strange marriage.

'Bonnie Dundee' stayed at Stobhall during the Whig revolution in 1689, on his way north to raise the Highlands for King James. Both Lord Perth and his brother Melfort followed the King into exile, where he rewarded them both with the Garter for their loyalty in adversity and made them both Dukes. These honours were of course not recognised by the Whig Government. But they were confirmed in their Dukedoms with the *honneurs du Louvre* by King Louis XIV of France, who gave their Duchesses the prized right of ' tabouret ': the right to be seated in the Royal presence. And the King of Spain is said to have made the exiled Duke of Perth a Knight of the Golden Fleece, the greatest Order in all Europe. Moreover, Perthshire always accorded them their Jacobite title, and it is probably after the first ' Duke of Perth ' that the well-known Scottish dance is named. For it ends with the characteristic ' reel of three ' of that period, instead of the ' poussette ' that later became fashionable.

In the 1715 Rising the 2nd Duke of Perth commanded the Jacobite cavalry at the battle of Sheriffmuir; and the 3rd Duke was one of the principal Jacobite leaders in the '45, throughout which he wore the Highland dress, riding in trews and plaid at the head of his men. He died at sea while escaping after Culloden, in which battle his Drummond kinsman, the 4th Viscount of Strathallan, was unhorsed and mortally wounded. As Lord Strathallan lay dying on the battlefield he is said to have been given the last sacrament in whisky and oatmeal because bread and wine could not be found in time. He was ancestor of the present chief, David Drummond, 17th Earl of Perth, P.C. (Duke of Perth in the Jacobite Peerage), former Minister of State for Colonial Affairs, whose father (the 16th Earl) was the first Secretary-General of the League of Nations, and who has restored the old castle of Stobhall to be once again the true home of the Drummonds.

Murray

The Murrays take their name from the great province of Moray, once a local Kingdom. Its name in Gaelic is *Moireabh*, in charter-Latin *Moravia*, from the early Celtic *mori-treb* or 'sea-settlement'. It was brought forcibly under the expanding Scottish realm in the twelfth century. The ancient royal house of Moray had merged with a branch of claimants to the Scottish throne (see Mackay); and their male line was ruthlessly discouraged. Scotland as we know it was then first being welded out of many different countries and peoples by the kings descended from Saint Margaret. The Flemish lords across the North Sea were both warlike and industrious, and a number of their younger sons found an outlet as settlers to help establish the King's Peace in the new realm.

The Scottish kings were related to the Norman kings of England, who found these Flemings equally useful in bringing law and order to the Welsh border. Among them, in the second quarter of the twelfth century, Freskin son of Ollec held lands in the west of what is now Pembroke. He was probably the Freskin who was also granted lands at this period by King David I in West Lothian and in conquered Moray. But it seems possible that he or his son William were wise enough to intermarry with the ancient royal house of Moray (in whose final overthrow they were taking part) for consolidation according to a common mediaeval practice. Their descendants certainly assumed the wide surname 'of Moray' or Murray—usually adopted in Scotland by the cadets of provincial dynasts, e.g. 'of Mar', 'of Lennox', 'of Atholl', 'of Dunbar', 'of Ross', 'of Argyll', 'of Menteith'—and took for their coat-of-arms the *three stars* with the colours blue-and-silver apparently associated with the Mackays and the ancient province of Moray.

Bothwell Castle, principal stronghold of the Murray chiefs until 1360: reconstructed from the ruins in a drawing.

Blair Castle at Blair Atholl, once the stronghold and still the home of the Dukes of Atholl, Chiefs of the whole Name of Murray.

Scone Palace, home of Mungo Murray, Earl of Mansfield & Mansfield and Lord Lieutenant of Perthshire, a former Lord High Commissioner to the General Assembly of the Church of Scotland (the nearest Scotland has to a Viceroy, for during his term of office he takes precedence even before the Duke of Edinburgh or Prince Charles). In the trees beyond the palace is a chapel on the old *moot-hill*, made of earth from all parts of the realm, where the ancient Kings of Scots were inaugurated on the Stone of Destiny, and where Charles II was crowned in 1651 at the last separate Scottish Coronation. The abbey of Scone, founded by King Alexander I in 1114-15, was given at the Reformation to the Ruthven earls of Gowrie (heirs of the senior line of the Camerons); but after their downfall in the mysterious 'Gowrie House Affair' in 1600, when the Murrays intervened on the king's behalf, King James VI gave Scone to his close friend Sir David Murray, whom he created Lord Scone and later Viscount of Stormont, both peerages still held by Lord Mansfield, as is that of Lord Balvaird. The Balvaird branch of the Murrays, of which Lord Mansfield is the chieftain, spring from a younger son of Sir William Murray of Tullibardine, who died in about 1511. Curiously, Lord Mansfield holds two different earldoms: being 7th Earl of Mansfield in Middlesex (a peerage of 1792), and also 6th Earl of a completely different place in Nottinghamshire that is also called Mansfield (a peerage of 1776): although the 1st Earl of both was the famous Lord Chief Justice, younger brother of the 6th Viscount of Stormont. Another younger brother was James Murray, created Earl of Dunbar by 'the King over the Water', which Jacobite peerage is now also held by Lord Mansfield (though of course not recognised by the Government).

The senior line of the Murrays took the surname of Sutherland and became Earls of Sutherland by about 1235. Thereafter the chiefs of the Murrays were the lords of Petty in Moray, who through an Oliphant heiress became also lords of Bothwell in Clydesdale before 1253. Sir Walter Murray, 1st lord of Bothwell, was co-Regent of Scotland in 1255. The 2nd lord was hereditary Pantler of Scotland in 1284; and the 3rd lord died a prisoner-of-war in the Tower of London. The heir, Sir Andrew of Murray, was the brilliant young general who led the Scots in 1297 in their first great rising against the English conquerors, but was mortally wounded in his famous victory at Stirling Bridge—after which his junior colleague, Sir William Wallace, fought on gallantly as an immortal guerrilla leader but unfortunately without the same success in pitched battle. His son Sir Andrew Murray, 4th lord of Bothwell, was killed in 1333 as Regent of Scotland, in battle against the English at Halidon Hill.

The last Murray lord of Bothwell married his own cousin and heiress Joan (daughter of Maurice Murray, Earl of Strathearn), and after his death of the plague—the 'Black Death'—in 1360, she carried the lordship of Bothwell to her second husband, the 3rd Earl of Douglas. After this, the famous 'Black Douglas' earls quartered the Arms of Murray with their own.

The chiefship of the Murrays then fell into doubt amongst the various scattered branches of the Name—from Sutherland and Murray itself, through Perthshire and Stirlingshire to Annandale and the Borders. But by the sixteenth century, the Murrays of Tullibardine in Strathearn (who had formerly borne the *three silver stars on blue* differenced with a Strathearn *chevron*) came to bear the chief Arms of Murray, *three silver stars within a golden royal tressure on blue*; and they were accorded the chief Arms by Lord Lyon Lindsay of the Mount in his authoritative MS. armorial of 1542, which ranks with Lyon Register. From this period, they assumed the leadership of the Murrays.

There is reason to suppose that the Tullibardine ancestor, Sir Malcolm of Murray, Sheriff of Perth in about 1270, was a younger brother of the 1st lord of Bothwell, and that their mother was the daughter of Malcolm, Earl of Fife and Chief of the Clan Macduff, Scotland's premier clan. Since Earl Malcolm was succeeded by his nephew in 1228, it would be necessary to account for some family arrangement (such as that made in about 1307 in the case of the earldom of Menteith) whereby his daughter had transferred the earldom of Fife to his heirs male; but it would certainly explain much else in Murray history. It was Sir Andrew Murray (son of the first Murray of Bothwell) who avenged the murdered Earl of Fife in 1288. The Earls of Fife claimed the first place in peace and war, but it was Sir Andrew Murray of Bothwell who was chosen as Regent of Scotland in 1332, and his youthful father who had been given place before Wallace himself as ' leaders of the army of the Kingdom of Scotland ' in 1297. It might explain the extensive holdings of the Murrays of Petty intermingled with those of the Earls of Fife on the Spey: and might account for the link between Petty and the Mackintoshes of Rothiemurchus (who claim to come of the Clan Macduff). It would certainly explain the possession of Aldie and Pitfar, that had formed part of Earl Malcolm's wife's *maritagium*, by the Murrays of Tullibardine; and their ancestor being named Malcolm.

James Moray, 14th of Abercairny, painted by Jeremiah Davison c.1739. His red cuffs are edged with gold, and his coat and plaid are of different tartans. It should be noted that his home was in the lowland part of Strathearn: although of course the Morays or Murrays have always been connected with the highlands.

Pitlochry and the surrounding countryside, in Atholl. The Butters of Pitlochry have helped to officer the Athollmen since before the Murrays themselves came to Atholl. For the Butters are a very old local family, and were seated at Gormack, between Dunkeld and Rattray, in the Middle Ages. They appear as landowners in Perthshire from at least 1432 and 1444, when Finlay Butter and Patrick Butter both sat on inquests together with such other local lairds as Sir David Murray of Tullibardine (ancestor of the Dukes of Atholl), Malcolm Drummond of Stobhall (ancestor of the Earls of Perth), Patrick Rattray of that Ilk, Finlay Ramsay of Bamff and Malcolm Moncreiffe of that.Ilk. Their crest of a drawn bow and arrow alludes to mediaeval archery at the *butts*.

In about 1508, Patrick Butter of Gormack married Lady Janet Gordon, daughter of the second Earl of Huntly (her sister was married to Perkin Warbeck, who claimed to be one of the two little princes actually murdered in the Tower of London). Lady Janet Butter was a dangerous wife, for she is accused by popular rumour (traceable to at least the sixteenth century) of having smothered her first husband, Alexander Lindsay, Master of Crawford (son of the Duke of Montrose), with a down pillow in the Castle of Inverqueich, where he lay wounded in 1489 after an affray with his own younger brother (afterwards the sixth Earl of Crawford). After this murder, she married Patrick, Master of Gray (later 3rd Lord Gray). However, this marriage was dissolved by more peaceful means and she next married Patrick Butter of Gormack, who was still alive in 1526 (when he witnessed an indenture between the Earl of Atholl and the Bishop of Dunkeld), but was dead by 1535 when the formidable Lady Janet had taken on a fourth husband. A local legend has it that, as a penance for smothering her first husband, she had to sit on a high rock opposite Gormack some two hundred feet above the Ericht near the present Craighall-Rattray, and spin night and day until the thread should reach the river below. The next laird, John Butter of Gormack, married Lady Janet's own niece, Lady Beatrix Gordon, daughter of Adam Gordon, Earl of Sutherland, by the tenth Countess of Sutherland in her own right.

This was the period when the Hay chiefs held the baronies of Logiealmond and Caputh in Gowrie on the frontiers of Atholl, as local inter-marriage shows. Thus John Butter of Gormack's daughter Elizabeth Butter married a son of the seventh Earl of Erroll, Lord High Constable, by his wife Margaret Robertson, daughter of the fifth Chief of Clan Donnachaidh. A later John Butter of Gormack was among those pardoned by King James VI in 1598, after being denounced rebels for taking part with the Earl of Atholl in a raid, when Ashintully Castle was set on fire and Andrew Spalding of Ashintully was carried off captive.

About this period, the Butter and Moncreiffe cadets in Atholl appear to have inter-married, or to have married two sisters who were ' heirs portioners ' of lands near Moulin, including Pitlochry itself and the hamlet of Kinnaird, about a mile and a half north-east of Pitlochry. The Butters got the ' sunny half ' and the Moncreiffes the ' shadow half of the town and lands of Kinnaird ', while the

Butters got the mill and mill-lands of Pitlochry, where the Moncreiffes held the Drum of Pitlochry and Tomnamoine, together with lands in Glenbrierachan. In 1606 there was a grant under the Privy Seal, ' to Alexander Moncreif in Kinnaird, his aires and assignis, of the escheit of John Butter in Pitloychere (Pitlochry) and Johne Moncreiff in Kynnard ', at the instance of a Reid in Atholl. In 1622, William Murray, Earl of Tullibardine (husband of the Atholl heiress), was put in possession of the notoriously lawless earldom of Atholl, and at once set about restoring order. Fifty-five Atholl gentlemen were promptly proceeded against for having worn hagbuts and pistolets and shot wildfowl and venison: among them John Butter of Pitlochry.

In 1638, the roll of weapons of heritors and their men, in certain Atholl parishes, includes Thomas Butter of Callemulling, heavily armed himself with two snap-work guns, a pistol, a bow and arrows, a sword and a pole-axe, followed by three of his men with swords. This roll has the following entry, from which various relationships can be deduced: '*Robert Moncreiff, portioner of Kinhaird*, himself and his men of his haill landis within the parochin of Moulin ar nyne. The said Robert himself hes ane snap vark gun, ane bow, ane sheaff, ane swird, ane tairge, ane poll aix, and thrie with bowis, sheavis and swirdis, and the remanent fyve hes bot swirdis onlie. *Thomas Butter, portioner of Kinhaird*, his men and himself of his landis ar bot tua, his awin wapines is ane bow, ane sheaf, ane swird, ane targe, and ane poll aix, and his man ane bow, ane sheaff and ane swird. The said *Thomas Butter* betuix him and Johne Robertsone of Croftmichie, ane man with vapins. *Johne Butter of Myln and Myl landis of Petlochrie*, himself and his men are thrie, his awin vapins is ane snap vark gun, ane swird, ane tairge, ane habershone and ane of his men hes ane bow, ane sheaff and ane swird, and the uther hes bot ane swird '. It may perhaps be wondered what happened to the shared man and his weapons if Thomas Butter had a feud with Robertson of Croftmichie. It is perhaps also instructive to think of meeting in Great Britain, on a moonlit night in Atholl, a Highland gentleman like John Butter of Pitlochry, armed with his breastplate and *round leather-covered wooden shield*, as well as his broadsword and more modern snap-work gun, accompanied by his attendants armed, one with a broadsword and the other with a *bow and arrows*, as late as the seventeenth century.

In the Hunting Roll of John Murray, Earl of Atholl's followers in September 1667 (for a sort of practice mobilisation of the leading Athollmen in the guise of a deer drive), calling out each principal feuar within the earldom of Atholl and lordship of Balquhidder, ' himself in proper persone, with a sufficient able man weel armed out of ilk ffourtie shilling land, and that by and attoure (as well as) the baggage men ', are Archibald Butter of Pitlochry, John Butter, portioner of Kinnaird, John Butter of Easter Dunfallandy and John Butter of Callemulling. Excluding Balquhidder, there were 113 Atholl feuars and wadsetters called out on this occasion, together with 247 of their unnamed men in attendance. In 1689, when the Athollmen were in fact mobilised to cope with the difficult political situation arising out of the Revolution, ten different Atholl chieftains were allotted captaincies and ' ilk captaine is impowried to name his own Lieutenant, Ensign, Serjants and ye particular souldiers and hold randivouzes at the places used and wont '. In this crisis, the Captains of Athollmen were four Robertson and five Stewart gentlemen, the only other being Patrick Butter of Pitlochry, who was appointed Captain of the armed Watch for Strathtummel. In 1705, the Roll of some 2,567 of the Duke of Atholl's Fencible Men (in fact he could raise about 4,000) included Patrick Butter of Pitlochry and his armed men, of two of whom, however, it is noted: ' William Duff, Merchant, excused; Robert Stewart, Miller, excused '.

During the 1715 Rising, when the Athollmen rose for the Jacobite Cause, Archibald Butter of Pitlochry was one of the five captains commanding companies (the others were two Robertsons and two Stewarts) in William Murray, 2nd Lord Nairne's battalion of the Atholl Brigade. He was among those taken prisoner at Preston, ' after a desparate resistance ', but was pardoned in the following year. ' It is said that Captain Butter of Pitlochrie, of Lord Nairne's battalion, being a handsome well-made young man, created considerable excitement amongst the fashionable people in London whilst he was a prisoner there '. During the next Jacobite

attempt, Patrick Butter, yr. of Kinnaird, was captured as a Jacobite officer in the Atholl Brigade and tried in 1746, but somehow got acquitted; and Archibald Butter at Faskally also appears in the ' List of Atholl Gentlemen ... who were concerned in the Rising of 1745 '.

After the Rising, the ancient Robertson barony of Faskally was forfeited, and when the Faskally estates were eventually sold by the Government a generation later, Henry Butter of Pitlochry acquired them. In 1797, his house in Atholl was surrounded by highlandmen rioting against the misunderstood Militia Act, as he was the local Deputy Lieutenant (the Lord Lieutenant of Perthshire being the Murray chief, the Duke of Atholl), and they forced him ' to come under an engagement not to act '. He had married the only daughter of Sir Robert Menzies of Menzies, Chief of that Clan; and had a gallant son, Archibald Butter, yr. of Faskally, who as a cavalry officer had been mentioned in a personal dispatch in 1795 from the Governor and Commander-in-Chief of Jamaica for his bravery during the Negro rebellion there: ' The command devolved on Captain Butter, of the 18th Dragoons, in a most awful situation indeed! To retreat to the New Town by the same track, through a tremendous ravine, over a road narrow, rugged, almost impracticable, and overhung with rocks lined by the enemy, was one alternative; the other—Forward!—to dash over mountains, an unexplored rocky country,

and in the face of forty Maroons—who were so far surprised as to be found standing in a body to oppose him. The sight of the savages decided the difficulty, and, after charging and cutting down eleven of them, he and his party rushed on, and, crossing at full gallop a country almost inaccessible, joined me at Vaughan's Field in the dusk of the evening, having traversed the whole of the Maroon district. This decision certainly saved the whole party, and Captain Butter has infinite credit in the adventure '.

In 1803, as Lt-Colonel Archibald Butter of Faskally, he was chosen to command the newly raised Atholl Battalion of the Perthshire Militia to meet the threatened French invasion. His descendant, Major David Butter of Pitlochry, M.C., is the present Vice-Lieutenant of Perthshire (the Lord Lieutenant himself being a Murray chieftain, Lord Mansfield). He won the Military Cross with the Scots Guards in the Western Desert during the Second World War; and is married to a granddaughter of the late Grand Duke Michael of Russia—she is also a descendant of the Russian poet Pushkin: immortal in verse, though killed in a duel. It was fitting that, in the Royal Family's box in Westminster Abbey at the Coronation of the present Queen, Major Butter of Pitlochry appeared in his full-dress uniform, with kilt and plaid, as Adjutant of the Atholl Highlanders.

Moreover, the heraldic ' beast ' of the Murrays of Tullibardine, that supported their shield, was the Fife *red lyon* collared with Moray stars. Their crest of two sleeved arms grasping a peacock's head by the neck also links the Tullibardine Murrays with those of Bothwell, whose overlordship of the thanage of Arbuthnott is still recollected in the Arbuthnott Arms and peacock's-head crest.

By two ' Bands of Association ' in 1586 and 1598, the various Murray lairds from all over Scotland (with their allies the Moncreiffes of that Ilk) recognised the supremacy maintained by the line of Sir John Murray, afterwards 1st Earl of Tullibardine. The signatories to one or other of these ' bands ' included among many others Moray of Abercairny in Perthshire, Murray of Polmaise in Stirlingshire, Murray of Cockpool in Dumfries-shire, Murray of Cobairdy in Buchan, and the Murrays of Falahill and Blackbarony on the Borders (of whom the Lords Elibank are a branch).

Ochtertyre, seen across the loch, is the Georgian seat of Sir William Murray of Ochtertyre, 11th Baronet since 1673, whose ancestor Patrick Murray, 1st of Ochtertyre (died 1476), was younger son of Sir David Murray of Tullibardine. The second Baronet was a Jacobite in 1715: but in 1745 his son, Sir Patrick, was a Highland officer in the Government service. He was sent in July 1745 with Campbell of Inverawe to arrest the Duke of Perth at Drummond Castle as a precautionary measure, and 'undertook to effect this under the guise of a friendly visit.

This treacherous scheme miscarried, for when after dinner they disclosed their errand he (the duke) asked leave to retire to a dressing-room, escaped by a back staircase, crept through briars and brambles past the sentinels to a ditch, lay concealed till the party had left, borrowed of a peasant woman a horse without saddle or bridle, and in September joined the Young Pretender at Perth. When Murray (of Ochtertyre) was afterwards a prisoner at Prestonpans, Perth's only revenge was the ironical remark, "Sir Patie, I am to dine with *you* today ".'

Penny issued by James Murray, 2nd Duke of Atholl, as Sovereign Lord of the Isle of Man. This sovereignty was inherited together with Castle Rushen (former capital of the whole Hebrides) and 170,000 acres by the 2nd Duke, together with the English Barony of Strange, as heir general of the Stanley earls of Derby. The Stanleys had been Kings of Man from 1406 until, in the reign of King Henry VIII, the 2nd Earl of Derby (no doubt seeing what was happening to the Irish local kings under English paramountcy) declared that he would rather be a great lord than a petty king, and altered the style. After the sovereignty of this Gaelic-speaking island had been forcibly purchased from them by an Act of the British Parliament, the dukes of Atholl ceased to be styled ' Lord of Man & the Isles ' but remained Lords Strange and retained their manorial rights in the island. John Murray, 4th Duke of Atholl and 9th Lord Strange, K.T., F.R.S., lived there at Port-a-shee (' Fairy Music ') until he completed the building of his new residence called Castle Mona, now the hotel in Douglas. At King George IV's Coronation he rendered the two falcons required by the Kings of England from the Kings of Man since 1406. But it was difficult to determine what manorial functions the dukes had retained on the loss of their sovereignty, and it caused much friction, so in 1828 he finally disposed of his remaining property and privileges in the Isle of Man to the British Crown for £417,144, then a vast sum. The items sold include ' Rabbit Warren, £1,816 '. Since the death in 1957 of James Stewart Murray, 9th Duke of Atholl and 14th Lord Strange, when the dukedom passed to a male-line descendant of the 3rd Duke, the present heir of the last Kings or Sovereign Lords of the Isle of Man is the descendant of the 4th Duke's eldest daughter: John Drummond, 15th Lord Strange, who lives at Tholt e Will in Sulby Glen on the Isle of Man.

The 1586 Band provided that ' We, Sir John Murray of Tullibardine, Knight, Sir Andrew Murray of Arngask, Knight [predecessor of the present Mungo Murray, Earl of Mansfield], William Moncreiffe of that Ilk, Robert Moray of Abercairny, with the whole name of Murray and others under-subscribing, taking the burden upon ourselves for our kin, friends, allies, servants, tenants and dependents, Being convened for the assurance and taking order of our own estates, the defence of our rooms, tacks, steadings, goods and gear, which by the incursions of Broken Men, and unthankful and unnatural neighbours, may appear to be in danger, and such other occasions as may fall out therethrough . . . We all with one assent bind and oblige ourselves . . . that the whole rest shall interpose themselves, their lands and gear, in their defence: so that one's cause shall be all, and all shall be one.' The Band goes on to set up a council composed of Tullibardine himself and eight lairds (seven Murrays and the Laird of Moncreiffe), with a *quorum* of four, always to be presided over by Tullibardine: with powers to settle quarrels within the Murray league and also to initiate action against outside aggressors. After the two Bands of Association, the Tullibardine hegemony among the Murrays was firmly established: and the present Iain Murray, Duke of Atholl and Marquis of Tullibardine, has been officially recognised in Lyon Register as Chief of the whole Name of Murray.

Lord George Murray, the brilliant Highland guerrilla leader and Jacobite general, in his campaigning dress with sword, dirk and targe, also a White Cockade in his blue bonnet. He was out in the Risings of 1715, 1719 and 1745. A Gaelic-speaking highlander himself, on the march he went on foot at the head of his men; although in battle he was mounted to be an effectual general. At Culloden, he led the charge of the Athollmen, galloping straight through to the rear of the Government Army and then breaking his broadsword as he hacked his way back on foot through the enemy ranks to remount and bring on the second wave of Jacobites. The Chevalier Johnstone said afterwards that 'had Prince Charles slept during the whole of the expedition, and allowed Lord George Murray to act for him according to his own judgement, he would have found the crown of Great Britain on his head when he awoke'.

Yet he had not wanted to take part in the '45 Rising. He had already spent ten years in exile (except when he was in hiding in the mountains after the 'Affair of Glenshiel'), and had been pardoned by the Government at the intercession of his Whig brother, Duke James, who then let Tullibardine to him and trusted him with a commission as his Sheriff Depute of Perthshire. At first he felt it would be a breach of trust to join in the Rising, but Prince Charles is believed to have sent him a personal letter from the Old Chevalier, the 'King over the Water' whom he adored.

So Lord George wrote sadly from 'Tullibardine, 3rd Sept. 1745, Six at night', to his brother, Duke James: 'Dear Brother,— . . . I was not a little difficulted when you left this place, . . . for, to speak the truth, I was at that time resolved to take a step which I was certain you would disapprove of as much when you knew it, as it would surprise you to hear it.

I never did say to any person in Life that I would not engage in the cause I always in my heart thought just & right, as well as for the interest, good, & liberty of my country.

But this letter is not wrote with a view to argue or reason with you upon the subject. I own frankly, that now that I am to engage, that what I do may & will be reckoned desperate, & though all appearances seem to be against me, interest, prudence, & the obligations to you which I lie under, would prevent most people in my situation from taking a resolution that may very probably end in my utter ruin.

My life, my fortune, my expectation, the happiness of my wife & children, are all at stake (& the chances are against me), & yet a principle of (what seems to me) honour, & my duty to King & Country, outweighs everything.

If I err, it is only with respect to you. I owe obligations to nobody else (I mean the Court of London), & if you find you cannot forgive me, yet sure you will pity me.

Think what a weight there is upon my **spirits**, my wife really in a dangerous state of

health (for it is no feigned illness) . . . But I must do her that justice to say that though she is much against my rashness (as she calls it), yet when she found me determined, she did not dispute with me upon it . . .

I will not venture to recommend her and my children to your protection. All I shall say on that head is, that a man of worth never repented of doing good natured offices. After what I have said, you may believe that I have weighted what I am going about with all the deliberation I am capable of, & suppose I were sure of dying in the attempt, it would neither deter nor prevent me . . .

As to the rents of this place that are unpayed, I have given my wife a bill of £90 sterling of Borlum's, endorsed to you, as I know there is a bond owing to his wife, which it will compensate so far. And my stock of cattle & furniture here, etc., will do much more than clear the byegone rents till Martinmas next . . .

I forgot to tell you that I never spoke or interfered with any of the Atholl Men, but now they are up (as I hear) you will excuse my doing my best, both with them & others.'

The Prince behaved with uncharacteristic shabbiness to Lord George Murray after the '45, but the Old Chevalier showed him every kindness. Lord George died in exile in 1760 in Holland; where the *seize quartiers* on his hatchment in the church at Medemblik remind us that his immediate ancestry included the great Continental houses of Montmorency, La Tremoïlle, Bourbon and the Nassau princes of Orange. His bookplate shows that he differenced the Arms of Murray of Atholl by adding a Douglas *crowned heart* at the centre point of the quarterings, and used the old Murray *peacock's head* crest with its accompanying motto but without the clutching hands. Lord George's son John Murray became third Duke, and was ancestor of the present Iain Murray, 10th Duke of Atholl.

The Moncreiffes of that Ilk, who were the only other surname to join in the Murray Band, have intermarried repeatedly with the Murrays in every century since the Middle Ages. The Chapel of Moncreiffe still has the grave-slab of Tullibardine's daughter Elena Murray who married Malcolm Moncreiffe of that Ilk, 5th Laird, and died in 1458: while the late 8th and 9th Dukes of Atholl were the sons of Louisa Moncreiffe, Duchess of Atholl, daughter of the 20th Laird. At least a dozen Murray-Moncreiffe marriages took place between 1526 and 1664. So it seemed natural for the Moncreiffes to ally themselves with the Murray league. Moreover Moncreiffe, like Tullibardine, lies in Strathearn: separated only by the lands of the Oliphants, with whom the Moncreiffes were then at feud.

Sir John Murray of Tullibardine, whose supremacy had been recognised in the two Bands of Association, became 1st Earl of Tullibardine in 1606. The 2nd Earl married Lady Dorothea Stewart, heiress of the Earls of Atholl (descended from a half-brother of King James II). The Murrays

In 1697, war broke out between Atholl and the cunning Frasers of Lovat. Simon Fraser, the 'Old Fox' destined to be beheaded as 11th Lord Lovat, had not only ambushed and captured Lord Mungo Murray but had also abducted the Marquis of Atholl's daughter, the Dowager Lady Lovat (ancestress of the present writer), and then married her by force while his Highlanders cut her stays with their dirks and his pipers drowned her screams. A punitive expedition of 600 Athollmen was promptly despatched northwards, commanded by Lord James Murray, with his brothers Lord Nairne and Lord Edward Murray and their cousin Sir James Moncreiffe as the principal officers. Simon Fraser took to the hills, the Athollmen occupied the Lovat country and castles, and the poor Dowager was restored to her own family at Dunkeld. This was probably the last full-scale inter-clan campaign ever to be mounted, although *Mac Shimi* was too wily to allow any pitched battle to take place.

In 1706 the Duke of Atholl, who was firmly opposed to the projected Union with England, mobilised some 4,000 Athollmen in arms, in order to put pressure on the Edinburgh government; but found himself insufficiently supported elsewhere in Scotland, and so disbanded them. In both the Jacobite Risings of 1715 and 1745 the Duke of Atholl stood by the Whig Government, and the district was saved from forfeiture. But on each occasion the bulk of the Athollmen rose for King James under William, Marquis of Tullibardine (son of the 1st Duke and elder brother of the 2nd Duke), one of the 'Seven Men of Moidart': and formed the Atholl Brigade in the Jacobite Army. His brother, Lord George Murray, had the effective command of the Jacobite army and led it through a series of startling victories that began at Prestonpans but ended in the inevitable tragic defeat at Culloden. The last Fiery Cross in Scottish warfare was that by which Lord George Murray summoned Atholl once more to arms in 1746, when the advancing Hanoverians had seized Blair Castle, and it became the last fortress in the British Isles to undergo a siege.

This too was the last time the Atholl Highlanders went to war. But the warlike Athollmen have always been proud to turn out peacefully as a ceremonial bodyguard for their Duke. Their uniform has not basically changed much from that worn by the highlanders for the Duke's 'tail' proposed at the time of George IV's historic visit to Edinburgh. Lord Glenlyon (afterwards 6th Duke) was attended by the Athole Highlanders, as he alone preferred to spell it, when he jousted at the famous Eglinton Tournament; and· in 1845 Lord Glenlyon wore his Athole Highlander uniform when he seconded the address at the Opening of Parliament. In the same year, Queen Victoria presented a pair of Colours to the Athole Highlanders, thus placing them in a unique position as the only private bodyguard in the realm. At this time they consisted of four companies of forty rank and file each, together with two 3-pounder mountain guns. Since then the principal duties of the Atholl Highlanders have been to furnish sentries or Guards of Honour for royal visitors to Blair Castle: and although the rank and file have not been kept up to strength in recent years, sufficient numbers have been raised *ad hoc* for such Guards as have been required. The Pipe Band flourishes, however, and the corps of officers attend their Duke twice yearly at the Perth Hunt and Royal Caledonian Balls.

The Atholl Highlanders with fixed bayonets marching past Iain Murray, 7th Duke of Atholl, K.T., at Blair Castle in 1890. The ducal 3-pounder mountain gun in the background is ready to fire a salute. The onlooker wears an Atholl bonnet with the characteristic red-white-and-blue dicing, and a kilt jacket of the 'Atholl grey'. The Duke wears the three eagle's feathers of a Highland chief, and all have sprigs of juniper in their bonnets.

When his ancestor John Murray, Earl of Atholl (grandson of the 5th Stewart earl) was retoured heir to the earldom in 1629, he took over its great martial strength. A roll of Athollmen and weapons in the parishes of Struan, Lude, Moulin and Logierait alone, taken in 1638, gives 523 men, armed with 110 guns, 2 hagbuts (short guns), 11 pistols, 149 bows and sheaves (quivers of arrows), 9 pole-axes, 2 halbert-axes, 3 two-handed swords, 448 swords, 125 targes (round shields), 8 head-pieces, 2 steel bonnets, 1 pair of plate sleeves, 11 habergeons (breastplates) and 1 jack (coat of mail). Only 21 men are returned as unarmed, while the exact weapons of a further 40 are not defined. Entries naturally include many Robertsons, Stewarts, and Fergussons, also some Moncreiffes and Butters, the Macintoshes of Tirinie and the Smalls of Dirnanean.

In 1640, the Earl of Atholl called out about 1,200 Athollmen to resist an invasion from Argyll. But the Earl was treacherously captured by the Campbells, who invited him to a peace conference and then violated the safe conduct; and he was so badly cared for during his captivity that he died soon after his release. The district of Atholl never forgot, and the feud with Argyll lasted a century. Eight hundred Athollmen supported Montrose against Argyll, who in turn ravaged Atholl in 1644. The Athollmen soon avenged themselves in the course of Montrose's invasion of Argyll, when forty Campbell barons and 1,500 Argyll men were slain at the battle of Inverlochy, and all Argyll laid waste. In 1646, a further 700 Athollmen on their way to reinforce Montrose fell upon and routed 1,200 of Argyll's men at Callander. The Argyll men, though commanded by Campbell of Ardkinglas, an experienced commander, 'fled like madmen, divers of them being slain in the fight, and more drouned in the river of Goodie, their haste being such that they staid not to seek the fords'. By 1650 the young Earl of Atholl was himself old enough to lead out his men for King Charles II: but two years later Cromwell's invading Englishmen occupied Blair Castle . in Atholl, and the following year the young Earl sent round the Fiery Cross and raised 100 horse and 1,200 foot in a vain attempt to drive them out of the Atholl country. By 1654 the ruler of Atholl was obliged to send his cadet, Lord Tullibardine, as his plenipotentiary to negotiate honourable terms with the Roundhead general.

After the Restoration, the Athollmen took part in the 'Highland Host' of 1678 against the Westland Whigs. The Marquis of Atholl also led them at Bothwell Brig, and was later painted in classical costume (but wearing a full wig) with the battle being waged in Roman armour in the background. In 1684, Atholl was given a commission as Lord Lieutenant of Argyll, whence the Campbell chief had fled into exile, and about 1,000 Athollmen occupied Inveraray. Next year, the Earl of Argyll landed in his own country, and seven Atholl Highlander companies were sent to oppose him. Dunstaffnage Castle was burnt, and after the Earl of Argyll's capture a few other Campbells were executed. Over 30,000 young trees were uprooted from Inveraray and transplanted to Atholl's own home at Dunkeld. In 1689, after the Whig·Revolution, the next Argyll avenged himself by occupying Atholl.

Medal issued by George Murray, Lord Glenlyon, afterwards 6th Duke of Athole, to the 5 officers, 3 sergeants, 4 corporals, 4 pipers, 2 orderlies and 56 privates of the Athole Highlanders, who attended him as his uniformed 'tail' when he went to the Eglinton Tournament in 1839. It was of course a romantick revival, but it was the last real tournament ever held. The combatants bashed each other pretty hard, and Lord Glenlyon, who jousted as the Knight of the Gael, had his gauntlet smashed and his hand injured by the Knight of the White Rose. His armour is still at Blair Castle, and tied to his lance-head is the tiny glove of his lady-love, Anne Home Drummond of Blair Drummond, whom he afterwards married. The medal was worn with Athole Highlander uniform on an Atholl Murray tartan ribbon, and the last of what were always known in Atholl as 'the Tournament Men' lived on until 1906.

thus acquired a vast Highland territory, eventually amounting to over 200,000 acres in Atholl, becoming Earls of Atholl in 1629, and Marquises from 1676. A seventeenth-century MS. (published in *Macfarlane's Genealogical Collections*) tells us that the Marquis of Atholl was styled in Gaelic *Am Moireach Mor*, 'the Great Murray'. They fought many wars throughout the rest of the century to curb the expanding power of Argyll, and to aid the Stewart kings against the Campbell chiefs. To their mediaeval peacock's head crest (still favoured by the great Lord George Murray), they had added in the sixteenth century the mermaid, as Lords of Balquidder (see MACLAREN), and in the seventeenth century they took also the demi-savage holding a sword and a key that commemorated the capture of the last Lord of the Isles by the first Stewart earl of Atholl in 1475: hence the motto FURTH FORTUNE AND FILL THE FETTERS.

Since 1703 the Murray chiefs have been Dukes of Atholl. For a time in the eighteenth century, moreover, the Murray dukes were also Sovereign Lords of the Isle of Man, with their own coinage and parliament, the House of Keys. The 1st Duke's younger son, Lord George Murray, was the brilliant Gaelic-speaking Jacobite general responsible for the Highlanders' astonishing successes throughout the greater part of the 1745 Rising. Lord George's descendant, the present Duke of Atholl, Chief of the Murrays, still lives at Blair Castle in Atholl: and the Perthshire chieftains and lairds—Murrays and Morays, Stewarts and Robertsons and Moncreiffes, Ramsays of Bamff and Butters of Pitlochry—are proud to be officers in his private bodyguard, the Atholl Highlanders.

Abercairny, the neo-Gothic seat of the Morays of Abercairny, was the largest house in Perthshire until its recent demolition by the present laird, James Stirling-Home-Drummond-Moray, 21st of Abercairny, Major late Scots Guards, who has replaced it with a more convenient modern house. Abercairny has passed by inheritance since the dawn of local recorded history, when it belonged to the Celtic dynasts who were Earls of Strathearn ' by the Indulgence of God ' and who were uniquely the superiors of their own Bishops of Dunblane. About 1320, the 7th Earl's daughter married Sir John Moray, baron of Drumsagard, a scion of the mighty house of Murray of Bothwell, and brought him as her tocher the lands of Abercairny in Strathearn. Sir John's eldest son Maurice Moray, Earl of Strathearn, was killed at the battle of Nevill's Cross, and his daughter Joanna Moray carried the lordship of Both-

well to her second husband, the 3rd Earl of Douglas. So these Morays must have been the nearest heirs of the house of Bothwell after the death of Joanna's cousin and first husband, the then Murray chief, of the plague in 1361; when Sir John's second son, Sir Alexander Moray, 2nd of Abercairny, presumably became heir male of the whole Name of Murray. Sir Alexander Moray of Abercairny married the Queen Consort's sister Janet, daughter of the 4th Earl of Ross; and was forefather of the Lairds of Abercairny ever since, although in 1850 the old barony passed again through an heiress, Christian Stirling-Moray, who married Henry Home-Drummond of Blair Drummond (in the male line, of the same original stock as the Lords Home) and was mother of William Augustus Stirling-Home-Drummond-Moray, 20th of Abercairny, father of the present Laird.

Moncreiffe

Moncreiffe is simply the Old Gaelic place-name *Monadh Craoibhe*: the 'Hill of the Sacred Bough.' The early tenures of the family connect them with Atholl and Dundas, both held by younger branches of the old Picto-Scottish kings, and the Moncreiffes have always borne the royal *red lyon* in their Arms. On the summit of Moncreiffe Hill the ancient Kings of the Picts had their stronghold, evidently called Dun Monaidh, centrally situated between their abbey of Abernethy, their palace at Forteviot and their inauguration place at Scone. So it seems probable that the Moncreiffes also sprang from one of the eleventh-century branches of the ancient Celtic dynasty whose dun was on the hill.

But their earliest surviving charter of Moncreiffe is that by which Sir Mathew of Moncreiffe (whose brother-in-law was co-Regent of Scotland) was confirmed in the lands of Moncreiffe in 1248. Sir Mathew also held the lands of Culdares and Duneaves in the Highlands, in the mouth of Glenlyon. These lands were formally incorporated with the rest into the Barony of Moncreiffe in 1455, giving the Lairds of Moncreiffe powers of life and death in their Highland as well as in their Lowland territory. William Moncreiffe of that Ilk was one of the Scottish barons who rode with the Earl of Atholl and other chiefs on the raid into Northumberland in 1296, when they burnt Corbridge and Hexham. A later William Moncreiffe of that Ilk appears on the Parliamentary Roll of Highland Landlords in 1587.

After Culdares was sold by the 11th Laird of Moncreiffe in 1598, a number of Moncreiffes remained in Atholl; where in the seventeenth century there were Moncreiffes of Kinnaird, which they shared with the Butters and which is not to be confused with the other Kinnaird, also in Atholl, bought in modern times by Sir John Ward, son of the celebrated beauty Georgina Moncreiffe, Countess of Dudley. As a result of the Moncreiffes' mediaeval and modern connection both with the Murrays and with Atholl, when tartan came into fashion they adopted that known as Murray of Atholl. A unique firing party of Atholl Highlanders attended the funeral of Sir Thomas, 20th Laird and 7th Baronet of Moncreiffe in 1879; and the 8th, 9th, 10th and 11th Baronets of Moncreiffe have all held commissions in the Atholl Highlanders—the Murray chiefs' private bodyguard, in which the present writer is a Captain. (*See also pages 226-7.*)

Easter Moncreiffe, home of Sir Iain Moncreiffe of that Ilk. The now ruined tower of Easter Moncreiffe lay 'a bow-drift lower eastward' from the castle of Moncreiffe. At the feast of St. Benedict the Abbot in 1312, Sir John Moncreiffe of that Ilk (who had traditionally sheltered Wallace in a cave on Moncreiffe Hill) resigned Easter Moncreiffe to his younger son Mathew, ancestor of the first separate line of Moncreiffes of Easter Moncreiffe: sometimes called 'Littill Muncreif'. In 1513, John Moncreiffe of Easter Moncreiffe was killed at Flodden with Sir John Moncreiffe of that Ilk. In 1592, Easter Moncreiffe was erected into a free Barony, giving its lairds the same powers of life and death as those already held by the Lairds of Moncreiffe. In 1674, Easter Moncreiffe was acquired by Thomas Moncreiffe of that Ilk, 14th Laird and afterwards 1st Baronet. As Sir Thomas himself lived at Moncreiffe, he allowed the old tower here to fall into ruin. But in 1707, the widowed mother of Norman MacLeod, 22nd Chief of MacLeod (she was daughter of the 9th Lord Lovat, and her niece Katherine Murray of Ochtertyre later married Sir Thomas Moncreiffe of that Ilk, 3rd Baronet) wrote to her uncle, the Duke of Atholl: 'I have desired Moncreiffe the use of his house as Easter Moncreiffe, which he readily granted . . . but I am told it needs to be put in some better order before I go to it, and Moncreiffe has given orders to make what reparation I desire, but before it can be done it will take some time'. It is thought that the old tower was then too far gone, and that the nucleus of the present house may have been built by Sir Thomas for Lady MacLeod's convenience.

Sir Robert Moncreiffe, 8th Baronet and 21st Laird of Moncreiffe, made extensive alterations and additions in 1890 to Easter Moncreiffe, where he lived awhile. Sir Robert was A.D.C. to King George V; and in 1915, at the age of fifty-nine and with the aid of an artificial stomach, this Laird commanded the Perthshire territorial battalion of the Black Watch (Royal Highlanders) in the trenches throughout the battles of Festubert, La Boiselle and Thiepval, being mentioned in despatches and awarded the C.M.G. Easter Moncreiffe was later the home of James Murray, 9th Duke of Atholl (grandson of Sir Thomas and Lady Louisa Moncreiffe of Moncreiffe), from whom it was acquired by his cousin, the present writer, to whom the late Sir David Moncreiffe of that Ilk, 23rd Laird of Moncreiffe, also assigned the old tower and Barony of Easter Moncreiffe.

Moncreiffe Hill, the original stronghold at *Monadh Chraoibhe* of the Pictish kings, from whom the Moncreiffes probably descend, although in the female line.

In spite of their turbulence, and an occasional rebellion during the difficult period of the sixteenth century (as when a Moncreiffe took part in the murder of Rizzio), the Moncreiffes have always had a firm tradition of loyalty to the Sovereign's person. The young 7th Laird of Moncreiffe was Chamberlain to the boy-king James III in 1464, and a branch of the name became a typical Scots courtier family that served in the Stuart royal household for a couple of centuries. To this branch, the Moncrieffs of Myres Castle, belonged two generals who both commanded the Scots Guards, but this line has long since taken the name of Skene of Pitlour on inheriting that estate. The Lairds of Moncreiffe have usually been archers of the Sovereign's bodyguard and indeed the 14th

Laird's name appears in the oldest known roll of the Royal Archers. Another line settled abroad as archers of the Scots Guard of the Kings of France, and formed three branches of French seigneurs. But one branch ended in an Academician, one of 'the Immortals', another perished when the Marquis de Moncrif was guillotined in the Terror, and the last was ended by a cannonball at Eylau.

There are three main lines left in Scotland today: each distinguished by its spelling of the name. The main branch of the whole name is that of Lord Moncreiff, who lives at Tulliebole Castle in Kinross-shire and is the 5th peer and 15th baronet. Between 1785 and 1905, the Moncreiffs of Tulliebole gave to Scotland three Lords of Session, a Moderator of the General Assembly of the Church of Scotland and a Moderator of the Free Church General Assembly; while to this branch belongs Francis Moncreiff, the present Bishop of Glasgow and Primus of the whole Episco-

palian Church of Scotland. From the 10th Laird of Moncreiffe's younger son, Alexander, condemned to death for rebellion in 1565 but pardoned, descend the Moncrieffs of Bandirran: also, in the female line, the Scott Moncrieffs and Moncrieffs of Kinmonth, the *ceann monaidh* or 'head of the hill' of Moncreiffe. This was the branch that produced the joint Founder of the Secession Church; also General Sir Alexander Moncrieff, inventor of the 'Moncrieff System' in artillery, and the late Lord Moncrieff, Lord Justice Clerk of Scotland. Among the Scott Moncrieffs are numbered the famous translator of Proust, whose translation is often said to have been better than the original, and also the present Admiral Sir Alan Scott Moncrieff. Finally, by a family transaction of the seventeenth century, the old baronies of Moncreiffe and Easter Moncreiffe are held by the line of Moncreiffes of that Ilk who were created baronets in 1685.

231

The House of Moncreiffe, completed in 1679 for Thomas Moncreiffe of that Ilk, 14th Laird (afterwards 1st Baronet), to replace the old Tower and Fortalice of Moncreiffe. The architect was Sir William Bruce, who afterwards designed the Palace of Holyroodhouse, Hopetoun and Kinross House: but Moncreiffe was his first complete building. It was destroyed by a fire in 1957, in which Sir David Moncreiffe of that Ilk, 10th Baronet and 23rd Laird, M.C., lost his life.

During the Second World War, Sir David had been longer in action than any other officer of the Scots Guards: serving in both battles of Monte Camino in Right Flank of the 2nd battalion (originally raised as No. IX Company by Sir John Moncreiffe of that Ilk in 1674) and then becoming Patrol Officer of the 1st battalion, in the Italian campaign. His sister, Elisabeth, who herself was badly hurt when she fell from a rope made of bedsheets during the fire, succeeded him in the mediaeval Barony of Moncreiffe.

Elisabeth Moncreiffe, 24th of Moncreiffe. Her Dunmonaidh Kennels, where she rarely keeps fewer than forty of the best-bred Alsatians of her own, have won many championship awards at Dog Shows.

The new House of Moncreiffe, completed in 1966 for Elisabeth Moncreiffe, 24th of Moncreiffe. It incorporates the front door of the older house, itself built three hundred years ago to replace the mediaeval castle of the family.

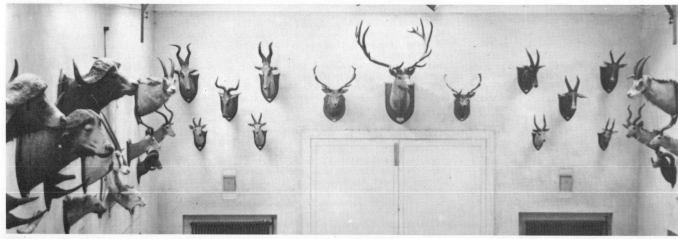

The old 'Moncreiffe Lands' by Loch Tay, at the mouth of Glenlyon. The lands of Culdares and Duneaves were confirmed to Sir Mathew of Moncreiffe by Sir Robert de Menzies, who was Chamberlain of Scotland in 1249. Sir John Moncreiffe of that Ilk was killed at the battle of Flodden with his brother-in-law and neighbour, Sir Duncan Campbell of Glenorchy, *Mac Chailein mhic Dhonnachaidh*. Sir John's son, the 10th Laird of Moncreiffe, had a blood-feud with Lord Oliphant. However, this feud quietened after the Master of Oliphant had been captured by Barbary corsairs, to die a slave in Algiers; and the Apparent of Moncreiffe had perished (with two fellow Scottish leaders) in an alleged plot to assassinate the King of Sweden, where he had gone in command of Moncreiffe's Regiment of Scottish mercenaries. They had not been adequately paid, and the idea (betrayed by a Colquhoun, whom they beheaded too late) was that their Highlanders should give an exhibition of the sword-dance in the royal palace (in 1573, an early reference to this Highland dance). At the critical moment, they were to have picked up their claymores and slain King John, thus reinstating the mad King Eric XIV on the throne and securing their arrears of pay. In 1590 Sir Duncan Campbell of Glenorchy received a bond of manrent from Duncan Bishop 'or Campbell', promising in return to protect him 'specially in any right of land which he may get from the Laird of Monchreif'. This was the unfortunate Apparent's son, William Moncreiffe of that Ilk, 11th Laird, who disposed of these lands to his neighbour, the chieftain of Glenorchy, in 1598: in order to buy the Barony of Carnbee in Fife. These old Moncreiffe lands later gave their name to the families of Menzies of Culdares and Campbell of Duneaves.

The Head Hall at Moncreiffe, showing the family Big Game trophies. Of the wapiti head in the centre, shot by William Moncreiffe in 1896, Frank Selous (greatest of all Big Game hunters) wrote: 'for symmetry and shapeliness, and every point that goes to make a deer head a beautiful thing to look at, I have never seen its equal'.

233

Menzies

The surname of Menzies, which is the same as the English surname Manners, is probably derived from Mesnières, about forty kilometres north of Rouen in Normandy. The *z* in Menzies should never be pronounced like *z* in zebra, for it is in fact the old Scottish letter for guttural *y* that was a cross between a *y* and a *g*. The present writer possesses a charter confirming to his forefather Sir Mathew of Moncreiffe the lands of Culdares in Glenlyon, and granted by the first Menzies to appear in Scottish records, ' as freely quietly fully and honourably as any Baron within the Kingdom of Scotland is able to give any such land '. In this early thirteenth-century document the granter (whose seal shews a shield *barry of six*) calls himself Robert de Meyneris, and the witnesses include *dominus* David de Meyneris and also Thomas de Meyneris.

This Sir Robert de Menzies, the first recorded chief, was at the Court of King Alexander II by 1224, and became Chamberlain of Scotland by 1249. He evidently received a grant of wide lands in Rannoch, in the west of Atholl. This area had probably formed part of the abbey-lands of Dull, of which King Alexander's own ancestors had been hereditary abbots. So it is possible that Sir Robert de Menzies had also been rewarded with the hand of a lady, legitimate or more probably otherwise, descended of the royal house. Certainly, two of his sons have the contemporarily royal names of Alexander and David.

The chief stronghold of the Menzies clan, who became known as *Mèin-nearach* in Gaelic, was at Weem near Aberfeldy in Perthshire. In 1510, Sir Robert Menzies of that Ilk, the then chief, resigned his Baronies of Ennoch and Weem into the hands of King James IV, who regranted them to him as the free Barony of Menzies, renaming the castle of Weem ' Castle

Sir Robert Menzies, Knight of the Thistle and former Prime Minister of Australia, in his uniform as Lord Warden of the Cinque Ports, an office in which his predecessors have included Sir Winston Churchill, Lord Curzon. the Iron Duke of Wellington, and William Pitt the younger.

Charter from Sir Robert de Menzies, 1st Chief of Clan Menzies, to Sir Mathew of Moncreiffe, 1st of that Ilk, confirming him in the lands of Culdares and Duneaves (in the mouth of Glenlyon), drawn up some time between 1224 and 1267. The oldest Menzies document in existence, it bears also the earliest surviving Menzies seal, but (for obvious reasons) is a valued possession of the present writer.

Castle Menzies at Weem. The lands of Weem were acquired by the then Menzies chief in the thirteenth century. But the chiefs lived at Comrie Castle on the river Lyon until it was burnt in 1487, when the then chief made his home at the ' Place of Weem ' until it in turn was destroyed in a raid by the Stewarts of Garth. By 1577 the present castle had been rebuilt (on the ' Z-plan ' suitable for enfilade defence against raiders) by James Menzies of that Ilk, who had sat as a baron in Mary Queen of Scots's Parliament. Considerable additions of 1840 have left most of the original main structure intact, but the castle has become ruinous in the twentieth century.

Dunalastair, or Mount Alexander, former home of Struan Robertson.

Menzies'. This charter mentions the loss of an earlier charter when the Place of Weem was burnt by malefactors.

In 1665 the then chief, Sir Alexander Menzies of that Ilk, was created a Baronet of Nova Scotia. His brother, Colonel James Menzies of Culdares (ancestor of the present chief), a veteran of the Civil Wars, had no less than nine *arrow* wounds in his thighs and legs in an affray with the marauding Macdonalds of Glencoe as late as the reign of Charles II. The larch, now the principal tree in Highland forestry, was introduced into Scotland from the Tyrol in 1737 by a later Menzies of Culdares. But the Menzies of Menzies baronetcy became extinct at the death of Sir Neil Menzies of Menzies in 1910; and Castle Menzies is now in a ruinous condition, though the Clan Menzies Society has done its best to save it.

The tinctures of the Menzies coat-of-arms are white and red, as is their tartan (although they also have the same sett in white and black when in mourning). So their war-cry is appropriately *Geal 'us Dearg a suas*: ' Up with the White and Red '.

The present chief descends in the female line from the 1st Baronet's brother, the gallant Colonel James Menzies of Culdares, and—although paternally a Steuart of Cardney (sprung in the direct male line from a natural son of King Robert II)—his late father was officially recognised as The Menzies of Menzies, *Am Mèinnearach*, as the nearest surviving heir of the Blood bearing the Name.

Robertson

The Robertsons of Struan take their name from their ancestor Robert *Riabhach* or ' Grizzled Robert ' Duncanson, 4th Chief of Clan Donnachaidh, whose lands were erected into the Barony of Struan in 1451 by King James II as a reward ' for the capture of that vile traitor the late Robert of Graham ' many years before, when Sir Robert Graham (under great provocation) had slain the late King James I. His capture by Struan is also heraldically commemorated in the rare ' single supporter ' beneath the armorial shield of the Robertson chiefs: *a wild man chained*.

But Struan Robertson's more ordinary heraldic ' supporters ' allude to something far more remarkable and ancient, to a descent that goes back beyond the Middle Ages to one of the gleams of light that illumine the Dark Ages at the dawn of Christianity in the Highlands. These ' supporters ' are a *serpent* and a *dove*, and they allude to the same proverb that is found on the privy seal of King Alexander III: *esto prudens ut serpens et simplex sicut columba*, ' be wise as the serpent and gentle as the dove '. The dove or *columba* is a pun, for both King Alexander III and the Robertsons belonged to the Kindred of Saint Columba himself.

In the ancient Celtic Church, monastic communities were regarded as families. Their abbots, who could marry, were administrators of the community and its lands, like temporal princes and chiefs. So a devout prince, who founded an abbey community, not only dedicated the lands to God and the patron Saint, but also expected either his own or else the Saint's family to take the trouble to administer them personally. Abbeys were called ' abbeys of the kindred of the land ' where the successive abbots were chosen from the local royal family who had founded them. But where the Founder Saint or Patron Saint was himself a royal prince, like Saint Columba, the abbey was usually an ' abbey of the kindred of the Saint ', and the abbots were chosen from his own kindred. Among the ancient Gaels the ' true family ' were the descendants in the direct male line from a common great-grandfather. Saint Columba's great-grandfather was

The winged head of Margaret Robertson, Countess of Erroll, crudely carved in stone at one corner of the rib-vaulted ceiling in the solar of the great tower at Delgaty Castle, erected in 1570; it is perhaps the oldest surviving attempt at Robertson portraiture.

Conall *Gulban*, King of Tirconaill in the fifth century A.D. So the 'kindred of Saint Columba' were the different branches of the Cineal Conaill, the royal house of Tirconaill.

After Iona was imperilled by the Norsemen, the great Saint's relics were divided between Ireland and Scotland. In Scotland, they were placed at Dunkeld, and thenceforward the hereditary Abbots of Dunkeld were the heads of the Kindred of Saint Columba in Scotland. It is not certain to which branch of the Cineal Conaill they belonged, but it might be worth investigating the branch called the Cineal Lugdach and referred to as 'in Scotland'. Abbot Duncan of Dunkeld was killed in battle in 964, for Celtic abbots used to go in the forefront of the battle bearing a reliquary of the Saint. Abbot Crinan of Dunkeld, perhaps his grandson, married the heiress to the throne and was father of King Duncan I, who was slain by Macbeth in 1040 and was buried with his Columban ancestors in Iona.

King Duncan's younger son Maelmare was father of Madadh, Earl of Atholl, whose grandson Henry, Earl of Atholl died in 1210 leaving heiresses to the earldom. But by an uncanonical union Earl Henry also had a son, Conan, to whom was given a vast territory in Atholl. This became the country of his descendants, the Robertsons or Clan Donnachaidh of Atholl. For its history and a map, see the writer's *The Robertsons: Clan Donnachaidh of Atholl* (Edinburgh 1954). Clan Donnachaidh means the Children of Duncan, who was their chief, known as Duncan of Atholl, in the early fourteenth century. Some of his descendants called themselves Duncanson or MacConachie or plain Duncan or Donachie. Many clansmen are said to have called themselves Macinroy or Maclagan, Stark or Collier. But the chiefs, and most of the clan, eventually came to be called Robertson.

Many Reids also took the surname of Robertson, for they adhered to the Clan Donnachaidh and believed themselves to belong to it in the male line. Indeed, the Reids share with the Robertsons the tendency to have an hereditary malformation of the fingers known as 'crooked crannies'.

Schiehallion, the 'Fairy Hill of the Caledonians', in the country of Clan Donnachaidh of Atholl. (*See also pp. 14, 16 & 41.*)

Curious tombstone in Moulin Churchyard, in Atholl, shewing the Robertson coat-of-arms. A captive man lies below the shield, for the Robertson chiefs have the rare distinction of such an extra 'single supporter' in commemoration of their capture of King James I's slayer in 1437. The crest, of a hand upholding the Crown of Scotland, relates to the same event. One of the three wolf's heads is (unusually) turned to 'respect' another. The Serpent looks rather like a pair of spectacles, and bird-watchers might not immediately recognize the 'Dove. Beneath this heraldic 'achievement', the hour-glass, skull and coffin tell their own tale. Above it, a winged head, representing the soul, affords much needed consolation. The Strachur Fergussons would tell us that it was really their *brideag*, but it is doubtless a pure coincidence that the Fergussons of Dunfallandy have lived hard by Moulin for centuries.

Their chieftain was Baron Reid of Strathloch (a barony held under the earldom of Atholl), who descended from Maud, heiress of Strathloch and daughter of the Chief of Clan Donnachaidh's younger son Thomas Duncanson (leader of the raid when the clan slew the Sheriff of Angus in 1392). Among the nearest neighbours of Strathloch to the south-east were the Ramsay barons of Bamff. So Maud's husband Patrick was perhaps Red Patrick or Patrick 'Reid' Ramsay, beloved esquire of the Black Douglas in 1408, who was certainly ancestor of the Reids of Colliston in Buchan. They bore the Ramsay black *eagle* in their Arms; and the Barons Reid of Strathloch quartered the Clan Donnachaidh *wolf's heads* with a red (i.e. 'reid') *eagle*. These Barons Reid were industrious Whig agriculturists, but not to be provoked: a seventeenth-century Baron Reid slew some marauders caught while eating his cheese. General John Reid, last Baron of Strathloch, composed the famous Scottish slow march: 'The Garb of Old Gaul'.

Rattray

The Rattrays are called after the Barony of Rattray, opposite Blairgowrie in Perthshire, which was already in their possession when surnames first came into general use in Scotland. The present chief still owns the grass-grown ruins of Rattray Castle, the Pictish *rath-tref* or 'fort dwelling' on a serpent-shaped sandy mound associated by local tradition with pagan snake-worship: and the supporters to his coat-of-arms are two knotted serpents, for the snake is the heraldic 'beast' of the Rattrays.

The chief's coat-of-arms, with the golden cross-crosslets on a blue field, indicates the Rattrays to have probably been either a branch of the ancient Celtic dynastic earls of Mar, whose territory is only separated from the Rattray country by Glenshee, or else closely related to them at the dawn of heraldry.

The first laird of Rattray to be recorded in an extant charter was Alan of Rattray, who witnessed several charters of King William the Lion (1165–1214) and King Alexander II (1214–1249). Sir Silvester Rattray of that Ilk, who sat in Parliament as a feudal Baron, and was an Ambassador to England in 1463, inherited wide estates around Fortingall in Atholl

SUPER SIDERA VOTUM

The town of Rattray on the river Ericht, taken from the air. The ruins of old Rattray Castle are near the town, but since the sixteenth century the Rattray chiefs have lived at Craighall-Rattray on the high ground further up Glen Ericht.

through his Stewart mother, daughter of one of the bastards of the ' Wolf of Badenoch ' (Alexander, earl of Buchan, son of King Robert II). This aroused the jealousy of the Earls of Atholl, whose opportunity came after Sir John Rattray of that Ilk was killed at the battle of Flodden. In 1516 the Athollmen drove Sir John's eldest surviving son Patrick Rattray from Rattray Castle and forced him to surrender his niece Grizel, the Rattray heiress, who was afterwards married to the 3rd Earl of Atholl. The Rattrays carried on their resistance from farther up Glen Ericht. Here Patrick Rattray was engaged in building the Tower of Craighall, when he was murdered by the Athollmen in 1533 in his own chapel, where he had sought sanctuary.

In 1648 the then chief's lands were erected into a new feudal Barony of Craighall-Rattray, and later in the century Rattray itself, with the ruins of the old castle of Rattray, were recovered by the family. The succession has twice passed through the female line, in 1799 and 1910. The present chief is James Silvester Rattray of Rattray, who fought in Africa, Italy, Holland and Germany as a Captain in the Scots Guards during the Second World War, and was mentioned in despatches.

Among their principal cadets were the Rattrays of Dalrulzion and the Rattrays of Rannagulzion. At Blair Castle in Atholl, there is preserved the targe or round bull-hide shield carried in action by the Rattray chieftain of Dalrulzion as a Jacobite in the 1715 Rising.

Water-colour sketch of Craighall-Rattray in the time of the Honble. James Clerk Rattray, Baron of the Exchequer, who was Laird of Craighall-Rattray (1799–1831) and declined a Baronetcy in 1830. The detached round towers are similar to those at some French *châteaux*, and remind us of the Auld Alliance between France and Scotland.

The Baron's grandmother had been daughter of Thomas Rattray, Bishop of Dunkeld and Primus of Scotland, the 20th Chief (1684–1743), a faithful Jacobite and non-juring Episcopalian, whose Greek scholarship had much influence on the present liturgy of the Episcopal Church of Scotland, and whose younger son, Dr. John Rattray, personal Physician to Prince Charles Edward in the 1745 Rising, was only spared after Culloden at the intercession of his old golfing comrade, Lord President Forbes.

Baron Clerk Rattray was a close friend of Sir Walter Scott, who often stayed with him here, and who modelled Tullyveolan (the Baron of Bradwardine's castle in *Waverley*) on Craighall-Rattray.

North view of Craighall-Rattray across the river Ericht. The oldest part is on the extreme left, where only the base remains of the original tower that was built by Patrick Rattray, rightfully 12th Laird of Rattray, when he was murdered by the Athollmen in 1533. It is perched on a rock 200 feet above the river Ericht, on a corner of the narrow tree-clad gorge, and originally could only be entered by walking across a removable plank.

David Rattray of Craighall, the 17th Chief, was a staunch Royalist: and Craighall was besieged and captured by the Cromwellian English. During the extensive alterations made by the 26th Chief, Lt-General Sir James Clerk Rattray of Craighall-Rattray, K.C.B. (who was wounded at the Redan in the Crimea and took part in the relief of Lucknow —riding in behind the pipes, ' dinna ye hear them? '—during the Indian Mutiny), a cannon-ball from the Roundhead siege was found lodged in one of the towers.

Ogilvy

When Princess Alexandra married the Honble. Angus Ogilvy, she was marrying into one of the most historic families in Scotland, a family of dynastic origin. In the twelfth century, when Her Royal Highness's ancestor in the direct male line was the Margrave of Meissen, Mr. Ogilvy's ancestor was the Earl of Angus, one of the Seven Earls of Scotland who were peers of the king himself.

We are told that the county of Angus was a kingdom in Pictish times, and that it was named (as Celtic districts often were) after King Angus who founded the local dynasty. Among the Picts, of course, succession always passed in the female line: the Gaels preferred the opposite. After the Union between the Picts and the Gaels, the rulers of the former Kingdom of Angus (like those of the other Scottish sub-kingdoms) appear with the Gaelic title of *mormaer*, which the Norse translated as *jarl*—certainly

David, Lord Ogilvy, the Jacobite, who raised a regiment of 600 men for Prince Charles Edward in 1745. Besides a number of Ogilvies, several of the officers were Stormonths, an old local family who take their name from the district of Stormont in Perthshire but have always been noted for their loyalty to the Ogilvy chiefs in Angus. Lord Ogilvy escaped to France after Culloden, and commanded Ogilvy's Regiment there, becoming a French Lieutenant-General, but was pardoned in 1778. This portrait is in the possession of Sir David Ogilvy of Inverquharity, at Winton Castle.

by 937, when Dubhucan, Mormaer of Angus, died.

Not enough records have survived for us to be able to trace any succession, nor to tell whether Angus passed in the female line to a branch of the Dalriadic royal house whose *red lyon* is blazoned *crowned* but *passant* on the Angus and Ogilvy shields of the Middle Ages. But outright dispossession of the descendants of the ruling house of Angus could only have been accomplished by war, and must have been such an event as to find its way into our chronicles. By the twelfth century, our mormaers had come to be styled in the Norman-English fashion as counts or earls, and so the former sub-kings appear as the Seven Earls of Scotland.

Among them, when they first appear on record in 1115, was another Dubhucan, almost certainly Earl of Angus. His successor by 1144 was Gillebride, Earl of Angus, who later took part in a devastating invasion of England. In Earl Gillebride's time Norman-French had become the international language of the West, and so his name was rendered 'Gilbert'. Before 1177, Earl Gillebride gave the lands of Ogilvy in Angus to his younger son Gilbert, who thus became Gilbert of Ogilvy.

The place-name Ogilvy itself is derived from the Ancient British *ocel-fa*, 'high plain', and so must have been in use in Angus in Pictish times before Gaelic became for a while the local language. From Earl Gillebride of Angus's son, Gilbert of Ogilvy, sprang the Ogilvy clan, gallant knights and Cavaliers, Jacobites and modern fighting soldiers.

Having been Earls of Angus at the dawn of local history, a branch of the family—the Ogilvies of Auchterhouse—became hereditary Sheriffs of Angus during the fourteenth and fifteenth centuries. So Sir Patrick Ogilvy was correctly styled Vicomte d'Angus when commanding the Scottish forces in 1429 with Joan of Arc against the English in France: as a Sheriff is a *Vicecomes*. From this branch sprang the present chiefs, who have been Lords Ogilvy since 1491 and Earls of Airlie since 1639. The spirit of a drummer-boy is said to be heard beating his ghostly drum whenever an Earl of Airlie is about to die. This warning of impending doom was last heard in 1900, when the late Lord Airlie was killed leading a cavalry charge at the battle of Diamond Hill in the Boer War. (His last order was 'Files about, *gallop*', and his dying words were 'Moderate your language please, sergeant'; and all the while, thousands of miles away, Lady Airlie heard the drummer drumming.) Today, the present David Ogilvy, 12th Earl of Airlie, K.T., G.C.V.O., M.C., who did so much for Highland development when he was Chairman of the North of Scotland Hydro-Electric Board, is still Lord Lieutenant of Angus.

Angus Ogilvy with Princess Alexandra on the steps of Airlie Castle in Angus. The Ogilvy Earls of Airlie descend in the direct male line from the original Celtic earls of Angus, who were among the famous Seven Earls of Scotland.

ENDURE FORT

Lindsay

The great chivalrous house of Lindsay long impinged upon the Highlands, both in Glenesk and in Strathnairn. Indeed, it was the then Lindsay chief who, with the Earl of Moray, arranged the celebrated 'Battle of the Clans' at Perth in 1396: when what the writer believes to have been the Shaws and the Cummins, fighting about their rival claims to Rait in Strathnairn, slaughtered each other manfully in the King's own presence— a rougher spectacle than any boxing-match or bull-fight.

The Lindsays were originally Anglo-Norman barons, and Baldric de Lindsay, who appears in 1086, held lands both in England and Normandy (where he granted tithes to the monastery of St. Evreux). Their name of Lindsay itself was derived from Lindsey (the 'island of the lime-tree' or *linden*) where they held the manor of Fordington. The great territory of Lindsey south of the Humber had once had a dynasty of its own in early Anglo-Saxon times: and it may just possibly be significant that the baronial house of Lindsay took their surname from the whole district and not from their particular lands there.

At the beginning of the twelfth century Cumbria and Lothian (modern Scotland south of the Clyde and Forth) were a separate principality from Scotland itself, and their ruling prince David was also earl of Huntingdon in England. A great lover of chivalry, David the Saint made many friends among the Norman aristocracy. Among them was Sir Walter de Lindsay, who was a member of the prince's Council that went into matters dealing with the See of Glasgow in about 1120. After St. David became King of Scots, the Lindsays sat as Barons in the Scottish Councils or Parliaments from at least 1147.

William de Lindsay, who was baron of Luffness and held (under Swan, son of Thor, ancestor of the Ruthven earls of Gowrie) the vast hill-district of Crawford in Clydesdale, had a son by his first wife whose descendants, the Lindsay barons of Lamberton in Berwickshire, also held Kendal and most of the beautiful Lake District in England. His second wife was the senior co-heiress to forty English manors; and their son William de Lindsay was steward to the Steward of Scotland. It was probably he who took for Arms the *fess chequy* of the Stewarts, differenced by changing the colours. So it was especially appropriate that at the Coronation of Queen Elizabeth in 1953 the present chief, David Lindsay, 28th Earl of Crawford, K.T., officiated as deputy for the infant Great Steward of Scotland, Prince Charles: and that the 26th Earl performed the same function for Prince George and Prince Edward at the Coronations of King Edward VII and King George V. In any case, the wife of Sir Alexander de Lindsay, lord of Crawford (whose father Sir David de Lindsay, Chamberlain of Scotland, had died in Egypt on the Crusade of St. Louis), was probably a sister of James, the Steward of Scotland 1283–1309. Incidentally, these Stewarts descended from the heiress of a branch of the royal house of Somerled, King of the Isles, thus bringing the highest blood of the Gaels to the Lindsays.

Although he had been knighted by King Edward I in person, Sir Alexander de Lindsay fought for both Wallace and Bruce, forfeiting his lands in England for the Scottish Cause. His son, Sir David de Lindsay, lord of Crawford, married in 1324 a great Celtic co-heiress, Mary, the younger daughter of the Lord of Abernethy, head of the abbotly branch of the famous Clan Macduff. So important was this match considered, that the great families descended from her and her elder sister (the Countess of Angus) were probably the first in Scotland ever to bear quarterly coats-of-arms: and the *red lyon on gold, debruised by a black riband*, of the old Abbots of Abernethy is still quartered with the *fess chequy* of Lindsay by the Earl of Crawford. Mary of Abernethy's grandmother had been Mary of Argyll, widowed Queen of the Isle of Man, and daughter of the

The old Airlie Castle, stronghold of the Ogilvy chiefs. Most of it was burnt down by the Campbells under the Marquis of Argyll in 1640, as is still recalled in the ballad song 'The Bonnie Hoose o' Airlie'. In revenge, Castle Campbell, Argyll's 'Castle of Gloom' in Clackmannanshire, was burnt by the Royalists five years later. A modern Airlie Castle, residence of the present Earl of Airlie, occupies the position of part of the old curtain-wall to the north. But the principal seat of the chiefs has long been at Cortachy, where Lord Ogilvy, the heir (a high-powered merchant banker), now has his home.

MacDougall chief Ewen of Argyll, King in the Hebrides and Lord of Lorn, 'the most prominent Highlander in Scotland in his day'. So, by the middle of the fourteenth century, the Lindsay chiefs were more than half Gael.

Sir James de Lindsay, lord of Crawford, who was captured by the Bishop of Durham in the moonlight fight at Otterburn in 1388, is generally credited with having organised the famous 'Battle of the Clans', the duel at Perth described by Sir Walter Scott. But it seems more probable that this was done by his nephew and successor, Sir David Lindsay, afterwards first Earl of Crawford (so created in 1398). Sir David's father (who died on a pilgrimage to the Holy Land) had acquired the great Highland district of Glenesk by marriage to the heiress of the Stirlings of Edzell (who themselves appear, from their alternate use of the Moray *stars* with the Stirling *buckles*, to have had a Moray descent), and also inherited the Abernethy lands in Angus: so that he held about two-thirds of the whole

Edzell Castle, stronghold of the Lindsays at the mouth of Glenesk in Angus from 1358 to 1715, commanded one of the more important passes to and from the Highlands.

county of Angus—the territory that became known as the Land of the Lindsays. The first Earl of Crawford (who married a daughter of King Robert II) was also overlord of the Highland district of Strathnairn, where the Clan Chattan feuded with the Cummins. In 1392, the Clan Donnachaidh of Atholl and the Stewarts of Garth, accompanied by some Roses and their adherents from far Strathnairn, made an historic raid upon the Lindsay lands in Angus. A mounted *posse* led by the hereditary Sheriff of Angus (Sir Walter Ogilvy, ancestor of the Earls of Airlie) set off in hot pursuit, but were ambushed by the Highland caterans in Glenbrierachan, where the Sheriff himself was killed and Sir David Lindsay (the future Earl of Crawford) was cut through his armoured steel-boot to the bone by the two-handed claymore of a clansman whom he had already pinned to the ground with his lance. It seems likely that this raid had something to do with the troubles in Strathnairn that led Lindsay and the Earl of Moray to arrange the 'Battle of the Clans' four years later.

Sir David Lindsay was the best tourneyer of his time, and as champion of Scotland jousted against the English champion, Lord Welles, on London Bridge at the Feast of St. George in 1390, in the presence of the King and Queen of England. The onlookers thought he must have cheated and been fastened to his saddle, when he unhorsed Lord Welles without moving in the saddle under the counter-shock of the English champion's lance. So Lindsay vaulted to the ground and back into the saddle, in full plate armour; and during the dagger contest on foot that followed, he lifted Lord Welles on the point of his dagger and threw him to the ground. After he was made Earl of Crawford, he was also Admiral of Scotland.

The Earls of Crawford became so mighty that their earldom (perhaps ultimately because of its Abernethy and therefore Clan Macduff element) has precedence before such older earldoms as Sutherland and Mar; and as Premier Earl of Scotland, in precedence, the present chief of the Lindsays bore the Sceptre when the Honours of Scotland were carried before the Queen to St. Giles's Cathedral in 1953. The Earls of Crawford had their own officers-of-arms, Lindsay Herald and Endure Pursuivant (called after their motto: 'Endure Fort'); their Swan crest shews that they possessed the necessary claim to descend (in the female line) from the Swan Knight, a descent so coveted by the chivalry of all mediaeval Christendom; their estates were a Regality; and in 1452 the fourth Earl of Crawford, known as 'Earl Beardie', entered into a treaty with the Earl of Douglas and Macdonald of the Isles (Earl of Ross) to partition the kingdom of Scotland among themselves. Their rebellion was, however, defeated by the Crown with the help of the Earls of Huntly and Angus (the Red Douglas putting down the Black); while the Lord High Constable was made Earl of Erroll, presumably for remaining loyally inactive although he was married to the Black Douglas's sister. The writer understands from Lord Strathmore that 'Earl Beardie's' ghost still sits in a secret room at Glamis, playing cards with the first Lord Glamis and the Devil.

In Angus, the Lindsays had a long blood-feud with the Lyons of Glamis. In 1382, Lindsay of Crawford had slain Lyon of Glamis; and in 1577/8 one of the 11th Earl of Crawford's 'tail' shot the 8th Lord Glamis, although both chiefs were endeavouring to calm their followers as they chanced to jostle past in a narrow Stirling Street. Similarly, the 3rd Earl of Crawford had been mortally wounded at Arbroath in 1445/6, while trying 'to prevent a conflict between his clan and the Ogilvys'. The Lindsays are said to have worn green on this fatal day: hence the saying 'A Lindsay in green should never be seen'. But a rival version substitutes 'Ogilvy' for 'Lindsay': and certainly this fits Ogilvy tartan better, for there is green in the Lindsay tartan. Moreover, the ballad 'Will ye gang tae the Hielands, Lizzie Lindsay?' tells us that she 'kilted her skirts of *green* satin, She kilted them up tae the knee'. The real reason for fussing about green, of course, is that green was the Fairy colour associated with witchcraft.

Mary Queen of Scots held a Privy Council in Edzell Castle in 1562, on her way North to overthrow the over-powerful Gordons. Sir David Lindsay of Edzell, son of the 9th Earl of Crawford (who had been temporary earl during the disinheritance of his cousin 'the Wicked Master' of Crawford), appears on the parliamentary Roll of Highland Landlords in 1587. His branch sprang from the ferocious Earl Beardie's brother, and were given Glenesk—the Highland part of the Lindsay inheritance in Angus—for their appanage. Sir David Lindsay of Edzell made a genea-logically interesting marriage to the tenth Earl of Crawford's daughter, whose mother in turn had been the famous Cardinal Beatoun's child by a daughter of Lord Ogilvy. In 1580, Sir David built the mansion attached to the older tower of Edzell Castle, which Dr. Douglas Simpson has called 'one of the noblest of Scottish baronial edifices' and which dominates not only the mouth of Glenesk but also the strategic Cairnamounth Pass through the great mountain barrier of 'the Mounth'. In 1589, King James VI received the submission of the Hay chief, the Catholic ninth Earl of Erroll, while staying with the Lindsays at Edzell Castle.

And in 1604, Sir David Lindsay (now a judge as Lord Edzell) also added the garden walls with their summer-house and bath-house, of which Dr. Simpson observes that 'The heraldic and symbolical sculptures associated with this pleasance are unique in Scotland, and give Edzell Castle a distinctive place in the art history of Europe'. For, though brave in war (the 24th Earl of Crawford's cousin Robert Lindsay, later Lord Wantage, won in the Crimea the first Victoria Cross ever awarded to the Army) and chivalrous in victory (the chronicler Froissart himself writes of the Lindsays' courtesy to the vanquished), the principal characteristic of the Lindsays throughout the centuries has been their great love of art in all its forms. In the Middle Ages, the Lindsays were almost alone among the Scottish nobles in appreciating the highly-cultured King James III, who made the then Lindsay chief a duke (the first duke ever in Scotland not to be a king's son). However, this dukedom was taken away again in 1488 by the successful Douglas & Home rebellion, during which the King was slain while leaving the battlefield of Sauchieburn (probably by Stirling of Keir, whose Tower he had burnt a few days before) after being thrown from the 'great grey horse' given him by Lord Lindsay of the Byres, who had vainly brought 1,000 horse and 3,000 foot to support the King's lost cause. Scotland's first dramatist was the poet Sir David Lindsay of the Mount, Lord Lyon King of Arms, close friend and childhood mentor of King James V: in 1540, he wrote 'Ane Satyre of the Three Estaits', re-enacted at the Edinburgh Festival some years ago. The Lindsay cultural tradition has been continued into modern times, and Maurice Lindsay is one of the pioneer Lallans poets of the new Scottish renascence, just as the late Ian Lindsay was one of our leading architects.

Their talented chiefs have led them well in this. To take only the last four generations, their record is still remarkable. The 25th Earl of Craw-ford 'acquired a high reputation for his works on religion, philosophy, and art, and was one of the most accomplished and learned men of his time'. The 26th Earl was a Fellow of the Royal Society, President of the Royal Astronomical Society and a Trustee of the British Museum: he 'presented to the nation for the Edinburgh Observatory the splendid astronomical equipment of his observatory at Dunnecht, Aberdeenshire'. The 27th Earl (whose brother, Sir Ronald Lindsay, was British Ambassador at Washington for nine vital years, 1930–1939) was Chairman of the Royal Fine Arts Commission, an active Trustee of the National Portrait Gallery and of the British Museum, also First Commissioner of Works and Public Buildings, as well as being a Cabinet Minister in 1922. His son David Lindsay, 28th Earl of Crawford and also Earl of Balcarres, K.T., G.B.E., present Chief of the Lindsays, was Chairman of the Royal Fine Art Com-mission and is now Chairman of the Trustees of the National Galleries of Scotland, was elected by the students as Rector of St. Andrews University 1952–1955, was Chairman of the National Gallery and a Trustee of the Tate Gallery, a member of the Standing Commission on Museums and Art Galleries, also Chairman of the National Trust, and still is a Trustee of the British Museum and the Pilgrim Trust, as well as being Chairman of the National Art Collections Fund. In true Lindsay tradition, his

The pleasure garden at Edzell Castle, with its summer-house and bath-house, is the finest of its period in Scotland. It was made in 1604 by Sir David Lindsay, Lord Edzell, and is enclosed on three sides with elaborately decorated heraldic walls. They are arranged in compartments of two alternating designs. One design has a single recess for flowers under different carved bas-reliefs: represent-ing altogether the Celestial Deities, the Sciences and the Theological and Cardinal Virtues. The other design represents the coat-of-arms of the Lindsays of Glenesk: *Gules a fess chequy Argent and Azure, and in chief three mullets silver*, that is a red field with a 'fess' across the centre chequered in white and blue, and three silver stars above. The chequers are arranged with recesses in such a way that the right colours can be brought out by putting flowers in them. Heraldic stars are often shown pierced, as spur-rowels. Garden walls needed to be defended in those days (Edzell was captured and recaptured in 1653); and these heraldic walls are most cunningly provided with gun-loops for defence, each loop-hole piercing the centre of a star.

younger son, the Honble. Patrick Lindsay (the present Endure Pursuivant) is an art expert with Christie's, the famous auction sale-rooms.

But the centuries-old holdings of the Lindsays in the Highlands have long since been lost, although the gallant Earl of Crawford-Lindsay was the first Colonel of the Black Watch. Lord Edzell's son, David Lindsay of Edzell, fell into disfavour at Court because he was accidentally responsible for the slaying of his uncle Alexander Lindsay, Lord Spynie, who had intervened in a brawl in Edinburgh between his two nephews Young Edzell and the Master of Crawford, and their respective 'tails' had got out of hand as so often happened in Lindsay history. Edzell became a Covenanter, and so the Great Montrose's highlanders ravaged Glenesk in 1645. The Royalists under William Hay, 4th Earl of Kinnoull captured John Lindsay of Edzell, the next laird, in the castle in 1653, but he was rescued the next day by Roundhead troops. Unfortunately, in 1715 his grandson, David Lindsay of Edzell, last Baron of Glenesk (which the Lindsays had held since 1358), was obliged to sell for debt ' his extensive barony extending over the whole north of Forfarshire from near Brechin to Invermark and Mount Keen'. The 'lichtsome Lindsays' impinged on the Highlands no more: although at the age of sixty-three Colin Lindsay, 3rd Earl of Balcarres (to whom his intimate friend Bonnie Dundee had appeared in a vision at the moment of his death at Killiecrankie) was out in the 1715 Rising and fought as a Jacobite at Sheriffmuir. He was the direct forefather of the present Chief of the Lindsays.

Appendix

The following is extracted from a personal Memorandum to the Minister of State, Scottish Office, about the Highland Development Bill then before Parliament, written in 1965 by the Earl of Dundee P.C., *Mac Mhic Iain*. Lord Dundee was President of the Oxford Union and later M.P. for West Renfrewshire, becoming Under-Secretary of State for Scotland. He was later Minister of State in the Foreign Office and Deputy Leader of the House of Lords.

OBJECTIVES

I think our generally agreed objectives are:—

1. To restore in the Highlands a large and vigorous population, among whom young people will be able to find the kind of life they want in their own country.
2. To increase the economic wealth of the Highlands. (This objective, of course, may not always coincide with the preceding one.)
3. To enable the Highlands to make a larger contribution to the general welfare of Scotland, and of Britain.

METHODS

Our principal methods are:—

1. IMPROVEMENT OF AGRICULTURE AND FISHERIES. In the last generation, agricultural progress has substantially increased the *wealth*, but not the *population*, of the Highlands. Rising wage standards require higher productivity, which means fewer men producing a larger output. If we want to preserve family farms and crofters, they must have additional part-time work, either industrial or sylvicultural.

2. AFFORESTATION. Experience has shown that large scale forestry, compared with medium-quality hill farming, will multiply both employment, and economic wealth tenfold, plus further employment in ancillary industry. Results, being slow, will always breed impatience, and sometimes antagonism. Answers—(a) if Highland recovery depended on forestry alone, repopulation would at least be quicker than depopulation has been for the last 80 years, and (b) immediate employment can sometimes be given by industry set up in anticipation of forest products, like the Fort William pulp mill, importing raw material until such time as new Highland forests shall have come into full production.

3. MODERNISATION OF THE TOURIST INDUSTRY, to provide a greater variety of accommodation (both luxurious and frugal), and more popular holiday attractions, could increase the earning power of the Highlands a great deal, and would also give new employment, some seasonal and some permanent.

4. NEW INDUSTRIES, either ancillary to forestry, or independent of it, can be established in any part of the Highlands, *either* with ordinary Development Area help, *or* with the help of extraordinary measures, like the Wiggins-Teape mill.

HIGHLAND AGRICULTURE

1. SHEEP. Hill sheep farming is still predominant in Highland agriculture. Sheep are excellent animals if they don't have the whole show to themselves. Like the goats which have transformed so many parts of the Middle East into desert, sheep monoculture in the Scottish Highlands has been slowly destroying fertility for the last 150 years or more, by eating out the finer grasses, leaving coarser grasses and bracken to predominate. Under our recent Hill Farming schemes, a little of this damage has been repaired by improved drainage, by expensive re-seeding on some selected parts of the lower ground, and by the introduction of more cattle, which eat down coarse grass, tread down bracken and drop more valuable dung than sheep. The problem of Highland sheep farming is human rather than economic. Economically, it would be in the national interest that most hill sheep farms of medium and poor quality should be transformed in one way or another. Some should be amalgamated into larger units, some should be wholly afforested, and some mainly or partly afforested. Wherever

possible (it is not always possible) the ratio of cattle to sheep should be raised. These changes can only take place gradually so long as there are numbers of established sheep farmers and shepherds with their families who do not want to vary their present occupation. Perhaps the best achievement of the Hill Farming Act has been the social benefit of providing a dwindling population of sheep farmers and shepherds with good modernised houses far more quickly than could have been done under any of the Housing Acts.

2. CATTLE. The hill cow subsidy was introduced by Tom Johnston when I was his Under-Secretary in the wartime coalition Government. We began with strict conditions concerning the breeds of cattle which could qualify, and the length of time for which they had to be kept out on hill grazings. Over the last 24 years these conditions have been wisely relaxed by D.A.F.S., for it has been found that many breeds of cattle previously thought unsuitable do very well in the Highlands, and that the best results may sometimes be obtained by using the hill grazing for only six or seven months in the year. The chief problem has always been that good hill grazings can sometimes carry a large stock of breeding cows, with their calves, in summer, but few Highland areas can grow enough hay or other winter fodder to keep the maximum summer cow population for the rest of the year. To buy winter keep and transport can be very expensive. Even more expensive can be the cultivation of poor-quality low ground with high-cost labour. Some farmers, instead of bringing fodder to the cows, find it better to bring the cows to the fodder, transporting them to the Lowlands in winter and back to the Highlands in spring.

The hill cow subsidy has been a success. It has enabled the Highlands to make a valuable contribution to our stocks of beef cattle, as they used to do in the droving days. It has helped in some places to restore fertility destroyed by sheep. The scope for further increase is considerable. But as in all other branches of farming, increased production is not usually accompanied by increased employment, but rather the reverse.

3. ARABLE FARMING. There is some good arable ground in all Highland counties except Zetland. Sometimes there is a pocket of good arable at the foot of the glen, surrounded by hill ground, but usually the best arable is in some homogeneous low-lying area. Most of it is well farmed. Marginal arable ground, as wage and other costs rise, tends to be converted into permanent or semi-permanent grass. Attempts to reclaim waste land for arable farming have occasionally succeeded here and there, but have sometimes been costly failures.

4. RECLAMATION. There is no more fascinating pursuit than the conversion of waste land to useful production, and no more rewarding sight than the spectacle of its successful attainment. In the Highlands, the main purpose of reclamation should be the growing of fodder crops, so that a larger stock of breeding cows may be wintered in the neighbourhood. But it would be a pity to risk too much Government money which could be spent to better purpose in other ways. Even successful reclamation has sometimes proved to be meretricious, giving initial results which do not endure.

5. INTEGRATION OF FARMING WITH FORESTRY. This is an unexceptionable platitude from which no one can dissent, but it is used to mean very different things. It can mean:—
(a) Leaving areas of ground unplanted which it would be in the national interest to plant, in order that patches of sheep monoculture may be perpetuated. This may sometimes be justified on personal grounds, although it retards the renewal of human population.
(b) Small holdings for permanent forest workers, of which the Forestry Commission has established a considerable number. This is an excellent policy which accords well with the Highland tradition of attachment to the soil.

(c) When a farm, or a number of adjoining farms, are mainly but not wholly afforested, it is sometimes possible to farm the best of the low ground, and the unplantable high ground, on a new pattern with a higher ratio of cattle to sheep, the intermediate ground being planted.

(d) The planting of large shelter areas on farms which continue to be used mainly for hill grazing. The biggest 'shelter belts' which could qualify for the Hill Farming Act grant of 50 per cent were usually too small to be of much use sylviculturally. But larger shelter plantations, though not acceptable under the Hill Farming Act, can be dedicated, earning the planting grant and other advantages. The Highland Panel make some suggestions for the encouragement of planting either by owner-occupiers or by tenant farmers. They point out that the Forestry Commission are willing to plant ground with an agreement that it will be taken over from them by the owner at a valuation after the young wood has been established. This can be particularly helpful to working farmers who have not the time or the knowledge to carry out planting work or to nurse the young trees until they are established, but who would like to have sizable woods on their farms.

(e) Integration of crofting with forestry is a special question because of the legal and procedural difficulties which may arise. The Highland Panel discuss some of these difficulties. Since it seems likely that the survival of some crofting communities will depend on integration with forestry, it is surely a pity that the obstacles are not being tackled with a greater sense of urgency than would appear to be the case.

(f) On the general question of integration, as I shall explain in the next section, I think it is reasonable that the Government should act with a bias towards forestry, and should not allow inhibitions against any kind of planting to prevail. No one in his senses would want to afforest really good arable except for some special topographical reason. But as for marginal arable, I think that every official report dealing with it, from the Royal Commission of 1909 to the Zuckerman Report of 1957, has held that some marginal arable would be put to a better use if it were planted. This is often done in Sweden, which no one could describe as an under-wooded country.

FORESTRY

1. PUBLIC FORESTRY. Our aims in the Highland counties are similar to our aims in the rest of Scotland. The Highland Panel, whose remit is limited to the seven Highland counties, recommend that in this area the annual rate of planting by the Forestry Commission should be increased to at least 20,000 acres. [This recommendation has since been accepted.] The Panel's Report, however, does not make it as clear as it ought to do, that to sustain a programme of this size over a number of years, more rapid encroachments will have to be made on ground at present grazed by sheep, and that the Forestry Commission's policy of acquiring land will have to be less cautious than it is now. Slowness of acquisition, and not Treasury restriction, is the reason why the Commission are not already planting a much larger annual acreage.

To get more land more quickly we shall need a good climate of public opinion (or at least not an adverse one) and a readiness to buy promptly and at a good price any land which is for sale, *whether or not it is all suitable for afforestation.* Compulsory powers, which already exist, must of course continue, though they have never been used. But nearly all the land which ought to be afforested has some sheep on it, and if compulsory powers were used with any frequency to hustle out sheep farmers who did not want to abandon their grazing, the Commission (or the new Highland Board) might become too unpopular to be successful.

In our approach to public opinion we have got to remember that the public usually likes to be told about plans which are expected to produce speedy and sensational results, and they are apt to be irritated when they are told of plans which will not fully mature until the next generation has grown old. They can easily be roused against changing the familiar appearance of a bare hillside, but they do not get so excited about measures to provide a better life for their unborn grandchildren. The best arguments for planting a bigger acreage now, and without delay, are to be found in those few areas where the Commission began planting

extensively in its first decade (1920s). None of these woods are yet fully mature, but they are already yielding a very satisfactory revenue from thinnings, and their results in terms of human population are already impressive. Forty-four years ago the parish of Dalavich, on the west of Loch Awe, had a population of 55 persons, of whom 11 (one-fifth) were children under 16. Now the number of people is 373, and the number of children 126 (over one-third). The whole population has thus been multiplied by seven, and the number of children by eleven and a half. The more quickly we can afforest now, the sooner we shall stop the exodus from the Highlands, then put it into reverse, and increase the number of young people with a future in their own land. Without more forestry this cannot be done, and if we cannot move more quickly than we are moving now, we may never overtake and outdistance despair. This is the whole reason for my belief that the Government ought to give priority to forestry, as a matter of principle, when any question of land use arises. Whoever our advisers may be, they are bound to make occasional mistakes. If we make the mistake of giving too much land to forestry, the costs of our error to future generations will be negligible. If we make the opposite mistake of giving too little, we may lose the battle for Highland regeneration. After this battle has been won, the time may come for a change of emphasis in land use, but that will not be in the lifetime of most of us who are now responsible for the making of public policy.

There are three ways in which the Forestry Commission can acquire land in Scotland; by purchase, by long lease, and by feu. If landowners have land which ought to be planted, but which they cannot plant themselves, and if they do not wish to part with the ownership, or with the superiority, the Commission is always willing to become the tenant, or the feuer, of the land. Alternatively, as mentioned above, the Commission is sometimes willing to act as planting agent for the owner if the land is dedicated and the Commission's expenses refunded.

How should State forestry in the Highlands be distributed geographically? It may sometimes be desirable that uneconomic planting should be done for special reasons, such as helping the crofters (if they will allow themselves to be helped!). And I think the Commission has always tried, as they ought to do, to give every Highland district some share in our planting programme, except where there is no plantable ground. But it would be in the general interest that most attention should be given to those areas where forestry will be most profitable both to the local inhabitants and to the nation, and where mature forests managed in harmony with ancillary industries will support a large population. For example, the county of Argyll, because of its soil and climate, is perhaps better suited than any other part of Europe or America to the cultivation of fast-growing conifers. And it is interesting to note that, except for the small county of Caithness, Argyll has a much smaller deer forest area (which usually means unplantable ground) than any of the five mainland counties. The area of 195,000 acres planted or about to be planted on September 30, 1963, is only 9.8 per cent of the county area, and anyone who measures the annual growth and the cubic content of the adolescent forests already planted in Argyll will be impressed by the great addition to the wealth of the Highlands which would accrue from a really large scale extension of forests in this area. Growth and quality are better than in Austria, where timber output since the war has played a major part in creating the modern prosperity of that country. In the counties of Inverness and Ross and Cromarty there are also very large areas, some already planted, where forestry will be a first-class national investment. In Sutherland and Caithness, growth is generally slower, but in these counties too there are considerable areas (like the big private scheme of the Westminster estate on the west coast) where forestry is undoubtedly the right answer. One factor in determining distribution will be distance from the Fort William pulp mill. The economic radius was first estimated at 80 miles, but this has since been greatly extended, and I shall be surprised if it is not doubled.

2. PRIVATE FORESTRY. Many farmers, and some landowners, are not only prejudiced against forestry, but are sometimes surprisingly unaware of the Government help which they could get if they did some planting. Until I joined the late Government in 1958 I was on one of the Forestry Commission's Regional Advisory

Committees, and I was also on the U.K. Forestry Committee and the Home-grown Timber Advisory Committee, both of which met in London. In conjunction with the Commission's Private Woodland Officers we did our best to persuade private owners that it would be to their advantage to plant. We had a little success, but often found them hard to convince. At that time the Commission were empowered to issue planting loans, which they tried to bring to people's attention by circulating pamphlets about them, but nobody seemed to read the pamphlets except those who knew all about it already. You will remember that in our debate on February 24 the Duke of Atholl, in a very helpful speech, asked if loans could be started, evidently not realising that they had been obtainable until only a few years ago. In fact we were just beginning to get a few people interested when the loans were suddenly stopped. This happened after I had come off the various Forestry Committees, and I do not know exactly why they were stopped. I thought it a senseless thing to do, for some of the people whom we had laboriously argued into a more favourable state of mind about planting schemes lost interest again when they found that the loans, which we had been using as one of the inducements, were no longer available. A long-term loan at fixed interest seems especially appropriate to a project like forestry which takes so long to yield returns. If the Treasury will not allow the Commission to do this for foresters in general, surely they could be asked to sanction it for crofters and farmers, or indeed for all foresters, in the Highland counties, where forestry is specially required for social reasons, and where it might help the Government to overcome lack of interest, or dislike, towards our forest policy.

In Scotland the most critical problem of our forestry is not how to manage old woods but how to create new ones. This is the reason why the State will have to do more than the private owner. In Sweden, where 50 per cent of the entire area of the country is woodland, four-fifths of the forests are privately owned. But Sweden suffered neither the slow deforestation which went on for a thousand years in Scotland, nor the sudden large compulsory fellings of the two twentieth-century wars. Our chief concern is how to re-afforest quickly, and we cannot expect that all heavily taxed landowners will be eager to spend capital which they haven't got for the benefit of descendants who haven't yet been born, and who may not be allowed to get the benefit when they do get born.

Although the tradition of private forestry is not universal in the Highlands, it is strong in parts of them. After the disappearance of most of the old natural forests, many owners began in the eighteenth century to establish new ones. The great plantations of Atholl, Cawdor and Moray, and all the Deeside woods, are outside the seven counties, but the very large Seafield forests in east Inverness-shire, largely devastated in World War II, are now being gradually restored, and in Easter Ross the Munros of Novar and Stirling of Fairburn have substantially increased their forest acreage. The first Chairman of the Commission, the late Lord Lovat, was a great forester on his own land.

In general, private forestry has so far fully achieved the target figures assigned to it in the 'Desirable Programme' worked out in the White Paper of 1943 which was the basis of our post-war forest policy. (The reason why State forestry has fallen so far behind its part of the programme is simply inability to acquire land fast enough.) In the seven counties, the ratio of private to public planting has been about 1 : 3 for the last six years. This is a little lower than the proportion for Scotland as a whole in 1963, when 12½ thousand acres of private forest and 33 thousand of State forest were planted. It is to be hoped that private as well as public afforestation in the seven counties, and elsewhere too, may be increased. Besides shelter plantations and small woods, there are also larger areas where private foresters may be able to plant and manage more conveniently than the Commission. Some estates are making a big contribution to our national forest acreage, and if more could be persuaded to do the same, we would attain our target more quickly and more easily than by State enterprise alone. I am sanguine enough to think it possible that, as more Highland forests come into production, and as their advantages become more generally visible, some landowners who are at present uninterested or sceptical may want to join the band-wagon.

In technique, public and private forestry can be mutually helpful. The Commission's high standards of sylvicultural education and of forest management, and particularly its growing facilities for research, are of incalculable value to the private forester. Private experiments in forestry may also be of value to the Commission. The late Sir John Stirling-Maxwell was a pioneer in trying out new methods of afforesting certain types of high peaty ground, previously thought unplantable, but which are now frequently planted. If I may be allowed to quote a personal example, I believe that the Commission, in the last ten years, have obtained over 20 million hybrid larch trees derived from hybrid seed orchards which I planted many years ago at home, and the parent trees in these orchards were obtained from the Atholl estate, where hybrid larch were first evolved sixty years ago, and from Cawdor, where some of our finest European larch strains have been bred for more than a century.

It has always been the policy of the Scottish Landowners' Federation, and the Scottish Woodland Owners' Association, to persuade landowners to do more planting, or, if they have suitable land which they cannot plant themselves, to offer it to the Commission as purchasers, feuars or tenants. The attitude of individual landowners, however, towards our present forest policy varies in the same way as that of all kinds of people who live in the Highlands—some are enthusiastic, some cautiously approving, some dubious, some ill-informed, and some antagonistic.

TOURISM

The Highland Panel's Report includes tourism in its section on sport and recreation. The first twelve of these paragraphs are about deer stalking, and in reading them I formed the impression that they may perhaps have been written by two or more members of the Panel whose ideas are in conflict but who have insisted that the whole of their views shall be embodied in the Report. Deer forests are in fact of small significance, either to our economy, or to tourism, but the Panel touch on a problem which might occasionally have to be considered by the Forestry Commission. On many deer forests, the patches of plantable ground are not large enough to be worth planting, so that no problem arises. But on some, there may be larger areas of good plantable ground which could be economically afforested, and if such ground should happen to coincide with the winter feeding ground of the deer, it may become necessary to reduce the deer stock on the high ground very heavily, otherwise they will die of starvation in winter. If we care to look far enough ahead, however, the reduction need not necessarily be permanent. The red deer lives on bare land against his own inclination; his natural habitat is woodland, and as soon as the afforested area ceases to contain sections of vulnerable young trees, the deer can then be admitted.

Venison is no longer popular in Britain, and since meat rationing ended it has become almost as much despised as rabbit. Fortunately for us the Germans have different gastronomic standards. Most of the Highland venison fit for human consumption is now exported to Germany, and the gain to our balance of payments, although small, is well worth the trouble required to get it.

Fishing is an old-fashioned tourist attraction which becomes relatively less important among the growing multiplicity of modern recreations, but it is still worth some attention. In Scotland there is some legal protection for salmon against poachers, but not for trout, except in a stocked pond, and trout fishing in the Highlands has been deteriorating for a long time. Most continental countries where there is good trout water take steps to preserve it by restocking and prohibiting fishing except by people who have paid for a licence, the licence fees being used to pay for improvement of the fishing, and policing against poachers.

The most important thing of all for Highland tourism is the future of the hotel industry, which may become more valuable economically than agriculture. The numbers of people who go to visit the Highlands, both from other parts of Britain, and from abroad, have multiplied enormously, and although some hotels have improved a lot since the war, there is too little room to satisfy the growing demand. Some of the most encouraging developments at the present moment are at Aviemore, where the new Rank motel of 500 units is already open, and where the Cairngorm Development Company has already started building work on the first of the large modern hotels which are planned (now completed). These are intended to be open all the year and to provide for all kinds of weather. Outdoor recreations like ski-ing, sailing, fishing, walking and pony trekking will be combined with indoor curling and skating rinks, heated swimming pools, tennis courts and bowling greens, conference halls, dance halls, cinemas and concerts. But probably the best thing which the management has done, is that they have gained the tolerance of the old-fashioned local hotel keepers who were naturally suspicious at first about the competition from the new arrivals, but who now perceive that their own businesses will benefit from the development of the town into a tourist centre which may one day become comparable to St Moritz, and which before long may have accommodation for two thousand visitors.

On the other side of the picture, it was a deep disappointment that the representatives of the Highland hotel proprietors, after first agreeing to the *Kur* tax, later withdrew their support. In Switzerland and other European countries the huge hotel industry has been largely built up over the last hundred years on the proceeds of the surcharge levied by law on the hotel bill of every visitor, and put into a fund from which the improvement of hotels and tourist attractions has been financed. In the Highlands, the demand for accommodation by people of all sorts, with money to spend, is so much in excess of the supply, that hardly any visitors would be put off by a levy of this kind, and all sections of the hotel trade would benefit. Suspicion and short-sighted individualism, however, have prevailed. Legislation would be needed to make the surcharge work fairly. Towards the end of the late Parliament, a Bill was prepared, but had to be abandoned. One can only hope that the industry will see more sense in course of time.

TRANSPORT

I am never satisfied with the progress of road construction and improvement, but at least the Highlands are getting a better share of it than they did before the transfer of administration from Whitehall to Edinburgh. As for rail transport, the most essential line, which must be preserved, is the line from Glasgow to the junction at Crianlarich Upper, from which one branch proceeds north-west to Fort William and Mallaig, and the other west to Oban. Further north, the local railway from Dingwall to Kyle must be kept at least until an improved road is made, which seems unlikely for a long time. This was stated in Parliament by the Secretary of State soon after the Beeching report came out, but everybody continued to behave as if nothing had been said about it, which caused a lot of quite needless anxiety. Further developments in air transport, which is a great boon to those who have to travel to and from the Hebrides and the extreme north, will no doubt depend on how much we can afford to subsidise it, and its value must be compared with the value of other desirable projects which may be competing for a share in the amount of public money available.

NEW INDUSTRIES

So long as our objective is to arrest and reverse the decline in population, we cannot rule out any viable new industry. Some would probably prefer to see a preponderance of small rural or semi-rural industries, like the weaving of Harris tweed, or the little coal mines at Brora and Machrihannish, and are probably glad to think the large scale manufacturing industry is, in any case, unlikely to spread itself throughout the Highlands. John Knox, a writer and lecturer who travelled extensively in the Highlands during the late eighteenth century, and who continually strove to persuade members of Parliament that Government measures should be taken to encourage new industries in the Highlands and to transform the unhappy condition of their inhabitants, wrote in 1786 ' The Highlanders continue to speak the ancient Celtic language in its purity, and to retain their ancient vigour, bravery, hospitality, and simplicity of manners '. Since 1786 the area of Gaelic speech has been sadly diminished. But Dr Fraser Darling, in his monumental work ' West Highland Survey ', published 1955, written with the help of the Department of Agriculture, research assistants from the North of Scotland College of Agriculture, an expert in population statistics (Dr R. S. Barclay), a succession of young Gaelic-speaking Highlanders who did much of the field-work and the township studies, and a substantial grant-in-aid from the Development Fund, writes ' We have taken the view that Gaeldom has been and still is a living culture, and that in the distant past it was an example of a culture finely adjusted to an environment which placed severe limitations on human existence. . . . Gaeldom, when it becomes conscious of its heritage, does not want to die, and if Britain is imaginative enough, she will not wish to lose the contributions to graceful living which the Gaelic culture can make. Both parties should forget the notion of numerical, financial, and technological dominance and face the facts, of difference and of environmental limitations, as intellectual equals '.

There are three courses, Dr Darling thinks, which Gaeldom can take: it can allow itself to be crushed out and absorbed by western commercialism; it can attempt cultural resistance by looking backwards and rigidly refusing to change, or it can accept change and evolution in the conscious poise of its own values. He admits that the third course is the most difficult, but believes that the Department of Agriculture, which is the biggest Highland landowner, and the Agricultural Colleges, can help a great deal, and that bodies like the Hydro-Electric Board and the Forestry Commission are more sympathetic than they used to be.

Government policy cannot compel the remnant of Highland culture to survive against its own will, but we can give it the chance to live, and perhaps even to recover a little of its lost territory if it has the virility to do so. We may have to bring in some new workers who will settle and breed in the Highlands, but we should also try to create conditions which will encourage the native Highlanders to work and rear families in their own native territory. The enormous growth of tourism and of hydro-electric power in Upper Austria, the Tyrol, Switzerland and Savoy has not uprooted the independence, nor destroyed the character of the mountain peoples who live there.

We must aim at spreading some industries, whether based on natural resources or not, which are not ancillary to forestry, so that the future economy may not be too dependent on timber prices. In the outer Isles, where the wind is too strong and too frequent for tree growth, and where there is a large crofting population, new industry must in any case be not directly dependent on forestry. But on the mainland we must have the forest industries too. The Wiggins-Teape pulp mill, which was very hard to get, will be a key point in our Highland economy, and we owe it to future generations to make sure *now, and not later on*, that our planting programme is big enough to ensure plentiful supplies for it in the next century. It will mainly consume thinnings. So will the chip board factory at Inverness. A great variety of other forest industries will come automatically, as later thinnings, and then final fellings, become more general. By increasing our planting programme now, we shall create more new small industries for the next generation, and the one after that, than by any other method. Meanwhile, thinnings from our not inconsiderable post-war plantations will soon begin to add progressively to the volume already being obtained from the inter-war planting. If only the inter-war planting had been four or five times as much as it was (which it could have been, if the land sold so cheaply in the farming depressions of the twenties and thirties had been boldly purchased), we would already be witnessing the turn of the tide in the Highlands.

I conclude this section on industry with another passage from Darling's survey. ' The greatest value the mass of Highland land could give to the nation would be as a continuing productive wild land in which perhaps twice as many people could live than are there at present. The very fact of successful growth would be a satisfying thing, helping to keep a forest population happy living there, cropping the wild lands but not mining them as they have been mined. This ecological continuum would yield more to the nation than the subsidised devastation, rendered the more macabre by imposed mechanical industries which have a habit of concentrating population and destroying the desired dispersal over the countryside.' (This is quoted because I think more attention should be paid to Darling's survey, on which a good deal of public money was spent. At the same time, I would make it clear that I approve the Highland Board's aim of starting one or two selected ' growth points ' for Highland industry.)

ECONOMIC BACKGROUND

The attached table shows the changes in the population of each of the seven Highland counties from 1755 to 1961. In 1755 Dr Alexander Webster, an Edinburgh minister, by correspondence with his brother ministers in every parish in Scotland, ascertained the numbers of people living in each parish in that year (in 1755 Orkney and Zetland were one county, and I have not tried to separate the parishes of one from the other). The official censuses for Great Britain began in 1801 and continued thereafter in every subsequent decade, except 1941 when wartime conditions prevented the decennial census from being held.

Until the middle of the eighteenth century, the clan system of social and judicial administration prevailed in the Highlands. After the rising of 1745, the Hanoverian Government set itself to eradicate the clan system, thoroughly and irrevocably, without being able to substitute anything which could effectively take its place. Territory administered by chiefs who had adhered to the House of Stuart was confiscated by the Government and managed for nearly forty years by Commissioners, conscientiously but without much understanding. The legal powers of the remaining chiefs were abolished by Act of Parliament, and they were treated in the same way as English or Lowland freehold landowners. As Dr Darling puts it, ' by the abolition of hereditary jurisdictions the common folk became technically free men, although in reality this freedom could be equated with the disintegration of their social system '.

One of the most important functions of a chief was the regulation of marriages. Marriage could not take place without the consent of the chief, who would only give his consent if the prospective bridegroom was in a position to support a wife and children. This patriarchal method of population control was abolished by Parliament together with the other powers of the chiefs. Its abolition was followed by a spate of early marriages, and a prodigious ' population explosion ', which caused almost continuous famine accompanied by mass emigration. The standard of living of the Highlander had never been high, but in the second half of the eighteenth century it reached depths which had never been touched before. ' There can be no doubt ' writes Darling ' that the general situation and standard of living of most West Highland and Island folk markedly deteriorated in the late eighteenth and early nineteenth centuries '. In a later chapter he writes ' It was too little realised that the factors which allowed an initial increase in the Highland population later brought about a much lowered standard of living which, once accepted, then allowed of accelerated increase in numbers until the population came up against the Malthusian ceiling. Our historical resumé did not reveal that landowners and the State between them were able to mitigate materially the grim consequences of a people having reached the Malthusian ceiling with a standard of living that could scarcely be lowered further '. This would not have happened if the State had left the clan system alone. The contemporary English traveller Pennant, who toured Sutherland in 1772, writes of the conditions he found there ' Numbers of the miserables of this country were now migrating. They wander in a state of desperation; too poor to pay, they madly sell themselves for their passage, preferring a temporary bondage in a strange land to starving for life in their native soil '. Later witnesses record that the winter diet of the Sutherland crofter was eked out by the putrid corpses of dead fish, and raw blood extracted from the hindquarters of starving cattle. John Knox (*A Tour through the Highlands of Scotland and the Hebride Isles in 1786*) says of the Highlands in general, ' In all these years of famine, the people must be supplied by the laird, or his factor, or some trader, with the actual means of existence, till the ground yields better crops. When one bad crop is succeeded by another bad crop, as in the years 1782 and 1783, the proprietor must either purchase grain from distant parts to support his tenants (many did so, but others lacked the necessary financial means), or turn them out of doors, or see them perish by slow degrees through want '. On the rate of emigration he writes in 1786, ' It is difficult to ascertain with exactness what number of people have emigrated since the year 1763. Some raise their estimates as high as 50,000, but certain it is that above 30,000 have in that time gone to America, besides a continual drain to other parts '. Telford (Survey and Report on the coasts of Scotland, 1802) states that in that one year (1802) 3,000 people left the Northern Highlands. It may be inferred from these contemporary estimates that considerably more than 100,000 must have emigrated in half a century. Yet the population which remained behind, in the seven counties, increased from 255,000 in 1755 to 302,000 in the Census of 1801.

Migration was of three kinds: emigration overseas, largely to Canada and the United States; emigration to the cities of the Lowlands and North of England, where the Industrial Revolution, even in times of low wages, offered a standard of life far above what the emigrant could hope for at home, and internal movement (which would not of course affect population figures) from the glens to the towns and villages, often occasioned by the introduction of large-scale sheep farming. Some emigration was unorganised, some organised, some voluntary and some compulsory. After the death of Francis Macnab (the subject of Raeburn's famous portrait) in 1819, the whole Macnab clan, together with their new chief Archibald MacNab, emigrated to eastern Canada, where the British Government gave them a grant of 80,000 acres of land. The compulsory clearances, and the harsh manner in which they were sometimes enforced, were all the more bitterly resented in Highland memory, because under the ancient Highland customary law, the land had been the property of the clansmen, and it had been the duty of the chief to protect each clansman's right to his own holding. The most notorious of all the clearances, which took place in Sutherland in 1814 and 1819, were conceived as well-intentioned slum clearance schemes. New towns with good houses were built along the fertile east coast, at Dornoch, Golspie, Brora and Helmsdale, where it was intended that the inhabitants of the interior, moved from the sub-human squalor in which they lived, could earn a decent living in a decent house. But many of them had no wish to quit the hovels which were the only homes they had known, and the inhuman methods by which some were compelled to do so (eviction from condemned property is not without parallel in modern local authority schemes), has left a deep wound in the soul of a people to whom hospitality and mutual personal loyalty were sacred duties. The wound, kept open by historians, has dimmed other memories, and few people remember the chiefs like MacLeod, or Macdonald of Macdonald, who spent their entire fortunes importing food for the hungry clansmen who had become too numerous to be supported on their native soil.

From 1801, in spite of continued large-scale emigration, the population continued to increase steeply for another half-century. Caithness, Orkney and Zetland reached their peak population in 1861, Ross and Sutherland in 1851, Inverness in 1841 and Argyll in 1831. The overall population of the combined seven counties probably reached its highest point between 1841 and 1851, in each of which years it is a little under 400,000. From 1851 to 1911, in sixty years, the numbers decline steadily, with an average loss of 900 a year, from 395,000 to 341,000, but the population in 1911 is still substantially greater than in 1811. The heaviest rate of decline, averaging 2,400 a year, is from 1911 to 1931, the numbers falling by 48,000 to 293,000. In the thirty years from 1931 to 1961 the fall is only 15,000, an average of 500 a year. The 1961 population is still greater than it was in 1755. But its age pattern is different, its distribution between small Highland towns and Highland country is different, and it is now only 5½ per cent of the whole population of Scotland, compared with 20 per cent in 1755.

In the period following the abolition of customary clan law, two great changes in agriculture took place, the introduction of the potato, and the arrival of the great sheep flocks imported from the south. In the long run both those changes were adverse to fertility, except on the best arable land where rotation of crops on large farms could be practised, as in the Lowlands. The potato helped at first to feed the rapidly swelling population (except when the crop was spoilt by early autumn frosts, which happened fairly often). As in Ireland, the potato blight in the 1840s was probably the chief reason for the downward turn of the population figures. As for the sheep, they overran the Highlands very gradually, but almost completely. The old sheep-cattle ratio of about 50 : 50 gradually changed, until by the mid-nineteenth century, it was becoming virtual sheep monoculture.

Sir Walter Scott, in the preface to one of his novels, tells of an old Highland laird who said to him 'In my grandfather's time, a chief took pride in the number of men on his estate, in my father's time it was the number of cattle, now it is the number of sheep, and I suppose in my son's time it will be the number of rats and mice'. While the good grazing lasted, sheep were profitable both to the flockmasters and the owners. But in the last quarter of the nineteenth century the collapse of world agricultural prices coincided with the steady deterioration of Highland hill grazings, and the sheep farming business, whose former profitability had pushed so many small tenants out of their sub-standard holdings, became itself a depressed industry, unable to afford a rent which could cover repairs and capital renewals.

Before 1745, deforestation had been proceeding for centuries. After the '45, and the social disintegration which followed it, the disappearance of the old natural forests was accelerated by heavy commercial fellings, and the fresh green sward left behind provided good pasture for the immigrant sheep, whose nibbling prevented any natural regeneration of trees. Artificial afforestation schemes, as mentioned in an earlier section of this paper, were carried out by a fairly large number of owners, and some of these were very extensive, but in the aggregate, they were not extensive enough to have any great effect on the ecology of the Highlands as a whole.

It is a pity that so good an ecological scientist as the compiler of *West Highland Survey* should have been carried off by the 'brain drain' to the United States. In some ways it is also a pity that his study was confined to the region west of the Drum Albyn ridge, but most of his researches and conclusions are applicable to the rest of the Highlands. The real value of his book lies in the wealth of evidence, carefully tested and diligently assembled, to show that nearly all Highland ground below 2,000 feet has been devastated by what he calls a millennium of fire, axe and tooth. But the erosion, the acidity, the flooding, and the sterility of soil have all increased more rapidly in the last 200 years, because

there have been too few trees, too few cattle, too many sheep and too many rabbits. 'The Highlands as a geologic and physiographic region are unable to withstand deforestation and maintain productiveness and fertility. Their history has been one of steadily accelerating deforestation until the great mass of the forests was gone, and thereafter of forms of land usage which prevented regeneration of tree growth and reduced the land to the crude values and expressions of its solid geological composition. In short, the Highlands are a devastated countryside, and that is the plain primary reason why there are now few people and why there is a constant economic problem. Devastation has not quite reached its uttermost lengths, but it is quite certain that present trends in land use will lead to it, and the country will then be rather less productive than Baffin Land.'

In another passage the author complains of 'subsidised devastation', meaning the expenditure of large sums of public money on restoring grazings ruined by sheep, with the intention of ruining them again in exactly the same way.

These passages may have been written some time before the publication of the Survey in 1955, for the Survey was begun in 1944 and was concluded soon after the 1951 Census. Since then, more cattle have been bred in the Highlands, more trees have been planted, and a nasty but providential endemic rabbit disease has reduced this arch-destroyer of fertility to very small numbers. When the Survey was being written, a great deal of the machair land, one of the most precious possessions of the Islands and West Coast, was in danger of complete destruction by rabbits.

In the last fifteen years we have been moving in the right direction, but we have not been moving fast enough. In the sections of this paper on forestry, I have tried to suggest how progress might be speeded up. Maybe I have not gone far enough. What I am sure of is that very much faster progress here is fundamental to any Highland policy, and that, if we can get moving on this thing now, then the other aims and features of our policy will soon become more easy to achieve.

TABLE showing CHANGES in the POPULATION of the SEVEN CROFTING COUNTIES from 1755–1961

	Argyll	Caithness	Inverness	Ross & C.	Sutherland	Orkney	Zetland	Total
1755	66,286	22,215	59,593	48,084	20,774	38,591		255,543
1801	81,277	22,609	72,672	56,318	23,117	24,445	22,379	302,817
1811	86,541	23,419	77,671	60,853	23,629	23,238	22,915	318,266
1821	97,316	29,181	89,961	67,762	23,840	26,979	26,145	361,184
1831	100,973	34,529	94,797	74,820	25,518	28,847	29,392	388,876
1841	97,371	36,343	97,799	78,685	24,782	30,507	30,558	396,045
1851	89,298	38,709	96,500	82,707	25,793	31,455	31,078	395,540
1861	79,724	41,111	88,888	81,406	25,246	32,395	31,670	380,442
1871	75,679	39,992	87,531	80,955	24,317	31,274	31,608	371,356
1881	76,468	38,865	90,454	78,547	23,370	32,044	29,705	369,453
1891	75,003	37,177	89,317	77,810	21,896	30,453	28,711	360,367
1901	73,642	33,870	90,104	76,450	21,440	28,699	28,166	352,371
1911	70,902	32,010	87,272	77,364	20,179	25,897	27,911	341,535
1921	76,862	28,285	82,455	70,818	17,802	24,111	25,520	325,853
1931	63,014	25,656	82,082	62,802	16,100	22,075	21,410	293,139
1951	63,361	22,710	84,930	60,508	13,670	21,255	19,352	285,786
1961	59,390	27,370	83,480	57,642	13,507	18,747	17,812	277,948

Tartans

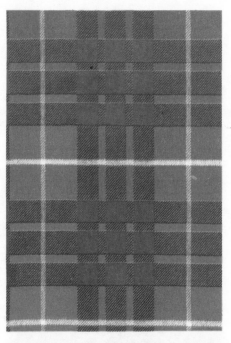

1	2	3
4	5	6
7	8	9

I	2	3
4	5	6
7	8	9

1   Morrison

2   MacLeod of Harris

3   Mackinnon (Hunting)

4   Maclean of Duart (Red)

5   Macfie

6   Macneil of Barra

7   Lamont

8   Maclachlan

1	2	3
4	5	6
7	8	9

1 Macmillan (Ancient)
2 MacEwen
3 Fergusson
4 MacNachtan
5 Malcolm
6 Campbell of Argyll
8 MacDougall
9 Cumming

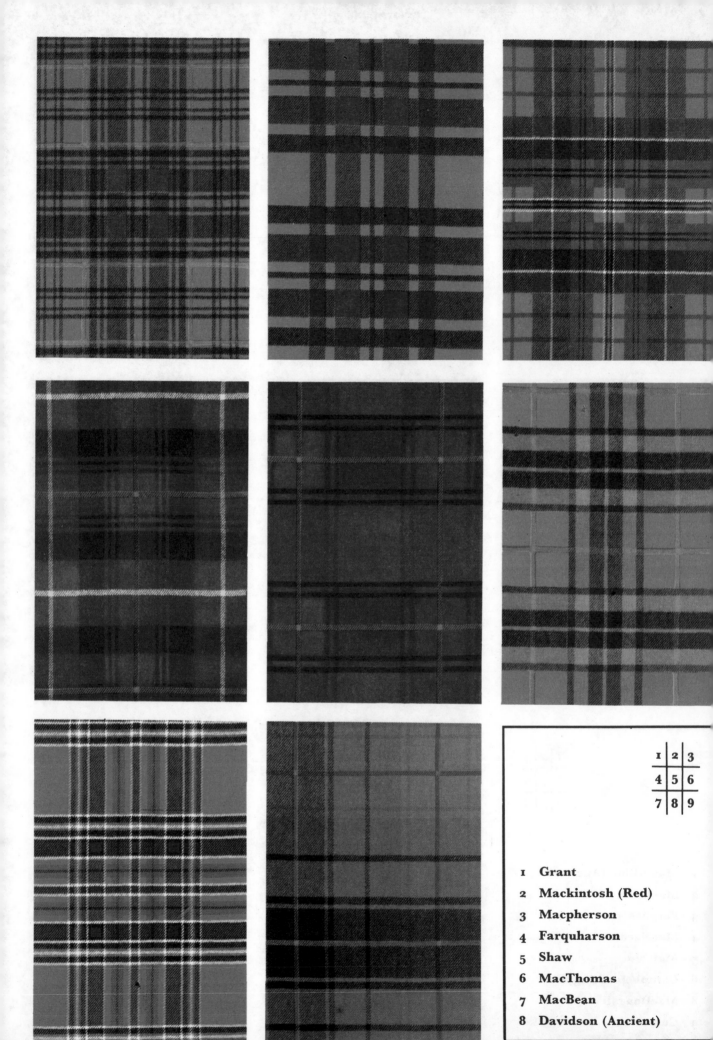

1	2	3
4	5	6
7	8	9

1 Grant
2 Mackintosh (Red)
3 Macpherson
4 Farquharson
5 Shaw
6 MacThomas
7 MacBean
8 Davidson (Ancient)

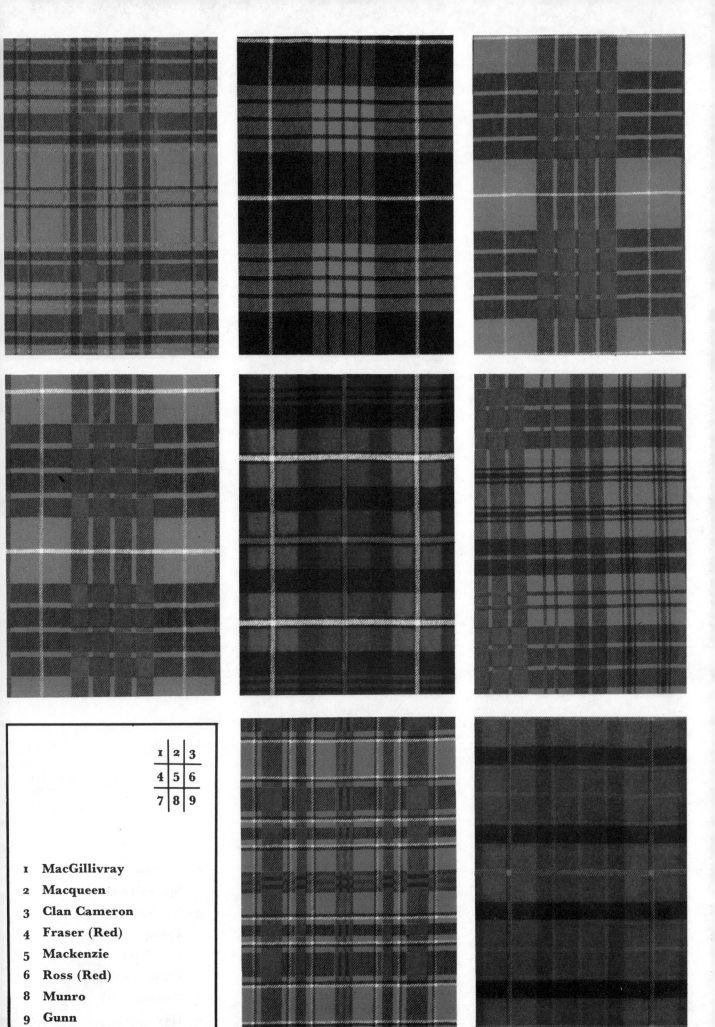

1	2	3
4	5	6
7	8	9

1 MacGillivray
2 Macqueen
3 Clan Cameron
4 Fraser (Red)
5 Mackenzie
6 Ross (Red)
8 Munro
9 Gunn

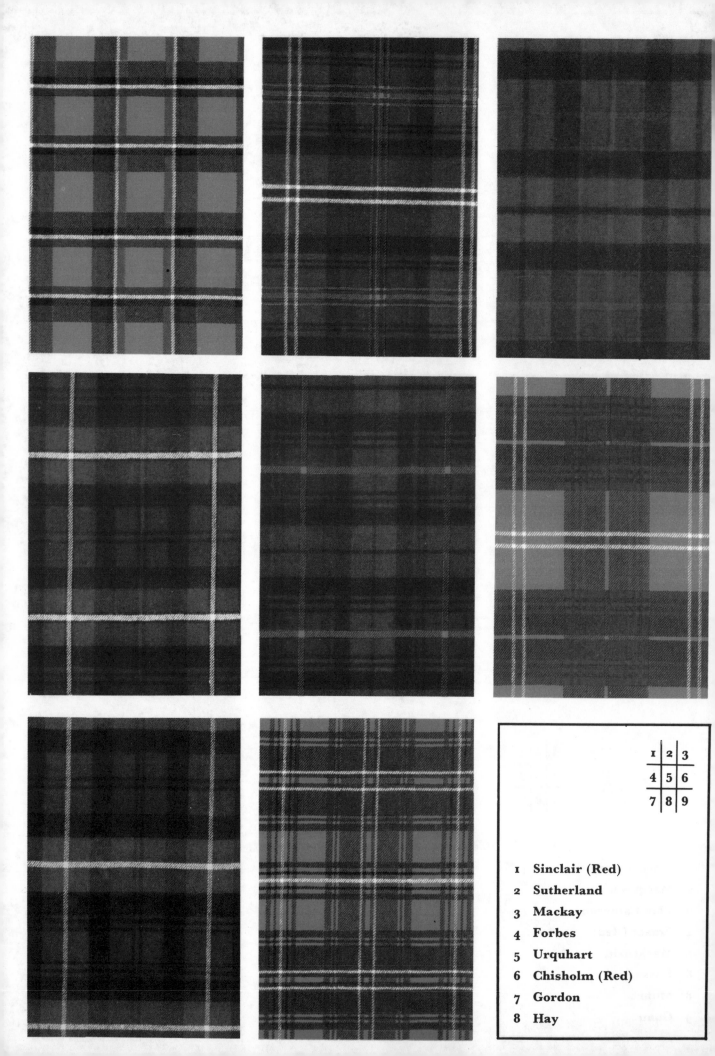

I	2	3
4	5	6
7	8	9

1   Sinclair (Red)

2   Sutherland

3   Mackay

4   Forbes

5   Urquhart

6   Chisholm (Red)

7   Gordon

8   Hay

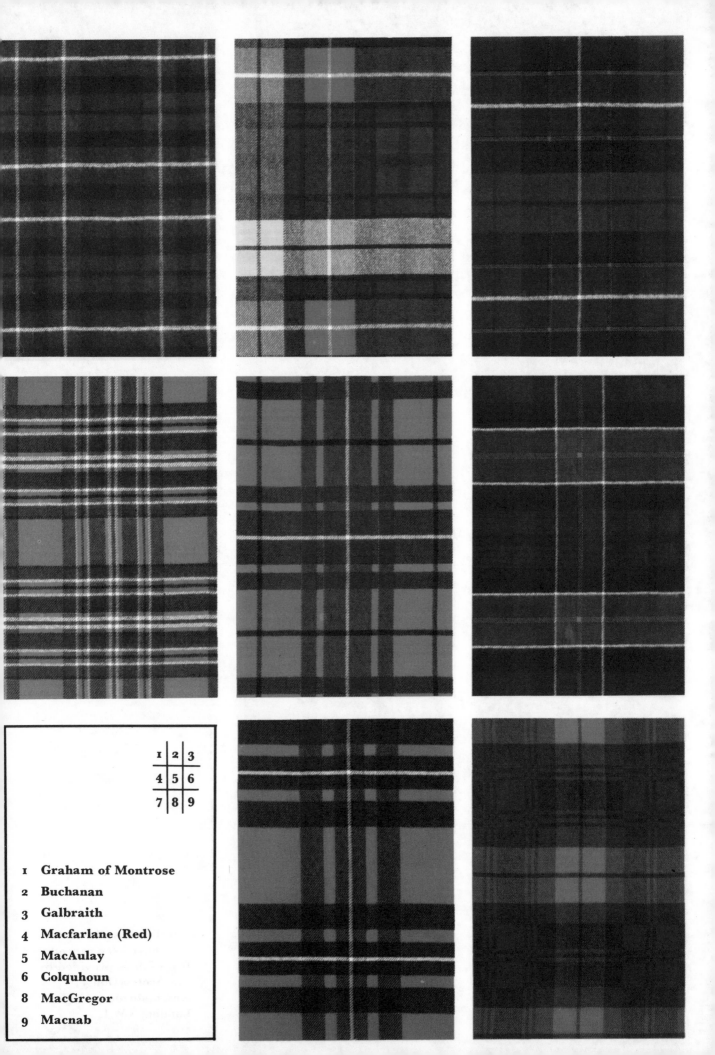

1	2	3
4	5	6
7	8	9

1   **Graham of Montrose**

2   **Buchanan**

3   **Galbraith**

4   **Macfarlane (Red)**

5   **MacAulay**

6   **Colquhoun**

8   **MacGregor**

9   **Macnab**

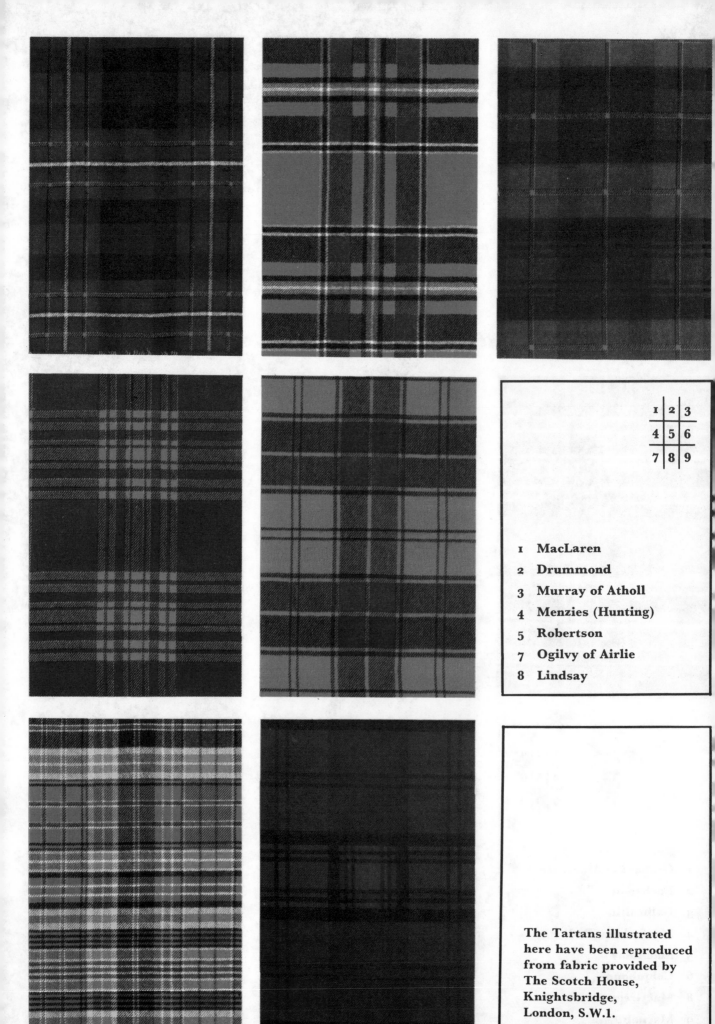

1	2	3
4	5	6
7	8	9

1 MacLaren
2 Drummond
3 Murray of Atholl
4 Menzies (Hunting)
5 Robertson
7 Ogilvy of Airlie
8 Lindsay

The Tartans illustrated
here have been reproduced
from fabric provided by
The Scotch House,
Knightsbridge,
London, S.W.1.

Index